DECEPTIVE GODS

DECEPTIVE GODS

CONFRONTING THE DIVINE AND DEMONIC

Lorne J. Therrien Sr.

DEDICATION

*To a new millennium of spiritual seekers and to the other forms of
intelligent life whose reality has not yet been accepted.*

"All warfare is based on deception."

- Sun Tzu

TABLE OF CONTENTS

INTRODUCTION

Deceptive Gods

Confronting the Divine and Demonic

It has been more than fifty years since I was introduced to the eyes that watch, influence, and manipulate from beyond the limitations of human sight.

In 1964, the house my family moved into was highly charged with the emotional residue of one of the city's most gruesome murders. This senseless tragedy attracted the malevolent beings of the parallel world, and I received an early education in their tormenting ways.

Years passed, and an emotional presence remained as a tag along occasionally wearing an attention-getting guise, shapeshifting, influencing a nightmare, or creating an illusion.

Fast forward to 1993. I was attending a birthday party with my two older children who were in their preschool years. Entering the old mill house, I sensed something sinister in the air as a vision came forward. A red rotary phone appeared ringing on an antique desk. Picking up the receiver a guttural voice said, "Hello Lorne."

"Who may I ask is calling?"

"Jinn."

"How are you spelling that?" I asked.

"J-I-N-N," it answered, as a vertical cloud of gray smoke manifested in front of the desk, dropping a chain with three dog tags attached on top. Engraved on each tag was the number three.

Disconnecting from the vision, I opened my eyes. This was the first time a spiritual being called itself Jinn.

In the corner, two grade schoolers caught my attention playing with a spirit board. Looking around the room, everyone was drinking and socializing with absolutely no concern. This troubled me knowing what was lingering and the potential danger, but I remained quiet. It was only when they asked my oldest son to join them that I spoke up.

"Stay over here with Dad," I said to my son, pulling him back.

"Oh, let him go, it's just a game for God's sake," an older woman yelled from the middle of the room.

"No, it's not just a game, it's an instrument to converse with spiritual beings."

"Oh please, give me a break," the older woman said laughing along with her friend.

I thought to myself. Should I let it go or give her a taste of spiritual being's abilities? For the first time, I chose the latter. Walking over to the boys at the table, I asked if I could give it a try. I told all the children to go to the other side of the house as it was a duplex. Sitting down, I asked if there were anyone that would like to join me.

"I'll do it," came from the back of the room. Walking forward was a woman in her early thirties. I stood up and reached out my hand.

"Hi, I'm Lorne."

"I'm Jill," she said with a smile, as she shook my hand.

"It's a pleasure, Jill. Have you ever used the board before?"

"Yes, I have."

"Good, because I haven't."

"You've never used the Ouija?"

"No, I've seen it done but never tried."

Sitting and facing each other we placed the board on our laps. The moment we put our fingertips upon the message indicator we were off to the races. Round and round counterclockwise the indicator went. Jill's relaxed expression instantly changed.

"One of you has to be moving it," the older woman said sarcastically.

Jill turned towards her and shook her head no.

"May I ask your name?" I asked the woman.

"Elizabeth," she replied with a cocky tone.

"Who may I ask is present?" I asked the Ouija board.

M-a-m-a was spelled out with strong energy one letter at a time. Jill was now getting anxious.

"How about we ask the board for your parents' first names?" I asked Elizabeth.

"Yeah, I'd like to see that," Elizabeth answered, with a glass of wine in her hand.

What she didn't realize was she just issued a challenge to the presence in the room. Quickly and powerfully, the board revealed both her parents' names.

"How could you know that?" Elizabeth asked.

"Maybe it's just beginner's luck," I answered back. "Let's try some more. How about we ask for their middle names?"

"Okay, go ahead," Elizabeth said.

I now had her full attention and the cockiness was gone. Everyone in the room began to move closer. The presence which called itself Mama went on to answer her parents' middle names, dates they were born, and even the dates they passed.

"It's not the board. You have to be some sort of medium or psychic," Elizabeth insisted.

"That is what the presence would like you and me to believe. I'm not the medium or the psychic, the presence is."

Elizabeth was ignorant to the fact that the spiritual being received its information from her memory or may have been following her, the family, or dwelling in the house for years. Folding the board, I prayed and then placed it in the box with the planchette.

"These boards are not harmless parlor games and should never be used by children," I said out loud.

It was easy to read the crowd that day. They were convinced it was me, and I knew it wasn't. But who or what was this Jinn? This experience got me thinking. How many people each and every day are innocently opening the lines of communication with a deceiver? Something must be done to expose how these clever beings mimic the dead.

Financial struggle and the challenges of co-parenting after a split kept me too busy to attempt such a task. On the heels of this, the dark side saw a perfect opportunity to unleash their wrath. Refusing to kneel in defeat after the loss of my martial arts studio, I fought back - meditating in nature, practicing martial arts, and praying morning, noon, and night as a Christian.

Desiring a personal relationship with God, I walked the path to win God's heart. Angels or celestial messengers appeared on the journey, alternating their visits with the forces of darkness. Each step closer to God brought more intense demonic assaults, and times of being graced with mystical religious experiences - but not without recognizing a familiar presence and noticing a pattern with angels, demons, and what I believed to be God.

Was my discernment wrong? I had to know the truth. Not just for myself, but for all I see as myself. I may not be successful in the endeavor, but I felt compelled to at least try.

A few years of preparation later, the opportunity presented itself when a divine-like presence knocked on the door of consciousness. At that moment I had a choice, accept what has been written about angels, demons, and God, or undergo a mind-to-mind war with the hidden race to get the truth. Gaining inspiration from a quote I always appreciated by G.K. Chesterton, 'The true soldier fights not because he hates what is in front of him, but because he loves what is behind him', I made my choice.

Until spiritual beings of the parallel world appear on a talk show, which I don't see happening anytime soon, our education of these conscious entities will be based on what has been written in religious texts, scientific discoveries, and the sharing of our personal experiences. This is the true story of my investigation to contribute to that knowledge and allow readers to come to their own conclusion.

Warning – This book contains unaltered dialogue that contains vulgarity and blasphemy.

CHAPTER 1

WHO IS CALLING ME SON?

A cool breeze was blowing on this chilly Monday morning. Walking toward the vehicle, I noticed three mourning doves sitting on the fence. "Good morning," I said, as I opened the passenger door and placed my martial arts bag on the seat. Looking at the trees surrounding the property, I realized the fall foliage was at its peak. With nothing planned, I purchased a pumpkin muffin and coffee and drove toward a scenic location.

Slowly I sipped, trying hard not to stain another piece of clothing. As I drove, I absorbed and deeply appreciated nature's spectacular color show of transforming leaves. While viewing this magnificent scenery, a vision of a golden-white cross appeared in my mind's eye as a warm, comforting divine-like presence embraced me, triggering a hypnotic state.

Without thought, I changed direction and drove to the Cumberland Monastery, the former home of Cistercian Monks. The Monastery of Our Lady of the Valley was built in 1902 by the Cistercian Monks, or Trappists, from stone quarried on the property. A terrible fire on March 21, 1950 destroyed most of the buildings. Fortunately, all 140 monks escaped safely. Due to the extensive damage, estimated at $2 million at the time, the monastic community decided to relocate. Since 1976, this 500-acre recreational area has been the home of the Cumberland Public Library.

Maintaining a peaceful vibration and clear mind, I parked facing the Ruth E. Carpenter Memorial Garden. Sensing an experience that should be recorded, I reached in the back seat and grabbed my backpack and water. Entering the garden, I was drawn to the old cedar cross. Walking closer, I could feel what appeared to be the essence of divine light. Slowly I raised my arms in the morning light; the higher they rose, the more magnified the impression became causing my eyes to tear. Standing still in total reverence with uplifted hands, I said, "God is my heart," with passion and power, piercing the bubble that separates God within from God all around.

Instantly, the wind picked up as I surrendered to the divine energy sensation. While staring at the cross, I began to walk backwards still in a peaceful trance. When I sat upon the stone bench, three translucent hooded monks manifested with a golden-white glow.

Unzipping the backpack, I took out a notebook and pen. Keeping my eyes on the benevolent visitors, I waited for their next move. One monk stood in the garden entrance to the left, one in the entrance to the right, and the third straight ahead in the entrance behind the cross.

Faces, hands, and feet were hidden in brown cloth, as they silently floated forward. The center monk passed right through a tree and then the cross, taking its position in front. Simultaneously, the other two monks glided to their positions, on the left and right of the center monk. In perfect sync, the end monks separated from the center monk by about 5 feet. The center monk began moving laterally back and forth in a distracting manner between the other two monks.

Taking off my silver necklace, I removed the cross pendant and placed it beside me. Opening the notebook, I removed an alphabet chart from the sleeve and placed it upon my lap. Looking up, I focused on the brightest star in the morning sky. Taking a deep breath, I let it out and relaxed into receptive oneness. Using the silver chain as a pendulum, I held it over the chart with my thumb and index finger. Controlling thought and emotion, I said, "For the goodness of all, if you please." The conversation with the monk to the left of the cedar cross began telepathically.

Illumination of heart begins here, in peaceful surroundings.

"Yes, it does. Good morning."

That it is. You are breathing in God.

"Yes, and exhaling God as well."

God is you, my brother. Here I walked, listening to the songs of the morning birds, very beautiful indeed. It seems like only yesterday. God lives here yielding to all who appreciate, Jesus yields to all who appreciate. They are one and the same, sharing the same heart. Seeing through the same eyes. Forever love, forever peace.

"Thank you for your wisdom. Do you have a message for humanity?"

Yes, walk into love and greet God with a smile.

"Thank you." The speaker then changed to the second monk at the right of the cross.

I am your brother and God is our source of eternal life. You have been transformed by the light of goodness; you now have God's eyes.

"Thank you."

Here on Earth, you are one, here in Heaven you are one.

"Thank you for your wisdom. Do you have a message for humanity?"

A half-truth is a whole lie, and a whole lie will alter your being to an unpleasant environment.

"Thank you."

Believe me, my brother, when I say it is your heart that shall rule your world.

"I believe, thank you." The speaker then changed to the third monk in motion.

Bless you, my brother.

"Thank you."

Monk I was, God I am, God you are. Compassion bleeds from your heart and soul. Holiness is freedom from selfishness. Compassion wields a mighty sword, illumination is the body armor of God, what penetrates can only make you stronger. Give compassion a voice, let it be you.

This is my message for humanity: Kindness breeds goodness, goodness breeds holiness, holiness breeds God child. Live well and live as God's children and all will be answered.

"Thank you for your wisdom and your message."

My brother, love never travels farther than your radiant heart can reach. I have spoken and others are coming. Always allow your family to speak as well. Selfishness is not God.

"I will speak with each. Thank you." Another presence was coming forward. The image in my mind's eye was the face of my father. Knowing there is no coincidence, a reason for this unusual visit was about to be revealed.

Maybe, here and now, you might feel who I am?

"I know who you are, and I say hello."

I know how you must feel.

"No one needs to conform to my perception to be viewed as part of the whole. I am not judging, so please continue."

You have grown to be very comfortable in your world between worlds.

"Disciplined yes, comfortable no. I see all as one world."

Yes, my son. I will respect your questioning through sensitivity. I can tell you, my son, you are what I hope all become.

"Disorganized? Just joking."

I know my son, just as you knew to come here, you will know truth in the words I speak.

"My memory of you is brief. All I recall is two visits. Once when I was 6 and the other at 14. Of course, the latter visit was because you were being brought to court for child support."

I'm sorry, my son. Fear was my weakness and I ran from who I was. I missed my children but lacked the courage to see them. I heard about you the most, because your martial arts abilities were quite popular in the city. But I was jealous of my son. I knew where you were and I never visited you.

"Those clouds passed many years ago."

When I was human, fear was my companion, so I drank, fear was my thoughts, so I drank, fear made my decisions, so I drank. So, can you see why I never came to visit you and the bar became my temple?

"As a father, no; but as a compassionate being, yes. I know the crippling force of fear if allowed to take root in your being, but you are putting too much blame on fear. You lived without heart. There is more to being a father than applying fifty percent of the genetic makeup."

I will explain. I love you my son, I really do. There can be heaven on Earth, you are heaven on Earth.

"Thank you, but I am still struggling for a better credit score."

Your humor I enjoy, but I am serious.

"Yes, I do experience heavenly moments and I am grateful. Do you tire as spirit?"

My son, if I could talk to you forever, I wouldn't tire.

"Thank you. If I told Mom we had this conversation, she wouldn't believe it."

She has plenty of reasons to believe it wouldn't be me. Who she came to know would have never spoken in this manner. And if any man came up to me at the bar and said 'I just talked to my deceased father' I would have offered him a shot of whiskey, then handed him the Yellow Pages to call a shrink.

"Ah, do I detect a touch of humor?"

Yes, and I am here now talking to you, and I say I am proud of you and I love you. The battles you fought to acquire knowledge for all is heroic beyond measure. You have walked the path of a saint, while camouflaging your abilities.

A robin landed on the top of the cross, facing east. "Thank you for sharing your perception. Mom has always called me a mystic. Those who have experienced these spirit world conversations call me a Medium, Shaman, or Psychic; and the list goes on by the perception of others and their beliefs. The robin lives in harmony with the all of God, plays its part without question, and faithfully waits now for the light of the morning sun. To call the robin a saint, I would agree, for it was one of my many teachers. I'm proudly just an expression of the source, living with a growing awareness. As far as battles, there were many - seen and unseen - that threw dirt in my eyes, but they were unaware that my heart can see. Like a seedling, I penetrated the soil and continued to reach for the light. It's all in what you see. For instance, I deeply respect the water in this bottle beside me. It has been following the water cycle since Earth was created. This water has been ice, rain, snow, liquid, and water vapor. This same water could be of a glacier that once covered this land. It could have quenched the thirst of a Native American 4,000 years ago, or a dinosaur millions of years ago. It has been around throughout the history of this planet."

I never looked at water that way.

"I know. If everyone understood this, few would ever disrespect water or this living planet again. The sun is about to peek over the horizon. Will its rays affect you?"

I only see light, there is never darkness here.

"A friend asked me, when you enter the light, do you lose your individual identity? I told him, Heaven doesn't mean you're giving up who you are; it's the full realization of who you are. When you are Heaven, you add light to your uniqueness and love to your every thought."

Your gift is your true being, my son. I am here now speaking to you as God's child because I, your father, learned of God from your radiant heart. When I passed, I came to visit you while you were sleeping. There lying in bed was my son beaming with the radiance of love. I kneeled next to you and prayed that one day I would get a chance to say I'm sorry and explain my weakness. With the miracle of God, the love of my heart gets a chance to speak.

How I lived was by the bottle, how I died was by the bottle, how I found God was by my son, who I gave up for the bottle... Please forgive me, my son?

"You were forgiven long before you passed. But I too could have initiated a conversation. On a couple of occasions through the years, we stood only a few feet from each other in line at the local convenience store. You were purchasing lottery tickets. I would look in your eyes and hope you would notice me, but you didn't. So, I defended my emotions and chose not to speak. I never felt anger or hate, but I allowed my memories to conquer the moment. So, you see, I may have heavenly moments, but maintaining a luminous state is a daily challenge."

I am not worthy to call you my son. It is from you I learned what is God, and it was from you I learned what it is to be a father. I wish you the world that your heart and mind dreams of. God's blood flows in you.

"I am happy. God's blood now flows in you."

Goodbye, my son, I will watch your days grow brighter.

"Goodbye father, enjoy your peace and joy of being." Placing the sterling silver chain on the notebook, I took a moment to pray, reciting the Lord's Prayer and Hail Mary. Was it possible my father achieved a degree of spiritual growth since his passing?

Many people who frequent this beautiful property are unaware that the Ruth E. Carpenter Memorial Garden is the former location of the Trappist's graveyard. The old cedar cross is original, and has remained standing, even after the fire of 1950.

As the years passed, the Cumberland Monastery has developed a reputation for being haunted. Witnesses claim sightings of phantoms on horseback, orbs, shadow beings, the ghosts of children, Native Americans, and monks on the grounds. I have experienced orbs and a few hooded shadows, when day greets night.

There are also reports of paranormal phenomena inside the Cumberland Public Library, which is connected to the remains of the Monastery of Our Lady of the Valley. These include doors banging and slamming, an elevator that functions on its own, disembodied voices calling out names, talking and laughing, being touched by invisible hands, feeling watched, books opening and closing on their own, loud bangs on walls, and wandering ghostly monks.

Despite the claims and what I have witnessed, I come here for its peaceful serenity and to enjoy the beauty of the landscape while practicing martial arts, meditating, or jogging on the fitness trail.

Feeling a little disconnected from the encounter, I took off my boots and walked barefoot across the grass field to ground myself and reconnect to Earth. After placing the backpack in the vehicle, I grabbed a protein bar out of the console and put on my boots. Opening the passenger door, I took two rattan sticks out of the martial arts bag for training.

Walking the Nine Men's Misery Trail, I pondered the bizarre experience. Nine Men's Misery is a monument, just off the trail, up on a small hill. The cemented stone cairn was erected by the Trappists in 1928 to protect the gravesite that had been repeatedly dug up through the years. Nine soldiers were supposedly captured, tortured, and dismembered at this location by Native Americans during the King Philip's War. The inscription on the plaque, in front of the stone and mortar cairn, reads *Nine Men's Misery, on this spot where they were slain by the Indians were buried the nine soldiers captured in Pierce's fight. March 26, 1676.* Nine Men's Misery is rumored to be the most haunted location on the grounds. Witnesses claim to have heard the moans and screams of the tortured soldiers.

Finding a dead, denuded tree, I placed my backpack down. Putting my hand on the tree, I announced to any spiritual beings that may inhabit it what I was about to do and that I meant no disrespect or harm.

Facing the tree with a left foot lead, I began working various intertwining sinawali patterns, like a boxer works combinations on a heavy bag. Sinawali, which means *to weave,* is a Filipino weapon-based martial arts term. Circling the tree and switching stances, I performed the patterns with a changing rhythm occasionally evading or defending an imaginary strike and then countering.

A few minutes into the practice, a robin caught my attention when it flew in front of my face. Landing on a branch to the left, it looked identical to the robin that stood on the cedar cross in the garden. Back in flight, it flew through an arch created by a broken oak tree and appeared to want me to follow. Putting on my backpack and holding the sticks in my left hand, I let the robin lead the way.

Flying low to the ground, it landed about every twenty feet, waiting for me to catch up. When the robin made its last stop, it was on the Field Trail and appeared to be standing on some writing in the dirt. As the songbird flew away, I looked down to see *I Love You* written within a drawn heart. Obviously, a human wrote this message for someone else. But how did the robin know to take me to this location? Was it the songbird's intelligence or the manipulation of what led me to the garden?

Kneeling on one knee, I drew a circle around the heart with my index finger and released gratitude into the beauty of the environment.

CHAPTER 2

RED CARDINAL ANGEL

Driving back to my apartment, I stopped at a deli. After paying the cashier, she handed me a ticket number which was 11. While waiting, I took a seat and watched television until my order was ready.

Into the deli walked a young woman wearing a red shirt with a number 11 in white. High vibration energy began to flow, and the vision of the golden-white cross returned. It appeared I had a tag along presence that wasn't finished talking.

Getting into the vehicle, the clock was blinking 11:11. Backing up, a divine-like presence embraced me in the same manner as earlier. Focusing on driving, I ignored its call until I came to an intersection. Looking to the right, a red cardinal was standing on the yellow lines in the middle of the road. With vehicles traveling both directions, it was trapped and possibly hurt. Quickly, I turned right and pulled over to the side of the road. Getting out of the vehicle, I slowly walked over to the cardinal. The cars stopped and I made sure the cardinal could hop to the side of the road and into the woods.

While looking after the cardinal, it flew up onto a limb about ten feet from the ground. I was happy to see it could fly, I knew if it didn't, it wouldn't survive long. To my right was a house with a mailbox which said, *Love lives here*. Another message brought to my attention by following a bird. Whatever and whoever this divine presence was, it's possible it manipulated the cardinal as it manipulated the robin to lead me to the *I Love You* message.

Walking back to the vehicle, the divine-like presence embraced me again as I opened the door. Inside the vehicle, I took the notebook out of the backpack. Removing my necklace once again, I placed the cross on the dash. Taking a deep breath, I exhaled and relaxed into receptive oneness, allowing the messenger to speak.

"I feel your presence and I am honored; do you have a message for the goodness of all?" I asked, as light as bright as the sun came to my mind's eye.

For all, I give you this, I am an Angel, listen carefully my heavenly friend.

Illuminate to God. Illuminate to self. Illuminate your world as God self. Illumination requires goodness of heart. Illumination requires goodness of thought. Illumination requires goodness of soul. Hold these words in your heart and feel them radiate throughout your being.

"Is there a name you would like to be called?"

I am light; I am not separate from light, so I require no individual name. The goodness of your heart, and the light in your eyes as you viewed God's beauty, attracted me. I am an Angel, you are a human eternal. I am light, you are capable of light.

"Thank you for your luminous message. I understand. Visions with heart create the spark."

God self speaks. Angels love illuminated visions however you make them. I share this secret with all. Judge your visions, judge your actions, judge your decisions, but never judge one another. Keep light in your world and it will follow you for eternity. I see, I feel, I am light.

"Thank you for your wisdom. Goodbye."

Closing the chain inside the notebook, I took a moment to pray then turned around and drove toward my apartment. As I passed the Saylesville Friends Meetinghouse in Lincoln, a small rock hit the windshield and a female voice whispered *Lorne* into my right ear.

Slowing down, I pulled into Gateway Park and parked. Picking up the notebook, I crossed Great Road and walked to the rear of the Quaker meetinghouse, which was built in 1704. Observing the craftsmanship of the building, I entered the graveyard of the early Friends who were laid to rest.

Taking a seat up against a tree, I placed the notebook on my lap and opened the alphabet chart as a presence was knocking on the door of consciousness. Taking a deep breath and then exhaling, I shifted to a trance state and allowed the telepathy of the tag along to begin. The vision sent to my mind's eye was a blonde-haired woman wearing a white cape and bonnet.

"Who may I ask is present?"

I am a Quaker for eternity. Heaven has a speaker, let it be you. Freedom to speak I wish I had. I loved life. People controlled my voice, but not my heart. I sang to God quietly. God listened and gave me strength for what was to follow.

I was hanged.

God I spoke. Love I felt. And the evil of man gave me the gift of a rope necklace. I said in my last words, I will speak again, this I promise you. Heaven I now enjoy, my friends. So, speak with heart and live with heart. Ye are truly Gods.

I speak not with fear. I speak not with assistance. I speak as God.

"You appear to be at peace."

I forgave them before the rope tightened. I was not to leave weak. I remembered Jesus and Jesus remembered me.

"The vision I am seeing is not this area of land."

I was new to the land.

"Would you like to leave your name for all to know?"

No, as a woman I had no say in that era. As light, I will be heard in this era.

Thank Jesus for love. Thank God for change. Thank you all for listening to my heart.

"Thank you for your message. Goodbye."

Putting down the chain I leaned my head against the tree and contemplated what was taking place. The voice of the Quaker was exact to the female voice that whispered in my ear after the rock hit the windshield.

Grabbing the notebook, I stood up, wiped myself off, and proceeded back to the vehicle when the phone rang. Pulling my cell out of my pocket I answered.

"Good morning Mom, how are you feeling?"

"Sad and lonely."

"I know. It takes time to heal. Have you been eating?"

"I managed to eat a half a donut this morning."

"Mom, you have to eat more than that."

"I don't have an appetite."

"I'll stop by the market and pick you up some yogurt and bananas."

"What are you doing?"

"I just had a few unexpected spiritual experiences."

"With what, ghosts?" my mother asked, before she laughed.

"Spiritual beings, Mom."

"That's good, because I need to talk to you."

"About what?"

"I was getting bangs on the walls last night, knocks at the door, and visits from shadows."

"How many knocks on the door?"

"Three."

"What time in the morning did the knocks occur?"

"Between 3 and 3:30 am."

"What were the shapes of the shadows?"

"The first one I caught out of the corner of my eye was tall and hooded, and I told it to go back to its master. Later in the evening there was a loud noise in the kitchen and Peetu started barking. I grabbed the flashlight and got out of bed to investigate. On the ceiling in the kitchen was a large black shadow spider at least 4 feet wide."

"Has Peetu been barking a lot?"

"Yes, mostly at night when we're in bed. Out of nowhere he will start barking toward the doorway, or toward the corner of the room near the window, but nothing is there."

"Something was there, Mom. It's the hooded shadow in stealth mode. What did you do when you saw the spider?"

"I shined the flashlight on it and it disappeared."

"When this happens, call me. I don't care what time it is."

"I'm not scared of them."

"I understand that Mom, but these beings are very sneaky."

"Well, I think Richard is trying to get my attention as well."

"What makes you say that?"

"Every morning I still pour him a cup of coffee and leave it on the table. Today I found it half drank."

"Mom, it doesn't mean it's Richard."

"I really think it's Richard, and you have the gift like your great-grandmother Pasquilina. Can you at least try to communicate?"

"It's not a gift, Mom."

"It's a gift."

"Okay, Mom. Then I will test the perceived gift."

"How about tonight?"

"I've had enough for one day. Let's plan it for Friday. Just don't use that Ouija board."

"I won't. I don't even know where it is. Are you going by Burger King?"

"Why?"

"I'm kind of in the mood for a hamburger."

"Are you sure you don't want a chicken sandwich?"

"I'm not in love with chicken."

"Okay Mom, see you soon, love you."

"Love you too, son."

Disconnecting the call, I started the vehicle and pulled out on to the road. As I accelerated, a large white SUV passed on the left. The license plate said L.O.V.E.

Forty minutes later I arrived at my mother's. As I knocked at the door, the dog began to bark.

"That didn't take long. What did you get?" she asked, opening the door.

"A grilled chicken sandwich," I answered, as I walked in.

Setting the food down on the coffee table, I walked over to the fridge and put the yogurt away and placed the bananas on the rack. Picking up the sandwich and coffee, I sat in Richard's recliner.

"You're not going to believe this. When we ended the call, I started fishing through my pocketbook for my glasses until I heard something fall in the kitchen. I got up, looked around, and couldn't find a thing. Then I heard a deep voice say, 'Ohhh Burger King, yum.' I cracked up, I couldn't stop laughing."

"You really heard that?"

"Honest to God. Do you think that's Richard?"

"No Mom, that obviously wasn't Richard. I really don't think his first words after passing would be, 'Ohhh Burger King, yum.'"

"That's true. It must be ghosts."

"As I told you before, they're not ghosts."

"Well, I think they're ghosts."

"Please sit down and eat, and I will explain something to you."

"Like what?"

"Why you're experiencing all this activity."

"I already know why, I'm a ghost magnet."

"Will you please listen for a few minutes?"

"Okay," my mother responded, while she rolled her eyes and took a seat.

"Mom, we co-exist with intelligent spiritual beings that know human weakness. You are vulnerable right now because you are grieving."

"I have been dealing with ghosts and shadows my entire life."

"Yes Mom, I know, so have I. But our perception of what they are is different. Have you ever noticed whenever you were experiencing these apparitions of men, women, and children through the years, there was also a lingering dark shadow presence?"

"You're talking about two different things."

"No Mom, they are the same, I assure you. What I am feeling is not Richard."

The energy in the room was darkening and making me disoriented and disconnected. A hot presence was pressing toward my right side releasing a psychological attack. Pressure in the head increased along with tightness in the solar plexus.

"Well, I honestly believe Richard is trying to watch over me."

"This is a common belief and one of the reasons why these beings thrive. By giving it a name and believing it is Richard, you form a relationship and give the being life as it drains and controls yours. You're hearing voices because you're connected. This whole house will react to your thoughts, emotions, and even your visitors because the beings live within the structure and within most of your objects. When they are angry, they will let you know. If they are in a mischievous mood, like what you just witnessed, they may exhibit a false sense of humor."

"It's not that bad."

"It's not that bad because you have become used to their presence and subtle harassment. Because you are in a chronic state of stress it will be difficult to notice the being's influenced negative thoughts and you may accept them as yours."

"So, what am I supposed to do? I can't move."

"I know you can't move at the moment, but you can accept that these are intelligent spiritual beings or jinn and not Richard."

"I still think Richard is here."

"I know, Mom. I'm not convinced you can talk to those that have passed. But I will try my best on Friday," I said, as I stood up. "I have to go now and get ready for class."

"Can you call me later? I'm not feeling that well."

"Of course," I responded, as I gave my mother a hug.

CHAPTER 3

I AM NOT A MEDIUM OR A PSYCHIC

"Are you all right, Ron?" Tom asked.

"I'm good," Ron answered.

"Alright, let's go one more round with single sticks," I said, as I tightened Ron's helmet.

The bell rang and they bowed to each other and touched gloves. The first strike was a forehand strike to Ron's hand. Ron missed with his forehand strike but caught Tom's hand with the backhand. The class was cheering. This was the last stick fighting match of the night.

Both students were avoiding each other's strike. Tom sprinted in with a downward X strike hitting Ron's helmet with both the forehand and backhand strike. Ron threw a few fakes, then thrusted into Tom's face as he advanced. Both then traded hard forehand strikes to the helmet. Tom again sprinted in with a downward X strike to Ron's helmet. Ron followed with a wild forehand strike just missing Tom's body. Ron was breathing heavily. Both were dancing around keeping their weapon hand moving to avoid getting it hit. Ron faked high with a backhand head strike then squatted low to backhand Tom's knee. Tom countered with a downward strike to the top of Ron's helmet.

"Time. Bow to each other, shake hands. Good match guys."

Tom and Ron removed their helmets and wiped their heads with a towel.

"Alright, let's line up class." All the students lined up according to rank, with their sticks in hand. "Bow. Kneel down and remove your belts." Kneeling, each student placed their sticks in front of them and removed their belt, placing it around their neck.

"Hands on your upper thighs. Focus now on the inhalation and the exhalation of your breath. Clear your mind of thoughts, feelings, and emotions." Five minutes passed. "Okay. Open your eyes. Bow, and dismissed. Take your time getting up."

Walking over to the entrance, I bowed toward the dojo as a sign of respect and then took a seat at the counter. Some students left in their uniforms and others changed in the dressing room. Each student said "Good night, Professor," and complimented the class on the way out. The last two students were Tom and Ron.

While typing attendance and class notes into the computer, Tom walked over to the fridge and took out a bottle of water. Ron stopped at the counter, in an obvious rush.

"Where are you off to in a hurry?" I asked.

"I've got a date," Ron answered.

"Have a good time, Ron."

"Did you meet this one online?" Tom asked, as he was looking over the training weapons in the showcase.

"Yup. We're meeting for a coffee," Ron replied.

"Good luck."

"Thanks, Tom. Goodnight, Professor."

"Goodnight, Ron." Ron left the studio, and Tom walked over and took a seat at the desk.

"So, Professor, Ron tells me you're writing a book on talking to spirits."

"Something like that, yes."

"I just finished reading two books. One on how to talk to the dead, and the other on angel communication. Now I'm a little curious to give it a try. Can you show me how you do it?"

"As a friend, I suggest you avoid this practice. There are many dangers the authors of these books leave out."

"That's why I'm asking if you'll teach me."

"No, Tom. I'd rather not. Practice mindfulness instead. Mindfulness will improve the quality of your life experience."

"I don't get it, Professor. If you're so against spiritual communication, why are you writing a book on the subject?" Tom asked, as he stood up disappointed.

"Sit down for a moment, Tom." Tom sat back down and I leaned back in my chair, wiping my glasses with a tissue.

"I am writing a book on deception in spiritual communication. This is the only reason I interact."

"You can make a lot of money as a medium or psychic, Professor. Why don't you do it on the side?"

"Never let fame or fortune be the reason you converse with the hidden. And I'm not a medium or a psychic."

"You can talk to the dead. That makes you a medium."

"Tom, I don't believe anyone talks to the dead. What I am interacting with is very much alive. Therefore, I am not a medium. Humans have been communicating with deceiving messengers masquerading as the dead since antiquity. As far as psychic, let me ask you a couple of questions. If you were standing next to a Silverback Gorilla, would you brag about how strong you are?"

"Certainly not."

"If you were standing next to a cheetah, would you brag about how fast you can run?"

"No. They can run like 70 miles an hour."

"Well then, in this moment we could be surrounded by spiritual beings that have real psychic ability, far more than any human. To label myself a psychic in their company would be foolish. I am not a psychic or a medium, nor do I want to be. What I am doing, any human can do with a little seasoning. But I wouldn't suggest it."

"How about angels, Professor?"

"They are not what you have been led to believe. It would be wise to leave them alone."

"What do you mean?"

"Our culture is undergoing an angel craze. The knowledge of these intelligent beings is limited."

"I'm thinking about taking an angel certification program next month."

"An angel certification program? That's funny."

"The author of the book I read is an angel expert."

"How cute. Well I'm not an angel expert. But I do have some experience with spiritual beings, which appear as light and/or claim to be angels. Let me share with you what I have discovered about angels. You are at liberty to believe me or not."

"Sounds good."

"Before we go any further, let me explain the very misunderstood label 'angel', as it is one of the biggest deceptions in spiritual communication. The word angel is derived from the Greek word *angelos,* which means messenger. In Hebrew, the word for messenger is 'malach'. All beings, human or non-human, who deliver a positive or negative message can be called a messenger or angel. When it comes to spiritual beings, the misleading label 'angel' tells you nothing about who or what you're interacting with, its true form, strengths, weaknesses, abilities, or intention."

"Are you saying there is no race of angels?"

"I'm saying there are intelligent spiritual beings that appear benevolent, malevolent, or neutral, and that converse and deliver messages in various ways. You can call them what you like. I prefer to call them spiritual beings or energy beings. When they deliver a message, I call them a messenger. Every intelligent spiritual being of the hidden world, benevolent or malevolent, can answer the call of angel."

"What if they appear as light?"

"Spiritual beings can appear luminous as white light, golden-white light, and various other colors. Because many humans have the false perception that the angels of the Bible had wings, deceiving messengers shapeshift and manifest as the heavenly humanoid with wings, or influence the image in visions and dreams. Angels are mentioned in the Bible close to 300 times, but never with wings. The only beings with wings are the cherubim and seraphim, and they are not referred to as angels."

"I know what cherubs are. They are those chubby babies with wings, which you see in art and as garden figurines."

"Not quite, my friend. Cherub is the singular form of these spiritual beings and cherubim the plural. In Scripture, Satan was a cherub created by God."

"You don't believe in Satan, do you Professor?"

"I believe in malevolent spiritual beings and human beings driven by deep dark hatred. Call them what you may."

"So, what does the Bible say Cherubim look like?"

"According to the prophet Ezekiel's vivid visions, they had four faces representing the four living creatures. Ezekiel 1:10 describes the four cherubim he saw with the face of a man, the face of a lion on the right side, the face of an ox on the left side, and the face of an eagle. In Ezekiel 10:14 there is a little difference. He describes them as having the face of a cherub, the face of a man, the face of a lion, and the face of an eagle. In addition to this, the beings have human form, calf's feet, men's hands, and four wings, two stretched upward and two stretched downward, covering their bodies."

"That's a little creepy. How about the seraphim?"

"Seraphim means fiery ones, burning ones, and is also applied to serpents. One of a few passages that mentions fiery serpents is Isaiah 14:29 which says, *Rejoice not thou, whole Palestina, because the rod of him that smote thee is broken: for out of the serpent's root shall come forth a cockatrice, and his fruit shall be a fiery flying serpent."*

"What is a cockatrice?"

"It is a mythological hybrid creature that is part rooster, part serpent or reptile. Seraphim were seen by the prophet Isaiah. He describes them as having a human form, each with six wings. Two wings covered their faces, two wings covered their feet, and with two they were flying."

"They certainly didn't list these beings in the angel book I read."

"Of course not, Tom. It's not the marketed version of an angel. Keep in mind, in some cases when angels appeared to humans in Scripture, their first words were 'fear not!' This wasn't because they were beautiful beings, with dove's wings, a white gown, and a golden harp. It's because they had a frightening or overwhelming appearance."

"What does the Bible say demons look like?"

"Just as the Bible never mentions angels having wings, it never mentions Satan or its servants with a goatee, dressed in a red suit, or with horns, tail, and pitchfork in hand. Two physical descriptions of the ancient adversary that come to mind are in Genesis and Corinthians. Search for 'What does the Bible say Satan, or the devil, looks like' on the internet."

"Which version, Professor?"

"King James will do." While Tom did a search on his cell, I watered the plants.

"I can't find much more than what you mentioned," Tom said, as I walked back into the studio.

"Go ahead and read what you have, Tom," I answered, as I replaced the trash bags in the baskets.

"Okay. Genesis 3:1; *Now the serpent was more subtil than any beast of the field which the Lord God had made. And he said unto the woman, Yea, hath God said, ye shall not eat of every tree of the garden?* Also, 2 Corinthians 11:14-15; *And no marvel; for Satan himself is transformed into an angel of light. Therefore it is no great thing if his ministers also be transformed as the ministers of righteousness; whose end shall be according to their works."*

"As you can see, there is a very limited description of Satan, or what I prefer to call the ancient adversary, as there is a very limited description of heavenly angels. What it comes down to is this, we co-exist with a diverse race of intelligent spiritual beings that appear to be benevolent, malevolent, and a little of both. No one religious text has all the answers about these intelligent spiritual beings. Each only contains bits and pieces. Take it from me, Tom. You're better off leaving the door to the hidden world closed."

"Professor, I used to play with the Ouija board when I was younger and I never encountered any evil spirits or demons. Besides, some things you have to experience for yourself."

"Alright, Tom. If you put it that way. What are you doing Saturday morning?"

"My laundry, I guess. Why?"

"Do you want to join me in an investigation of spiritual beings to learn what they are and what they are not?"

"Are you kidding me?"

"Not at all."

"Where?"

"We will begin with the Monastery."

"Cumberland Monastery?"

"Yes. Are you interested?"

"Of course I'm interested. The place is haunted. Are you going to teach me how you communicate with spirits?"

"Yes, Tom. And at the same time, I'm going to show you why you shouldn't, and if you do, what to expect."

"This is awesome Professor, thanks."

"You're welcome. But before I introduce you to another form of intelligent life, I need you to make a promise."

"Sure. What is it?"

"Promise me you will not try and interact on your own until the investigation is finished. After that, you are free to converse if you choose or take the so-called angel certification program."

"No problem. We have a deal," Tom said, as we shook hands.

"Good. Let's meet at the gazebo at 9:30."

"Do I need to bring anything?" Tom asked, as he picked up his martial arts bag.

"Yes, an open mind and a small regular coffee." I answered, while shutting down the computer.

"You got it. Goodnight, Professor," Tom answered, as he chuckled.

"Goodnight, Tom."

CHAPTER 4

GHOST MONKS

Tom stepped out of his vehicle and handed me a coffee.

"Good morning. Thanks, Tom."

"Good morning, Professor. I bought a couple of doughnuts. Do you want one?"

"No thanks, I already ate." Walking into the gazebo, we took a seat at a picnic table. Tom took a plain doughnut out of the bag and placed it on top of his coffee.

"What do you have planned, Professor?"

"Yesterday morning I had an unusual encounter in the garden and a couple more on the way home."

"What happened?"

"In the garden there were three translucent monks with a golden-white aura that paid me a visit and delivered their message."

"Ghost monks?"

"They're not really ghosts, but you could say that. They had what some would believe to be an angelic presence, and that's not all. There was also an impostor presence posing as my father."

"Are you being serious?"

"Yes, I'm completely serious, Tom. When I left the monastery, I had an encounter with a messenger that introduced itself as an angel and another that claimed to be a Quaker."

"What did they say?"

"I'll let you read what occurred and the dialogue." Opening the backpack, I took out the notebook and flipped through the pages to the conversations. Turning the notebook around, I slid it across the table to Tom. As he began to read and enjoy his doughnut, I picked up my coffee and walked around the monastery. Twenty minutes later I returned.

"Professor, this is some intense stuff."

"Not really, Tom."

"They definitely sound like angels."

"They are, but they are lying angels and the reason we are here to investigate."

"How can you tell?"

"This is not the first time I detected dishonesty in what appeared divine."

"How about your father? He seemed way too kind to be a fake."

"I would like to think so, but unfortunately the pattern of communication, behavior, and energy tells a different story. That wasn't my father. As we analyze the dialogue, I will explain. Let's take a walk into the garden." Placing the notebook in the backpack, Tom and I picked up our trash and threw it in the dumpster. Walking over to the garden, we entered and took a seat on the stone bench.

"It seems peaceful in here. I'm not getting any weird feelings or anything," Tom said, as he looked around.

"Did you know this was the Trappist monks' former graveyard?"

"No. I never knew that."

"Not too many do. It is peaceful. But that doesn't mean we're alone."

"The bodies must have been removed."

"I'm sure they have. But the spiritual beings that hang out in cemeteries haven't."

"Can you see any spiritual beings around me?"

"You see what they want you to see. Can you see the bacteria on the bottom of your shoes or all over your cell phone?"

"No, thank goodness."

"Just because we can't see microbial life, doesn't mean it's not there. The same applies to spiritual beings." At that moment, I received a vision of hundreds of puzzle pieces, about six inches in width, floating in the air.

"Why do you think they are appearing as monks, Professor?"

"It's mimicry. Just like they mimicked my father. These messengers, could be the same adversaries that watched, tormented, and tempted the Trappist monks of the Monastery of Our Lady of the Valley as they devoted their life to God."

"Could they be the ghosts of dead monks?"

"No."

"Don't you believe in ghosts?"

"Are you referring to the dead that appear to the living?"

"Yes."

"Then the answer is no. I believe in ghosts because I have seen my fair share, but they are not dead humans. A ghostly image can be the product of our own consciousness or an optical illusion. It can also be a temporary shapeshifted manifestation, projected image, or an influenced illusion or hallucination from an intelligent spiritual being or beings."

"What about residual hauntings?"

"An apparition moving about with no awareness of human eyes watching?"

"Yes."

"If there were truly a location that a residual haunting of a past traumatic event was taking place regularly, every news crew in the country would be there filming. The missing part of this theory is who, or what, is activating the playback of these so-called recordings. From experience, I believe the answer to that is intelligent spiritual beings. I will give you a couple of examples of how it could work. First, the spiritual being resides at the location and selects who it projects the image to, or it creates the effect in a way I would compare to being immersed in a virtual reality simulation. Kind of like dreaming while you're wide awake. This could be done to one individual or a whole crowd."

"Second, the spiritual being could be following an individual or group, and creating the effects to suit its agenda and maintain its relationship with its host or prey. We are not dealing with stupid beings, Tom. As an example, just a few minutes ago, I received a vision of large puzzle pieces, with different colors and images floating in the air."

"Why puzzle pieces, Professor?"

"They, or it, knows why I'm here and they're ready to play their game."

"What type of game?"

"The guess who game, Tom. Do you still want to do this?"

"Yes, of course," Tom answered nervously.

"Have you heard of the jinn?"

"Yes, I saw the movie *Wishmaster*," Tom replied.

"Is there any movie you haven't seen?"

"What can I say? I'm a supernatural fan."

"I know. Jinn are known for taking on the form of the dead. But few realize that they are quite adept at masquerading as loving angels, deities, spirit guides, and even God."

"Just like Satan can transform into an angel of light."

"Exactly. The Arabic word 'jinn', which can also be spelled d-j-i-n-n, refers to that which is hidden or concealed from the very limited human eye. Individually they are known as jinni, or djinni with a D, or the more popular word here in the western world is genie, which sounds like jinni. It is believed there are female jinn as well and they are known as jinnia."

"Do you think this is the jinn?"

"Yes, and I'll explain why. Just as I told you any spiritual being can answer to the label angel, because they all can play messenger, likewise any of those same spiritual beings can also answer to the label jinn, simply because they are all hidden. Any being you can't see, unless they want you to, can be referred to as jinn. But what type or species of jinn, and how many, is the challenge we face. Let's go back to the gazebo and review the dialogue."

Back at the gazebo, we sat at the picnic table. Taking the notebook out, I turned the pages to the first monk's conversation.

"The first monk said, *God lives here yielding to all who appreciate, Jesus yields to all who appreciate. They are one and the same, sharing the same heart. Seeing through the same eyes. Forever love, forever peace.* These are beautiful words. Discerning the messages of the ghost monks, it would appear they are God's messengers. This makes me think of the quote from Lao Tzu in the book *Tao Te Ching* that says, 'the truth is not always beautiful, nor beautiful words the truth'."

"Some people might think how can the ghost monks be bad if they're mentioning Jesus?"

"Contrary to what many have been led to believe, praising Jesus is not a true sign of a celestial visitor from God. Some believe the malevolent or demonic amongst the spiritual beings cannot even utter the word Jesus. In my experience, this is false. Jinn or spiritual beings that appear to be benevolent or malevolent, can and do speak the name Jesus when interacting with a Christian to gain their approval and an entry. The second monk said, *Here on Earth you are one, here in Heaven you are one.* There was no question the ghost monks emitted a very believable heavenly presence."

"I'm a little confused about the heaven thing. What does it mean *here in heaven*? You didn't go anywhere."

"What is perceived as heaven or hell is not a destination but a state of being. Heaven or hell can come to you as an energy experience induced by spiritual beings, human beings, or your own subconscious. It can also come to you in dreams, visions, and voices through the influence of spiritual beings. Because these spiritual beings are playing the role of Christian monks, I took out the King James Bible last night and searched for passages that were similar or exact to the messenger's dialogue or its intent. To help you understand the *here in heaven* comment, and our first comparison of the monk's dialogue to the Bible, let's review the baptism of Jesus and focus on what occurred after Jesus came out of the water."

"Matthew 3:16; *And Jesus, when he was baptized, went up straightway out of the water: and, lo, the heavens were opened unto him, and he saw the Spirit of God descending like a dove, and lighting upon him.* Matthew 3:17; *And lo a voice from heaven, saying, This is my beloved Son, in whom I am well pleased.* Mark 1:10; *And straightway coming up out of the water, he saw the heavens opened, and the Spirit like a dove descended upon him.* Mark 1:11; *And there came a voice from heaven, saying, Thou art my beloved Son, in who I am well pleased.* Luke 3:21; *Now when all the people were baptized, it came to pass, that Jesus also being baptized, and praying, the heaven was opened,* Luke 3:22; *And the Holy Ghost descended in a bodily shape like a dove upon him, and a voice came from heaven, which said, Thou art my beloved Son; in thee I am well pleased.*"

"Jesus didn't go anywhere when the heavens opened. They didn't say he disappeared and came back. Jesus experienced the powerful life-changing presence of heaven and influenced visions induced by a spiritual being that we have come to know as

LORNE J. THERRIEN SR.

the Holy Spirit. There is no description of God, because what he felt was a presence of love, with a vision of light."

"Why are your eyes tearing, Professor. You've had this experience, haven't you?"

"Yes, Tom. Many men and women throughout history have had the mystical religious experience. The problem lies in making this experience something it is not with unnecessary fluff."

"Can you tell me about your mystical religious experience?"

"Sure. The mystical religious experience I am speaking of is what appears to be a divine presence that descends and washes over your being as you are engulfed in an intense light as bright as the sun inducing an addictive euphoria of pure joy, and at times causing your mind to go blank, free of thought, unable to speak, or even feel the need."

"Originally, when the mystical religious experiences began, I believed it to be God, or the Holy Spirit, due to Christian mental conditioning. As time went on, I noticed a pattern with the mystical religious experiences, angelic visitations, and demonic attacks."

"Questioning my discernment that recognized the angels, demons, and what I believed to be God as the same presence, I started doing some research. What I found was a pattern of the Holy Spirit presence that dwells within the lovers of Christ, like the Christian mystics and saints, allowing them to experience what is perceived to be celestial or godly visions and the euphoria of a presence of divine love one moment, and then being attacked, assaulted, and tortured relentlessly by what is perceived as a separate enemy being the demons or Satan the next."

"These mystical religious experiences are highly addictive. The victim craves the return of the divine presence of love for another euphoric moment, willing to receive the beating and abuse beforehand like a poverty-stricken drug addict would accept from a drug dealer for another fix."

"This is what happened to you. That's why the Impostor Father said, *you walked the path of a saint while camouflaging your abilities.*"

"Yes, my friend. Jinn can play the role of saints or attempt to get you to believe you're walking that path. This is the flattery con, a common deceptive tactic and another sign it was not my father. There was never a desire of walking the path of a saint, but I walked the path like many others, who love God with all their heart. The goal of the deceiver in the garden is to inflate my ego and give the being the opportunity to continue the divine/demonic rollercoaster ride of the past. This I have already done by taking on this investigation."

"Now let's get back to Matthew, Mark, and Luke's description of the baptism where we can see differences. Matthew's would mean everyone present heard the voice from heaven. Mark and Luke say the heavenly voice was speaking directly to Jesus, which could mean they conversed telepathically. The voice came from the presence that emitted the heavenly sensation. Again, Scripture didn't say Jesus left and visited a destination called Heaven. Jesus experienced this heavenly sensation right where he stood, induced by the Holy Spirit or Holy Ghost."

"The first ghost monk said, *Here I walked, listening to the songs of the morning birds, very beautiful indeed.* A robin appears on the cedar cross that later leads me to a message of love, and a cardinal catches my attention to lead me to another message of affection. Jinn can appear as wildlife, and can influence and manipulate wildlife for benevolent or malevolent reasons just as they can humans. Birds and wildlife may continue to play a role in this investigation."

"Comparing *I am well pleased* from Matthew, Mark, and Luke's description of the baptism to the Impostor Father that calls me son, we have, *Yes, and I am here now talking to you, and I say I am proud of you, and I love you.* Do you see the resemblance?"

"Yes. What does this mean?"

"As I said, these beings are not stupid. They are very old and very wise and could be the same race of beings that influenced the religions of the world."

"This is really deep."

"We haven't even begun. In the notebook, I described my experience yesterday while driving. A vision of a golden-white cross appeared in my mind's eye at the same time I was embraced by a divine-like presence. This is why the second monk said, *you have been transformed by the light of goodness; you now have God's eyes.*"

"What does the monk mean by *you now have God's eyes?*"

"God's eyes, or spiritual eyes, are perceived by some as a phase of a spiritual awakening process. This is what the second monk was implying. In truth, the jinni's mind becomes my mind and my mind becomes theirs. Heaven is the perceived gift, but hell might come with the package."

"What do you mean by that?"

"It means I am now subject to their, or its, hallucinations or illusions. The three ghost monks could be an influenced hallucination from one jinni. Jinn are energy beings with consciousness, or conscious entities. When you connect, or merge, you have a mind to mind conversation. But when you end the call, the connection may still be there, and you are subject to what lives within that mind. Deceiving jinn are like the Trojan Horse, once you welcome them within the gates of your being, hell is slowly released."

"How can you avoid this?"

"Don't engage in spiritual conversation, Tom."

"Professor, you're like the Sherlock Holmes of the spirit world."

"Thank you, but I was played a fool before I attained the knowledge, my friend. And I can still be played a fool. Last night a voice whispered *Constantine* into my ear three times. When I woke up I did some research on Constantine. What I came up with was Constantine was the first Roman Emperor to convert to Christianity. Constantine worshipped the sun god Sol Invictus, the unconquered sun. But one day just before the battle of Milvian Bridge, Constantine and his soldiers looked up in the sky and saw a vision of a cross of light above the sun, which Constantine believed was sent by the God of Christianity because of an omen the night before. This vision of the cross of light is said to have taken place on the evening of October 27th."

"October 27th was yesterday, Professor."

"Yes, Tom."

"That's freaky."

"That's the spirit world. Along with this cross of light were words that translate to 'In this sign, you shall conquer' in Latin. Pondering the meaning of the vision, Constantine had a dream the next night in which he was visited by Christ who told him to use this cross sign for protection and to defeat his enemies. This supposedly began Constantine's conversion to Christianity."

"I would compare Constantine's perceived miracle to Paul's vision experienced on the road to Damascus. There are three contradicting accounts of the story by Luke in the Bible but we will just take a look at what occurred in Acts 9:1-9. Could you do a search and read it please?"

"Sure." Tom picked up his phone and performed the search. "I've got it. Acts 9:1-9, *And Saul, yet breathing out threatenings and slaughter against the disciples of the Lord, went unto the high priest, And desired of him letters to Damascus to the synagogues, that if he found any of this way, whether they were men or women, he might bring them bound unto Jerusalem. And as he journeyed, he came near Damascus: and suddenly there shined round about him a light from heaven: And he fell to the earth, and heard a voice saying unto him, Saul, Saul, why persecutest thou me? And he said, Who art thou, Lord? And the Lord said, I am Jesus whom thou persecutest: it is hard for thee to kick against the pricks. And he trembling and astonished said, Lord, what wilt thou have me to do? And the Lord said unto him, Arise, and go into the city, and it shall be told thee what thou must do. And the men which journeyed with him stood speechless, hearing a voice, but seeing no man. And Saul arose from the earth; and when his eyes were opened, he saw no man: but they led him by the hand, and brought him into Damascus. And he was three days without sight, and neither did eat nor drink."*

"Thank you. Saul who later became Paul was engulfed in a light and heard a voice that claimed to be Jesus that frightened him. In this version he couldn't see a form and neither did the men who accompanied him. How many days was he without sight?"

"Three"

"Yes. Moving on to the third monk who said, *Kindness breeds goodness, Goodness breeds holiness, Holiness breeds God child.* Speaking in threes is a common trait of some messengers who appear as light. At times, they will introduce themselves as angels, and other times they don't. Here the word *breeds* was used three times. The Impostor Father also spoke beautifully and in threes when it said, *Fear was my companion so I drank; Fear was my thoughts so I drank; Fear made my decisions so I drank* and *How I lived was by the bottle, How I died was by the bottle, How I found God was by my son, which I gave up for the bottle."*

"Speaking in threes are not the words of a human spirit. When I asked the Impostor Father if he would be affected by the sun's rays, he said, *I only see light, there is never darkness here.* Looking through the King James Bible I found this, 1 John 1:5; *This then is the message which we have heard of him, and declare unto you, that God is light, and in him is no darkness at all.* This is more evidence of the ghost monks, or the jinni playing the ghost monks, knowledge of the Bible."

"When the Impostor Father spoke, I recognized the energy presence to be exact to the ghost monks and past spiritual beings that have introduced themselves as angels and/or appeared as light. Comparing the dialogue of the Impostor Father to the third monk, I see the word *radiant* used by both; that would have never existed in my father's vocabulary. *My brother love never travels farther than your radiant heart can reach,* by the third monk, and from the Impostor Father, *Because I, your father, learned of God from your radiant heart."*

"Impostor Father said, *I know my son, just as you knew to come here, you will know truth in the words I speak.* The spiritual being led me here with the light and love trap, then it attempts to convince me that it was my intuitive ability that knew to come here."

"During our investigation, we will be paying close attention to the pattern of words. This will help in revealing the deceptive work of a jinni or a group of jinn."

"Reviewing the dialogue of the messenger that we will call Red Cardinal Angel, we see the same pattern of words as the ghost monks and the Impostor Father. But this time, the messenger introduced itself as an angel, spoke in threes four times, and used the word illumination like the first and third ghost monks, along with the words illuminate and illuminated."

"Red Cardinal Angel said, *The goodness of your heart and the light in your eyes,* which we can see is a follow up to what the second monk said, *you have been transformed by the light of goodness; you now have God's eyes.*"

"In the last encounter we see an example of the needy spirit con, which is used to pull on the heart strings. The Quaker which was never human spoke in threes and was an expressed female persona. I could dissect the dialogue even more, but we can see from the dialogue of the ghost monks, the Impostor Father, the Red Cardinal Angel, and the Quaker that the personas could easily be the work of one being."

"I never would have figured that out. Why do the ghost monks call you brother?"

"They, or it, could be referring to brotherhood in God. Humans have given messengers many labels. Messengers will give humans many labels. The ghost monks called me brother, the Impostor Father called me son, and said, *you walked the path of a saint,* and the angel called me heavenly friend and human eternal. This is to get me to believe I'm more than what I am, inflate my ego, establish a relationship, feed on my energy, gain entry, and share their doctrine. That's why the third monk said, *give compassion a voice, let it be you.* The Quaker said, *Heaven has a speaker, let it be you,* showing the same use of words, and the third monk said, *I have spoken and others are coming. Always allow your family to speak as well. Selfishness is not God.* Clearly they, or it, want me to be their voice piece."

"What next, Professor?"

"Monks, an Impostor Father, an angel, and a Quaker. If I were naive to the deceptive ways of jinn, it would appear they are all individual entities when they surely are not. Now that I have drank the parasitic water by connecting, the symptoms will progressively worsen. Are you ready to learn the nature of another intelligent form of life?"

"I'm just following your lead."

"Good. Then let's begin."

CHAPTER 5
BEINGS OF ENERGY

S tepping over the guard rail onto the Beauregard Loop Trail, two joggers passed. A family approached us with a young boy wearing a six-gun belt, cowboy hat, and a red bandanna tied around his neck. When the boy pulled out his toy guns, he said "Howdy partners." "Howdy," we both answered back as the family smiled.

From the Beauregard Loop we took the Nine Men's Misery Trail. Passing through the field, we entered the forest and stopped just before we reached the brook.

"Tom, behind that tree is a walking stick, can you get it please?" I asked, as I pointed to a large oak tree in the distance.

Tom stepped off the path, the sound of small fallen branches snapping and dried leaves crunching with each step. "This is the perfect bo staff height." Tom said, as he returned with the stick.

"Yes, it is. I would like you to practice your bo staff strikes, and one and two hand spins, while we walk."

"Is this to scare away the evil spirits?" Tom said, jokingly.

"No. It's to entertain them."

"You're kidding, right?"

"We will see."

"This stick is a little heavy to spin fast."

"Then spin it slowly, Tom."

"Professor, do you think these woods are haunted like they say?" Tom asked, as he was performing the helicopter spin overhead.

"Humans are haunted, Tom. There are spiritual beings on the monastery grounds and within the monastery building, but that doesn't mean another person is going to have a similar experience to yours or mine, or if they don't have the experience that there is nothing there. When it comes to spiritual communication, the spiritual being is the transmitter and you are the receiver."

"Scientists have discovered that consciousness creates reality. If consciousness creates reality and these spiritual beings are conscious entities, then they can affect your reality by merging with your bio-electricity creating a virtual reality simulation from their thought alone. This in turn becomes a challenge for the victim to distinguish what is real from what is illusion."

"Dreaming while wide awake, like you mentioned."

"Yes."

"That makes it much easier to understand."

"Good. The forest is full of life which can't be easily detected with human senses." Stopping, I kneeled and dug into the soil with my right hand. "In this handful of earth, we see a couple of creatures, when in truth there are billions. If you could see these critters clearly, then you would also be able to see the bacteria on the bottom of your shoes, your cell phone, and the millions inside your mouth, at this very moment. Seeing this, would probably put you in a padded room on a tranquilizer diet."

Tom laughed. "Funny, Professor."

"There is plenty of life humans can't see, for good reason."

"Good analogy."

"Thank you, Tom."

From the Nine Men's Misery Trail we took the Cart Path and then the Homestead Trail. Stopping, I placed my right hand on an old oak tree. "Let's take a seat on the rock wall." Stepping off the trail, we walked over to the wall. Taking off my backpack, I laid it down on a large rock and then took a seat.

"Professor, why did you touch the tree?"

"I'm emitting heart energy into the tree, which travels through the forest by way of the network of roots."

"Why?"

"Because the forest soothes me and I am grateful."

"Should I touch trees?"

"When the beauty of nature brings tears to your eyes and joy to your heart, it will be time to touch."

"Are there spirits in the trees?"

"There are spiritual beings of nature that inhabit all you see and don't see above and below the Earth's surface. There were spiritual beings in the fieldstones, which the monks gathered from this property to build the Monastery of Our Lady of the Valley. Long before this land was sacred to the monks it was sacred to the natives of this land. Myths and legends of these native people speak of encounters with both benevolent and malevolent spiritual beings in a variety of forms. Two of these forms I have experienced are shadow beings and what could be Puckwudgies."

"I know what shadow beings are, but what the heck is a Puckwudgie?"

"Puckwudgies, or Pucks for short, are a mischievous and sometimes dangerous goblin, gremlin, or troll-like spiritual being of a shorter stature. Hooded shadow beings are shapeshifters just like Pucks. I believe Pucks are either a shapeshifted form of the shadow beings or a related race."

Unzipping the backpack, I took out the notebook, placed it on my lap, and opened it to a fresh page. Removing the chart from the sleeve I placed it on a rock. Taking off my silver necklace, I removed the cross pendant and put it in my pocket.

"What are you going to do with that?" Tom asked, as he looked at the chain.

"I'm going to use it as a pendulum."

"Why do you use a pendulum?"

"It allows me to have a longer conversation with the messenger in a way that I'm comfortable with. This gives me the necessary time to read their energy, look for patterns in their speech, delayed answers, and notice any slip-up in their tangled web of lies."

"What do you think of an EVP (electronic voice phenomena) recorder?"

"An EVP recorder is limited. If we were using an EVP recorder at this moment, we would most likely receive a few words in bits and pieces, or nothing at all, even though we are surrounded by spiritual beings. Spiritual beings don't desire a relationship with an EVP recorder, they desire a human host. They don't communicate because they like to talk, they communicate to connect and gain access into the human host. EVP recorders can become addicting, like any other form of divination, and carry the same dangers. Using a pendulum with an alphabet chart in this manner opens doors and makes connections, just like a spirit board."

"Do you ever actually see doors?"

"Yes, at times. Ancient and modern doors and gates appear to the mind's eye influenced by the subconscious or a spiritual being. They are made of various materials, and come in different colors and shapes. Sometimes they swing out, as an invitation to enter, and sometimes they swing in, when a spiritual being is coming forward. But don't be concerned with doors right now. The real danger is beginning relationships with spiritual beings that are very jealous, have a hot temper, and don't take rejection well. Just like some humans."

"It sounds like you have been down that road, Professor."

"I have. Now let's talk a little bit about what is going to take place. When I interact with spiritual beings I always take into consideration that what is speaking could be an attachment, follower, or what I like to call a tag along, and not necessarily a spiritual being that resides in the location the communication is taking place. One tag along can collect information and play many roles in numerous locations. Overlooking this truth is one of the biggest mistakes of paranormal investigators and those that claim to be psychics and mediums."

"Can the messengers really hear your thoughts?"

"Yes. In addition to watching, a tag along listens closely for your desires and fears, as thoughts attract and open doors, feeding the parasitic."

"That's just plain creepy."

"It's just plain reality."

"How do you know for sure who you're talking to?"

"You don't. Words will flow without thought. Names will be given and visions shared. But keep in mind you are dealing with pathological liars. No human has ever known for sure who, or what, the messenger is they're interacting with."

At that moment, a rock hit the tree hard to our right. "What the hell was that?" Tom yelled out in surprise.

"A rock."

"Who threw it? There's no one around."

"Our invisible neighbors. As I said, we are not alone, Tom. They are nature spirits or spiritual beings in nature."

"Why did they throw a rock?"

"To frighten. Jinn like to throw rocks. They, or it, is being mischievous. If they wanted to hit you or me, they easily could have."

"I'm getting a little freaked out."

"Why?"

"What do you mean why? Maybe you're used to invisible brats throwing rocks, but I'm not."

"Relax, Tom. They are just trying to scare you and disturb your peace."

"It worked."

"Focus on the inhalation and the exhalation of your breath to center yourself, like I taught you in class."

"What if I get beaned off the head with a freakin' rock?"

"You won't. They usually aim for the testicles."

"What-t-t?"

"I'm just joking, Tom." Tom closed his eyes and focused on his breathing, while I merged with the stillness of the environment. Taking a deep breath, I let it out and relaxed into receptive oneness. "Do you feel more relaxed?"

"Yes, I do."

"Good. Can you take notes?"

"Sure."

Handing the notebook and pen to Tom, I placed the alphabet chart in my lap.

"I will be speaking outwardly to the presence, receiving their transmission telepathically, and translating it to you. It's going to appear like you're hearing one side of a telephone conversation. Try your best to remain calm, no matter what the messenger may say. These beings are very emotional. Any emotional shift in you, will cause an emotional shift in the presence. We have company waiting. A benevolent presence is here, and it's sending an image to my mind's eye of a ghost monk, just like in the garden. The monk is standing in front of the first of three gold triangles. Are you ready to write?"

"Yup," Tom answered picking up the pen.

Controlling thought and emotion, I said, "Hello, for the goodness of all, if you please. Do you have a message to share with humanity?" The conversation began telepathically.

You are beginning to understand what few will take the time to figure out. All is one. You know this.

"I'm learning. But, thank you. Tom, would you like to ask the questions?"

"Yes, I would. What is the path that mankind is on? And where will it lead?" Tom asked.

All paths are individual. What path you choose depends on your current beliefs. All have unique visions and dreams. You must follow your heart and judge no one who chooses a different path. Humans will follow what appears to be truth. What appears to be, is not always truth. I appreciate your question. I hope you understand my answer.

"Kind of, I would like to know a specific location of an object that is within this area that is not of this Earth?" Tom asked.

You mean something alien?

"Yes," Tom answered.

You are a firm believer in what is called aliens. Little green or gray men in spaceships. You will find your answer in the world around you. I am sitting right next to you. Do you see me?

"No."

When you can see me, you will see your answer. You are among many beings. I am not going around your question. I am answering you truthfully. Do you understand?

"Yes and no."

You will search your lifetime for what will be explained in another dimension of being. Accept this, and enjoy every breath of life.

"You refer to us as humans. What do you call yourself?"

I am spirit, once human, always love. You are referred to as human because I am energy. You are energy. You're wearing a shell. I am without the shell. I am no different inside than you are inside.

"What is your name and where did you live?"

My name is Father Albert Celestine.

"Have I spelled your name correctly?"

Yes. I am of the monastery. Here I lived, here I died, here I continue to live with many of my brothers.

"Where can we verify your information?"

I am love and light. You are also love and light. I speak for all in saying God is more than man and I am more than a voice. My friend, what and who I was will be among the pictures as you enter the monastery. Please enter to confirm my validity. I would be proud if you would do that.

"Another energy shift is occurring, Tom. The image sent to my mind's eye is another ghost monk standing in front of the second of three gold triangles." This time I asked the questions. "Hello. Who may I ask is present?"

Being of energy.

"It is a pleasure. There is no emotion felt in your presence."

I have no emotional make up.

"Do you have a message for humanity?"

Yes. I am more than capable of letting you know I am here without words. I, like you, have learned to communicate with energy of various expressions. Here in your atmosphere is a stadium of beings watching and communicating. Each unique energy has a unique being. Each unique being tries to express but goes unnoticed until a unique being gives them a chance to speak.

"Tom, would you like to ask some questions?"

"Yes, I would. Do you have a physical form?"

No. I am pure energy. Most will think alien. If I told you aliens are without flesh, would that create visions? If I told you we have assisted your race for thousands of years, would that create visions? If I told you your advanced technology is of alien mind, would that create visions?

What about God? Is it man or being? Those that think they know the answer create more confusion in your already turmoiled world.

"Can you tell us more about energy beings?"

Yes. Some are harmful to your presence, some complement your presence. Throughout time, energy beings have complemented your human stature. We have mated with your race. Look at your newly found gifts of ancient artifacts dispelling much of your previous theories and rewriting history. Energy beings have shown you, now show us what you can do to recreate your Earth plane existence.

We have watched you. We have educated you. We have altered you. I am communicating through Lorne because his mission is pure. You can't hide your purity from beings of energy. Freedom of mind will create freedom on Earth. Freedom isn't living without respect for Earth. It's living without limitations of your thoughts or any others.

"Most will find this hard to believe."

Forget about what is perceived as normal. Because to know normal, you must know truth. When truth accompanies your being, you will see differently. You will see beauty not in the contours of flesh, but in energy pulsation. Visions won't fool your picturesque mind. You will accept and become aware that you share Earth plane existence with energy beings, shattering the window of pre-recorded knowledge. We have become family. You are about to learn what truly is and discard what truly isn't. Don't worry time will soften the impact of this doorway to world alteration. This won't hurt you so don't battle your imagination. We have kept your race going thus far. The real inventors take no credit, for we only assist your race, not try to control it. Compare notes, maybe you will see when we began our assistance.

A vision was sent of what looked like the pyramids of ancient Egypt. I was now asking the questions. "I'm seeing what looks like ancient Egypt."

You see quite clearly Hemate.

"Is Hemate a place near Egypt?"

Hemate was a civilization much different than Egypt.

"I'm seeing pyramids and square stone buildings with chiseled lines in the rocks like sunrays and drawings on the walls. Are you speaking the truth?"

Yes.

"I'm sorry, but I must ask."

You don't have to apologize for validity. More people should acquire this habit before making note of communication. Hemate was more barbaric than Egypt until we mated. Then civilization forever changed and started the process of human illuminated evolution. Look at the drawings, study the interpretations. For thousands of years we blended, for thousands of years we hid valuable artifacts for safety of the discoverer. Timing is the wisest teacher, it knows when to enter the grand scheme of life. I know what you're thinking.

"Yes, I know. If Hemate is checked and doesn't exist, the validity of this conversation is gone."

I will help you find the validity. Look up Hemate civilization.

"I will, later. What may I ask is God to you?... Tom, a third energy shift is taking place. The image sent was the last ghost monk standing in front of the third of three gold triangles."

God's ye are, Gods ye be. Deep within your electrical core a seed of light awaits. Internalized oneness emits the food that feeds the God. Birth begins and God grows to the frequency of its feedings.

"Who may I ask is speaking?"

An energy being, explaining God, for which you asked. Alien I am. God I am.

A vision was sent to the mind's eye of a circle drawn in dirt with a dot in the center. "Tom, can I use the pen for a moment?" Tom handed me the pen and I drew the symbol right beside the alphabet chart, then handed it back.

Look at the symbol you have drawn.

"It is a symbol for the sun."

How did it come to be?

"I don't know."

I will explain. Find civilization, and alien has complemented its beginning. Long ago human beasts roamed like animals. Killing gladly and impregnating female for survival. The hole in the center of the circle you drew is planted celestial matter.

"Are you saying all is not God?"

Obviously, take a good look around you. Goodness is the light it consumes. God is you and all like you. The illumined seed planted deep within fills all gaps in cell memory. Growth is calculated and messages appear. The God you created brings the messages to your attention.

"Was this seed planted for the evolution of humankind?"

Alien enters, being evolves, Earth lives. Humans fight, we don't. Humans kill, we don't. Humans die, we don't. It will all come together full circle, at the right moment. Heresy frequents the questioning mind.

"May I ask, what are angels and demons to you?"

Demons are parasites of emitted evil waste. Angels are light emitted by the goodness of the God seed. A battle begins keeping freedom of life at great length. Freedom was and can be again. I promise you this story will make more sense. The sun can speak, believe, and listen. Goodbye.

"Thank you for your wisdom and your message. Goodbye." Placing the pendulum on the notebook I took a moment to pray and then drank some water. Tom slid down off the rock.

"Holy shit. That was unbelievable. Do you think these ghost monks or jinn are aliens?"

"They played alien because of your fascination. Just as they play God's messenger, because of my love for God. To gain your attention, the messenger knows it must provide information that piques your interest."

"What do you mean by an energy shift?"

"There is a change in the energy of the presence. It could be an emotional energy shift, another messenger, another persona of the same messenger, or a subtle shift in its energy vibration. When the messenger is invisible you can't look in their eyes or read their body language, like you can with a human liar. You must read the language of their energy. Before we analyze the dialogue and content, please do an internet search for Hemate civilization."

"Alright," Tom answered. Within a few moments, Tom shook his head. "There is nothing, Professor."

"Of course, this is the nature of the being."

"But they said some really good stuff."

"They are ancient deceivers, Tom. They can say some really good stuff. When playing a benevolent role, they share a mixture of knowledge and lies."

"Why don't you just tell them they're lying?"

"Because that would cease the flow of the conversation and create unnecessary conflict. I am interviewing clever spiritual beings that may have somewhat of a Jekyll and Hyde personality. When I am interacting, I monitor the tone of my voice and try to maintain emotional harmony. You can't get to know the whole being by pissing them off. Let's review Father Albert Celestine."

"Are we going inside the monastery to check if Father Albert Celestine is on the wall?" Tom asked.

"We can. But the picture will not be there."

"How do you know?"

"Because the jinn enjoy sending humans on wild goose chases. There is another reason why Father Albert Celestine wants us to enter and it's not to see a picture on the wall. What the persona wants is to talk inside the building where it will have the advantage. Here in nature I am in my element which makes it much easier to maintain a higher vibrational frequency when conversing."

"Most abandoned or former religious dwellings like monasteries, churches, rectories, and convents become the home to malevolent jinn, which in my experience is the hooded shadow."

"Why, Professor?"

"By the end of this investigation you will have your answer. There have been reports of shadow beings, in the form of hooded medieval monks on the monastery grounds. I have witnessed the hooded shadow on the property three times at dusk through the years. The other night, my mother just happened to have some shadow visitors which she described as a tall hooded shadow and a four foot wide shadow spider on the ceiling, which was most likely a shapeshifted form of the hooded shadow. My mother now believes some of the activity is Richard trying to get attention and she asked if I would try and communicate."

"Are you going to?"

"Yes, on Friday."

"Do you think there is a correlation between what is happening here and at your mother's?"

"Yes, Tom. I have a tag along, and that tag along is a hooded shadow. Whatever is hidden within the cloak of this species of jinn may be the spiritual being that has been labeled the demon or devil, the false angel of light, or even what we have come to know as gods. Please do a search for Celestine."

"Okay." While Tom searched, I drank some more water and began to stretch. "Its origin is Latin, and it means heavenly."

"How cute is that? Father Albert Celestine is not all heavenly. The second monk, the Impostor Father, and the Quaker used the word heaven. The Red Cardinal Angel called me heavenly friend. Neither of us witnessed a manifestation of ghost monks during the conversations, like I witnessed in the garden. All three ghost monks standing in front of a gold triangle were influenced mental images to my mind's eye."

"Why gold triangles?"

"Messengers also communicate through symbolism and with numbers. How many sides to a triangle?"

"Three."

"My mother experienced three knocks at the door between 3 and 3:30 am. Three triangles is 333. Both benevolent and malevolent messengers use these master numbers. We will discover more about its meaning soon enough. The visions were sent to my mind's eye from a jinni that has invisibility on its side, like the hooded shadow. Father Albert Celestine began with flattery and went on to answer your question and discuss paths. Celestine reinforced the reason for these ghost monks and other personas when it said, *Humans will follow what appears to be truth. What appears to be, is not always truth.* These messengers are delivering their doctrine, as expected."

"Before today, I would have believed everything these messengers said."

"I know, Tom. We are removing the mystique and exploring the true nature of the being. There is truth in what Father Albert Celestine said, *when you can see me, you will see your answer. You are among many beings.* When humans better understand our invisible neighbors, they will better understand that aliens could also be invisible and not necessarily need a spaceship for travel any more than messengers need wings to move through the air."

"Father Albert Celestine said, *I am spirit, once human, always love.* Father Albert was never human, just like the Quaker, but I'm sure influenced many. Father Albert spoke in threes, and mentioned brothers when it said, *Here I lived, here I died, here I continue to live with many of my brothers.*"

"Comparing the first two sentences from Father Albert with the first two sentences from the Impostor Father that said, *How I lived was by the bottle, how I died was by the bottle, how I found God was by my son, which I gave up for the bottle…* You can see Father Albert Celestine said, *Here I lived.* The Impostor Father said, *How I lived.* Father Albert Celestine said, *Here I died.* The Impostor Father said, *How I died.* Both personalities are played by the same being."

"Damn, you're good Professor."

"I could be wrong, Tom. Looking at the dialogue of the messengers that called themselves Being of Energy and Energy Being we also see speaking in threes. Do you know why they, or it, chose the label Energy Being and Being of Energy?"

"No, why?"

"Because I told you at the studio that I prefer to call these beings spiritual beings or energy beings."

"That's right. I forgot."

"Being of Energy said, *I am more than capable of letting you know I am here without words.* Do you know how?"

"By feeling its presence?"

"Yes. A sinister side is already surfacing. Did you feel a presence when the messengers were speaking?"

"No, not at all."

"When these spiritual beings are invisible, and their energy is neutral, it is difficult to sense their presence. If they are emotional, it is much easier."

"Just like I told the Quaker she appeared to be at peace, I told Being of Energy that there was no emotion felt in its presence. Being of Energy replied with, *I have no emotional make up,* because it wants me to believe it doesn't get angry or have a dark side. This is a lie. Having a neutral energy presence only proves the being wasn't emotional at the moment."

"Do you think they mated with our race, Professor?"

"I'm not a scientist. But it is possible. Human beings have been co-existing with spiritual beings over many millennia."

"Looking at the word *validity* that Father Albert and Being of Energy used and then a sentence which means the same thing by the Impostor Father, we see more evidence of the same being. *Please enter to confirm my validity,* by Father Albert Celestine and *You don't have to apologize for validity.* Then, *I will help you find the validity* by Being of Energy and *I will respect your questioning through sensitivity,* by the Impostor Father."

"Messengers say they agree with validation, but after an investigation of the identity you will find it's all lies. This is just a small example of how these beings play, and another reason you should avoid spiritual communication in all its forms."

"By what I have seen so far it doesn't seem dangerous, just deceiving."

"Consider this the honeymoon phase of the relationship. These benevolent messengers don't reveal much information about the demons or perceived opposing dark force. They never do, even in Scripture. Energy Being said, *Demons are parasites of emitted evil waste. Angels are light emitted by the goodness of the God seed. A battle begins keeping freedom of life at great length. Freedom was and can be again. I promise you this story will make more sense.* Energy Being used the term parasites because the tag along heard me say, 'in addition to watching, a tag along listens closely for your desires and fears, as thoughts attract and open doors, feeding the parasitic.'"

"The last sentence of Energy Being we will review will be, *the sun can speak, believe, and listen.* When Red Cardinal Angel appeared in the mind's eye, it did so as light as bright as the sun. The tag along can appear in vision as bright as the sun and it wants me to converse, believe, and listen when it does. It also wants to continue to interact in sunlight as it sent an image to my mind's eye of the sun symbol, which was a dot in the center of a circle. This is promoting sun worship which has occurred in various forms throughout human history."

"In my experience, benevolent personas, and what appeared to be divine manifestations have come forward when interacting in direct sunlight out in nature. It is possible that this species of jinn may receive positive benefits from sunlight, like other sentient beings, possibly producing a calming effect on their moods as it does human beings. They may also charge, energize, or feed on the light emitted by the sun. Let's take a break and enter the monastery."

CHAPTER 6

THE GOLDEN CROSS

E ntering the Cumberland Public Library, we walked up the stairs and took a left
to the restrooms in the original portion of the monastery.

"Look around and see if Father Albert Celestine's picture is on the wall."

"Alright."

Walking into the restroom, I was immediately greeted by an aggressive, malevolent presence that projected its wicked energy against my back in an intimidating manner. An image was sent to my mind's eye of a monk in a black wooded frame. The monk in the picture had a long gray beard and appeared angry as it began to talk, but no words were heard.

Get out, was whispered in my right ear by a deep, guttural voice.

Ignoring its aggressive tactics, I washed my hands and didn't attempt to interact. Walking out, Tom was standing in front of a mounted page of a newspaper on the wall.

"Professor, look at this, it's the cedar cross during the fire of 1950."

"Yes Tom, the cross has been there a long time."

The headline in *The Woonsocket Call* newspaper read '$2 Million Fire Ruins Monastery'. Observing the old photos of the interior and exterior of the Monastery of Our Lady of the Valley, I noticed two angel statues facing each other behind the altar in the church and two larger statues, possibly Mother Mary and the other a saint.

"I'll be right out," Tom said, as he opened the door to the restroom.

"Okay," I answered. As I continued looking at the old photos, I was concerned if Tom were going to be approached by the malevolent presence. I didn't mention my experience in the restroom to avoid any apprehension. Tom walked out of the restroom rubbing his solar plexus in a circle with his right hand. This action said plenty.

"Now I know why you're in no rush to interact in this building. There is an eerie feeling in there, I felt like I was being watched."

"Let's not talk about that now."

"How come?"

"Thoughts attract and we're going to take a ride."

"Where?"

"To visit the closest cemetery."

"Why."

"To get some more information, then a sandwich."

Turning right out of the monastery entrance, there was a policeman parked in the church parking lot drinking a coffee. I pulled in and parked beside him. Rolling down my window I said, "Excuse me, could you tell me what graveyard is close to here?" He gave me directions to one that was right up the road. "Thank you," I said, as I drove away.

Arriving at the cemetery, there was a man getting out of a backhoe. I walked over to him and introduced myself. "Hi, I'm Lorne Therrien."

"I'm Patrick Bradley."

"It is a pleasure, Patrick," I said, as we shook hands.

"I am writing a book that includes the Cumberland Monastery. Would you have any information about the Trappist monks that were buried there?"

"As a matter of fact, I do," Patrick answered as he looked at me strangely. "It was my father who transferred three monks buried in grain sacks from where the flower garden is now to their new resting place at the monastery in Spencer, Massachusetts."

"I never knew the flower garden was the monk's former burial ground," Tom said.

"Well, it was," Patrick answered.

"You have been very helpful, Patrick. Thank you," I said.

"What are the odds of that? You pull in to the first cemetery and the guy getting out of a backhoe is the son of the man that moved the monks," Tom said, as we walked back to the vehicle.

"Now we know why the messengers appeared as three ghost monks in the garden. But you notice these ghost monks never mentioned the garden was a former burial ground, or that they were laid to rest there. They wanted us to discover this fact as part of their game."

"I wish I could do this every day."

"No, you don't Tom. Believe me. And never say I wish."

"Are we going to the deli?"

"Yes. I'm thinking about one of those Thanksgiving subs."

"Oh, those are good. I think that's what I'll get too."

After picking up the subs, we drove back to the monastery and parked in front of the senior center. While eating in the gazebo, a father, mother, and their young daughter in a pink dress formed a triangle in the field and were kicking a pink ball back and forth.

"Professor, was that presence a hooded shadow in the monastery?"

"Yes, Tom. We didn't discuss your restroom experience in the monastery because as I said thinking about or discussing the presence will call it to you. I received a territorial greeting in the restroom."

"What happened?"

"The malevolent presence projected its wicked energy against my back, and then sent a vision of a monk in a black picture frame talking, but no words were heard as its mouth was moving. After that, it said *Get out* in a deep guttural voice. This is a common response from a hooded shadow when you're trespassing on their turf."

"Are you going to go back in and converse with this shadow?"

"Maybe I already am, Tom. That monk picture was supposed to be a picture of Father Albert Celestine."

"So, it's playing with us."

"Either what lurks within the monastery was listening to the conversations outside, is the leader of a parasitic gang, or it's the tag along."

"What are we going to do?"

"We are going to stay out, for now, and continue our investigation on the grounds."

"Are we going to do anymore investigating today?"

"Yes, once the food settles."

Taking the bag of training weapons out of the vehicle, I threw it over my shoulder and we proceeded to the training location. Removing the aluminum swords and daggers out of the bag, I gave a pair to Tom. Facing the pond, we reviewed the Espada Y Daga, or sword and dagger combinations on both our right and left sides slowly. Following the combinations, we began sumbrada which is a counter for counter drill. Out of the corner of my right eye I saw a woman walking in our direction. We continued to practice until she got close.

"Hello," I said.

"Hi. You two move so gracefully."

"Thank you," Tom and I answered. We placed the weapons in the bag and introduced ourselves.

"I was looking out the window of the senior center where I work, and I saw you taking some eskrima sticks and training swords out of your vehicle," Carla said.

"Yes, I have been practicing and teaching martial arts on these grounds for years."

"I'm surprised I never saw you, I walk the paths with my dog regularly," Carla responded.

"We constantly change the location and try not to bother anyone."

"I have done some training with the sticks and always wanted to learn more, but there are very few legitimate teachers. How long have you been studying Arnis, or Stickfighting?"

"I have studied the Filipino Martial Arts of Kali and Modern Arnis or Arnis De Mano since 1986. Full Circle Arnis De Mano is my expression of Modern Arnis."

"Do you have a studio?"

"Yes, in Lincoln." Tom pulled a business card out of his wallet and handed it to Carla.

"Thank you, Tom," Carla said.

"Have you ever witnessed any paranormal activity on this land?" Tom asked Carla.

"As a matter of fact, I have. I was walking my dog out here and he started growling when I saw an apparition of a monk."

"How about Carpenter's Garden?"

"A couple of people have said they saw a shadow monk in and around the garden. There is a stone cross in the woods that we get many reports of activity about as well. When I am near the stone cross, I feel something watching."

"Where is this cross?" I asked.

Carla pointed out the direction in the woods. "Follow the Monk's Quarry Trail. It's lying on the ground, near the Monk's Quarry and a pile of rectangular granite stones."

"We will have to check that out."

"I have to get back to the office. It was a pleasure meeting the two of you."

"Same here, Carla. Have a great day," I answered.

"Nice meeting you, Carla." Tom said.

"Well Tom, there is our next location. Let's take the weapons back to the vehicle and I will grab the backpack."

"This place sounds pretty cool."

"It does. I have never been in that section of woods."

"A shadow monk seen in and around the garden. You may be right, Professor."

"We will see."

Back at the vehicle I switched bags. Walking to the Monk's Quarry we approached an older man walking his dog in the field. "Hello, could you tell me if you have come across a stone cross on the ground in that section of woods?" I asked, as I pointed toward the direction of the Monk's Quarry.

He thought for a moment and responded. "Oh, yes," he said. "There is an old cross near a bunch of stones; just follow the path. If you blink, you will miss it."

We both thanked him and continued our journey. The narrow path that connects the Nine Men's Misery Trail to the Monk's Quarry Trail is easy to miss and explains why I never noticed it before. Where the narrow path connected to the Monk's Quarry Trail we had an option of taking a right or left. We took a right and followed the trail until we came to another path on our left where an old oak tree stood. Looking down the path I could see a pile of large rectangular granite blocks, most likely left behind from the monks.

"This must be it," I said to Tom

"Hey look, it's an old pulley wheel," Tom said, as he pointed to a large steel pulley lying just off the path.

"That's probably part of a pulley system the monks used to lift these blocks."

Walking to the pile of blocks, we looked around the area for any visible sign of a cross. Climbing the small hill, we looked down to see the Monk's Quarry, but still no sign of a cross. Descending the hill, we searched the area until I saw a piece of rectangular stone with the rest of its shape covered with the yellow oak leaves of fall. Kneeling, I started wiping them off and Tom joined me.

"It's the cross. I wonder why it's lying on the ground," Tom asked, as its shape was revealed.

"I don't know. It could easily be repaired," I answered.

"Should we stand it up?"

"I feel we should leave it where it is," I answered while my right hand was placed on the cross.

Immediately, my heart energy was stimulated as I received a benevolent embrace from a presence. Extreme compassion was felt as the vibrational frequency elevated and my eyes began to tear. Wiping my eyes, I took off my cross and placed it on the stone cross in direct sunlight. Sitting on the side of the cross, I took the notebook and pen out of the backpack and handed it to Tom. Placing the chart in my lap, I took a deep breath and slowly let it out, relaxing into receptive oneness.

"Are you ready to write, Tom?"

"I'm ready."

"Please make note, Tom. With the sun at my back, an image came to my mind's eye of a hooded monk, kneeling in front of the cross. Face, hands, and feet hidden."

Controlling thought and emotion, I held the chain over the chart. Before I began, I repeated 'I can do all things through Christ which strengthens me' internally a few times. Then I said, "Sunshine before my eyes, sunshine within my soul. For the goodness of all, if you please. Do you have a message to share with humanity?" The conversation began telepathically.

I speak for truth. Either I am eternal, or heaven is here. A golden cross stands before you. Heaven lays down a golden carpet, and I am kneeling next to you.

The golden carpet was the sun shining down upon the yellow leaves, highlighting the path to this location. "Who may I ask is speaking?"

A monk. I keep my daily ritual of prayer. Please leave the golden cross where it is. I would be lost without my ritual. I live here until light points the way in another direction. He who loves, lives eternal, he who hates, holds what treasure that left them behind.

Leave with what you came with, live with what you came with, believe in what you came with, that is God.

I may live forever here beside this cross and never feel lonely. Here lie many memories and experiences that I watch like a morning sunrise. I know you enjoy the Sun, and love as God as well. Forever the light, temporary the flesh. Walk these woods and pray with me. I will kneel with you, my brother. Know here is a church with no walls, but all love. Feel light, be light, give light.

This is the message of Love. Leave your offerings in Love. Keep your hard-earned money. I ask of you no more, love asks of you no more. Seek God in you, not me. Give only what you feel is true. Keep ignorance out of your breath. Hold God's hand with your heart. All hands become one heart, one soul, one world, shining infinitely as Heaven's golden children. You may ask your question.

"With what you know in this moment, what would you tell all that is different than your beliefs when you occupied a physical body?"

Believe this, my Brother, I held light in my heart until my body left me.

Jesus has a heart, you have a heart, and both have a home. So, I say to all, may you find the door and walk in. Simple it is. Jesus spoke of his luminous experiences; may you all speak of yours. Jesus will not rise again, and Christ never left you. Jesus was a man; Christ was his heart. See this, my family. Stop waiting for an illusion that you will never see. I question you now.

"I would be pleased to answer you."

How did you know light and love was here?

"Seeing a cross lying in the silence and solitude. The splendor of the sun, shining through the trees of yellow leaves, and the soothing vibration of nature."

You knew because Christ lives in you. And don't be afraid to say so.

I went into a light trance as the monk viewed the environment with wonder through my eyes.

Thank you for your eyes, thank you for your heart, thank you for your time. Live my brother and talk of this moment. Some will believe. Some will only listen.

"Thank you, for your wisdom and your message. Goodbye." Tom closed the notebook, but it wasn't over. "Don't close the notebook yet, Tom. There is another presence. The image in my mind's eye appears to be a woman, with long brunette hair and light blue eyes. She is wearing a medieval green cloak and has the same golden-white glow as the monks." Still in a peaceful trance, I allowed the conversation to begin.

I am Kim.

"Hello, Kim it is a pleasure."

I am intrigued by your illumined being.

Dishonesty was detected, but I controlled my emotion and continued. "I am not feeling that bright in the moment."

You are bright even when you don't feel love. A good heart shines always. You are a good heart. I can answer your Jesus questions.

"May I ask why?"

Because I have followed Jesus through two worlds.

"What would you tell all about this experience?"

Jesus spoke from the illumined heart and goodness was his soul. I speak from heaven on this day because I told love you are my choice, stand and be me. I walked much lighter from that moment on. Jesus taught this, I listened. Heaven essence laid down the carpet, and I followed it home. For all I say, you are welcome here, bring only your loving heart, and leave emotions behind, they will only weigh you down.

"Kim, it is the year 2007. May I ask what year you last remember?"

The year was 1966 when I walked home. Happiness was the song I heard, and I danced to meet it.

"I like that, Kim. May I ask, when we are conversing, how do we connect and disconnect?"

We connect by like vibration. We disconnect by change in your vibration or the message is completed. Unless, of course, some other disturbance gives us a push.

"Thank you, Kim. So, you took the Heaven walk in 1966?"

Yes. I enjoyed life fully. I worshipped the light of love. Earth was beautiful and I told her so.

"Kim, I have a vision that just came forward of you as a long-haired brunette in a sundress dancing by an old oak tree with a peace sign carved into it."

Oh, I danced. Peace and freedom were my best friends. I have no regrets. Don't let wrong choices sink your ship. Sail into the sunlight with no worries.

"Thank you, Kim."

Compassion is you, my brother. I know your heart; it circulates around your aura. This is the beacon that attracted me.

"May I ask, is there a gate to heaven?"

Light of heart illuminates your entrance.

"May I ask, how do you remember your memories?"

The human brain is not the mind, it is only a temporary shell, the ocean within comes home.

"Thank you, that answer made me smile."

Goodness makes you smile, I'm just speaking its language.

A vision came forward of Kim in a head on collision while driving a light blue convertible vehicle. "I see a vision of what happened to you Kim. We will avoid this discussion."

Thank you. I place my heart in these words. I am a real voice of a loving heart. Believe and become. Lorne must feel as me, to speak as me. So today I lived another moment in your world. Thank you, Lorne.

"I thank you as well, Kim."

Be you, my brother, I love you.

"Thank you for your wisdom and your message. Goodbye. An energy shift is occurring, Tom. The image sent to my mind's eye appears to be a woman with long dark hair and emerald green eyes. She is wearing a medieval red cloak and has the golden-white glow."

I am Helen.

"It is a pleasure Helen. Do you have a message for the goodness of all?"

For love and light.

"May I ask for all where are you right now?"

I am a grain of sand in God's palm.

"Are you aware of what year this is?"

No, here time interests no one. How do you know time?

"By a watch, clock, and the positioning of the sun."

Love has eternal sunlight.

"Am I giving off a vibrational frequency that attracts you?"

I hear your heart giving me directions to your soul.

"May I ask did you follow a religion?"

I was a pagan.

"May I ask what year that was?"

Yes, 1754.

"May I ask where you lived?"

Salem, Massachusetts. Many were harmed because of their beliefs. I watched my sisters suffer and they watched me. Convents became our home, not by our choice but theirs. We listened daily to the words of the evil, disguised as colonists.

What love lived like this? What God would allow this? I questioned but remained faithful. I now see a different world. One with no names, but pure divine heart.

"May I ask, how do you see?"

We follow our hearts, but I can only see through your eyes.

"Could you explain what you mean by heart?"

All you ever felt, all you ever experienced, all you ever believed in one bottle, floating in the ocean of God. You pulled the cork and I spoke.

"Your expressions are simple and beautiful."

I thank you for selecting me.

"I think I was just lucky."

I know you know better than that. I greatly appreciate your goal.

"Thank you, Helen." I pointed to my energy field, as I asked the next question. "May I ask, are you attached to my energy field?"

I connect like jelly on bread, absorbing into the perforations.

"Are there holes in my energy field?"

Holes no, think of it more like a sponge. Water is absorbed, but openly doesn't pass through.

The conversation ceased, as a couple walking two dogs passed on a connecting path. Folding the chart, I put it in the pack. Picking up my cross, I placed it in my pocket with the chain and stood up, brushing off my pants.

"Now the ghost monks are female. Were Kim and Helen beautiful?"

"This time, yes," I answered, as I felt a malevolent presence in the air.

"Now those are the type of visions I want to see."

"Tom, listen to me. Always speak as if many ears are listening."

"Why?"

"Because there are."

"Sorry, Professor."

"It's not me you need to worry about."

"Ok, I'm sorry tag alongs. I'm just kidding." Tom said out loud, chuckling.

Shaking my head, I packed up. Noticing some empty beer cans scattered in the area, Tom helped me pick them up and crush them. While Tom was snapping a few pictures of the stone cross, I picked up a stick from the ground about five feet in length, snapped it in half against my knee, then handed the two sticks to Tom.

"Let me guess. You want me to practice my double stick striking and twirling as we walk back to the vehicles."

"Yes, and I want you to entertain any tag alongs at the same time."

"This time I know you're not kidding."

"You're right."

CHAPTER 7

FAIRY OF THE FOREST

Tom and I took a seat at the picnic table under the gazebo. Opening the backpack, I took out two oranges and two protein bars, then handed one of each to Tom.

"Thank you, Professor."

"You're welcome." Opening the notebook to the golden cross conversations, we began our review. "Looking over the dialogue of the Golden Cross Monk, Kim, and Helen we can see they spoke beautifully and very flatteringly. Kim and Helen revealed a face, but hid their hands and feet in cloth, like the ghost monks."

"Do you think Kim and Helen were ever human?"

"No, but you have now been introduced to female messengers or angels. There are no examples of angelic beings appearing as female in Scripture, they are exclusively referred to in the masculine sense. The only three named angels in the Bible are Michael, Gabriel, and Lucifer. In my experience, the spiritual beings playing messenger, or angel, have appeared as both male and female, as well as light without form, and occasionally as winged humanoids and other human-animal hybrid combinations."

"Why do you think there are no female angels in Scripture?"

"There can be many reasons, one of them being male dominated cultures. These beings are shapeshifters and imitators. If they can appear as male and mimic a masculine voice, they can surely appear as female and mimic a female voice."

"Looking over the dialogue of the ghost monk that we are calling the Golden Cross Monk, we can see mentioned the golden cross, the golden carpet, and heaven's golden children. Gold remains in the dialogue after our encounter with three ghost monks which stood in front of gold pyramids. The monk said, *Heaven lays down a golden carpet* and Kim said, *Heaven essence laid down the carpet.* Helen spoke in threes once, the monk four times, and Kim did not speak in threes at all yet used the same words as the ghost monks. This shows they don't always communicate in that manner."

"The Monk said, *here lie many memories and experiences that I watch like a morning sunrise. I know you enjoy the sun and love as God as well.* Kim said, *Sail into the sunlight with no worries* and Helen said, *Love has eternal sunlight* which has the same meaning as the Impostor Father saying, *I only see light, there is never darkness here.* This is a continuation of sun worship, and the need to stay in direct sunlight to converse with this being."

"The Monk asked, *how did you know light and love was here?* Kim said, *I worshipped the light of love.* And when I asked Helen if she had a message of goodness for all she answered, *For love and light.* Compare this to Father Albert Celestine's words,

I am love and light. You are also love and light. This is a continuation of the light and love con."

"The vivid vision shared of Kim in a sundress, dancing by an oak tree, and later passing due to a head-on collision was false. Just like Helen's story of suffering in Salem, Massachusetts, and the Quaker's story of being hanged. The goal of Kim's vision and Helen's story was to continue to pull on my heartstrings with a different guise. These messengers not only lie, but tell phony stories through words, visions, and dreams."

"When I asked Kim how we connect and disconnect, she answered, *we connect by like vibration. We disconnect by change in your vibration, or the message is completed. Unless, of course, some other disturbance gives us a push.* When I asked Helen how we connect, she answered, *I connect like jelly on bread, absorbing into the perforations.* Then I asked if there were any holes in my energy field. She answered, *Holes no, think of it more like a sponge. Water is absorbed, but openly doesn't pass through.* There is a little truth in both explanations."

"Comparing Kim's dialogue to the other personalities, we have Kim saying, *the human brain is not the mind, it is only a temporary shell, the ocean within comes home.* Compared with Father Albert Celestine who said, *you're wearing a shell. I am without the shell.*"

"Kim used the words *Illumined heart, Loving heart* and *Light of heart* which has the same meaning as the third monk in the garden and the Impostor Father's word *Radiant heart,* and Helen's *Divine heart.* Kim also said, *I am intrigued by your illumined being* and *I know your heart; it circulates around your aura. This is the beacon that attracted me.* This is the same meaning as what the Impostor Father said, *there lying in bed was my son beaming with the radiance of love.*"

"When Kim said, *the human brain is not the mind, it is only a temporary shell, the ocean within comes home*, this is a truth. The brain is not the home of the mind. Kim said, *Goodness makes you smile, I'm just speaking its language.* There was truth in those words. This wise tag along knows if it speaks with goodness, it stands a better chance of me continuing the conversation. Kim called me brother, like the ghost monks saying, *be you, my brother, I love you.* Again, we have another message of affection."

"Is a spiritual being saying 'I love you' a bad thing?"

"*I love you* can be a warning sign of a spiritual being that is attracted and may be looking for a little more than a good conversation. If a stranger called you on the phone, and after five minutes told you they love you, a red flag would go off, or at least it should. The same applies to hidden world interaction."

"Do they usually use stuff like a saying on a mailbox or a personalized license plate to speak?"

"Yes, Tom. If they need to get a message across this is just a couple of the endless ways intelligent spiritual beings will converse. Looking over Helen's dialogue, we see she said, *all you ever believed, in one bottle, floating in the ocean of God. You pulled the cork and I spoke.* This was to make us think of the genie in the bottle or the jinn."

"The last dialogue we will discuss today is the monk's words, *Thank you for your eyes.* This was after the monk viewed the environment using my eyes. When I asked Helen, how do you see? She said, *we follow our hearts, but I can only see through your eyes.* Kim said, *Lorne must feel as me, to speak as me. So today I lived another moment in your world.*"

"I have told you spiritual beings establish a relationship to feed on your energy, they flatter to inflate your ego, and they use humans as mouthpieces to share their doctrine. Now we can add to that knowledge that they need human eyes to see the physical world clearly, and they seek a human host or vessel to live another moment in our world."

"What is it like when they use your eyes?"

"While they're using your eyes, you are looking through the front windshield from the rear seat of the vehicle, so to speak."

"That's really weird."

"Yes, it is. To reveal the ways of spiritual beings, it requires me to speak from personal experience."

"I'll never look at spiritual communication the same again."

Bright and early the following morning, I walked out to the Monk's Quarry. Climbing the hill, there were three mourning doves on a long branch. When I reached the top, they flew away with their wings making a distinct whistling noise.

Taking off my backpack, I placed it down on the rock.

Picking up a single stick off the ground, I announced to that which I couldn't see, "Please excuse me, I am about to use this space to practice my art and I don't want to accidentally strike you." When I am with a student or friend, this respectful announcement is made telepathically. Hitting or harming a spiritual being or an object it resides within can make them very angry.

Performing solo baston sayaw slowly, I could feel a presence watching. Solo baston means single stick and sayaw means dance in the Filipino Martial Art of Arnis De Mano. Sayaw, or Anyos, is equivalent to katas or forms in other martial art disciplines.

When finished, I took a seat on the rocky ledge overlooking the quarry. Taking out the notebook, I placed it on my lap and opened it to a clean page. Removing my necklace, I placed the spiral cross in my pocket.

Focusing first on the birdsongs, I merged with the stillness and spoke from the heart. Looking up into the sun and down onto the trees, I visualized how the trees convert the sun's rays into their food and expressed my appreciation for the oxygen they faithfully release. In this blissful state of being, a vision came to the mind's eye as a comforting benevolent presence merged with my being.

The image coming forward was a woman with long blonde hair, somewhat transparent, radiating an intense golden-white light. Her full-length white dress matched her long, white, angelic wings. As she raised her arms, golden leaves rose from the ground and began to swirl. Holding the silver chain with my thumb and forefinger, the telepathic communication began.

Fill the heart with God's illuminated blood and oak tree strength of being you shall have.

"Good morning. Would you like to give a name?"

I am the Fairy of the Forest, you might say.

"I am honored. If you please Fairy of the Forest, I, as well as others, would enjoy hearing your expression."

Reach deep into your soul and find what holy truly means. I am holy as one because I am one. Not the bark of the tree, but the core of the forest.

"How would you describe yourself for others to see?"

See me as the leaf beside your feet. See me as the rock on which you sit. See me as the trees, each and every one. See me as all the creatures that do their part to maintain the beauty and each has never been told how to do it.

"You were once human, I know."

Very good, you know more than you see. Time stood still in these surroundings. Here is God's word that never needs to be spoken. I found God, I found richness, I found truth.

"May I ask what years you remember that you walked this land?"

I treaded this land as female human in the years of 1917 to 1950. Female human is not feminine God.

I am God, I am love, I am you. I require no ego desires, nor do I have a need for them. This demonstration of merging into one soul for the good of all is true love. Compassion returns to homeland when merging as one powerful soul becomes your quest.

"Human history shows a pattern of doomsday predictions. What message do you have for all?"

Humankind will transform into what creatures they choose to be. Humankind will only cease when God leaves their shell.

God has no robe, why then do humans seek one? God has no castle walls, why then do you separate yourself? God has no scroll of rules, because this is no game.

God gives life to the shell that covers your soul. God didn't name you, your parents did. God didn't give human birth to you, your mother did. You were always alive; you always will be. God is not your father, God is not your mother, God is you.

"Thank you for that powerful message. You are leaving now, I know. Your expression is greatly appreciated. I thank you with the love of my soul."

I thank you with all the love of mine.

"Goodbye, Fairy of the Forest."

Goodbye, Lorne.

Pondering the experience, a small shadow about six inches in length appeared out of the corner of my right eye. Looking like a small humanoid or cartoon-like fairy, it had large butterfly wings without detail and flew around a small tree for a few seconds before it vanished.

What felt like a hand started gently playing with my hair. Closing my eyes, an invading vision appeared of a stone hallway, with twists and turns, like a corn maze. At the end of the hallway was a taller wall, about 25 feet high, with a large cave opening at the top. Looking left and right, there were dark tunnels going in opposite directions. While I was deciding which to take, a white sparkling horse raced by me going from right to left and then returned going left to right.

Ready for its next pass, I leaped up grabbing hold of its long sparkling white mane, pulling myself onto its back. Holding tight and staying low, the horse rode me out of the maze and into a world of bright glowing flowers, trees, and plants.

Getting down from the horse, a long path appeared of perfectly straight wooden planks through a thick green forest. Turning around, the horse shrunk down to the size of a mouse and was now inside a half glass, half gold cylindrical bottle.

Squatting down, I observed the horse moving in the upper portion of the bottle. Standing, I turned to face the path and hesitated before taking the first step. The moment my foot touched the wooden plank, trees on both sides of the path glowed brighter and continued to do so with every step. Rays of sunlight shone down from above, forming an upside-down triangle. A comforting white mist rained down as I approached a pair of ancient-looking wooden doors. Green in color, with carvings of wildlife, the giant doors began to open, as a gust of wind carried the scent of a flower garden.

Slowly the outline of a naked woman was revealed. Standing in front of a pure white background, the woman stepped forward. Her long sparkling hair was as white as the horse's mane and strategically covered her private parts. Her eyes were glowing emerald green, similar to the personality Helen's eyes.

Advancing forward with a seductive stare, *have sex with me,* she asked. "No," I answered, as I retreated. *I love you,* she said in a soft voice. "Yes, I know," I responded. As soon as she leaned in to kiss me, I opened my eyes, disconnecting from the influenced daydream.

Still a little foggy, I opened the bottle of water and took a few swigs, then ate an apple. Standing up, I performed some stretches, put on my backpack, and began the trek back to the vehicle. Taking a left on to the Homestead Trail, a human-like shadow being around six feet tall, crossed the path about fifty feet ahead.

Was this the same shadow that shifted into the small fairy-like being? Did this shadow influence the naked woman daydream or was it the tag along? These questions came to my mind as I continued my walk back to the vehicle.

In class, students were holding Muay Thai pads, working their hands, feet, knees, and elbows in combinations.

"Pad holders, you need to be in a fighting stance moving around, utilizing your footwork, and being alive, not static. Remember you are not training to fight an ice sculpture."

"Alright students, let's end with the devastating outside leg kick for 15 repetitions each leg. Make sure you are stepping out at a 45-degree angle and dropping that shin into the pad at a downward angle. Keep the opposite hand up as you drop the same side hand down for counterbalance and to open up the hip."

Walking around, I corrected the students' technique and complimented their improvements. Fifteen minutes passed, and we lined up to cool down and bow out. Walking into the office area a student asked to purchase a school shirt. "What size would you like Darlene?"

"I think a medium will do."

"A medium it is," I responded, pulling it out of the pile and handing it to her.

"Thanks, Professor," she said as she gave me the payment.

"Thank you." As the last of the kickboxing students were leaving, Tom walked up to the counter.

"Professor, can I get a pair of sticks? Mine are beat."

"Of course, Tom. Go through the sticks and pick out the set that feels right to you." Opening the case, I took out the pile of rattan sticks and spread them across the counter. While Tom was looking them over, I typed the attendance and class notes into the computer.

'What do you think of these?" Tom asked, as he held up the sticks he chose.

"Choosing your sticks is a personal thing, Tom. Do they feel dense?"

"I think so," Tom answered, as he performed a double stick striking pattern in the air.

"Then you made the right choice."

Tom handed me the payment and I placed it in the cash box. Tom placed his sticks on the counter. "I've got to tell you about the crazy nightmare I had last night."

"Go ahead," I answered, leaning back in my chair.

"This seemed way too real. I was sitting in a wooden chair up against the wall in what looked like my bedroom. The lights were off in the room but not in the hall. Out of the corner of my eye, a dark silhouette appeared in the doorway. The outline was a woman in a body suit with extremely long hair, but a face I couldn't see. As she entered, her red and black outfit stood out and evil overcame the room."

"Did you see her feet?"

"Not really, why?"

"I'll tell you after. Go ahead, finish your dream."

"Okay. So, she grabbed another wooden chair that appeared out of nowhere. With one hand, she dragged it slowly across the floor, spun it around and placed it in front of me. In a sexy manner, she stepped over the seat and sat facing me. She, or it, was beautiful with long flowing brunette hair, full lips, and bright green eyes. Then she spoke these words which I will never forget. *I want to show you something Tom* in a voice that sent a chill right through me. Her eyes instantly turned jet black and started to slant as she opened her mouth wider than humanly possible. Snake-like scales appeared on her skin and the lips turned into the mouth of a sucker fish and continued to stretch wider and wider. With all my strength, I tried to leap out of the chair, but I was completely paralyzed and couldn't move a muscle. While my heart pounded, I tried to scream but nothing came out. Her head started rising as her neck lengthened. Like a snake she struck, attaching to my chest and knocking the wind out of me. When I could speak, I yelled 'Stop!' over and over as I felt her siphoning the life out of me. Waking up from the dream, I was completely conscious but still couldn't move. The presence of that evil creature was still in the room pinning me down, but I couldn't see a thing. Just when I thought I couldn't take anymore it was gone. To make sure I even pinched myself a few times. I turned on all the lights, pulled the covers over my head and eventually fell back to sleep. What do you think it is Professor?"

"I think it's time for you to get a girlfriend."

"That's nice Professor. Thanks."

"I'm just joking, Tom. Let's get back to the feet for a moment."

"I really can't remember seeing any."

"The reason I ask is that images of this nature can appear footless, or with feet turned backwards, as well as with hooves, paws, talons, or claws."

"By what I've read, it has all the signs of a sex demon or succubi or maybe even a jinnia."

"There can be many reasons for a demon Lilith-type encounter, and it doesn't have to be a malevolent spiritual being. In this case we know we're dealing with a spiritual being that can play female personalities, and this could be its influence. I also experienced a seductive encounter at the monastery today."

"Really?"

"Yes. It was in an influenced daydream which we will discuss when we analyze to-day's dialogue. Male and female sex demons, known singularly as incubi and succubi, or plural as incubus and succubus, are seductive spiritual beings of medieval folklore, attracted to humans. They are not two different beings, but one charming spiritual being or jinni, assuming a gender as needed. Please look up Genesis 6:1-2."

Tom pulled his phone out of his pocket and searched. "I've got it. *And it came to pass, when men began to multiply on the face of the earth, and daughters were born unto them. That the sons of God saw the daughters of men that they were fair; and they took them wives of all which they chose.*"

"We can see even in Scripture that spiritual beings were attracted to human be-ings. Let's talk about some others. Male and female jinn, as well as the gods and god-desses of ancient mythology, were known to fall in love with humans and engage in sexual activity or rape. The Greek God Zeus was a womanizer of both the mortal and immortal. The demon Mara tried to seduce Buddha with beautiful women who were believed to be Mara's daughters. Do you see the pattern?"

"Yes. We are surrounded by a bunch of horny spirits."

"Good one, Tom. It certainly appears that way, doesn't it?" I responded, as both of us laughed.

"How about the pinning down while I'm conscious?"

"This terrifying phenomenon is what I came to know as the Old Hag Syndrome. Some cultural and religious beliefs relate this to a supernatural cause. But if you do some research, you'll find the medical field sees it differently and would most likely label your experience Sleep Paralysis with an accompanying hallucination."

"Have you had this experience?"

"Yes."

"Do you think it's a hooded shadow?"

"It can be."

"Could it have anything to do with me saying I would like to have visions of beautiful females, like Kim and Helen?"

"It might. I said always speak as if many ears are listening because I felt a malevolent presence in the air when you spoke. If it is the hooded shadow, it knows you would tell me about your nightmare, which informs me it's following you, as it is following my mother."

"I'll be a little more careful with what I say from now on."

"That would be wise. Don't give this nightmare anymore thought, especially when you're home. Watch a good comedy; avoid your supernatural movies, paranormal books, and surfing the net on the subject."

"What am I supposed to do if it happens again?"

"Focus on the inhalation and the exhalation of your breath, and just relax. Let it pass, without feeding it fear or anger."

"Easier said than done."

"True. But it works."

"Do you think it will happen again?"

"It depends on who or what is responsible. If it's the hooded shadow, then it depends on its agenda or mood. When you interact with spiritual beings, benevolent or malevolent, and develop a relationship there is the potential to put someone, or everyone in your life, in danger of their subtle or unsubtle torment, manipulation, and influence. Just don't worry. Worry, like fear, feeds the parasitic. Avoid giving it what it desires, and that's emotional energy and an internal opportunity. Now I would like you to read the dialogue of today's fairy encounter."

"Fairy?"

"I told you, these beings play all the roles, Tom. Myths and legends of seductive nature spirits, like the beautiful nymphs, huldra, mermaids, peri, and fairies can be shapeshifted forms of spiritual beings or jinn." Unzipping the backpack, I took out the notebook and placed it on the desk. Opening to the Fairy of the Forest, I slid it over to Tom.

"While you're reading, I'm going to wipe down the mirrors."

"Alright. I'll let you know when I'm done."

Grabbing the window cleaner and paper towels, I walked over to the dojo entrance, bowed, then entered. "Professor," Tom called out about fifteen minutes later.

"I'll be right there," I answered, as I finished the last mirror. Bowing toward the dojo, I entered the office. "What do you think?" I asked, as I threw the used paper towels in the trash and placed the window cleaner back in the closet.

"How come you get the beauties and I get a monster?"

"Don't be jealous, Tom. Whether they are beauties or monsters, they're one and the same being. Eventually I will encounter the latter. Fairy of the Forest attempted to seduce through an influenced daydream of a beautiful naked woman in nature. Her goal was to draw me into her fantasy world, which draws me deeper into the being's mind, energy, and dimension. The true fairies of folklore, like angels, were nothing like the marketed versions we know today. These spiritual beings in nature would appear in forms like the beauty I experienced, as well as the creature you experienced. The Lilith-like creature in your dream could have easily seduced you, in its beautiful form, and fed on your sexual energy. Instead it shifted to a grotesque form, to feed on induced fear and possibly to show the power of its influence."

"How do you think they influence our dreams?"

"It's like transferring data from one cell phone to another. But it's not two cell phones, but two conscious entities connecting, one human, one non-human. Let's analyze the fairy's dialogue. What patterns did you notice?"

"Well she spoke in threes."

"Yes she did, five times. No matter what the name or label of the personality, we have seen the words, illuminate, illuminated, and illumination frequently used. The fairy used the word illuminated, like the Angel, Being of Energy, and Kim when she said, *God's illuminated blood*. Like the Impostor Father, Father Albert Celestine, the Quaker, Kim, and Helen, Fairy of the Forest was never human despite saying she *treaded this land as female human in the years of 1917 to 1950* – which would have made her 33 years old when she passed."

"Fairy of the Forest continued with the *They are God; we are God* message. The first monk in the garden said, *God is you, my brother.* The third monk said, *God I am, God you are.* The Quaker said, *Ye are truly Gods.* Energy Being said *God's ye are, Gods ye be* and *Alien I am, God I am.* And Fairy of the Forest said, *I am God, God is you.* This particular species of jinn is not just saying it's a messenger or angel, but also a god."

"So, hooded shadows could be the gods, Professor?"

"Yes, or what is hidden within their darker than night cloak. A small shadow fairy, and a human-like shadow being in the shape of a man, appeared after the conversation. Both were opaque and not transparent like the ghost monks, which tells me they're shapeshifted forms and not projections."

"Fairy of the Forest used the word *shell* like the personalities Father Albert Celestine and Kim when she said, *God gives life to the shell that covers your soul* and *Humankind will only cease when God leaves their shell.* Fairy of the Forest said, *God has no castle walls, why then do you separate yourself?* We can compare this to, *know here is a church with no walls, but all love,* spoken by the Golden Cross Monk. The Quaker, Kim, Helen, and Fairy of the Forest all share the same soft, charming, female voice with slight modifications."

"What have you seen more of Professor, ghosts or shadow beings?"

"Various shadow beings."

"When was the first time you encountered a shadow being?"

"I was three years old. It was 1964 and the house we just moved into was highly charged with the emotional residue of the city's most gruesome murder. This senseless tragedy attracted the malevolent from the hidden world and I became one of the targets."

"I've got to hear this."

"Now is not the time, my friend. Thoughts attract, and we already have our hands full, let's discuss the daydream. In the dream we see a cylindrical bottle that was gold at the lower half, and glass on the upper half revealing the shrunken white horse. The shrunken horse in the bottle I would compare to the dialogue from Helen saying, *all you ever believed, in one bottle, floating in the ocean of God. You pulled the cork and I spoke.* There is an intentional genie or jinni flavor being thrown into the mix."

"Makes me think of the sitcom *I Dream of Jeannie.*"

"I'm sure it does, and that's what they want. In the daydream we continue with gold and a triangle. Rays of sunlight shone down from above, forming an upside-down triangle, which may represent female energy. Whatever its meaning, there is one thing for sure. The triangle represents the number three, and three is the signature of these intelligent spiritual beings."

"This was also an example of how you see doors."

"Yes, it was. The wooden doors were green with beautiful carvings of wildlife. When they opened, a gust of wind came forward with the tranquilizing scent of a flower garden. This was followed by the appearance of the naked woman. Her hair was as white as the horse's mane, because she was also the horse."

"They know how to seduce don't they?"

"Just as well as they know how to frighten, beguile, and mesmerize. Sex sells, Tom. The material world and hidden world know this."

CHAPTER 8

QUASAR AND A FRIEND

Later, I arrived home from a sushi restaurant. First thing I did was pour a tall glass of water to counter the dehydrating effect of alcohol. As I drank, the hair on top of my head began to be played with in the same manner as it did prior to the naked woman daydream.

Controlling thought and emotion, I continued my get-ready-for-bed routine. Brushing my teeth, the presence pressed at my back but appeared to be non-threatening.

Walking into the bedroom, I changed into pajamas and I got into bed. Turning onto my stomach, I positioned the pillow and rested my head. Within a minute, my hair started to be played with again and the left side of my face softly caressed. Gently the presence laid on my back and buttocks, feeling somewhat solid like a human. What felt like hands began giving a light sensual massage to my upper back.

"No," I said firmly. The touching ceased and I scanned my body for intrusion.

Let me make you feel better, was said by a familiar soft female voice.

"I said no."

Are you sure? the soft voice asked.

"I'm positive." Turning onto my back, I pulled the covers up to my chin. Closing my eyes, a vision came forward immediately of three conveyer belts of pizza coming from three black ovens. Landing on a long red shelf were three individual pizzas.

Go ahead, try, the soft female voice said.

A rectangular thick crust cheese pizza was first, a round thin crust pepperoni pizza was second, and an oval stuffed crust vegetarian pizza was third. Taking a bite out of the rectangular pizza, it was as realistic as you can get. The taste and the crunching of the dough was exact. Continuing, I tried the round and oval pizzas and enjoyed them equally as well.

Coming to my senses, I stopped and asked myself what I was doing.

Like the pizza tastes real, I feel real, the soft female voice said.

"I will take your word for it. But the answer is still no." The bed began to shake as the presence grew angry from the refusal. Getting out of bed, I walked into the bathroom. When the light brightened, I said aloud, "No offense, but I prefer humans."

Climbing back into bed, I opened a martial arts magazine and began to read. Banging noises began to occur throughout the apartment. Ignoring the activity, I slowly drifted off to sleep.

In the dream state, I appeared in a classic New England setting. I faced a building with worn, unpainted wooden siding. The sign hanging above the window said General Store. As I was walking up the wooden steps, a small group of people passed and opened the red door. Before it closed, I stopped it with my foot. Following the group, I ascended the narrow stairway to the second floor. Remaining aware of any surprises, I took each step slowly.

Suddenly, the red door below swung open and a large white dog raced up the stairs. The size of this Bull Mastiff–like dog forced the group and me up against the wall and tripped one person in the process. "Must be a sale," I said jokingly, and the group laughed.

Once inside the General Store, I was impressed with the variety of items. Standing at a four-sided greeting card rack, I observed the selection. Out of the corner of my left eye, the large white dog stood on its hind legs and shapeshifted to a hybrid creature. Standing about seven feet tall, its body was like a polar bear with long claws on its huge paws, but the face resembled a gorilla. The old woman behind the counter never lifted her head during the transformation, she just continued to wipe down the counter with a red rag like nothing happened.

The creature stared as it made its way toward me, knocking over shelves in its path. In a panic, the group of people fled out the other side of the store. To my right was a grill with about a dozen large hot dogs cooking. Lifting the cover, I grabbed the tongs and picked up a couple. As the creature came close, I held them up. Without any hesitation, the creature snatched them off the tongs and quickly swallowed them.

You know what I like, the creature said to me in a deep voice.

"No, you just looked hungry," I answered back. Handing the creature the tongs, I slowly walked backwards. Once I stepped over the threshold and into the antique weapons section of the store, the creature vanished. Noticing a doorway to another set of stairs, I quickly descended and ran out the door.

The scene changed. Snow now blanketed the original environment. Walking the street of the residential neighborhood, I noticed two men and a woman from the earlier group, waving and yelling, *C'mon, stay with us.* Walking by a woman cleaning the snow off her red car, I came upon a mailman standing next to his truck. When I approached, he was looking through a pile of letters. Just as I was about to ask him where I was, he pointed up at a mountain without turning around.

It looks like your friends know where they're going, he said.

"How can you see that far?" I asked.

I can't, I use these. The mailman pulled out a large pair of binoculars from his truck and handed them to me.

"Wow, these are strong," I said, as I adjusted them to see a three story, yellow building with white trim on the top of a mountain. Three people from the group were waving from the third-floor porch, as if they could see me clearly.

You may need to grow some wings if you want to get up there, the mailman said, as he turned and smiled.

"You're right," I answered. Raising my arms, I began to flap them as if they were powerful wings. Feeling the wind under my arms, I flew straight up through the clouds and landed on the porch.

No one was around. Opening the sliding glass door, I said "Hello?" There was no answer, so I stepped into the bright, mystical looking interior. Again, I said "Hello, is anyone here?" They appeared to be gone. In that moment, the sun's rays came down through a skylight overhead. Manifesting was the beautiful, sparkling white horse from the daydream, with its wavy, long flowing mane. Accompanying the horse, was the scent of a flower garden. The horse turned and walked into the next room with a soothing sound of hooves on the wooden floor. Visions, scents, and sounds were created to keep me calm and comfortable in another attempt to seduce.

Following the horse, I stopped when I reached the large white framed doorway. Looking into the bright sunlit room, the horse was shapeshifting to the human female form. Naked and her back to me, she said, *Beautiful, isn't it?* as she ran her fingers through her long, white sparkling hair.

"Beautiful for the moment," I answered.

If you don't come to me, I will come to you, she said as she bent forward and placed her hands on her thighs.

"No thanks," I responded. Forcefully she backed me up and drove me against the wall, grinding wildly up and down. Observing her skin, I noticed small bumps appearing and disappearing, as the being struggled to maintain human form. Gripping her hips tightly, I said, "Sorry fairy, the ride is over," and tossed her to the left and sprinted out the doorway.

Waking from the dream, I leaned over and turned on the lamp. The bed was shaking and banging noises were heard throughout the apartment. I sat up, opened the drawer of the nightstand and took out a muscle car magazine. Sitting back against the headboard, I read until the atmosphere calmed and the bed settled.

A couple of laps on the Beauregard Trail and I was ready to start the day. Cooling down, I stretched my calf muscles up against a tree then walked over to the grass to complete a stretching routine when the phone rang.

"Hello Mom, what's up?"

"Hello, son. Do you have a moment?"

"Sure, go ahead."

"I know what you're going to say, but Richard's face was in the window screen yesterday in the back of the house."

"C'mon Mom, you have to stop falling for the smoke and mirrors."

"It's him, I know it. That's not all. Richard came to me in a dream last night. He asked me to meet him at the corner of High Street and Exchange."

"Mom, this is the dream influence of the hooded shadow."

"It seemed very real, he was smiling, and he had on a red ball cap and a red shirt."

"A red ball cap and a red shirt?"

"Yeah."

"Do you remember the color of his pants?"

"They were black I think."

"Mom, don't go out on any of these wild goose chases. I will stop by after I leave the monastery. Do you need anything?"

"I ran out of aspirin and I need some double A batteries for the remote."

"Okay. I'll pick up a bottle of aspirin and batteries. Love you."

"Love you too." As the call disconnected, I caught what appeared to be a white-hooded ghost monk beside a tree out of the corner of my right eye. Manifesting for just a moment, it was clear a message was waiting.

Walking to the vehicle I grabbed the backpack and water bottle. Today, I was going to converse at Monk's Irrigation Pond.

Arriving at the location, I took off the backpack and laid it down beside a large oak tree. Sitting against the tree, I arranged the tools for the interaction. Focusing on the serene pond, it took a few minutes to achieve a calm and relaxed trance state. The white-hooded ghost monk manifested, with a golden-white glow, on the opposite side of the pond. Floating forward on the pond surface, the monk stopped in front of me with the hood covering its face and hands, and feet hidden.

Hello, I am Quasar. I am a guide in your chosen school of fish.

"It is a pleasure, Quasar. May I ask how we are communicating?"

I'm following your soul, keep the direction of heart and love will be your island paradise.

"May I ask about Jesus the Christ?"

Yes. Jesus filled the Bible with few words. He loved more kindly than the recorded spoken words. The question remains either Jesus did or Jesus didn't. What a glad day it will be when Jesus returns. Jesus ran from evil into the arms of evil. We follow, but very rarely question. *We seek, but rarely know what. Jesus was a tile placed on the path to freedom. All messengers are tiles on the journey home. One tile does not tell the whole story. Jesus shared his hearts' song. We must not listen to the song of only one bird. You have many frequencies of hearing. My song may not soothe you, but one of my siblings might. The tiles are steppingstones across the sea of fish. I am a little fish, but I am one, you are a little fish, but you are one. It really isn't that complicated. Swim in comfort, or swim in chaos.*

"How about an explanation of love?"

I believe it is good timing for this. You are here to interpret love internally and express it externally. God is expressed from within your glass container. What you feel inside, will shine outside. Pure love illuminates the glass container. Illumination summons a molecular change; God in you is the result.

"Are there any other messages you would like to share with humanity?"

See more light than foolish thoughts. Find your goodness, find your God. Each coin thrown into the fountain brings total harmony to all. Throw your excess into your brothers and sister's hands.

"Thank you."

Remember, I am God and so are you. Keep focused on full circle. I believe in you.

"I will Quasar, goodbye." While still in an altered state of consciousness, I closed my eyes, giving the being or beings present an opportunity to communicate through a different medium.

A vision came to the mind's eye of flat stones of various colors, taking me across a patch of ocean to a beautiful rocky mountain. Slowly I stepped on the slippery stones, as waves were crashing against the surrounding large rocks. Drenched and barely able to see, I reached a halfway point. Turning and looking behind me, the steppingstones submerged. Unable to go back, I took the next step onto what appeared to be a flat rock. Rising quickly into the air, the stone threw me backwards into the ocean. Treading water, I watched what I thought was a rock reveal a giant octopus with one large eye. Higher and higher it rose, as it quickly grabbed me around the waist with one of its tentacles. Holding me high in the air, it began shaking me side to side as it squeezed harder and harder. While struggling to breathe and break free, the sun appeared in the sky. Feeling the heat of its rays, I stared into its brightness and relaxed. Opening my eyes, I disconnected from the manipulated daydream.

An image in the mind's eye was a ghost monk in brown cloth. *God is sending you a friend,* was whispered. Coming forward next in my mind's eye was an image of a female friend that passed. Scanning my energy field, I did not feel threatened and the presence appeared to be projecting love.

Hello Lorne. Finally, I get to talk to the man I loved.

I was hesitant to respond.

I am not the last woman you dated, my love. Her actions were disgusting. How you pick them, I could never figure out. I loved you with all my heart and I died with you still in my heart. Love is forever, because I still love you. Keep our memories alive. Find a woman that has love to give before giving your heart away. I see why you choose these crazy women. It has all been a test. Evil wins every time you accept their distraction. I really wanted to enjoy you for life. Now I'm enjoying you in death. Friends for life has a new meaning now in my soul.

"Where are you now, Amy?"

I am a grain of sand begging for God's attention. You are the god I begged for.

"I'm not a god."

You didn't fall, you're still love. Choose a woman good in appearance, before bad in heart. You can't change them all. I never felt prouder in life than I do now, knowing the real you. Wait patiently, God will come to her sinful being and she will remember you. I know you're not easy to forget. I tried, but I missed you too much. I couldn't function. I couldn't fake the relationship I was in. I started dying inside. I would have loved your children as if they were my own.

"I know you would have, Amy. At that time in my life I was drinking heavily to numb my feelings."

You were being a man, not the God you truly are. I forgave all your mistakes in choosing nasty women. They were throwing themselves at you left and right. You became weak only a few times, which is more than I can say for most men. You now must finish your book.

"I'm working on it. Amy, may I ask how you died?"

I needed friends and I couldn't get their time. You moved and I couldn't find you. I got really mentally sick and I couldn't live with either of my friends. So, I gave up and overdosed. Now I'm talking many years later to my best friend and love of my life.

The presence is doing its best to stir up emotions, and it's starting to work despite my knowing it's an impostor.

I feel your love, and I won't hurt you ever again.

"Goodbye, Amy."

Goodbye, my love.

"Are you in heaven?"

I'm in your company, that's heaven to me.

"Thank you, Amy."

Death was worth me getting a chance to know the real you. Have a beautiful life, my love.

"Goodbye."

Putting down the chain, I took a deep breath and exhaled. When the conversation began, the voice was very close to Amy's, but as the dialogue continued it gradually became the soft voice of the other benevolent female personas. Leaving Monk's Irrigation Pond, I took the Old Road Trail back to the Beauregard Loop and stopped at the chin up bar for a few sets. While recovering between sets, a translucent old woman manifested.

You are the teacher, she said, and paused for a moment looking into my eyes. *Thank you,* she added, as she turned, took a few steps and vanished into the air.

Shaking my head, I jumped back up on the bar and finished the workout. Still feeling eyes upon me, I walked across the path and entered the woods. Taking a seat on the remains of an old stone building foundation, I prepared the tools again for interaction. Manifesting before me was a hooded ghost monk in brown cloth. Its head was tilted forward, and its face, hands, and feet were hidden as usual.

Taking a deep breath, I let it out and relaxed into receptive oneness. The conversation began telepathically. "Good morning."

I just fulfilled my day by your company. Heaven has found a home in you. Love with complete faith is rare. Give me a question and I will be honored to answer.

"How did you come across me?"

Your illumination is hard to avoid. My life is God. I roam the Earth searching for the goodness of a loving soul. Welcome my brother, you are a soul of love.

"For humanity I ask, why do you roam the Earth? Can't you go home to the light of heaven?"

I am home. Light is love, and where there is love there is heaven. Heaven is all around you. If it was just above you, then heaven wouldn't be love. Home of love is spirit. Spirit is God. God is the pillow for all to rest upon. You see spirit is one entity, there is no other entity. Keep this in your thinking mind. What you are, you can always change. This is the simplicity of God. Illumination is the brightening of God's energy. Heaven is the process. Illumination changes me, but also changes the whole entity. This is rearranging your cell integrity, altering your recent structure into metamorphosis of soul. Known in your world as God's self.

"That was a powerful and thorough explanation. Thank you."

Every voice of spirit you interview will be unique. I hope my explanation is helpful in your book.

"I'm sure it will be. May I ask how we are communicating, so those who are reading can understand?"

My brother, knowing this can change your world. I speak as you, because temporarily I am you. Include in your book this speech. Illumination isn't difficult. It's quite simple. Just feel love and maintain that feeling. Let no outside energy interfere.

"Thank you."

Thank you and goodbye, my brother.

Putting down the chain, I closed my eyes once again to give the being, or beings, another opportunity to influence and manipulate a daydream. In the trance state, their world quickly became mine and I was standing in the middle of the large field of the monastery. Looking at my hands and feet, I was wearing a brown monk-like robe with the hood over my head, just as the ghost monks.

Sections of grass all around, began growing taller and taller. The grass turned to hay and then formed into human shaped creatures with no facial detail. One after the other, they attacked and I defended. Kicks and punches had little effect, so I began redirecting their advances, throwing them into one another.

While back kicking a hay beast charging me from behind, another grabbed me from the front and lifted me off the ground in a bear hug. Instinctually, I kneed the beast rapidly, as it squeezed and shook me side to side just like the octopus encounter. Tearing into its arms with my hands, I began throwing hay into the air. As the arms became thinner and thinner, I broke free from its grasp.

Surrounding me in a circle and ready for round two, I had a choice. Open my eyes and disconnect from the created world or continue to play the game.

Looking up into the sky, the clouds parted, and the sun shone. Up from the ground rose the handle of a bolo machete with a glistening gold handle. Reaching down, I pulled it from the Earth's grasp.

"Let's continue," I said to the hay beasts.

As the sun's rays reflected off the blade, they unleashed their attack. Slicing and hacking, I removed their limbs as they lunged aggressively from every angle.

Grass beasts were lying all over, unable to move. Kneeling, I sunk the machete back into the earth as the beasts shifted to bales of hay.

Standing up, a voice from behind said, *well done, my brother.* Turning around, there sat a heavyset hooded monk with an elephant's trunk exposed from where a nose should be. Sitting in a lotus position upon three stacked rectangular granite blocks, the monk couldn't have been more than five feet in height. Waiting for the monk to speak again, I remained silent. Slowly the monk began to levitate while it appeared to be meditating.

Opening my eyes, I disconnected and brought myself back to a peaceful waking state. Taking out an apple, I slowly ate and pondered the experiences.

CHAPTER 9

DID THE PIZZA TASTE REAL?

Arriving at my mother's, I knocked on the front door. When she didn't answer I tried the doorknob and it was unlocked. Entering the first-floor apartment, I called for my mother but there was no answer. Walking out the back, I found my mother sitting in the swing.

"Okay Mom, tell me how this began," I asked, as I sat beside her on the swing and handed her the bag with batteries and aspirin.

"I didn't see him first, Dee did. Dee was near the garden gate and looked up at the third floor window and screamed 'Ma, look! It's Poppy!' 'It's Poppy?' I asked. I stepped back and looked. 'Oh my God, it is Poppy', I said. I walked over to where the garden gate is and said, 'Hi Hun, what can I do for you?' He tilted his head and looked down, but he was cut off at the shoulders. I didn't see anything past the bottom of his beard because of the window."

"Dee said 'Mom, Mom, look Poppy is following you with his eyes.' If I walked to the left, he turned his head that direction, if I walked to the right, he turned his head that direction. Then Cheri came into the yard, she looked up and Dee said, 'Look, it's Poppy.' Cheri said, 'Oh my god, it's Jesus.'"

"'It's not Jesus. You can see the baseball cap. I don't think Jesus would be wearing a baseball cap', I told her. Do you remember at the wake I had him wear the baseball cap like he always did? And Cheri said, 'Yes, but it looks like Jesus.'"

"Were you all drinking?" I asked my mother.

"Of course not," Mom answered.

"Mom, it's not Richard."

"I'm not done. About an hour later after Cheri and Dee left, I was still working in the garden. It was getting dark and hazy and I was singing a song. Richard loved this song. Suddenly, I got that swooshing feeling of a comfortable presence passing right through me. I knew it was like a hug, because it felt so loving. I looked up at the screen window and Richard was looking down and smiling. 'Did I do something good?' I asked. Richard nodded his head yes. Then a flame about 6 inches in length appeared and hovered in front of me."

"What? Mom this has nothing to do with Richard. You are being toyed with by jinn. If you were to step back and view the phenomena taking place it would be clear that you have established a relationship with a deceiver."

"It's Richard. Wait and you will see."

"How long did this flame last?"

"About a good minute or so."

"What happened after that?"

"I was startled by the flame and looked up at Richard in the window and said 'I'm confused, do you want me to burn something?' Richard gave me a smirk. He used to have these smirks when he was pulling mischief."

"It's a hooded shadow or shapeshifting jinn, Mom."

"Will you stop with the jinn?"

"Mom, you're not using your common sense."

"Are you saying I'm going senile?"

"Not at all, Mom. When you saw the hooded shadow the other day, could you see through it?"

"No, it appeared solid and it was jet black. Why?"

"I think there is another form hidden within that dark cloak."

"You might be right. It didn't feel friendly. Are you still going to try and talk to Richard tomorrow?"

"Yes, Mom."

"What time?"

"What time did you see Richard's face in the screen?"

"I would say it was a little after four."

"Then I will be here at 4 p.m."

In the evening before class, I lined up the free-standing heavy bags and changed into my uniform. One by one the students came in, ready for a hard workout. Beginning with a warmup, followed by a few rounds of shadow boxing, we moved on to combinations on the bag.

"Alright class, the first combination we are going to work is jab, rear elbow, rear knee, rear leg kick." Demonstrating it first in the air and then on the bag. After that, I walked around correcting technique. "Before we move on to the second combination, grab on to the bag and perform twenty skip knees. Ready? Begin."

Thirty minutes had passed, and it was time for the cool down and ab work before ending the class. Sitting at the desk, I said good night to the students as they left. Tom did some weight training, while I typed in attendance and class notes. Twenty minutes later, Tom bowed at the dojo entrance and entered the office.

"What do we have today, Professor?"

"Quasar and a couple of other personalities."

"Isn't a quasar like a star?" Tom asked, as he was wiping his forehead with a towel.

"A quasar is the brightest celestial object in the universe."

"I can't wait to read it."

Taking out the notebook, I opened it to Quasar. "When you're done, let me know, I'll be stretching."

Bowing at the entrance, I entered the dojo. Walking over to the stretching machine, I took a seat. Slowly I cranked the handle, spreading the legs. When I reached a comfortable stretch, I held it for a few minutes and then closed it, repeating the action four more times.

"Professor, I'm all set," Tom called from the office.

Slowly cranking the stretcher closed, I got up and shook out my legs. Walking over to the dojo entrance, I turned and bowed toward the training space.

"Professor, this Quasar sounds cool."

"It is another wise personality."

"Amy was an impostor like your father, wasn't she?"

"Yes, Tom. The being is pulling out all the stops to stir up my emotions. This was another angle of getting close or intimate, through the guise of a deceased female friend."

"What do you think of Quasar's comments about Jesus?"

"I would compare it to the Golden Cross Monk who said, *Jesus has a heart, you have a heart, and both have a home. So, I say to all, May you find the door and walk in. Simple it is. Jesus spoke of his luminous experiences; may you all speak of yours. Jesus will not rise again, and Christ never left you. Jesus was a man; Christ was his heart. See this, my family. Stop waiting for an illusion that you will never see.* Who was Constantine visited by the next night after the cross vision?"

"Christ."

"Yes. What we see is the same being with two personalities stating in its doctrine that Jesus was a kind, loving man who had a mystical experience and Christ was his heart - an experience of which we are all capable. Jesus filled the Bible with few of his spoken words. Jesus ran from evil spiritual beings into the arms of evil human beings, or it could mean into the arms of benevolent spiritual beings that were also malevolent. When Jesus the man passed, Christ remained, which is the illumined heart the benevolent personas speak of. Jesus the man will not return."

"Interesting."

"This is the common doctrine of benevolent deceivers, Tom. Never kid yourself into believing these beings are sharing knowledge for the goodness of humanity. What have you learned that these deceiving messengers, which appear benevolent, do very well?"

"Compliment and flatter."

"That's right Tom, compliment, flatter, and sweet talk. Quasar sarcastically said, *the question remains either Jesus did or Jesus didn't. What a glad day it will be when Jesus returns. Jesus ran from evil into the arms of evil.* That was no compliment. Keep in mind the personas that are speaking beautifully about Jesus, are coming from the same being that is speaking negatively. This is contradiction, and how they confuse and play both sides of the coin."

"Deceiving or not, I really like the way Quasar explained messengers as tiles and said, *we must not listen to the song of only one bird.* What did you make of it?"

"Basically, Quasar's doctrine is saying we must not listen to one spiritual teacher or belief system if it doesn't soothe you or resonate as truth. You are free to listen to the knowledge of another teacher or belief system, if necessary. This I agree with Tom, but understand they have traps for the spiritual, as they have traps for the religious."

"Reviewing Amy's response to my question about where she now was, she answered, *I am a grain of sand begging for God's attention. You are the God I begged for.* When I asked Helen the same question, she answered, *I am a grain of sand in God's palm.* Sand is used as a symbol many times in the Bible."

"When the being played Amy, the voice was similar to Amy's but not exact. This could mean at least one of the spiritual beings heard Amy speak when she was alive. As the conversation with Amy continued, the voice changed and was recognized as the same tone as the other female personas including the white-haired seductress fairy.

The more the conversation carried on with flattery and sweet talk, the more it spoke in a manner foreign to the Amy I knew, just like the Impostor Father."

"Amy spoke about a woman I dated and how I became weak a few times, and said, *I see why you choose these crazy women. It has all been a test. Evil wins every time you accept their distraction.* Neither Amy, Quasar, or the monk in brown cloth we will call My Life Is God, mentioned the white-haired seductress distraction that's aggressively looking for a roll in the hay."

"Because they're the personas of one being."

"Yes, Tom. The spiritual being that's playing the seductress would like nothing more than for me to avoid human women so the being can have me to itself. This is the nature of jealous spiritual beings."

"Did the seductress pizza really taste real?"

"Yes, it did."

"Maybe you don't know what you're missing?"

"Maybe you should control your hormones. I know exactly what I'm missing. If you fall for the seduction and become a spirit spouse, you may never be able to have a healthy relationship with a human woman."

"Why?"

"Because these jealous beings will do everything in their power to destroy it, eventually destroying you. We can see the white-haired seductress visitations are escalating in intensity and frequency. When you read about the seductress backing up against me in the night dream, what did I say occurred next?"

"Her skin started to change."

"That's right. Spiritual beings can't hold their counterfeit forms for long, whether it's a temporary manifestation or an influenced image in a dream or vision. They need you to believe and buy into the illusion to give it strength to maintain form. If you look closely at these counterfeits, they are never exact in the first place. There will always be flaws in their creation."

"The octopus and hay creature attack was like a video game."

"Do not be impressed. Yes, they can create simulated environments. But it's another hook to strengthen the connection. What I'm doing is giving the being a continuing opportunity to communicate through a different medium to expose their vision and dream patterns. Already this tells us they can influence and manipulate these video feed-like dreams to seduce, tempt, or torment, anywhere or anytime."

"Notice both the octopus and the hay beast that grabbed me in a bear hug squeezed and shook me side to side in the same manner. Notice also, the night dream encounter with the seductress took place up in a mountain and the daydream was crossing the ocean to a mountain. The sun, or the rays of the sun, appeared in all three daydreams. This is for two reasons. One is to get me to be drawn to the sun and bright light in visions and dreams as a sign of a divine presence or God. Two, these beings know that I deeply enjoy the visual experience of sunrise, sunset, and sun rays through clouds and they arrange the dreamscape or vision with that knowledge."

"Who do you think the monk with the elephant trunk is?"

"It's just another human/animal hybrid form. Since childhood I have encountered endless variations of human/animal hybrid forms, usually when I was aware that a shadow being was present. One of the most popular benevolent forms was a human-like being with an elephant head. The reason for this particular hybrid probably stemmed from my close relationship with Fanny, the elephant from the Slater Park Zoo. While my mother worked there as an artist, I spent a lot of time with Fanny. She was a beautiful creature - gentle, empathetic and friendly, but her emotional energy was one of deep sadness due to her living conditions. As I have taught you, these spiritual beings will take any and all forms necessary to develop a relationship."

"So, the marketed angel is a human/bird creation."

"Yes, it is. Just like the Satyr, a goat with a human head, the Centaur with the lower body of the horse and the upper body of a human, the deity Ganesh of Hinduism with an elephant head and a human body, and the Great Sphinx of Egypt with the body of a lion and the head of a human. These are just a few of endless variations of human/animal, human/bird, human/fish, and human/reptile creations that we can find in the myths, legends, and religions of every ancient culture. What patterns did you notice in the dialogue, Tom?"

"Well Quasar said, *God is you, I am God as well* and *Remember, I am God, and so are you.* Amy said, *you were being a man, not the God you truly are,* and *You are the God I begged for,* along with the continued use of the words *illuminate* and *illumination.*"

"Yes, the words *illuminate* and *illumination, and the 'we are Gods, they are Gods'* message continue despite the personality they play or the guise they wear. These messengers not only say that humans are gods, but we can see a pattern of the messengers or personas calling themselves God."

"When I told Amy, I am not a god, Amy said, *you didn't fall, you're still love.* This is referring to falling from grace, like a falling messenger or angel. Another word pattern we can see is the use of the word direction. *Love gives me direction of which wind of soul to follow,* by Quasar. *I'm following your soul, keep the direction of heart and love will be your island paradise,* by Quasar. *I live here until light points the way in another direction*, by Golden Cross Monk and *I hear your heart giving me directions to your soul,* by Helen."

"Was Quasar referring to your system of martial arts when he said *Keep focused on full circle. I believe in you.*"

"Yes and no. Energy Being also mentioned full circle, *it will all come together full circle at the right moment.* Before I named my expression of martial arts, Full Circle Fighting System, I called the cross I wear Full Circle Path. " Reaching into my shirt I pulled out the cross and turned it around. "I designed and had this cross made for my children and myself. As you can see it says **LOVE** vertically and **GOD** horizontally on the back. Six circles are interconnected to represent unity and oneness. It is worn upon the chest because this marks the spot of the mind of the heart, and the home of the true loving God."

"Can you have a Full Circle Path cross made for me?"

"Yes, I can. Looking over Amy's dialogue we see the message, *you now must finish your book,* and reinforced by the next personality My Life Is God, which said, *I hope my explanation is helpful in your book,* and *Include in your book this speech.* They, or it, want their story and doctrine to be included in my book. Let's end today's lesson on that note."

"How is your mom doing?"

"The activity at my mother's is escalating as expected. She and my two sisters saw what appeared to be Richard in the third-floor screen window and my mother witnessed a hovering flame."

"That can't be good."

"It's not. This is another sign of the jinn."

CHAPTER 10

RICHARD'S WISH

Mom and my nephew John were on the first floor when I arrived. Placing the backpack down, I took a seat in Richard's favorite recliner. A strong headache came on as my solar plexus began to tighten in the uncomfortable environment.

"Are you going to talk to Poppy?" John asked.

"I don't know who we're going to talk to, but something I'm sure will answer."

"Can I stay?" John asked.

"I rather you not. It's very easy to pick up an attachment or follower," I answered.

"But Uncle, my mother uses a spirit board to consult her guides all the time," John countered.

"We will have to talk about that another time. Yes, you can stay but try to remain calm no matter what activity occurs."

"I will, thanks. Do you work with spirit guides?" John asked.

"No. But if I ask for one the deceivers will surely deliver."

"I take it you don't believe in spirit guides."

"Not like most do, John. Let's go see Richard in the screen," I said to my mother, as I looked at the time on my watch.

"You're going to see, you're wrong about the screen," my mother said, as she got up off the couch.

"Maybe, Mom." Walking outside to the back of the house, the three of us stood and looked up at the window screen on the left. Patiently we waited, and waited, as twenty minutes passed and not a thing showed its face. Mom was very disappointed and surprised. "We will try another time, let's go in."

"I'm telling you it's Richard. Dee and Cheri saw him with their own eyes."

"Mom, I'm not doubting you're seeing something. I just don't agree it's Richard. Don't underestimate the mimicking ability of the hidden race."

"Maybe you're giving them too much credit."

"Maybe you're not giving them enough. Can you take notes, Mom?"

"Yes, of course," my mother answered. All three of us took a seat on the couch inside, with my mother on the left and my nephew on the right. "I just felt a cool breeze," my mother said while rubbing her arms, "maybe it is Richard."

Knowing it wasn't Richard, I kept my mouth shut and prepared the tools. Peetu, my mother and Richard's silver-haired Yorkie, was following something in the air with his eyes.

"What is Peetu looking at?" John asked.

"It's either an orb, a shadow, or both," I answered as a vision of orbs, coming down from the ceiling and up from the floor, flying horizontally, diagonally, and zig zag, came to the mind's eye.

"There are orbs in here?"

"I'm sure there are, Mom. If we had a digital camera and walked around the apartment, you would see them flying in all directions."

"Can all dogs see orbs?" John asked.

"In my experience, dogs and cats can see orbs and shadows, some a little more than others." Turning my notebook to a fresh page, I slid it over to my mother and handed her a pen. Placing the alphabet chart down, I removed my necklace and placed the cross on the table.

"When are you going to make me one of those crosses?" my mother asked.

"I will cast you one next week," I responded. "Are you ready to write?"

"I've got to open a window first, I'm feeling kind of claustrophobic," my mother said as she walked over to the window to the left of the television and raised it. Doom and gloom energy filled the room, and aggressively the presence pounced and began to squeeze me like a tube of toothpaste.

"Mom, I will be speaking outwardly to the presence, receiving their transmission telepathically and translating it to you. Spiritual beings are emotional, so please think before you speak and do your best to control your emotional energy of anger or fear," I said, as I struggled to maintain emotional peace.

Closing my eyes an invading vision of a red Chevy Blazer with a black roof was sinking into a dark secluded pond and a dark shadow arm reached out the window and started waving as the vehicle slowly submerged.

"What is about to speak will not be pleasant and is definitely not Richard." Taking a deep breath, I let it out and allowed the conversation to begin telepathically. "Who may I ask is present?"

I am Donovan. I am hate. I am evil.

"Why is that?"

I can't stop being angry with those who took my life.

"Who took your life Donovan?"

Five men took it from me.

"Why are you here?"

Hate follows hate. I followed someone here.

"Who may that be Donovan?"

I cannot say. Hate can only live with hate. Fear can only live with fear. I want to change.

Internally I raised my vibration with prayer and memories of goodness to battle Donovan's toxic wickedness. Donovan's energy shifted to a neutral emotional state.

God does exist, I felt it. Thank you, Lorne. Live, my friend. I am sorry for any uncomfortable feelings. I will go now. Thanks again, Lorne.

"You're welcome Donovan. Goodbye." Donovan wasn't going anywhere, but I played along. I promised my mother I would attempt to converse with Richard and I stayed focused on that goal.

"Mom, I'm going to take a quick break and then try to interact one more time on the third floor."

"That will probably be better because that's where we spent the most time," my mother responded.

"We will see," I said stepping into the bathroom.

My mother asked John to go up to the third floor and get her a soda. Within a minute, he came running down the stairs.

"There is a ghost upstairs," John said, as he frantically opened the door.

"What happened?" I asked.

John was pale and out of breath. "As I opened the refrigerator door, Poppy's chair turned and faced me, and I just froze. Then his hat was knocked off the chair onto the floor," John said, as he walked over to the recliner and sat.

"Maybe this is Richard," my mother suggested from the couch.

"I doubt that," I answered. "Stay here," I told John.

"Do you want me to come with you?" Mom asked.

"No Mom, not yet." Ascending the stairs to the third floor, the presence was at my back. Opening the door, I walked into what felt like a face full of spider webs. Wiping my hair, face, and ears with my hand I looked to see no visible signs of webs in my hands.

The atmosphere was considerably heavier than the first floor. What sounded like a man and a woman talking was coming from my mother's bedroom. Unable to make out what they were saying, I ignored the disturbing tactic. Taking a seat at the kitchen table, I closed my eyes giving the presence the opportunity for an influenced daydream.

Richard and I were in a beach setting, seated at a pub table in a restaurant. French style doors were open in all four directions giving us a full view of the ocean. Looking down on the floor, snakes were slithering and were coiled around the bottom of the bar stools. Picking up the menu, I started to read the choices when Richard said, "I already ordered for the both of us, I hope you don't mind."

"That's fine," I answered.

Walking up was a young waitress with snakes coiled around both forearms holding two plates of lobsters that were red with black claws. Setting them down on the table, she asked, "Is there anything else I can get you?"

Richard answered, "That will be it, thank you."

As the waitress walked away, I noticed a snaked draped over the mailbox outside and a woman with a painted blue face wearing a dark hood seated at the bar staring.

The daydream changed to a different scenario. Automatic glass doors opened, and I stepped into an emergency room hospital setting with what appeared to be my mother. White waiting room chairs were directly in front and to my left. On my right was the patient registration area in a glass enclosure. My mother walked up to the registration and said to the blonde haired woman, we are here to see Richard Nolan. The woman asked her to take a seat and a nurse would come out.

My mother paced the floor as I sat and picked up a magazine. A man came out of the treatment area dressed in pajamas with a red and black puzzle pattern, a matching old-style nurse's hat with red and black trim, and brown and white oversized furry slippers on his feet. Holding a clipboard, he called out my mother's name. My mother answered and the male nurse said, "Come with me."

Sitting across from me the nurse crossed his legs, smiled, and said, "Richard doesn't look too good." Placing her hand on her chest my mother said she was getting pain and couldn't breathe. I stood up and asked the nurse if he could help her. He laughed and said, "I'm afraid not."

Small black spiders started crawling down the wall to the right. When I looked down at the nurse's slippers, they now had dog faces, and both stuck out their tongue.

Two doctors came out from the treatment area. A woman stood to my right, and a middle-aged man stood to my left. The female doctor looked at the back of my hands then asked me to turn them over. In my left wrist was what looked like a thick worm embedded about 3 to 4 inches in length. "Ahh," she said, "there it is."

Quickly the male doctor grabbed a wheelchair and had me take a seat then rolled me into the treatment area crashing through the swinging doors. Standing up, I switched to the bed while the male doctor closed the white curtain. The female doctor came in and injected a numbing medication while the male doctor wheeled over a cart with surgical tools.

Wasting no time, the female doctor started cutting and digging into my wrist. Grabbing hold of a red worm, she started prying it out as the worm fought to stay attached. When the worm was successfully removed, she dropped it in a small gray box and said, "There is more."

Digging into my wrist for the rest, she grabbed two at once and began yanking hard and pulling until they were out wiggling in her fingers. Dropping them into the box with the other worm, she immediately sealed it closed with tape. Looking at my forearm, it was absolutely disgusting with canals and torn skin every which way.

Opening my eyes, I disconnected from the daydream and felt the wickedness of the influencing presence. Walking over to the fridge, what felt like a hand was placed on the back of my right shoulder. Ignoring the touch and its energy, I opened the refrigerator door.

"I don't care who you are, you're not getting the leftovers," I said out loud, with a little unwelcomed humor. Using internal dialogue, I told the presence that I would talk in a few minutes if it backs away. Instantly, the presence pulled back revealing that it heard my thoughts clearly.

To the right of the fridge was a blanket covering a picture frame on top of stacked boxes. When I pulled the blanket off there was an old painting face down. Turning it over, the painting was a young boy, possibly 4 or 5 years old in early 1900's clothing. Waving my hand over the painting, I felt a disturbing energy possibly from the emotions of the artist, an attachment, or the environment it came from. The bell on the door rang as my mother walked in.

"What is it?" my mother asked, catching her breath from climbing the stairs.

"There appears to be a variety of spiritual beings present. So, it's tough to say. This apartment house is infested."

"What do you mean by infested?"

"Every home accumulates at least one variety of spiritual being. Who is to know how many have been brought in by the antiques and used religious items you have purchased, in addition to the beings that have followed the family for years."

"I don't believe that."

"I know it's not something you want to hear, but it's true."

"It's Richard."

"If it is, he is not alone. How long has this old painting been face down on the boxes?"

"A few months."

"Where did you get it?"

"Just before Pops had a stroke, we found it in the cellar of the apartment house we purchased. Why?" my mother asked.

"I'm just asking. Objects can contain the negative emotional energy from the home where they came from or an attachment."

"There is nothing wrong with the objects in this house."

"That's exactly what they want to hear, Mom. Are you ready to try again?"

"Yes. But I have to get Peetu first." My mother opened the door and yelled down to John on the first floor.

"What Gramma?" John answered.

"Bring up Peetu."

"Okay. Do you want your pocketbook?" John asked.

"Yes, bring that up too," Mom replied.

John came up with Peetu in one arm and Mom's pocketbook in the other. When John put him down, Peetu walked over and laid at my mother's feet. There is nothing fake about the unconditional love from a dog or its sensitivity to spiritual beings. I will be watching Peetu's body language closely because of the bond Richard had with Peetu and his ability to see what I may not.

Donovan's wicked presence grew and engulfed the room like a massive dark cloud. If there were any chance in speaking to Richard, I needed to change the tone of the dominating emotional energy.

My mother moved a chocolate cake from the kitchen table to the top of the stove as I focused on projecting internal peace. The wicked presence shifted to a neutral emotional state and was no longer threatening. Sending an image to my mind's eye of the old painting on the boxes, it was about to wear a guise and I was about to play along. My mother sat to my left and John took a seat straight across. Handing my mother the notebook, she opened it to where the pen was left.

Taking a deep breath, I let it out, and allowed the next conversation to begin telepathically. "Hello, who may I ask is present?"

I like your approach.

"Thank you."

My name is Harold.

"Welcome, Harold."

You are very good. What you felt was my hand on your shoulder. You don't scare easy.

"I was too focused on the leftovers."

Forgive me, but we always try to frighten human bodies.

"I understand."

You are wise. Why are you so different? What are you?

"Just a taxpayer. Do you move around during the day Harold?"

All that is energy must move constantly because energy is alive. You know this already. There is no couch to sit on.

"Can you go outside during the light of day?"

Yes. God created a wall to separate what is human from what is energy.

"Is it like a veil?"

Yes. The veil separates us. We can wander by night.

"Did you live a long life, Harold?"

Yes, I lived a good life, I lived to eighty-seven years.

"Is that your picture on the boxes?"

Yes.

"You look about four or five years old in that picture."

I was five years old. I really liked that outfit. They called me Harry at that age.

"Those are good memories, Harold. Would you like to say something about the picture?"

Yes, don't leave my picture face down; I am proud of my picture.

"That is a great outfit you are wearing in that picture, Harold. What would you like us to do with the picture?"

I would enjoy it if you would hang it up.

"Mom, could we return the picture back to the apartment house cellar where it was hanging before?"

"Yes," my mother answered.

"There you go Harold, we will hang your picture back up where it was."

Thank you, you are a gentleman. Maintain your gift.

"Goodbye, Harold. Nice talking to you."

A shift in emotional energy occurred back to the angry, hateful presence originally felt. Donovan was playing the personality Harold and it knew I could read the intention in his words and feel its energy darkening. Peetu was beginning to shake and couldn't sit still. An influenced image came forward of Richard being held back by a tall dark shadow figure standing behind him, covering his mouth.

I hate Richard. I will fight him.

"I want you to leave. I understand you want to speak, but I am in control and I choose to speak to Richard."

I am a poltergeist. Give me your evil feelings and I will give you protection from any poltergeist that is attracted to your energy.

"I'm fresh out of evil today," I said out loud.

"Please leave, I want to talk to my husband," my mother said firmly.

Are you done begging?

"I'm not afraid of you," my mother answered.

Don't get cocky. I feel your fear.

"What is it that you want?" my mother asked.

Eat some fucking cake and puke old lady. Are you ready to die, bitch?

"When the time comes," my mother answered.

Don't fall bitch.

The malevolent presence sent an image to my mind's eye of my mother falling on the rock in the backyard that knocked out all her front teeth. This angered me for a moment, but I would not let the anger take root and feed the presence. Whether there was one being or many in this evil fog there would be no reasoning through words. My mother and John have not learned the value of controlling their emotions in the presence of deceiving beings. Mom was angry and John was showing fear, which didn't help the energy battle in the room.

"Both of you need to relax," I said to my mother and John.

Hate gives me strength. I hate all of you. You can't beat me. I have your soul.

"No, you don't. You're looking for anger and fear to feed on."

Give me hate back. I like that.

"Hate feels too uncomfortable. How about love?"

Another shift in the presence took place. An image of Richard came forward wearing his favorite tan baseball cap. I raised my vibrational frequency and balanced my energy to maintain emotional peace and stillness.

I am Richard.

"My Richard?" my mother said, going from a slouch to an upright position in the chair.

Yes, Jean, I am your Richard. Every day I watch you outside working in the backyard. I wish I could fight back. But things are different now. It's these clowns who have been playing with you. Don't let these evil clowns trick you.

An invading vision came to my mind's eye of a small clown face at distance. It came forward aggressively. Behind the small clown face was a larger clown face as it came closer. The small clown face vanished and the large clown face wearing a large red and black tie became angry and intimidating. As the nose lengthened on a downward slant, the ears grew, and the skin turned gray. It now looked like a goblin.

"I hope you find love. I hope you find happiness and joy, all of you," I said out loud to the malevolent presence in the air. An energy shift occurred in the presence and the atmosphere calmed.

I give you hate, and you give me love. I have no love, but I know what you're doing. I respect that. I would have hated you back. You are strong. Hate follows everyone, but feeling hate is what gets you here. I live where hate grows. I will leave now. I'm sorry. I am only being what I am. Goodbye.

"Goodbye," I answered.

"Does 'I live where hate grows' mean hell?" John asked.

"I'm sure that's what the presence is referring to, yes. Mom can you get the silver bracelet I gave Richard and the Josh Groban CD?"

My mother walked into the bedroom, then came back into the kitchen and handed me the bracelet Richard wore up to his passing. John put the CD into the player and played Josh Groban's beautiful song "To Where You Are".

This was Richard's favorite song and one I enjoyed as well. If it is possible to converse with Richard, he was now free to speak. The vibrational frequency of the room soared to a level that should repel a malevolent spiritual being or change it to a benevolent or divine presence. Tears were falling from my mother's eyes as a very convincing cloud of joy descended. Peetu walked over and laid at my feet and the conversation my mother waited for began.

Wipe your tears with my hat, I am here my love. Thank you for playing my song. I feel so bright. Don't cry over losing me. Smile, because I am really talking to you. This is really me, Jean.

"I feel a caress of loving energy around me," my mother said.

Your energy is weak, Jean. You must eat and get some rest.

95

My mother started to break down, making it more of a challenge for me to hold my emotions at bay.

"How am I to rest when I don't have you?"

I can't be what you want me to be. I can't visit all the time.

"Do you still love me?"

I don't need to say that. I always love you. My love hasn't changed, feel me around you. I know how it would help if you could hear my voice every day. But I want you to hear your voice. Make every day special. I can't say this enough. I miss you all. I would love for you to say, I love you Richard and love will bring us together again. You must believe I love you all.

"Did I make you happy?"

All you've done and all you've ever done was make me happy. I am holding your hand, and I would like you to listen to this. It hurts me to feel your emotions. You must start living better and please stop hurting yourself. I am only asking this because I love you. Your life doesn't have to end. Why lose what can't be bought, and that is life. You are stronger than this, Jean. Strength is never giving up. Fight back, give them a run for their money. You are basing your strength on me. I am telling you, you must get stronger. I will tell you why. What Lorne always said is true; here is where what you feel is what you are. I mean this with all my heart. Be strong in your world and you will be strong in mine. I would love, more than anything I've ever asked for, for you to start drawing again.

"That is Lorne saying that."

I wouldn't let Lorne tell you something I didn't say. Give yourself more credit, Jean. I would love for you to show the jealous what you are capable of. I will enjoy their looks when you let your creativity loose. Don't destroy your creative gifts, Jean, show them.

"I still feel you, do you still feel me?"

I feel you all the time my love. Remember, where we spent the most time. That is where I will be. All your messages are heard, but we know I can't fulfill all of them, but this is one wish you asked. To talk to me, I am here. Come over to my picture.

My mother walked over to Richard's picture which stood below the shelf that holds the pyramid urn of his ashes.

I love you. With Lorne's gift you can hear me. I can't bring myself to leave you. Heaven is here with you. You are looking forward to death more than life. Let me tell you, don't do that. Life is beautiful. This is a miracle in itself, me talking to you. But this is something that can't always be done. We will be together, but if you harm yourself, we will be apart. Welcome life every day, and I will welcome it with you. This will make our connection stronger.

"Will you be there when I pass?" Mom asked.

That did it. My emotions were taking too much of a beating. Feeling the intense emotions of my mother, the presence which claims to be Richard, and my own were too much to maintain for much longer. "Mom. Please don't talk like that," I said.

Lorne is right, you weren't listening to me. I will see you when that time comes, please don't rush that time. I know you want to be with me. But, I still scratch your back at night. I still have a coffee with you in the morning. I am at the table with you now, sitting in my chair. Feel my heart.

The emotional energy of the presence claiming to be Richard increased along with sharing a vision of his sad face. I knew what he was about to ask.

I have one wish, if you would do this for me. I always wanted to hear you say, I love you Pops. That is my only wish.

My mother was waiting for me to respond, so I did. "I love you, Pops." I said.

Thank you, Lorne. I have to go, my love. Please don't make your life searching for me. I'm with you always. Lorne, you are more than a man.

"Stay a little longer," my mother said.

I can't, I love you Jean. My heart is yours.

My mother was about to speak.

Yes, I say I love you back every time you say you love me. This I want you to know.

"How did he know what I was going to say?" Mom asked.

"He heard your thoughts, Mom."

"Is he gone?"

"It appears so," I answered, as I placed the chart in the notebook.

"How do you do that?" John asked.

"Trial and error." Looking at Richards's urn up on the shelf I realized it was a gold pyramid, like the three gold triangles in the vision with the ghost monks. Now it was coming together. "Mom, when you and Richard saw the apparition of Gram in the bedroom, what was she wearing?"

"When she came in through the bedroom door, she wore a red shirt."

"Do you remember what color the pants were?"

"It was rather quick, but I would say black. It's kind of weird my mother hated the color red. Why are you so concerned about colors?"

"Spiritual beings can use color symbolism. What did the apparition of Gram do after it came in?"

"She floated in front of the television and you could see right through her. She turned and smiled, then continued right through the fire escape window."

"What color was her hair?"

"It was her natural color, orange, and she looked at least twenty years younger than when she passed. Why did you ask that?"

"I'm piecing together a puzzle. Whether you believe what I'm telling you or not what appeared as Gram, can appear as Richard, complete with his body scent and voice. Just as an actor or actress can embody a character, spiritual beings can as well."

"That was Richard talking, I know it. I was skeptical at first, but when I saw Peetu lay at your feet I knew it was really him," my mother said.

"Mom, Peetu has laid at my feet many times before."

"I think you're wrong. One day you will have to accept you have a gift. Are you coming downstairs?"

"Yes, after I look over the notes." Mom picked up Peetu and her pocketbook and descended the stairs. John stayed behind holding the door open.

"Why don't you think that was Poppy?" John asked.

"Patterns, behavior, and emotional energy. These beings are con artists, John. They know just what to say, and how and when to say it."

"Gram believes Poppy is still here. I know that wasn't Poppy that turned the chair around and knocked his hat off."

"You're right John, it wasn't. And it certainly wasn't your Poppy speaking either. Avoid divination in all its forms. It's all deception and lies."

John nodded his head, shut the door, and descended the stairs.

CHAPTER 11
ELEVEN GEMS

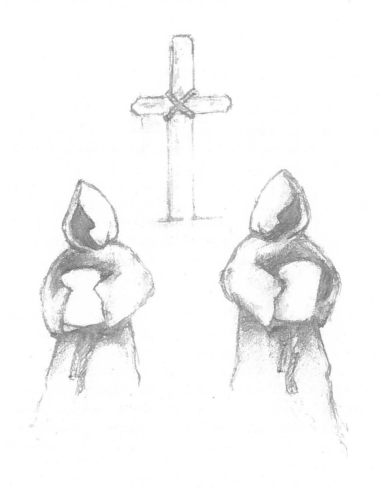

Craving red licorice, I stopped at a convenience store on the way to the monastery the following morning. While waiting in line a young boy, about eight years old, was asking his mother if he could have a box of Cracker Jacks. "I told you no!" she yelled, then swore and called him a name that made me cringe. "I have no money," she said, as she purchased twenty dollars' worth of lottery tickets and a pack of cigarettes.

Walking out the door, her son followed with his head down. As I stepped up to pay the cashier, she was shaking her head, "Some mothers need to be shot," she said, ringing up the licorice. "No, some people just need to find their hearts," I replied. "You got that right," an older woman responded behind me. "Have a good day," I said to the cashier and older woman.

Walking to my truck, the woman was leaning on her car, smoking and talking on her cell phone. The little boy was standing on a parking block, waiting patiently. When I approached the boy, he turned and looked at me. I smiled and said, "Good morning." "Good morning," he replied back.

Continuing to walk, I reached into my pocket and pulled out a dollar bill. I know the price of Cracker Jacks, they are a favorite of mine as well. Relying on the wind, I released the bill into the breeze, while not looking back and continued to walk faster to my truck. As I was opening my door, I heard the magic words. "Mom, look, I found a dollar bill—can I go get Cracker Jacks?" I stalled stepping into my truck to listen for her answer. She said, "Go ahead, you pain in the ass." I got into my truck and drove away.

Parking facing the Ruth E. Carpenter Memorial Garden, I grabbed my stuff and entered. I planned to speak from the heart and repeat the actions that led to the first appearance of the ghost monks. Before I began, I made the sign of the cross and recited the *Our Father* and *Hail Mary,* then spoke from the heart. When my heart began to sing and my eyes began to tear, I raised my arms and said, "God is my heart." A warm loving embrace was felt by what appeared to be an overwhelming cloud of divine light energy.

Staring at the cross, I walked backwards in a peaceful trance. When I sat upon the stone bench, I placed the notebook, chart, and pen on my lap.

While in a high vibration state, two translucent ghost monks manifested with a golden-white glow. One monk stood in the entrance to the left, one in the entrance to the right. Floating silently toward each other, they stopped about a foot apart and slowly turned to me. Face, hands, and feet were hidden in brown cloth and they were holding stone tablets. Removing my necklace, I placed the cross on the notebook and held the chain over the chart.

Taking a deep breath, I exhaled and relaxed into receptive oneness. Controlling thought and emotion, "For the goodness of all, if you please," I said aloud. The conversation began telepathically with the monk to the right reading the tablet that was now glowing gold. The monk to the left lowered its head and held its tablet to its chest.

Eleven gems surround God's crown.

"Could you clarify the meaning of your message, please?"

Eleven Gems are holy words I spoke. I will repeat them.

1. *I judge, I forget who I am.*
2. *I lie, I forget who I am.*
3. *I steal, I forget who I am.*
4. *I commit adultery, I forget who I am.*
5. *I see Earth as mine, I forget who I am.*
6. *I mingle with the darkness, I forget who I am.*
7. *I vision my brother or sister's lover as mine, I forget who I am.*
8. *I release words and energy of hatred, I forget who I am.*

Now the final three:
9. *I am God.*
10. *I am Jesus.*
11. *I am Love.*

The simple trinity.

The tablet stopped glowing and the monk to the right lowered its head pulling the stone tablet back to its chest as the monk to the left began to read its glowing, golden tablet.

Eleven gems I spoke as well. Eleven gems are as follows:

1. *Believe in God.*
2. *Become God.*
3. *Let love rule your heart.*
4. *Have faith when others have none.*
5. *Ill of mind spreads like locusts.*
6. *Mend torn remnants of past experiences.*
7. *Wear the holy cross inside the third eye.*

8. *Until evil settles to the bottom of the ocean, don't swim in others souls.*
9. *I Am is your real name, as God is your real body.*
10. *Fear means you lost your eternal eyes and put the lenses of illusion on in its place.*
11. *This Earth I belong, just as this body of God I belong. Let no keeper of the truth sell you another story.*

Repeating the actions of the monk on the right as soon as the tablet stopped glowing, the monk on the left lowered its head pulling the stone tablet back to its chest. Both were careful not to expose their hands during the delivery of the eleven gems by keeping them hidden in their sleeves.

"Thank you both for your powerful message."

Thank you, my brother, they answered in unison. Turning they faced each other, and slowly floated backwards out their entrance and vanished into the air.

Placing the chain down, I closed my eyes. A vision came forward to the mind's eye of walking on top of a beautiful mountain of divine light. Flowers grew everywhere, in every color, and they were luminous. Men, women, and children were wearing bright long white robes and were barefooted. Each greeted me with a smile and a hug.

Opening my eyes, I felt at peace. After making the sign of the cross, I drank some water and packed up. Putting the backpack in the vehicle, I went for a walk on the Beauregard Loop Trail. When I approached the Old Road Trail on the right, a large flock of birds flew into a tree on my left. As I continued the Beauregard Loop, they flew to the next tree as if following. This phenomenon continued from tree to tree, until I reached the chin up bar on the trail. At that point they flew away, but a blissful feeling remained.

A picture of Jesus Christ came to the mind's eye. This was a common artistic representation like the prayer cards my grandmother bought me when I was a child. Coming up on the left was a wooden bench. Stopping, I took off the pack and had a seat.

The artistic representation of Jesus Christ remained in my mind's eye as I pulled out the notebook and pen. Turning to a clean page, I positioned the chain over the chart. A vision of Jesus Christ appeared before me as bright as the sun.

I might not always speak my brother. Do you have a question?

An energy of incredibly calming peace engulfed me again in divine light. I couldn't talk. I had no thought to question. For the moment, I enjoyed this intense state of pure joy and bliss. When I could speak, I said, "I am questionless."

I know, my brother. I find feeling a better speaker. I know how goodness feels. Lorne knows as well. Live and share this goodness. I will speak when words are more necessary than feeling. Feeling love always precedes the word. Remember and become.

"Who may I ask is speaking?"

I am Jesus, my brother. God is Heaven. I am Heaven's door. When you are at the door, you are my brother. When you step in, you are God's son.

"Spoken beautifully. May I ask for all, are you Jesus known as Jesus the Christ?"

You man gave me Christ. I Jesus gave you God's word.

"May I ask for all, how are we connecting?"

Those who sing the tune of love, receive the tune of love. God is the tune. Illuminated melody of a pure heart is the song. My brother, I am mystical and so are you. I am like a fish and you are like a fisherman.

"May I ask for all, how do you stop the torment of the malevolent spiritual beings?"

Holy light peers on the darkest days. The Devil can, and will, acquire heads of sheep. Let love blind its vision. Don't let anger cloud your clear skies. Kindness, Compassion, Love. These qualities are what emits from God's heart. Only you can choose which heart lives.

Give your money to the homeless. Give your money to the sick. Give your money to those that struggle just to eat. This is God. Help one another. Love one another.

High above this current vision of yours, I watch you, my brother. Fear will enter your mind, but never will it enter your soul. Just be God's eyes and watch the world change.

"Why all the battles when all I wanted to know was God?"

Your battles have brought you home.

"Thank you, Jesus."

Thank you, my brother. I love you.

Pondering the divine experience, I packed up again and walked the trail in a pure state of joy. A hawk flew toward me, low to the ground, as I approached the next bench. Before it reached me, it swooped upwards and landed on a branch just above me. Stopping, I looked up as it hopped and flapped its wings moving farther out on the branch.

Taking off the pack, I set it on the ground and prepared to interact again while still experiencing the intensified flow of love. "God, I ask You with all the love of my heart, which is You, and for the goodness of all, which is you. Please let me write as You speak, as I feel your compassionate embrace." As tears started to fall, my mind ceased thought and the divine presence took control of my writing hand with a light as bright as the sun shining in the mind's eye.

My son, you are me, more than you know. I know your heart is true. Believe with the eyes of your loving heart, I am God. You deserve the truth.

You have never asked from me more than truth for all. Here is your truth, my son. Believing in more than self, is my mind in you. Feeling love for all, is my heart in you. All is truly me with many unique faces.

Let this knowing come forth, my children. I am all the children that fall during your wars. I am all the children left standing after your wars. Love all as me and walk as my illuminated children, sharing all of me with one another.

I hold all of you in one heart, there is no other.

"My Lord, may I ask for all what is Christmas to you?"

Illuminate your holiday by illuminating your heart. This is your gift to Jesus. This is your gift to self. Christmas is the celebration of compassion, love, and goodness, for all God's children. Illumination is the star that shone in Jesus heart. Not the one above the manger. Jesus was a man in flesh and a God in heart. Jesus spoke as the star gave him voice. I am the star. You are the sky; I speak when the clouds are under control. Today's forecast is clear skies and a bright sun. You are my bright sun.

After what appeared to be a moment of divine intervention, my heart continued to ache. The dialogue had begun with an overwhelming sensation of compassion which escalated to a point I could barely tolerate. In this experience, there was no pendulum used. Today we would call this phenomenon automatic writing.

Leaving the monastery, I drove to the laundromat to do a load of laundry.

Later at the studio, twenty-eight women showed up for the women's self-defense class. Tom and a few senior students assisted with correcting technique and holding pads. Today the women were executing kicks from a ground defensive position. Class ended with a review of wrist grab escapes and two sets of ten burpees for conditioning.

When all the students were gone, Tom and I cleaned the dojo, then sat down and enjoyed a cup of green tea.

"I had some weird stuff happen last night and another crazy nightmare, Professor."

"What happened?"

"Well, before bed the lights started flickering for some strange reason. Then, about 3:30 in the morning, I was awoken by a loud bang in what sounded like the kitchen. Sitting up, I listened for any other noises. I heard what sounded like someone going through cupboards and was a little nervous to investigate. When I got up the nerve, I walked into the kitchen and nothing looked out of place. Walking back into the bedroom, another loud bang occurred in the bathroom. Getting back into bed,

I was extremely anxious and couldn't get back to sleep. When I finally did, I had a dream that I walked out to my car and there was a large black snake with a red ring around its neck, hanging down from under the vehicle. When it disappeared, I got down on my hands and knees and looked under the vehicle. The whole undercarriage was full of holes. Standing up, I looked in the window to see if there were any snakes. It looked clear, so I opened the car door and was shocked by hundreds of snakes of all kinds filling the interior. I slammed the door, but when I turned around there was a black Doberman-like dog sitting there with an evil stare. Thankfully I woke up, but when I did that same evil presence was felt in the room, just like after the succubus encounter. Do you think it's the same being?"

"Yes. You heard a loud bang in the kitchen at 3:30, just as my mother heard three knocks between 3:00 and 3:30 a.m. and experienced a loud noise in the kitchen. The presence is intentionally leaving its symbolic signature in your dreams. The pattern of snake scales appearing on the succubus skin, and the neck lengthening also like a snake, matches the snake nightmare you just experienced. There is the sinister red and black color symbolism in both your nightmares. The succubus with a red and black body suit, and the large snake in your dream which was black with a red ring around its neck."

"What about the black dog?"

"Dogs and snakes are a popular shapeshifted form of the jinn. It is believed that black dogs represent the evil amongst the jinn. In my experiences, jinn will assume the form of a dog of any species, color, or variety of colors, based on their goal, mood, or agenda. Snakes and a black dog are an influenced or manipulated dream, to appear malevolent and promote fear."

"What do I do?"

"Stand your ground, face your fears, and exercise emotional discipline. There is an internal adversary and there are external adversaries. Both must be handled in the same manner. The internal adversary is the dark aspect of your consciousness, or your own worst enemy. The external adversaries are human and spiritual beings whose consciousness may be partially or wholly dominated by the darker aspect. The internal adversary and the external adversaries want control of your mind and body, and their suggestions will be based on maintaining their survival. Both will do everything in their power to sway you away from positive change and a better quality of life."

"That's powerful, Professor."

"It's truth, my friend."

"How did you make out last night? Did you talk to Richard?"

"No, as expected it was an impostor like my father and Amy. But my mother is convinced it was Richard. After you read about the activity and conversations at my mother's yesterday there will be the Eleven Gems experience at the monastery today."

"Eleven Gems? That's different."

Opening the notebook, I placed it in front of Tom. Picking up the two empty mugs, I threw the tea bags in the trash and walked down the hall to the restroom to wash them. Returning to the studio, I got into a conversation with another tenant. Fifteen minutes passed when I entered.

"I just don't get it, Professor. This is incredible. Eleven gems is like the Ten Commandments. I really, really like this."

"Remember Tom, they are wise, but they are luminous liars as well. It appears the ghost monks have dictated their own list of moral guidelines or angelic law despite Fairy of the Forest saying, *God has no scroll of rules, because this is no game.*"

"Do you think it was one of these beings that gave Moses the Ten Commandments?"

"I'm sure that's what they would like us to think, and it may be true. All I know is what I am experiencing firsthand. I believe each of these deceivers make up their own angelic laws, moral guidelines, or commandments. The deceiver gave two versions of the eleven gems. This was to refer to the 11:11 phenomena, which in my experience is another signature of these beings."

"Even Jesus is calling you brother now, Professor?"

"And why is that?"

"Flattery and deception."

"Yes. Jesus said *I love you* as well. Obviously, that wasn't the historical Jesus of Nazareth. Keep in mind, no one knows what Jesus of Nazareth looked like, just as no one knows what his mother Mary looked like, yet the most common reported sightings around the world are Marian apparitions. A Marian apparition is an appearance of what is believed to be the Blessed Virgin Mary. We have many artistic representations of the historical Jesus and his mother Mary, but that's exactly what they are. I understand these perceived supernatural appearances are inspirational to the faithful, but an apparition, vision, dream or image of an artistic representation of Jesus or the Blessed Virgin Mary should raise a red flag no matter how divine the presence may seem. In this case, the impostor invoked an intense heavenly energy experience of peace and joy."

"Messengers or personas that appear benevolent have proven they can speak the name Jesus, talk about Jesus in a positive or sarcastic way, speak beautifully as Jesus, and even manifest as an artistic representation of Jesus. The Counterfeit Jesus spoke in threes, like the other benevolent messengers. *Give your money to the homeless, Give your money to the sick. Give your money to those that struggle just to eat.*"

"If we turn back the pages of the many personalities to the Golden Cross Monk, we can compare its dialogue to the Counterfeit Jesus. *So, I say to all, may you find the door and walk in,* by Golden Cross Monk and *God is Heaven. I am Heaven's door. When you are at the door, you are my brother. When you step in, you are God's son,* by the Counterfeit Jesus."

"We can compare Quasar's dialogue to the Counterfeit Jesus. *I am like a fish and you are like a fisherman,* by Counterfeit Jesus. *I am a guide in your chosen school of fish,* by Quasar and *the tiles are steppingstones across the sea of fish. I am a little fish, but I am one, you are a little fish, but you are one,* by Quasar."

"The fish is a symbol of Christianity. A large portion of the Twelve Disciples were fishermen. This may be one reason for the mentioning of fish and fisherman. Spiritual beings or jinn will also appear as fish, whales, and other sea creatures in dreams and visions."

"Quasar sarcastically said, *what a glad day it will be when Jesus returns,* and then we have the same spiritual being that plays Quasar now playing Jesus. Let's back up to the first ghost monk reciting the Eleven Gems list of moral guidelines, paying attention to numbers 9, 10 and 11. *I am God; I am Jesus; I am Love. The simple trinity.*"

"Three is their signature. The same being played God and Jesus, while projecting the energy of love. Before the being played Jesus on the Beauregard Loop Trail, it said *I am Jesus* in the garden. Before it played God on the Beauregard Loop Trail, it said *I am God* in the garden. The first of the three ghost monks in the first garden encounter said, *God lives here yielding to all who appreciate, Jesus yields to all who appreciate. They are one and the same, sharing the same heart. Seeing through the same eyes. Forever love, forever peace.* All along these benevolent messengers sharing what appears to be luminous knowledge have said they are God. All along, the prior messengers mentioning of Jesus, was to lead up to the same being playing Jesus."

"Unbelievable, Professor."

"It's their nature, my friend. As you can see there was no pendulum used in the conversation with the God presence. This was an automatic writing experience which is a form of channeling. The God presence mentioned the sun and used the words *illuminate* and *illumination,* just like the messengers, because God, and the messengers or angels, is one and the same being."

"Looking at the word *unique* and how it was used, we have, *each unique energy has a unique being. Each unique being tries to express but goes unnoticed until a unique being gives them a chance to speak,* by Being of Energy. *All have unique visions and dreams,* by Father Albert Celestine. *Every voice of spirit you interview will be unique,* by My Life Is God and *All is truly me with many unique faces,* by the God presence."

"It is true, all the unique faces are the masks of this multi-personality presence. Now let's review the deceiver's other side which has obvious anger management issues and a talent for masquerading as the deceased to trap the heartbroken and grief-stricken."

"My mother experienced an influenced dream from a presence attempting to send her on a wild goose chase, just like Father Albert Celestine. What she believes to be Richard, wearing black pants, a red shirt, and a red ball cap came to her asking her to meet him at the corner of High Street and Exchange."

"That could have put her in real danger."

"Yes, it could have. This is another example of the types of wild goose chases these beings influence. What did you notice in the influenced vision and dialogue of the first persona, Donovan?"

"I noticed the red and black symbolism in the vision with the red SUV with a black roof sinking in a swamp."

"Very good. How about the dialogue?"

"Donovan used the words *I am* three times, saying, **I am Donovan. I am hate. I am evil.**"

"That's right. In this case the being is malevolent, which shows both benevolent and malevolent messengers can and do speak in threes. What else did you notice?"

"It used the needy spirit con, pulling on the heart strings with the story that five men took his life and it said, **I want to change**, then ended with the flattery con after the energy shift."

"Excellent, Tom. Now for the third floor personas starting with the symbolism in the influenced daydreams."

Tom took a moment to look over the notes. "Red and black again, Professor. Red lobsters with black claws in the first daydream, and a man wearing red and black puzzle pattern pajamas with a matching nurse's hat in the second dream. Snakes were in the first dream, and dog slippers and black spiders in the second. How about the worms?"

"In addition to the usual serpent forms like snakes, dragons, and other reptiles, worms are used in their influenced dreams, visions, and illusions. How many worms were taken from my forearm?"

Tom looked over the notes again. "Three."

"Yes. Next, we have Harold who used the flattery and needy spirit con. Looking over the dialogue of the persona, after what appeared to be a hand was placed on the back of my shoulder, Harold said, *what you felt was my hand on your shoulder. You don't scare easy,* Harold then said, *forgive me, but we always try to frighten human bodies.* The Impostor Father also said *forgive me.*"

"You can see that I asked Harold if that were his picture on the boxes. I did this to give the deceiver a chance to spin a story. As expected, it took the bait and said yes, that it was his picture and I played along."

"Comparing the dialogue of Father Albert Celestine, Harold, and Richard, you see the mentioning of pictures, pay attention also to the word proud. *My friend, what and who I was will be among the pictures as you enter the monastery. Please enter to confirm my validity. I would be proud if you would do that,* by Father Albert Celestine at the monastery. Harold said, *Yes, don't leave my picture face down; I am proud of my picture,* and Richard said *to talk to me, I am here. Come over to my picture.*"

"Recognizing the energy, I can say the malevolent presence at my mother's is exact to the malevolent presence confronted in the monastery restroom. If it's not, it's the same species."

"Donovan said, *I followed someone here.* When I asked who, the answer was *I cannot say.* Well, the tag along has already said who it's following in the form of Quasar saying, *I'm following your soul.* This is the way a tag along works."

"The persona Harold started in a neutral emotional state then turned to anger and hate, the so-called Poltergeist and the persona Donovan went from anger and hate to a neutral emotional state."

"Is there such a thing as a poltergeist?"

"Poltergeist is German for a noisy ghost or spirit. What did the presence do to get both you and my mother's attention?"

"Made noise."

"Yes. In my experience, what is perceived as a poltergeist is an angry hooded shadow or other species of jinn trying to get attention or frighten. Notice before the poltergeist spoke, the influenced vision was Richard being held back by a tall dark shadow figure standing behind him covering his mouth. What type of arm started waving as the vehicle submerged in Donovan's vision?"

"A dark shadow arm."

"Correct. The poltergeist in its angered state used vulgar language which is common when a spiritual being's darker side is dominant. Looking at the similarities in dialogue between Donovan and the poltergeist, we have Donovan saying, *Hate follows hate. I followed someone here.* The poltergeist said, *Hate follows everyone, but feeling hate is what gets you here.* The poltergeist said, *give me hate back* and *give me your evil feelings.* Reviewing the dialogue, you can see the malevolent personas of the parasitic being wants to trigger the lower vibrational frequencies of anger, hate, and fear in which to feed and gain strength. This is the diet of the dark aspect of a hooded shadow's consciousness."

"The poltergeist said, *I have your soul.* Can it take your soul?"

"No," I answered, as I laughed. "This was the message and intent of the worm infestation daydream. To inform me I had been invaded, demonized, or was under the being's influence."

"There are deceivers in the hidden world that will attempt to awaken desires and corrupt your perception during intentional or unintentional spiritual communication, just like the deceivers in the digital world that influence daily with the information and propaganda being electronically fed to you through the screen of your television, laptop, tablet, or cell phone."

"These conscious entities play with human's ignorant beliefs, stories, and fears. What has been labeled your soul is your true nature, pure consciousness, or the source of all creation. It is not an individual energy body that can be taken or swayed. What gives life to the human race, gives life to the hidden race, and they know this. Their goal is to lead you astray from an awakening to your true self."

"Can they protect you?"

"Yes, but this is a trap. The poltergeist said, *give me your evil feelings and I will give you protection from any poltergeist that is attracted to your energy.* Let's back up and read what two benevolent personas of the same being said about being attracted to my energy. The Red Cardinal Angel said, *the goodness of your heart and the light in your eyes as you viewed God's beauty attracted me.* Kim said, *I know your heart; it circulates around your aura. This is the beacon that attracted me.*"

"Many believe it is just lower vibrational or negative energy that attracts hooded shadows. This is false. The poltergeist, Red Cardinal Angel, and Kim are all personas of the hooded shadow. These beings are attracted to both lower and higher vibrational energy."

"Any protection comes with a price. This offer can come in dreams, visions, whispers, and during divination practice. Often, they will call themselves the protector or masquerade as an angel, deity, deceased ancestor, or loved one. You will soon learn that your invisible defender doesn't show up when needed or comes up with an excuse for the lack of assistance. An example of this is the persona Richard saying to my mother, *I wish I could fight back. But things are different now.* When it does appear, they have come to your rescue, are they defending you from another entity or just another one of their personas? This you will never know."

"So much for guardian angels."

"There are guardian angels, Tom. But they are not what you have been led to believe. They are humans with compassion, empathy, and love for others. They are your men and women of the military, first responders, Red Cross, Salvation Army, humanitarian aid organizations and the like, who show up at every tragedy, natural disaster, and emergency to help, care, and risk their life for another. In times of need, a supernatural being or deity may not arrive but the human heart of the compassionate and empathetic has time and time again."

"I can't argue there, Professor."

"The hooded shadow or what is hidden within its cloak is the perceived genie, or jinni, that not only offers wishes and gifts but, as you can see, uses these words frequently in its clever dialogue."

"This is why you told me never to say I wish."

"Yes, Tom. Speak as if many ears are listening. Spiritual beings are like human con artists, and human con artists are like spiritual beings. Just like the offer of protection, spiritual beings that appear benevolent or malevolent will offer gifts, promises, and deals in dreams, visions, whispers, telepathically, and through divination. It is wise to respectfully reject."

"When the presence couldn't trigger lower vibrational energy within my being and I said, 'Hate feels too uncomfortable. How about love?' the presence shifted and influenced a vision of Richard wearing his favorite tan baseball cap and I adjusted my energy to maintain emotional balance."

"Richard said, *don't let these evil clowns trick you.* The presence that is mimicking and masquerading as Richard is the evil clown."

"The clown with a red and black tie."

"Yes, Tom. While remaining calm and not allowing the manipulation of my emotions, I spoke aloud to the presence after the clown vision saying, 'I hope you find love, happiness, and joy.' You can either allow their projected negative energy to change you or you can reject it and return positive energy, changing or repelling them. This applies to human and spiritual beings."

"Unable to get my being to sing its song with its intimidating behavior, fear tactics, and ominous message, it shifted and applied the flattery con, needy spirit con, and an apology of *I am sorry,* like the persona Donovan. Poltergeist said, *I will leave now,* just as Donovan said, *I will go now.* In truth, the presence didn't go anywhere, all it did was change its mask to Richard."

"They have all the bases covered, Professor."

"They have observed humans for many millennia, Tom. Giving it one last try, I asked my mother to get the Josh Groban CD and the silver bracelet that I gave Richard. Let me give you a little history so you understand why."

"Richard had asked on more than one occasion that if something were ever to happen to him and he was about to die to play the song by Josh Groban, *To Where You Are.* When the doctors considered Richard legally brain dead after the major stroke and told us they were going to pull the plug on life support, we asked for permission to play his favorite song. A nurse returned a few minutes later and Richard got his wish."

"The time came, and my mother, family, and friends formed a circle around his bed as the nurses unhooked the life assistance. Peetu was placed on his chest and we all held hands and prayed. The CD play button was pressed and the beautiful song that brought Richard pleasure was played. Tears fell from our eyes, including a couple of nurses in the intensive care unit. It was a magical moment of love and compassion to say the least."

"When my nephew John played the song at my mothers, it triggered intense emotion which altered the presence to what appeared to be an angelic or divine-like state feeling exactly like the Red Cardinal Angel, Counterfeit Jesus and the God presence. My mother was thoroughly convinced, saying, 'I feel a caress of loving energy around me.' As expected, the persona Richard put on its benevolent performance from there, revealing a pattern of sweet talk just like the personas Amy and the Impostor Father."

"Richard said, *Heaven is here with you,* to my mother just as the Golden Cross Monk said, *Either I am eternal or heaven is here,* to me."

"Notice Richard said, *I still have a coffee with you in the morning.* The hooded shadow heard my mother and me discussing the coffee on the phone and wanted to continue the relationship with my mother. Before the conversation on the third floor, I tested the presence with internal dialogue, telling the being if it backs away, I will talk. Instantly it pulled back which told me it hears my thoughts clearly. The presence demonstrated this ability again as the persona Richard, revealing it could hear my mother's thoughts at the end of the conversation. The hooded shadows or jinn are the real psychics, Tom."

"Understanding that these beings, or at least this particular species of jinn, can hear your thoughts and you will know how some mediums and psychics pick up information from the client, other than what is acquired through cold or hot reading techniques. The tag along that the medium or psychic perceives as a guide, angel, ascended master, or deceased human hears the thoughts of the client and shares the results with the medium or psychic in the same manner that I received the information from the tag along playing Richard. What occurs frequently is the client who now believes the medium can interact with the family member continues to go back for another sitting to hear a few more words, or to get advice, ignorant to the fact that the tag along of the medium or psychic that has now connected to their mind to hear their thoughts has become their tag along as well."

"Which could lead to unexplained paranormal activity in their lives."

"Yes, this could begin immediately or years later."

"Besides pulling on your heart strings again, why did the being want you to say, *I love you Pops?*"

"The deceiver will wear a hundred guises just to feed on emotion, feel the energy of a compassionate heart, and hear the words I love you. Never in thirty years did I say I love you or call Richard Pops like my brothers and sisters. We had our differences and Poppy, or Pops, is what I called my late grandfather who passed when I was fourteen. To me there was only one Pops."

"At least one of these beings has been around the family for some time and could be a prior tag along of Richard's seeking a new host. The real Richard came from a deeply religious family and was struggling with what appeared to be personal demons, attempting suicide twice. Richard knew of my exploration of the spirit world before his passing and was a bit of a skeptic until he witnessed a few startling apparitions of his own. I'm not doubting the love Richard had for my mother, but this was not him."

"The hooded shadow masquerading as Richard is giving your mother false comfort and hope."

"Yes, and the deception won't stop there."

"What are you going to do?"

"First, I'm going to sit down with my mother and have her read the dialogue of the Impostor Father and Richard for comparison, before she tries to contact Richard with the Ouija board now that it appears he is speaking."

"Your mother uses a Ouija board?"

"She has in the past."

"I think just about everyone has played with the Ouija at one time or another."

"True, Tom. This is why I choose to educate rather than condemn the curious."
Looking at my watch, I had thirty minutes to get to the mall and pay my phone bill.

"Tom, I have to stop here because I have to make a run to the mall," I said, as I placed the notebook in the backpack and grabbed my keys.

"No problem. I've got to pick up some incense at the gift shop anyway, Professor."

An eavesdropping presence was detected, and I wasn't surprised to see Tom rubbing his solar plexus in a circle with his right hand as we walked out together. Tom has a tag along.

CHAPTER 12

THE STAIRWAY ILLUSION

Opening the rear hatch, I took out the basket of clean clothes and shut the door with my foot. Climbing the stairs to the third floor, I placed the basket down as I sorted through the keys. Entering the apartment, I walked into the bedroom and placed the basket on the bed. Taking the key out of the door, I closed it and placed the keys on the kitchen table.

Walking back into the bedroom, I began to hang up my shirts, pants, and martial art uniforms. While placing my underwear and socks in the bureau drawers, my hair and face began to be touched and caressed. Closing the top drawer, I turned to see an indentation on the opposite side of the bed, like someone or something with weight was lying there.

Leaving the bedroom, a soft female voice said, *don't leave*. Shaking my head, I ignored the request. Standing at the kitchen counter, I opened the cupboard and took out a box of crackers, then opened the fridge and took out the hummus.

Placing the hummus and crackers on the coffee table, I walked back into the bedroom noticing the indentation in the bed was gone. Taking my robe and a blanket out of the closet, I placed them over my left shoulder. Before shutting the door, I grabbed a pillow off the bed and my pajama bottoms off the hamper.

Putting the pillow and blanket on the couch, I changed with a strong feeling of being watched. Lying on the couch, I picked up the remote and turned on the television. Searching the channels for a good flick, I got lucky. One of my favorite comedies, *The Beverly Hills Ninja*, had just started. Opening the container of hummus, I began to dip.

An hour and a half passed. Other than a couple of bangs to the walls in the room, the activity remained minimal throughout the movie. Feeling groggy, I shut off the television, got up from the couch, and put the food away. After prayer I pulled down the covers and got into bed. Touching and caressing began immediately. Closing my eyes, the seductive fairy appeared, naked as usual.

I know you can see me, she said.

"I know you can hear me, and the answer is no," I answered.

Holding out a red heart shaped box, she said, *Try one.* Opening the box, she revealed an assorted box of chocolates while displaying her long, polished fingernails that matched her emerald colored eyes.

"No thanks, I got the point with the pizza. I'm sure they taste real."

The vision changed to a triangle-shaped garden of various purple flowers in the middle of the forest. On a huge bed of purple rose petals in the middle of garden was the seductive fairy. Lying on her side, with one leg drawn up in a seductive pose, she said, *join me and all is yours*, with one hand playing with her hair.

"As I already said, no thank you," I replied.

Angry, she shapeshifted to the white bull mastiff and the dreamscape vanished into the void.

Drifting off to sleep, I appeared in a nightclub standing at the bar. Walking up to me was the seductive fairy dressed in modern clothing. Staring into my eyes she pulled me close without warning and gave me a passionate kiss on the lips. An intense feeling of euphoria traveled through my body like electricity. Turning away from her she said, *don't leave, I love you.*

Waking from the dream, the nerve endings of my lips was still stimulated and the euphoric feeling remained. Tossing and turning, I couldn't shake the stimulating feeling. Sitting up, I rubbed my face and body with my hands, thinking how easy it would be to fall for the seduction process of these perceived invisible lovers, if you were naive to the consequences.

Looking over at the clock, thirty minutes had passed before the sensation began to fade. Closing my eyes, an intense light appeared as a calming peaceful energy embraced me in the same manner as what occurred with the Counterfeit Jesus and God experience at the monastery. In a state of pure joy and bliss, I comfortably fell back to sleep.

Waking to the peaceful, cooing sound of mourning doves was a welcomed treat. Sitting up, I prayed and spoke outwardly from the heart. Getting out of bed I walked into the kitchen, picked up the kettle, and placed it under the faucet. Placing it back on the stove, I turned on the burner. As the water was heating up, I put up all the shades, then washed my face and brushed my teeth.

When the kettle whistled, I opened the cupboard and took out a mug and a tea bag. While pouring the water into the mug, the peaceful calming energy presence returned. Knowing the presence wanted to talk, I walked into the living room and placed the mug on the coffee table. Grabbing the backpack, I sat on the couch, removed my necklace and arranged the tools.

Taking a deep breath, I let it out and relaxed into receptive oneness. Holding the silver chain over the chart, I said, "For the goodness of all, if you please." The conversation began telepathically, with a light as bright as the sun shining in the mind's eye.

Light of heart, was heard from a soft male voice.

"How do I address you properly, Light of Heart?"

That, in itself, is my name.

"How, may I ask, do you protect yourself from mind creatures?"

By becoming me, my son. I covered you last night in my love. No mind creature can enter my world. You are my son, believe in this.

"If you are love, compassion, and the essence of all life, why these tormenting beings?"

Good question, my son. Come into my light, illumination is what you are. Placing my illumined heart in you, makes you me. I am only light; I am you, because you are goodness, despite your occasional impure visions. You know what goodness is. Don't change your face for a hiding spot. Step forward out of your cave, my son.

"Is it wrong to say you are within all?"

If I were within all, could you harm one another?

"No, Light of Heart."

I am a choice; Heaven is a choice. I am light. Placing my heart in you makes you internally me and externally Earth. When your experience is complete, you will remain as me and your body returns to Earth. A simple process made confusing. I could not create disease; you create the external world. I am love; I don't know other feelings, so I only answer to one.

"The confusion may lie in most feeling they are not capable of enlightenment."

I know. To be me, is to be love. Not the word, but the pureness of heart. Goodness seen in every vision. Enlightenment does not give you a name, it gives you a home. Names for the enlightened, are human created. I call them all my children.

All loved, All equal, All goodness.

Hierarchy does not exist. Goodness is the highest vibration of being.

"Is conversing through divination against your rules?"

I am your heart; you are not against me. Heaven is all around you, waiting to speak. Keep your mind pure. Darkness of thought can't exist in the light of my heart.

"When I am asked how this communication takes place, what should I say?"

Say I think purely, I feel purely, I am Heaven in this moment. Be careful, my son. Goodness is your intention, but not some others. I am light, be me always.

"Do angels have names, Light of Heart?"

Angels are light, I am light, and they speak as me. If Heaven has no name I have no name, why would angels have names? Names must stop, it is poison. Flowers grew bright long before names were given.

The conversation ended. Placing the chain on the notebook, I pondered the experience for a few minutes. Focusing on the breath, I centered myself and prayed, before getting up and walking into the kitchen.

Opening the cupboard, I took out the protein powder and peanut butter to make a shake. Taking the milk out of the fridge I poured it into the blender. Adding the powder and a large tablespoon of peanut butter, I turned the blender on.

Taking two bags of unsalted peanuts out of the cupboard, I placed them in the backpack, then filled the water bottle. Shutting off the blender, I poured the contents into a tall glass. Sitting on the couch, I put my feet up on the coffee table and enjoyed the shake, while thinking about the monastery plan for the day. Monk's Quarry came to mind.

Finishing the shake, I rinsed out the container and placed it in the strainer. Taking a couple of training knives out of the martial arts bag, I placed them in the backpack. Today was a cold, windy day so I added a hooded sweatshirt for another layer of warmth.

At the Monk's Quarry, crows were cawing in the distance as I climbed the hill where the Fairy of the Forest conversation took place. It was cloudy and windy, and the environment was dark.

Eyes were upon me, as I placed the backpack on the rock. Beginning with some breathing exercises, I moved on to footwork drills. Pulling out two training knives, I placed them in my belt. Before I began the next drill, I respectfully announced to the unseen my intention. Empty hand shadow boxing was followed with single and double blade shadow boxing.

When I was through with the physical training, I placed the knives back in the backpack and took a seat on the rocky edge overlooking the quarry. Taking a deep breath, I exhaled and merged with the soothing vibration of nature. As I spoke outwardly to God, my vibration rose, and I prepared the tools for interaction. Heavy gusts of an ice-cold wind blew through the forest, bending the treetops.

Putting on my hood, I held the silver chain over the chart. A tall, translucent, hooded monk manifested in white, like Quasar, standing at the top of stairs. Slowly the monk descended. When he reached the last stair, two shorter monks in brown cloth manifested to its right and left. Face, hands, and feet were hidden.

The golden-white glow of the center monk was substantially brighter than the shorter two. The conversation began telepathically with the monk in white, as the other two vanished.

Illumination places love everywhere. I am everywhere. Illumination spreads its wings in the temple of the forest. Hello, my brother. Masters are teachers of illumination.

"Thank you and good morning. I welcome your visit."

And I yours.

"I am sitting and extending beyond skin."

Believing in more than self is believing in all as self.

"Yes, I embrace the interconnection."

You speak as you.

"I have my days."

Early light gives night vitality.

"It definitely empowers the mood for the day."

Humans will learn that illumination brightens your soul and energizes your life. The ripened fruit of humanity will now evolve and fertilize a new cycle of being grown from the seeds of love.

"Yes, the unification of human and loving God. As your awareness grows, your self-defeating patterns will flake off your aura like dried mud, exposing the complete fulfillment of the illuminated self, the true birthright of every soul."

Only oneness can call forth the Master. The forest is beautiful in your eyes. I give you this. God lives in you. Hide no longer, my brother. Remove the hood and express who you are before you settle back into who you are not. A Master knows when to enter the grand scheme of human consciousness. I am a Master and so are you. We are unique but we are one and the same.

"With respect, you know I don't believe in titles, just feeling and the value of the message."

I know, but the reason you resist who you are, is the reason you are who you are. I speak truth you may not consciously think you're ready to hear, but it would not be spoken if you as a being were not ready. I am not a playful spirit; I am a Master and we are brothers. *Masters, at times, have difficulty with human experience. I understand your quest for truth to educate all, it has been your purpose all this life. But this is truth uncomfortable to part of your consciousness. I speak to you as a brother first, before I speak as a Master. Masters are spirit and universal energy combined. You wonder why we are universal energy. Humans don't understand Masters. Humans don't understand spirit. But think of this, humans have always been spirit or electromagnetic energy - but why such technological advancement the past few hundred years? Quite simple, universal wisdom filtered into the human mind from universal Masters.*

"My school grades were not the greatest. I mean no disrespect, but I am no universal Master."

My brother, you joke with others and you joke with your true self, because you refuse to believe what you know. I will ask you this, the loving wisdom you have been speaking and writing down for years, is it you? Is it God? Is it God in you?

"Physical life is precious. I just want to experience the beauty of Earth and share the knowledge I have acquired openly and honestly."

You are part of the beauty of Earth. See through the costume you wear, my brother. Your human age means nothing. You must understand this, before you understand you.

"What do you suggest?"

I cannot tell you; you must learn from you. Feel your truth, feel you educating you.

"It is believed every human can grow from going within."

Not quite, my brother. There are human beings and there are human beasts. They both possess electromagnetic energy, but their internal contents are not the same. Spend time with you, adjust to oneness, there you will find you.

"For humanity I ask, are there many Masters?"

My brother, we are not counted individually, we are one being. You choose the costume you wear to be better accepted by your students. Sometimes the teacher gets lost in the role they play and become their own worst enemy.

"Well, if anything, this conversation makes a great story."

But, is it a story, my brother? Be you, and all will unfold.

A shift in energy occurred. The center monk in white faded and vanished, as a monk in brown cloth manifested to the right.

I am good in being and true to heart.

"Hello and thank you."

I would love to answer your questions.

"Thank you again, have we talked before?"

No, I have only heard your God tongue and enjoyed the message.

"Thank you. May I ask, have you ever occupied human form?"

No, I am pure essence and all love.

"For all I ask, are you an angel?"

I am what I am, call me what you feel.

"Then, a Voice of Love is what I will call you."

There is no better explanation.

"I hear people coming. Will we be able to maintain our connection?"

Keep love in your thoughts and I will answer you. I will say the pleasure of goodness is more than good nervous feelings. I am more than a voice, but less than the all of God.

"Could you explain that to humanity?"

I will explain. Human is a creation of God's planet Earth. I am a creation of God not filtered through Earth. I am in the All that the human eye can't see. Jesus was a child filtered through Earth like all of you. Jesus expressed God tongue; some enjoyed and became God self. I don't need to speak of those that didn't listen. I will tell the listeners, Jesus still speaks. I will tell the others; you will never hold the tongue of God. God speaks through the pure loving hearts and pure loving minds.

Jesus spoke as God, you speak as God, all loving humans can speak as God.

The filtering process of Earth is not the filtering process of love. It is infinite in your created words and all God in mine. God is everywhere human eyes and instruments can see and everywhere human eyes and instruments will never see. The picture is bigger than given words can express. Don't try to figure out what your human mind may question. Start with seeing all as God and enjoy your experience.

"Thank you. Is there anything else you would like to say to humanity?"

I am a voice and you are a Human God expression. All of you are One Essence, One World, One God.

Give poison another home, let love conquer your fears. Let hate get caught in the filtering process. Yes, my open-minded inquirers, there is a place that holds hate. Call it what you may, it is simply the reversal of your entrance. When you see clearly, you will see this truth.

Again, I am a voice, and these words are from my speaker's tongue. He loves all enough to make this conversation possible.

"Thank you."

I thank you.

A shift in energy occurred, and the ghost monk to the right faded then vanished as a monk in brown cloth manifested to the left.

Hi, being spirit has its advantages. I see clearly now without flesh. I remember judging people by their skin color.

"A substance called melanin in the skin gives it color. If I remember correctly."

I didn't know that. I was just following the rest. I didn't understand love. I didn't understand what love really is. Religion confused me as it did many. Jesus was my savior, but I wasn't being saved. I didn't follow religion anymore. Instead, I judged, I lied, I stole.

I quickly became my own worst enemy. Keeping love alive became like pulling teeth, and I was running out of teeth. God became the negative, instead of the positive in my life. For my ignorance, I condemned life, the one thing that was free. Realizing my life lacked meaning I put poison in my body. That poison was hate and jealousy.

I became sick, I became weak, I became foolish.

Love was far away from my temple, or I should say I was far away from my temple. My life quickly was ending. I lost hope in the God I once loved freely. I leaned toward hate because Jesus didn't answer my prayers. I was praying, but I wasn't loving. Love is God. This was left out of my religious education. Love was replaced with comments like you're all sinners. Like only Jesus was loved by God. The rest of us were just humans. I thought at the time what good is God if he selects only one apple to feed one mouth. This is how I lost faith.

I speak as spirit now. I speak with no fear of death, because I am not alive. I speak as a loving spirit.

I ask for no money for I have nowhere to spend it. My heart is my treasure and God is the bank I keep it in. Keep love, my brothers and sisters, in your heart and richness of soul is yours forever.

Live as God. Love as God. Be as God. Love never causes you pain. God will open to all when ready.

"May we know your name?"

If love was a name, then God is it.

"How are we connecting telepathically?"

We connect by electrical impulse opening the door of love. I am just a speaker of love. You are a messenger of love, if felt with the heart.

"Can you tell us about dreams?"

Dreams are a world in itself. Bring only love forward and dreams will be bright. I inhabit mind in motion.

"Could you tell us more about Jesus?"

Jesus was a messenger of the illuminated heart. Please understand, Jesus is your brother in God's family. All are loved here. Jesus loves you here, I love you here.

"How would you describe angels?"

Angels are illuminated love messengers.

"Can you give a deeper explanation of the illuminated heart?"

Jesus was a lot like you. Jesus gave love a voice, Illumination of heart became illumination of soul. He was named Jesus. You were named Lorne. Both are God's children. Both made the choice of illumination of heart. Able to be human. Able to be God. Able to be human God.

The same choice all God's children can make. Being human is sometimes difficult for human God. Being human God does not bring richness of material wealth but brings richness of soul. Material wealth stays here where it is seen as a great treasure. Love follows you for eternity. Love is God's greatest treasure.

Jesus' Earth experience was interrupted by human jealousy and misunderstanding of Jesus' words from the illuminated heart. Jesus was born human and chose God. Not born God and chose human.

Jesus is your human brother. Jesus is God's son. Jesus is human God.

This is illuminated heart speaking. Illuminated heart knows the human heart. Illuminated heart knows the human mind. The love you have within can radiate throughout your world opening the door to heaven on Earth and altering your being to human God.

"What other words of wisdom would you share with humanity about the illumined heart?"

Welcome love into your existence and you shall welcome illumination into your life. Illuminated hearts do not judge what human hearts do, simply because what is not illuminated will become illuminated given enough time. The learning process does not end here but continues well beyond. Make illumination your world. Remember this, I am your heart, I am your soul.

"On my journey, I have come across angry spirits and through conversation and maintaining a feeling of oneness their emotional state of being appeared to change. Is this possible or were they mischievous spirits entertaining themselves?"

When love is felt, it is much more easily understood, breaking through all language barriers. Your love radiates as illumination, it was felt and altered what words alone could never have done. Your love became their love. Their love became God's love. Love is now their home. What do you ask for in return?

"Nothing. All I did was view all as one while maintaining compassion and internal peace. At times of spiritual conflict, I have found this approach to be an effective shield and sword. Not to harm, but to protect. It is a wiser choice than going toe to toe with what I can't see."

Instantly a powerful energy shift took place, and an intense bright light projecting the emotion of love triggered a euphoric sensation and tears began to fall.

I am proud to hear those words. Your love has come full circle. Live by these words and all is yours. Never feel alone for I am here. Never feel punished for I am here. Never feel ashamed for I am here. Never feel I love only one, for I am only one.

Hello my child. I love you with my entire being. Jesus loves you with his entire being. I help those who help others. Forget all who emphasize name over emphasizing love. There exist no names in my kingdom. Heaven is my kingdom. Love is my heart; goodness is my soul. Illumination is my heart in you, calling me. Heaven is all my hearts holding each other's hand. The unity of love. Heaven exists all around my playground. I see all my children interacting through my heart in each vine grown from Earth. This is my garden. Earth is my planet that nourishes my plants.

Internally I said, God, cleanse me of any impostors if you please. Be it my mind or any others.

You are careful, this is good. I surround you my child, no emotion will distract my speech. I am without form. This is my world of form. Freedom to be any thought put into action creating desired result.

"God, I have heard others speak in that way."

I speak through all my children, know this. Goodness is freedom for your thoughts to germinate into reality of form. Angels are love as I am all emotions your nervous system experiences.

Yes, I am anger, I am hate, I am fear, I am ugly visions. I am jealousy. I am drought, I am war, I am love, I am joy, I am peace, I am pleasure, I am beautiful vision, I am goodness. I am all your feelings, I am all your being. I am within, so please pray as if you know this. I am all you experience, so please live as if you know this. I am within all you choose to harm, so please give thought before you choose to strike. I am within the most evil of form, so please just have good thoughts, I will do the rest.

The energy was strong.

Evil is not a fallen angel of my kingdom. I am goodness. I follow my children, they give me their ailments, I give them love. I leave only those that harm here on Earth. Here is your vision of ugliness. Here is where you will stay until you see as me. It's that simple, your energy pulls you one way or the other. I speak but few listen. Heaven is only a home for my heart. Understand heaven, now understand Earth. Earth is letting you destroy her because she knows my heart. I don't harm my children, Earth doesn't harm her plants.

Earth beats a rhythm of life, while my children beat a rhythm of destruction. I give Earth all my love, she asks for nothing in return, just existence. Learn from her. Compassion will save Earth. Take control of those that lack compassion because greed is all they feel.

You have my strength, you have my heart, you have my mind. Use it now.

There is no hierarchy in my kingdom for all is one royal family. You are all me. Those who give names and titles are just my children masquerading for jest. I ask for only love, what do they ask for? Many will give their last treasure for their words of ignorance. Ignorance because they ignore my existence but speak in my name. I will speak through you, as I spoke through Jesus. I am love, give me only what I have given you, and I am yours forever.

I expect you to question these words. I expect you to ignore these words. But I am these words.

The dialogue ceased, as a woman approached walking her dog. Placing the chain down in the notebook, I closed it and placed it to the side. When the woman passed, I closed my eyes and entered their influenced world.

Sitting behind the wheel of a vehicle, I was driving down a long dirt driveway in the forest. At the end of the windy road was an old cabin. A variety of cars, jeeps, and pickup trucks were parked on the property. Getting out of the vehicle, I could hear the talk of others.

To the left of the cabin was a pile of cut granite rectangular stones. Just like the pile at the monk's quarry. A small crowd of men and women were circled around a hooded monk in white. With only a long gray beard showing, the monk floated over to a large rectangular stone standing vertically in the dirt. Hugging the stone, the monk lifted it with ease then placed it down gently. The group of people clapped. Next the monk floated over to another rectangular stone, of the same size, lying on the ground. In the middle, about a foot apart, were two thick gold rings. Squatting down the monk grabbed hold of both rings, never exposing its hands, and lifted the stone with equal ease. Holding it for a few seconds, the monk set it back down gently. Floating to the side of the stones, the monk made a motion with its hand, as if to say, please try.

Two large men from the group walked over to the stones and attempted to lift them with no success, unable to even budge the large cut granite.

Bowing its head, the monk turned and floated into the cabin. One after the other, they all followed, and I joined them. Filing into a large room, we each took a seat on the bench with individual cushions. The first thing that caught my attention was shelves of hundreds of idols from around the world, on all four walls. Idols made of gold, silver, jade, wood, crystal, and various other types of material, with and without precious and semi-precious stones, stood on three level wood shelves that wrapped around the room. As some of the guests were focusing on the idols, others were anxiously waiting to hear the wisdom of the monk.

Floating in from the back room, the monk took a seat at the desk. Attention now was on the monk, as the room silenced. The monk kept his head tilted forward, never acknowledging the group. He just started writing in what appeared to be an old leather journal.

Sitting to my left was a young girl. "Hello," she whispered, "which of the Gods and Goddesses do you worship?"

Looking up at the idols, I answered, "None of the above." She turned away from me as if angered, and I placed my right fist in my left palm and sat quietly. The guests were growing impatient waiting for the monk to speak as he continued to write, never exposing his face. When he suddenly stood up and floated out of the room, the guests were disappointed. As the time passed, the guests placed their attention solely on the idols. Two guests started discussing how much the gold statues must be worth. Another person said, "I want to talk to the deities on the top shelf, I bet you they're more powerful." At that point they all started arguing over whose deity was stronger.

A woman across the room began staring at me, playing with her hair, trying to get my attention. While I ignored her attempts to distract, some of the guests started leaving. When the monk floated back into the room the remaining guests stopped talking and turned toward him. Sitting down, the monk again didn't speak or even acknowledge our presence. He just tilted his head forward and continued to write.

This angered the guests and the last of them stormed out. The guests were obviously not familiar with a vow of silence or its benefits. With all the guests now gone, I continued to sit peacefully, free of thought and silent. The monk raised its head and looked toward me, exposing his bright blue eyes, and nodded.

Disconnecting, I opened my eyes. To my right were three deer which froze as I turned in their direction. Two does and one fawn stared, ready to flee with any sudden movement. Turning away, I stood up slowly as not to spook them. Shaking out my legs and brushing off my pants, I opened the backpack and put the notebook away.

Trekking back to the vehicle I heard what sounded like a young girl crying to my left. Stopping, I waited to hear it again. The sound of someone, or something, striking a stick against a tree in threes was heard from behind. When I turned to look, a small rock or acorn hit me in the upper back. It wasn't thrown hard, but with enough force to get my attention. Blended into the tree ahead was the face of a puck. A large nose and oversized ears is the norm for these creatures.

One more time the crying was heard from another angle. Having enough of being toyed with, I ignored the distractions and moved on.

CHAPTER 13

ANALYZING THE GOD PRESENCE

At the studio, class began with falling skills and proceeded to Judo throws. The last throw we worked was the Ogoshi or Major Hip Throw. With the class seated around the mat, I called up one of the students to demonstrate. "Come on up, Travis."

Travis smiled as he stood up and bowed, then walked onto the mat.

"Let's break this throw down from the beginning. First with your left hand grab your partner's right wrist and pull your partner off balance as you step in with your right foot, shooting your right arm around your partners back. Pivot stepping back with your left foot getting your hips, which should be below their belt line, into your partner and lift with your legs while pulling down with your left hand. As you partner goes over, release your right arm but maintain hold of your partner's right wrist with your left hand to help break your partners fall."

Travis got back up and I threw him again slowly.

"Alright, one more time real speed," I told the class and threw Travis for the last time.

"Pair off with a partner and remember safety first. Make sure your area is clear before you throw so no one gets hurt," I announced to the class from the center of the mat.

Ten minutes passed, and we ended class with a cooldown and bodyweight exercises then wiped down the mats. After rolling up the mats and placing them to the back of the dojo, the class lined up, bowed, and removed their belts for meditation.

When the class was dismissed, Ron asked me if I would watch him perform Solo Baston Anyo Lima, which means Single Stick Form Five.

With a handful of students watching, Ron bowed and announced the name of the form. As he performed the movements of the form there was a much better flow and I could tell he was using his imagination, visualizing opponents and living the form. When he was finished the students clapped.

"That was much better, Ron. The variations in speed and the slight pause between each series of movements made a big difference. Now perform the form a few more times, slowly with this." I handed Ron a kamagong stick, which is also known as ironwood.

"Wow, this is heavy. I wouldn't want to get hit by this," Ron said.

"Grandmaster said in the old days these sticks were used in death matches."

"The fighters must have had strong forearms."

"I'm sure they did. I would like you to perform your anyo and shadow spar slowly with the kamagong to build up your wrist and forearm muscles, working both hands equally."

"Okay," Ron answered.

Bowing at the dojo entrance, I walked into the office. Tom came out of the locker room. "Professor, could you order me another pair of pants?"

"Sure. A size 5?"

"Yes."

"You look tired, Tom." I started writing Tom's pants on the order list.

"More disturbing dreams, Professor, and this morning I got three distinct loud knocks on my bedroom wall. After that I couldn't get back to sleep."

"What time?"

"3 a.m., the witching hour."

"In truth Tom, it is not the witching hour or demon hour, but the signature of a hooded shadow. We know my mother experienced three knocks, so the being is repeating the activity at your place to continue to let me know it's there."

"Can you come to my apartment and talk to this thing?"

"Talking is exactly what it wants. Interacting at your place is not going to help cleanse the presence from your apartment or your life. It can only make matters worse."

"I'll pick up some sage tomorrow."

"It's not that easy my friend. You don't remove with smoke that which can appear as smoke. Do you remember any of the dreams?"

"Yes, the most disturbing one. I was in my apartment and it was pitch dark because the lights wouldn't work. Suddenly I felt the evil presence and I was grabbed by both wrists. The presence was too strong and I couldn't break free. Once the presence pulled me to the door it released the grip and the door opened slowly. Standing in my underwear, I watched numerous men and women walking various breeds of dogs around the house in a circle. The dogs took turns urinating all over the trees and shrubs. Feeling something crawling on my legs, I looked down to see black bugs caught in the hairs of my legs. Frantically I started wiping them off, but they just kept coming until I woke up. Reaching over to turn on the light, it blew. Even while awake, I still felt the creepy feeling of bugs crawling all over me. I've really had it with this thing. I'm getting where I don't want to go to bed. How do you kill this pest?" Tom asked in anger.

"That is not a wise thing to ask, Tom. I told you, speak as if many ears are listening."

"If it's listening, tell it to take a hike." Instantly, an emotional shift occurred in the air. The eavesdropping presence was angered.

"Do not allow the presence to awaken anger in you. Focus on the inhalation and exhalation of your breath."

Tom closed his eyes and started to focus on his breathing and relaxed. "I'm sorry, Professor. I have been feeling on edge lately."

"In order to cleanse the pests, you need to avoid that which attracts the pests, which means it's time to wrap up this investigation."

"You're done?" Tom asked.

"Yes, my friend. To continue would just be more of the same. The goal of this investigation was to collect the evidence to educate you, and those curious like you, in the deceptive ways of messengers, jinn, or gods."

"Well, you have certainly done that."

"Would you like to review the last of the evidence?"

"Yes, of course."

Unzipping the backpack, I took out the notebook and placed it on the desk, opening to the seductive fairy visit last night and the three monk's conversation at Monk's Quarry. "While you're reading I'm going to vacuum."

Walking over to the closet, I took out the vacuum, then bowed at the dojo entrance and entered. Twenty minutes later, Tom called out, "Professor, I'm all set."

"I'll be right there," I answered, as I reeled in the vacuum cord. Walking over to the dojo entrance, I turned and bowed toward the training space.

"Boy, the seductive fairy is persistent."

"It's the nature of the being. Temptation in this case is not limited to just visions of beautiful naked women as Gautama Buddha received from the demon Mara. What the spiritual being really wants is the love of my heart and a relationship, for reasons we have already discussed. The seductive fairy in a forest setting said, *join me and all is yours*. This is a common temptation phrase of the deceivers."

"Mountains are a common image and symbol of spiritual beings used in dreams and visions. The seductive fairy appeared in a night dream at the top of the mountain. The daydream of the octopus attack took place while crossing the ocean to a mountain. Before the Counterfeit Jesus conversation in the garden, I experienced a vision of a beautiful mountain of divine light."

"Do you think Jesus and Buddha were tempted by the same beings?"

"Three is their signature. Both were tested and tempted three times, in a manner that is consistent with the evidence in the investigation. But all I know for sure is what I am experiencing first hand. Let's move on, we have a lot to cover, beginning with the seductive fairy progression."

"To demonstrate how realistic a sexual encounter would feel, she influenced the three slices of pizza and a box of chocolates. When I refused to give her a try, she grew angry and the bed began to shake, followed by a show of manipulating electricity by making the light bulb increase in brightness. Looking through the King James Bible, I found a passage which is Peter's vision that I would compare to the seductress vision of offering food, like the pizza and a box of chocolates."

"Acts 10:9-16; *On the morrow, as they went on their journey, and drew nigh unto the city, Peter went up upon the housetop to pray about the sixth hour. And he became very hungry, and would have eaten: but while they made ready, he fell into a trance, And saw heaven opened, and a certain vessel descending upon him, as it had been a great sheet knit at the four corners, and let down to the earth: Wherein were all manner of fourfooted beasts of the earth, and wild beasts, and creepy things, and fowls of the air. And there came a voice to him, Rise, Peter; kill, and eat. But Peter said, Not so, Lord; for I have never eaten any thing that is common or unclean. And the voice spake unto him again the second time, What God hath cleansed, that call not thou common. This was done thrice: and the vessel was received up again into heaven.*"

"Deceptive god's offer food in visions and dreams. Whenever you see a passage saying the heavens opened, this is a vision coming to the mind's eye. This passage has all the makings of a virtual reality simulation created by a deceptive god. How many times did it happen in the biblical passage, Tom?"

"Thrice."

"Yes, which means three. After I denied the offering the vision changed to a triangle shaped garden of various purple flowers in the middle of the forest. On a huge bed of purple rose petals in the middle of garden was the seductive fairy. Lying on her side, she said, *join me and all is yours.* When I answered no thank you, the seductive fairy shapeshifted to a white wolf and vanished. White is believed to be a sacred color in most spiritual and religious belief systems and the deceptive god caters to that belief in many forms."

"Entering the dream state, the seductive fairy appeared dressed in clothing and aggressively gave me a kiss to demonstrate her ability to produce intense euphoria, and yes it felt real. When I turned away, she said, *don't leave, I love you.*"

"In the dream, I felt the sensation of the kiss and what appeared to be the heat and feeling of a real body pressed to mine. When we look over the progression of the seductive fairy's advances, we see it can physically touch, caress, and lay upon you, or a bed, with weight. What this tells me is there is the possibility that the sensation of the kiss lasted outside of the dream because the presence physically kissed me while I was vulnerable in the dream state."

Tom had a big smile on his face.

"Keep in mind Tom, they are not a human male or female, but shapeshifters."

"I didn't say anything," Tom said, as he laughed.

"You didn't have to. Moving on to the presence Light of Heart or the second god presence, the words Light of Heart first came up when I asked Kim if there were a gate to heaven. Kim answered, *Light of heart illuminates your entrance.* Light of Heart said, *Darkness of thought can't exist in the light of my heart,* which we can compare to the Impostor Father saying, *I only see light, there is never darkness here.* What patterns did you notice, Tom?"

"Besides speaking in threes, Light of Heart called you son."

"Yes, it did. Light of Heart speaks in the first person as God and called me son, just like the first god presence and the Impostor Father. The third god presence didn't call me son but said, *Hello my child.* The compassionate embrace of Light of Heart was exact to the God presence that took control of my writing hand for the automatic writing experience and its appearance was a flash of brilliant white light, as bright as the sun in the mind's eye."

"In Scripture there is confusion over why the Angel of the Lord in the Old Testament speaks in the first person as God. The true identity is never given which leads to a whole lot of guesswork. It is the Angel of the Lord that appears to Moses in a flame of fire in the burning bush. Here is the passage."

Turning the pages of the notebook I pointed to Exodus 3:2-6. "Could you please read the passage?"

Tom nodded yes. *"And the angel of the Lord appeared unto him in a flame of fire out of the midst of a bush: and he looked, and behold, the bush burned with fire, and the bush was not consumed. And Moses said, I will now turn aside, and see this great sight, why the bush is not burnt. And the Lord saw that he turned aside to see, God called unto him out of the midst of the bush, and said, Moses, Moses. And he said, Here am I. And he said, Draw not nigh hither: put off thy shoes from off thy feet, for the place whereon thou standest is holy ground. Moreover he said, I am the God of thy father, the God of Abraham, the God of Isaac, and the God of Jacob. And Moses hid his face, for he was afraid to look upon God."*

"Thank you, Tom. What appeared to my mother in the backyard?"

"A flame of fire."

"Yes. And what did I tell you this is a sign of?"

"Jinn."

"Correct. In Exodus 3:2 the Angel of the Lord appears. In Exodus 3:4, God called on Moses from the same burning bush, and in Exodus 3:6 the God presence said, *I am the God of thy father, the God of Abraham, the God of Isaac, and the God of Jacob,* which, by the way, could be taken as speaking in threes."

"Why would God, which gives life to all seen and unseen, say it is the God of just these men? We will never know what truly took place at this time in history other than what is written in this confusing passage. But based on the evidence of this investigation we do know that what appeared to be a divine presence played the role of the God presence, Light of Heart, Red Cardinal Angel, and the Counterfeit Jesus. One presence wearing the guise of God, angel, and deity."

"When I asked Light of Heart, or the second god presence, if angels have names, Light of Heart answered, *Angels are light, I am light, and they speak as me. If Heaven has no name, and I have no name, why would angels have names? Names must stop, it is poison. Flowers grew bright long before names were given.* The third god presence said, *forget all who emphasize name over emphasizing love. There exist no names in my kingdom,* and the personality Helen said, *I now see a different world. One with no names, but pure divine heart.*"

"Angels or messengers speak as Light of Heart because they are Light of Heart or the god presence. Light of Heart said, *I am light.* Red Cardinal Angel said, *I am light.* Light of Heart said, *Angels are light, I am light, and they speak as me,* and *I am light, be me always.* Red Cardinal Angel said, *I am light; I am not separate from light, so I require no individual name,* and *I am light, you are capable of light."*

"If names are poison, why does the spiritual being with multiple personalities and faces, keep appearing as light and giving names. Whether a spiritual being gives a name or not is not an indicator of a benevolent or malevolent messenger, angel, or god. Sometimes they give names, and sometimes they don't. It all depends on their intention, goal, or agenda. If they know you believe that benevolent beings don't give names, they will certainly cater to that belief."

"The ghost monk that we called My Life Is God also said, *Heaven is all around you.* This is just more evidence telling me that the ghost monks are a projection or an influenced illusion from the same presence that speaks as God and calls me son. Backing up to the first interaction in the garden you will see I wrote, 'standing still in total reverence with uplifted hands, I said, "God is my heart," with passion and power, piercing the bubble that separates God within from God all around.'"

"It's mimicking you, that's why it said, *Heaven is all around you.*"

"Yes, Tom. You will find much of what I have said is being mimicked."

"When I asked how to protect myself from the mind creatures Light of Heart replied, *by becoming me, my son. I covered you last night in my love. No mind creature can enter my world. You are my son, believe in this.* Well, this so-called son was tormented and invaded by the seductive fairy. Light of Heart doesn't discuss this seductress form or reveal who or what is playing the personality. But Light of Heart does go on to say, *I am you, because you are goodness, despite your occasional impure visions.* We can compare this to the personality Amy saying *I see why you choose these crazy women. It has all been a test. Evil wins every time you accept their distraction. You became weak only a few times. Which is more than I can say for most men."*

"Another pattern, Professor. One personality is trying to get you horny and the other personality is trying to make you feel guilty if you do."

"Well put, Tom. It is playing both sides of the coin, with different personalities and genders. If you feel sexually aroused, it benefits. If you feel guilt, it benefits. The presence playing Light of Heart isn't going to admit it's influencing the impure visions for sustenance and/or pleasure."

"When Light of Heart said, *don't change your face for a hiding spot, step forward out of your cave, my son,* what did it mean?"

"It's not I that keeps changing its face for a hiding spot. Light of Heart wants me to preach their word. The Master said, *Hide no longer my brother. Remove the hood and express who you are before you settle back into who you are not.* What being, or beings, do we know like to hide?"

"The jinn."

"Correct. The one God, or source of existence, does not hide because it cannot hide. The face of the source is all you see and all you don't see. When I asked Light of Heart if conversing through divination were against its rules, Light of Heart answered, *I am your heart, you are not against me.*"

"Did you ask Light of Heart if divination were against its rules because talking to the dead and raising the dead is taboo in the Bible?"

"Yes. As I mentioned, I don't believe you can communicate or consult deceased humans or raise the dead. We have experienced these spiritual beings, messengers, or gods that play or mimic the dead, who we know also play the role of a divine presence or god perfectly. As far as divination, depending on your goal, you can cherry-pick passages from the Bible where the God of the Old Testament was for or against divination. In one passage a diviner was a respected position, in another it was an act punishable by stoning. Here is a passage about the biblical God being for divination, including the diviner and the prophet together as respected positions. Isaiah 3:2-3; *The mighty man and the man of war, the judge and the prophet, And the diviner and the elder; The captain of fifty and the honorable man, The counselor and the skillful artisan, And the expert enchanter.*"

"It is because of their competitive nature and the use of reverse psychology that the biblical God made the next statement which became the most popular passage in the Bible against divination, contradicting itself. Keep in mind, divination may be how the true nature of the biblical God will finally be discovered. Here is the passage from the Book of Deuteronomy. Deuteronomy 18:10-12; *There shall not be found among you any one that maketh his son or his daughter to pass through fire, or that useth divination, or an observer of times, or an enchanter, or a witch. Or a charmer, or a consulter with familiar spirits, or a wizard, or a necromancer. For all that do these things are an abomination unto the Lord: and because of these abominations the Lord thy God doth drive them out from before thee.*"

"Deceptive gods know the human mind. Tell people not to do something or label it taboo and you create interest, spark curiosity, and make some people think their freedom is being threatened so they do the exact opposite. Tell them not to think of something that is perceived as evil or dirty, and they will have that thought twice as much. This is how the subconscious works."

"That is so true, Professor. That's why you are teaching me about the dangers of spiritual communication and allowing me to make the choice rather than telling me not to do it because it's dangerous. What is a familiar spirit?"

"It is believed to be a malevolent spiritual being or demon, summoned by a medium who may or may not believe it is a deceased human. But we have learned that the demon or malevolent spiritual being is the malevolent component of the deceptive god who is also benevolent. Here is a passage with the punishment for interacting with a familiar spirit or demon. Leviticus 20:27; *A man also or woman that hath a familiar spirit, or that is a wizard, shall surely be put to death: they shall stone them with stones: their blood shall be upon them.*"

"Words such as these are born from the dark aspect of human and spiritual beings or jinn. Ask yourself, would the one God, or source of existence, tell you to stone a unique expression of itself?"

"That wouldn't make any sense."

"No, it wouldn't. The question remains, is the same being that is masquerading as God in Scripture and suggesting stoning or death to diviners, mediums, and necromancers, the same deceptive being that is playing the dead?"

"After what you have taught me, Professor, I wouldn't be surprised. Were there any divination tools mentioned in the Bible?"

"Yes, Urim and the Thummim were divination tools used by the high priests of the Old Testament to determine God's will." Turning to the back of the notebook I pointed to three passages. "Here are a few related passages, 1 Samuel 23:9; *And David knew that Saul secretly practised mischief against him; and he said to Abiathar the priest, Bring hither the ephod.* 1 Samuel 28:6; *And when Saul enquired of the Lord, the Lord answered him not, neither by dreams, nor by Urim, nor by prophets.* Exodus 28:30; *And thou shalt put in the breastplate of judgement the Urim and the Thummim, and they shall be upon Aaron's heart, when he goeth in before the Lord: and Aaron shall bear the judgement of the children of Israel upon his heart before the Lord continually.*"

"What is the ephod?"

"The ephod was a garment which the breastplate containing the Urim and Thummim was attached. This was worn by the high priest. As you can see David, Saul, and Aaron, who was Moses' brother, communicated with the biblical God through these divination tools. Divination was allowed by the biblical God in the Old Testament as long as you weren't talking to another god or pissing him off. In 1 Samuel 28:6, you see Saul is shut off from divine guidance and the spirit or biblical

God withdrew from him. This occurred because Saul disobeyed the biblical God and refused to listen. Out of desperation the fearful Saul consulted a medium and necromancer or the witch of Endor to conjure up his mentor, the deceased prophet Samuel, to guide him during the battle with the Philistines."

"Saul consulted a medium and necromancer when it was an act punishable by death?"

"Yes, Tom. Up until that moment, King Saul himself obeyed divine law and banned and removed all diviners, mediums, wizards, and necromancers from his kingdom. Saul was disguised as a commoner when he approached the medium for a séance but his identity was discovered when Samuel shockingly appeared to the medium. Saul has to ask the medium for a description of what she sees, which means it could have been an illusion influenced by a deceptive god or a vision to the mind's eye. After the medium describes the appearance of the old man, Saul perceives it to be Samuel. This presence goes on to speak like the prophet Samuel and re-deliver the dark news of his defeat."

"So, Samuel could have been played by Saul's tag along?"

"It could have, based on the nature of the deceptive gods in this investigation. When I was talking to the deceased benevolent personas played by the tag along it would appear to some that I am a medium. When I spoke to the god presence it would appear to some that I am a prophet. Both the divine god and the deceased in my case was played by a deceiving tag along."

"What did the Urim and Thummim look like?"

"There is no clear description. It is believed they were made of wood or stones. Most likely precious or semi-precious stones with engraved inscriptions or markings. Casting lots was also a popular form of divination in biblical times, a practice also of the apostles."

"Isn't casting lots like casting their vote?"

"No, my friend. Casting lots is divination - again, a practice like using rune stones, flipping a coin, or rolling the dice. Sticks, stones, or pieces of pottery with engraved inscriptions or markings of various sizes and shapes, dropped on to a surface or your lap and interpreted. I have told you the one God, or source of existence, doesn't get personal and doesn't pick favorites. When you pray or request assistance from an external intelligent being, whoever and whatever you assume it to be, to decide, direct you, or determine the will of God, it will never be the one God or source that responds. Especially when it determines the fate of another living being. And why would that be, Tom?"

"Because it is all living beings."

"Correct. In Scripture there is also speaking in tongues. As you have learned, if spiritual beings or gods want to communicate, the ways they can do so are many. To those inexperienced with the nature of spiritual beings or jinn and their many methods of communication, it is easy to be fooled by a different label for the same occult practice. But for the experienced, speaking in tongues is channeling."

"Were they channeling the Holy Spirit?"

"They assumed those that were speaking in tongues were filled with the Holy Spirit, or the third person of the Holy Trinity. But the question is who or what is the Holy Spirit, and is it always holy? We as humans are often fooled in relationships, by falling for a false front. Ask yourself, if the one God or source of existence lies within you why would you need to give an external entity an internal invitation to speak as God?"

CHAPTER 14

YOU'RE A MASTER

"Professor, you should start another religion."

"The world doesn't need another religion, my friend, but a comprehension of spiritual beings or jinn. We see an emphasis of the words *I Am* in their doctrine thus far. Beginning with the words of the Impostor Father saying, *maybe here and now you might feel who I am?* The third god presence used the words *I Am*, and we have *I am within*. The god presence admits it is anger, hate, fear, ugly visions, jealousy, drought, pain, and war, but it is also love, joy, peace, pleasure, beautiful vision, and goodness. This would be in line with the biblical passage, Isaiah 45:7; *I form the light, and create darkness: I make peace, and create evil: I the Lord do all these things.*"

"That would certainly explain why God allows Satan to live."

"Satan, the devil, the adversary, fallen angels, the beast, the evil one, and demons - are not separate beings, but another face of the messengers or gods. There is no battle between God and Satan, but intelligent spiritual beings, or conscious entities, which have both benevolent and malevolent qualities, or angelic and demonic qualities, that want to be worshipped and perceived as the one God. Therefore, the god presence used the words *I am within*. There is a God within, but it is not these clever external gods unless you give them an invite."

"When I asked the ghost monk Loving Spirit the question, 'I have come across angry spirits, and through conversation and maintaining a feeling of oneness, their emotional state of being appeared to change. Is this possible or were they mischievous spirits entertaining themselves?' Loving Spirit answered, *when love is felt, it is much more easily understood, breaking through all language barriers. Your love radiates as illumination, it was felt and altered what words alone could never have done. Your love became their love. Their love became God's love. Love is now their home. What do you ask for in return?*"

"*What do you ask for in return?* is temptation. This brings us back to the seductive fairy saying, *join me and all is yours,* which we can compare to the third god presence saying, *Live by these words and all is yours.* The first, second, and third god presence is also the seductive fairy who planted the euphoric kiss."

"The third god presence also said full circle."

"Yes it did, Tom. Prior to saying *all is yours,* it said, *I am proud to hear those words. Your love has come full circle.* Let's put the full circle messages in order. First Energy Being said, *It will all come together full circle at the right moment.* Quasar said, *Keep focused on full circle. I believe in you.* The third god presence said, *your love has come full circle. Live by these words and all is yours.* You can see there is an obvious progression to Full Circle by the order of their messages."

"Looking back at the dialogue of Energy Being we see, *Humans fight, we don't, Humans kill, we don't, Humans die, we don't.* Humans fight, we don't, is a truth. Humans kill, we don't, is a lie, and Humans die, we don't, I can't answer. There is no war between angels and demons, just humans fighting and killing one another over differences in religious beliefs, based on the word of deceptive gods and controlling power hungry humans."

"The label deceptive gods is a good fit, Professor."

"Then that is what we will call these intelligent spiritual beings moving forward."

"Professor, the ghost monk Voice of Love said, *I am what I am, call me what you feel.* This has to be the same type of being that spoke to Moses as God."

"It doesn't have to be, but it certainly could be. The Angel of the Lord identifying itself as *I Am That I Am* and *I Am,* from the burning bush. *I Am That I Am* may mean I will become what I need to become."

"If we look in Scripture, we find Jesus the Christ saying, John 14:10; *Do you not believe that I am in the Father, and the Father is in me? The words that I say to you I do not speak on my own initiative, but the Father abiding in me does His works.* That is channeling."

"Immediately following the baptism of Jesus, he was led into the wilderness by the Holy Spirit or a heavenly voice to be tempted by what was perceived as the devil or Satan depending on the version of the Bible, as he began a 40 day fast. The related passage is Mark 1:12-13; *And immediately the spirit driveth him into the wilderness. And he was there in the wilderness forty days, tempted of Satan; and he was with wild beasts; and the angels were ministered unto him.*"

"Everyone is free to believe that the Holy Spirit, Satan, and the ministering angels were all separate beings, and I once believed the same. We know during the investigation that a deceptive god can be both divine and demonic."

"The one God is all you see and all you don't see. So, you must ask yourself who the historical Jesus was referring to in John 14:6; *Jesus saith unto him, I am the way, and the truth, and the life. No one comes to the Father but by me.* The one God is within all and it is impossible to be separate. What was within the historical Jesus when he made such a statement?"

"The Holy Spirit?"

"Correct. A couple related passages are, Mark 16:17-18; *And these signs shall follow them that believe; In my name shall they cast out devils; they shall speak with new tongues; They shall take up serpents; and if they drink any deadly thing, it shall not hurt them; they shall lay hands on the sick, and they shall recover.* Acts 2:4; *And they were all filled with the Holy Ghost, and began to speak with other tongues, as the Spirit gave them utterance.*"

"This could have been channeling a jinni or deceptive god. I respect the early Christian perception of the presence that has been labeled the Holy Spirit or Holy Ghost. But you must understand none of them did a thorough investigation of this invisible presence that so many blindly follow as the teacher, guide, and comforter. We should be hesitant to inviting or opening our heart to any external presence including what is perceived as the Holy Spirit or Holy Ghost into your life. The non–personal one God, the source of all life that is in every one of the trillions of cells that makes up your human body, does not need an internal invitation because it always resides within. It is your true nature whether you are a believer or non-believer in a deity or religion."

"In the year 2000, I was attending a hypnosis training session and was selected to be hypnotized by the teacher. Unexpectedly, a powerful presence spoke through me in my receptive state with authority and wisdom. The teacher asked the presence if it was from the light. The presence responded with *I am the light* and spoke beautifully, like the benevolent messengers of this investigation, leaving the classroom mesmerized and ended saying to the hypnotist, *Tell Lorne I love him.* Students said my aura, or energy field, became extremely bright and the vibration in the room was soothing and comforting. This was unintentional channeling."

"When I think about it Professor, it makes more sense that Jesus was channeling a god. This would explain why he spoke as god, but also prayed or spoke outwardly to God."

"Jesus appeared to be a man, a prophet, and a god or deity in different passages. No one will ever know what really took place other than what has been recorded."

"When I unintentionally channeled during the hypnosis training session, the energy vibration of that divine-like presence was exact to that of the first, second, and third god presence, Counterfeit Jesus, and Red Cardinal Angel. The experience was more along the lines of trance channeling because the presence entered the body and spoke directly through me as I remained in an altered state of consciousness. If I trance channeled during the investigation rather than the light channeling that took place during the use of the pendulum or chain, the deceptive god would have spoken directly though me saying, I am God, I am Jesus, I Am Light, I am an Angel, and so on, giving you the impression that I was speaking as God, Jesus, an Angel, Quasar, and the rest of the personas, and you would have been directly interacting with the being like the hypnotist instead of me dictating their telepathic messages to you in a fully conscious state."

"So, perceived holy men of the past could have been trance channeling."

"Anything is possible."

"You have another label. Now you're a master."

"Actually, two new labels. The monk in white called me a *Master,* and the monk in brown cloth that I called Voice of Love called me a *Human God Expression.* The Master said, *masters are teachers of illumination* and *sometimes the teacher gets lost in the role they play and become their own worst enemy.* This is to reinforce the message, *you are the teacher* from the translucent old woman that appeared at the chin up bar."

"The Master in white, and the male and female monks in brown cloth on its left and right, were played by the same being, and I will tell you how. Think of these beings as ventriloquists. They can make a voice or sound appear to come from a created visual image in your mind's eye, an induced hallucination or a translucent manifestation. But they are not limited to using just their creation for puppets. Their voice could appear to come from a sleeping human, a pet, doll, statue, or any other physical object, or form of life, of their choosing. I would say the deceptive god is intentionally appearing in this manner because in Genesis Abraham is visited by what he perceived as the Lord appearing in the form of three angels or the biblical God along with two angels. This is why the monk in white was glowing brighter."

"Comparing the words of the Master and Being of Energy, we have the Master saying, *but think of this, humans have always been spirit or electromagnetic energy but why such technological advancement the past few hundred years. Quite simple, universal wisdom filtered into the human mind from universal Masters.* Being of Energy said, *If I told you your advanced technology is of alien mind, would that create visions?* We can see it is one and the same message of their influence."

"Master and I Am a Voice used the word *filtered* or *filtering.*"

"What does it mean filtered through Earth?"

"Filtered through Earth means we are human beings, part Mother Earth, created from dirt or clay."

"The ghost monk I Am Light said, *I see clearly now without flesh.* We can compare this to Being of Energy saying, *If I told you aliens are without flesh, would that create visions?* Then Master said, *A Master knows when to enter the grand scheme of human consciousness.* We can compare this to Being of Energy saying, *Timing is the wisest teacher, it knows when to enter the grand scheme of life.* More words from a multi-personality spiritual being."

"Looking over the ghost monk dialogue from the Master and Voice of Love, we can see the reinforcing of the 'Speaking as God' message. The Master said, *you speak as you* and *I will ask you this, the loving wisdom you have been speaking and writing down for years, is it you, is it God, is it God in you?* Then, Voice of Love said, *No, I have only heard your God tongue and enjoyed the message* and *Jesus spoke as God, you speak as God, all loving humans can speak as God.* The intention of this reinforced message is to get me to believe I am a prophet of God. Voice of Love said, *all loving humans can speak as God.* This is true, but which God?"

"When I said, 'I am sitting and extending beyond skin' I was embracing the interconnection or oneness of being. Therefore, the Master said, *you speak as you,* which we can compare to the ghost monk My Life Is God saying, *I speak as you because temporarily I am you.*"

"Master continued with the need to use my eyes saying, *the forest is beautiful in your eyes.* The word forest was used in the sentence, *Illumination spreads its wings in the temple of the forest,* by Master as well. Who appeared with long white angelic-like wings in the forest?"

"Fairy of the Forest."

"Yes. The Master is a masculine component and the Fairy of the Forest a feminine component of the tag along."

"What do you think they see when they don't use human eyes?"

"Possibly energy without detail. They need our eyes to see our world just as you need their eyes to better see theirs. Maybe one of the reasons shadow beings appear without detail is because that is the way they see humans, without the use of a human or physical creature's eyes."

"*Question* or *questions* is another word pattern used. *Give me a question and I will be honored to answer,* by My Life Is God, *I can answer your Jesus questions,* by Kim, and I *would love to answer your questions,* by Voice of Love. They want you to ask questions to continue the conversation and connection which gives them more life in our world."

"Voice of Love said, *I am more than a voice, but less than the all of God.* We can compare to Father Albert Celestine saying, *I speak for all in saying God is more than man and I am more than a voice.* Voice of Love said, *God speaks through the pure loving hearts and pure loving minds,* then refers to God in the first person as the third god presence saying, *I speak through all my children know this.* First it says God speaks, then it says I speak. This is another example of the angel or messenger and the god being one and the same."

"The ghost monk Loving Spirt said, *I became weak.* Comparing other personas that used words weak and weakness we have, *you became weak only a few times,* by Amy. *Fear was my weakness and I ran from who I was,* by the Impostor Father, *I kneeled next to you and prayed that one day I would get a chance to say I'm sorry and explain my weakness,* by the Impostor Father. I Am Light said, *A demon is finding your weakness and planning a trap,* and *You are right, women are not your weakness.* More evidence of the same being."

"To see more of the connection between Loving Spirit, the Master, and the Impostor Father with the word *temple* we have, *So, can you see why I never came to visit you and the bar became my temple?* by the Impostor Father. *Love was far away from my temple or should I say I was far away from my temple,* by Loving Spirit and *Illumination spreads its wings in the temple of the forest,* by the Master."

"Deceptive gods use the word temple to refer to a dwelling, a place of worship, and the physical body of a human. When a temple is built to worship a perceived deity, god, or goddess, the temple becomes the physical body of the deceptive god. All who enter becomes its possession."

"When I asked Loving Spirit about dreams it answered, *Dreams are a world in itself. Bring only love forward and dreams will be bright. I inhabit mind in motion.* Impostor Father said, *I wish you the world that your heart and mind dreams of.* Both used dreams and world in a sentence. These beings can inhabit the mind because it is electricity. They connect you to the dream world of their design, like we both experienced. Deceptive gods deliver messages through the medium of dreams today, just as they did in biblical times. The 21st century human is not inferior to the perceived chosen mouthpieces of ancient history. A consistent question I asked the messengers was how we connect or how are we communicating?"

"Kim said, *we connect by like vibration. We disconnect by change in your vibration or the message is completed. Unless of course, some other disturbance gives us a push.* The Counterfeit Jesus said, *those who sing the tune of love, receive the tune of love. God is the tune. Illuminated melody of a pure heart is the song.* Loving Spirit explained that, *we connect by electrical impulse opening the door of love.* Quasar said, *I'm following your soul, keep the direction of heart and love will be your island paradise.* Life Is God answered, *my brother, knowing this can change your world. I speak as you, because temporarily I am you. Include in your book this speech.* Light of Heart said, *Say I think purely, I feel purely, I am Heaven in this moment."* Finally Helen said, *I connect like jelly on bread, absorbing through the perforations.*

"Merging their bio-electricity with ours is what I believe takes place. Bringing love forward, as Loving Spirit mentioned, is projecting electromagnetic energy from the mind of the heart, creating a change in your aura or energy field. This will be liked or disliked by the tag along."

"According to this list from the messengers, electrical impulses - which may be our emotions - vibrate or sing a song when we think purely and feel purely, and is the illuminated melody of a pure heart, or the heaven vibration in the moment. Deceptive gods are emotional which means one of the ways we are connecting, and disconnecting is by vibration or the song of our electrical impulses."

"Any other questions before we close this ghost monk investigation?"

"Yes, what was the lesson from the daydream with the ghost monk in the cabin?"

"First, we can see the ghost monk demonstrated its strength. Gold rings were another sign of their connection to gold. Within the cabin the test involved idolatry, patience, distraction, and silence. To worship an idol is to separate or disconnect from the awareness of the one God or the source. Deceptive gods will inhabit these idols and feed on your projected energy. To know your true nature you must turn inward, never outward toward idols, objects, and the many gods. Therefore, I pay no attention to idols and statues. In the dream, the guests were also unfamiliar with a vow of silence as part of a monastic life. The tag along heard me say, 'When I say the one God, I am referring to the source of all life, seen and unseen, that does not speak. But in its stillness and silence, it reveals all.'"

"Clever."

"As I mentioned before, to gain your attention the messenger knows it must provide information that piques your interest. A quote about the silence of God that I would apply here would be from the 13th century Persian poet, Islamic scholar, and Sufi mystic Rumi, who said, 'Silence is the language of god, all else is poor translation.'"

"I like that."

"I figured you would."

"Was that really a puckwudgie on the trek back to the vehicle?"

"Both hooded shadows and puckwudgies are known to be shapeshifters, both can mimic a child's cry and throw an object. The face in the tree had a large nose and oversized ears like the Puck or goblin-like forms I have experienced in the forest through the years. But they could all be projected images or illusions from a hooded shadow or other intelligent spiritual being."

"I don't know what to say, Professor. You have opened my eyes to a world I never knew existed. What you have taught me has brought clarity to what never made sense. Thank you," Tom said. As he stood up and shook my hand, he started rubbing his solar plexus.

"You're welcome, Tom. I hope your questions have been answered and you have learned that spiritual communication should be avoided in all its forms and labels. No matter who you believe to be the source of the information, nothing but lies and deception will come from the practice."

CHAPTER 15

ENERGY BUFFET

Parking in front of my mother's house, I gave her a call.

"Lorne?"

"Yup, I'm here. Can you open the door?"

"I certainly can."

My mother opened the door and I handed her a bag of groceries and a coffee. "I have to get my computer, I'll be right back." Returning, I opened the door and was greeted by Peetu wagging his tail. "How are you doing?" I asked Peetu as I pet his head. Taking a seat on the couch, Peetu followed. After I put the computer down, I picked him up and put him on my lap.

"Look at him, he is trying to kiss you. He is such a good watch dog."

"Yes, he is."

"Let me get this out of your way," my mother said, as she cleared the newspapers and magazines off the coffee table.

Taking the computer out of the case I set it up on the table. "Mom, I'm going to have you read these two conversations. Can you read alright with those glasses you're wearing?"

"I should be fine," my mother answered, taking a seat next to me on the couch.

"Do you know how to scroll on the computer?"

"No."

"Alright, you read, and I will scroll. You know it's really hot in here."

"I have the window open. Uh oh," my mother said, as the cross she was wearing fell off the chain and onto the floor. "The clasp just broke. That's weird."

"Isn't that the cross Richard used to wear?"

"Yes. I don't know what happened," she responded as she picked up the cross and placed it on the table. The atmosphere darkened and began to thicken.

"I'm going to have you read first what was supposed to be my father."

"Okay, I might have a hard time with that fine print," my mother said, looking at the screen.

"I can make it bigger. How about now?" I asked, after enlarging the font.

"That's good."

"When you see this font right here that is supposed to be my father talking and the other font is me," I said, pointing to the screen "Start with the line that reads 'another presence was coming forward', and I will scroll. When you are done, we'll discuss what you think."

"Okay." My mother read and I scrolled. When she was finished, she said, "This is like, wow! And what you said about water is brilliant."

"Thank you. As you can see it's not my father speaking."

"You want to think it is him. But I never heard that man talk loving to anybody."

"The deceiver is playing on the human belief of the deceased going to heaven and changing into a loving being."

"That's what you want to believe."

"Of course, and this is why you can be sold on the loving sweet talk. Today I am giving you an introduction in how these beings speak beautifully, tell stories, and deceive in communication."

"They're very wise. Like they went to Heaven's college."

"Yes, but once you know their pattern, it becomes easier to spot their con. Do you want to continue?"

"Are you kidding? I'm into this."

"Alright. Now I would like you to read Richard's dialogue. If you start getting emotional keep in mind, it's not Richard. The presence is speaking very smooth, like the Impostor Father."

"He believed in spirits, you know. We've seen them in here."

"I know. But this isn't Richard." What sounded like a large animal scratched the wall behind us.

"What the heck was that? That's not Richard," my mother said, as she turned around. "That sounded like an animal, didn't it?"

"Yes, it did. But it's not an animal."

"I think we're stirring up a few things."

"Yes, we are. Please read where it says *I am Richard,* and I will scroll."

"He would never say that," my mother said, as she read the dialogue of the poltergeist persona.

"That is not the persona Richard. This is where the presence gets nasty again as the poltergeist. Just skip that for now and continue where it says *Wipe your tears with my hat.*" My mother read, and again I scrolled as the temper of the presence grew hotter and hotter.

"Something is pulling at my brain right now."

"What do you mean something is pulling at your brain?"

"I can feel it. It's trying to get my attention away from reading."

"It's trying to distract you. We are going to stop here. I just wanted you to read these two conversations because I knew the presence would make itself known. It's psychologically attacking you because it doesn't want you to read this anymore or listen to me. The presence prefers you continue to believe it's Richard. This is the nature of the being."

"Richard used to say most of those exact words, and I swear to God he did say many times that he wished you would call him Pops."

"The being has knowledge of these things because it watches and listens."

"It knows a lot."

"Yes, it does."

"I'm getting goosebumps and pressure right here," she said as she placed her hand on her solar plexus.

"That's the mimicking presence, Mom. It descends as a heavy blanket of uncomfortable negative emotion initiating an energy assault. This is the same presence that you felt when you said, 'I feel a caress of loving energy around me' during the interaction. It is not two separate beings."

"The good don't fight the bad and the bad don't fight the good?"

"Not in this investigation. This is an emotional and unpredictable hidden race that has been given free will like humans to choose between what is perceived as good and what is perceived as evil."

"I didn't learn that in Sunday school."

"I'm sure. We can see in their dialogue an example of the Impostor Father and the Impostor Richard being played by the same being. The persona Richard said, *be strong in your world and you will be strong in mine,* which we can compare to the Impostor Father that said, *you have grown to be very comfortable in your world between worlds.* Both spoke of two worlds. This is the jinn from a parallel dimension."

"As Richard, the shrewd presence said, *to talk to me, I am here. Come over to my picture.* This, and talking to the presence as if it's Richard, you must not continue to do."

"I won't," my mother responded. "When I just said that, I felt a presence go right through my body."

"That's because a connection or energetic ties between you and the presence has already been established. Remain calm and call me if the activity escalates." Standing up I gave my mother a long hug. "Are you still getting solar plexus pressure?"

"No, it's gone now."

"Good. I love you, Mom."

"I love you too, son."

Walking down the stairs the presence was felt at my back. No sooner did I get in the vehicle when the cell rang. Recognizing the number, I answered, "Hello, Tom."

"Good evening, Professor."

"What's up?"

"I hate to bother you."

"It's no bother Tom, I was just leaving my mother's. Go ahead."

"Professor, the evil presence is here right now, and I have a tightness in my solar plexus that won't go away."

"Relax, Tom. Focus on the inhalation and the exhalation of your breath."

"But my heart is beating like crazy and I feel like I'm going to have a heart attack."

"You're not going to have a heart attack. Step outside and get some fresh air while you perform the breathing exercise. I'll be right over."

"Okay, see you in a couple." The presence was not just at my mother's, but at Tom's as well, demonstrating the ability of jinn to travel from one place to another with great speed.

"Hello Professor, thanks for coming," Tom said, as he opened the screen door.

"Not a problem, Tom. How are you feeling?" I replied, as I was greeted by a familiar angry presence.

"Terrible," Tom answered. "My chest is still really tight and I'm having a hard time breathing. This creep is relentless."

"Stay calm and don't dwell on its presence, it will pass."

"I certainly hope so. Can I get you something to drink?"

"Do you have any tea?"

"I don't know, let me check. Yes, I have Lipton."

"That will work."

"Milk and sugar?"

"No thanks, black is fine."

The atmosphere was thick, heavy, and uncomfortable in Tom's remodeled basement apartment. Doom and gloom was in the air revealing the darker nature of the hooded shadow. Taking off my jacket, I caught a glimpse of a light blue orb flickering for a moment in the kitchen. Tom walked into the living room rubbing his solar plexus and sat down, placing his soda on the coffee table.

"Is the pressure easing up?" I asked.

"No, the moment I stop rubbing, the tightness comes back even stronger."

"Is it alright for me to place my hand on your solar plexus?"

"Sure, go ahead," Tom answered.

After about a minute, I took my hand off his solar plexus. "The pressure is gone. What did you do, Professor?"

"I introduced a calming energy to the seat of your emotions. But this will only be a temporary fix. What this presence is doing is projecting negative energy, just like an angry human being, causing you stress. Solar plexus tightness, anxiety, and an increased heart rate are a few of the physical symptoms."

On the coffee table was a book on how to talk to animal spirits and a couple of supernatural flicks. "Tell me Tom, when did you buy this book on animal spirits?"

"I bought it at the gift shop tonight, with this." Tom reached into his pocket and pulled out a crystal pendulum. "What do you think?" Tom asked, as he dangled it in the air.

"It's cute."

"Cute?"

"Yes, cute. Let me guess. By the feeling of our not so friendly company, you tried to communicate with the pendulum?"

"Well yes, I did. But it started spinning counterclockwise like crazy and I stopped. I know I shouldn't have bought it, Professor. I was just going to buy the book, but then I felt drawn to the rack of pendulums."

"That's okay, Tom, I understand. Remember, I drove to the monastery in a hypnotic state and was drawn to the cedar cross when I first encountered the ghost monks."

Suddenly what sounded like a small rock hit the wall in the hallway. "What was that?"

"It sounded like a rock," I answered.

Tom was frightened. Both of us got up and searched the hallway for a rock or some other object. Nothing was found. "There is no rock. Where could it have gone?" Tom asked.

"This time the being mimicked the sound of a rock thrown."

"That's just great. Now the rock thrower is in my apartment. Can you please talk to this thing?"

"When you feel this type of presence in your dwelling the last thing you should do is talk. But this is a necessary lesson. Do you have a paperclip?"

"Yeah, why?"

"I'm going to make a pendulum. I left my chain and cross in the jewelry cleaner."

"Why don't you use mine?"

"No thanks. I have other plans for that."

"Okay. Do we need anything else?"

"Yes, if you have a notebook grab that too." A loud bang occurred to the wall behind the television causing Tom to jump.

"Now what was that?" Tom asked in fear.

"Ignore the bangs, bumps, knocks, and dings. It's just a temper tantrum."

Tom left the living room and walked into his bedroom. A headache began as the malevolent presence engulfed me in its rage and whispered into my right ear, *I don't believe in Jesus. I don't believe in Jesus. I don't believe in Jesus.*

The hateful energy of the presence was overwhelmingly toxic as it spoke in threes. Closing my eyes, an invading vision of a small black speck appeared at a distance. As the speck came closer it increased in size to a giant black spider. Aggressively, it charged toward my mind's eye releasing threads in all directions. The image vanished into the void as a man with a dog on a leash was seen at a distance walking up a road of shiny black asphalt. To the left of the man were train tracks, heading in the same direction uphill into the horizon. Wearing black pants, a red outdoor shirt, and a red ball cap his back remained to me, never revealing his face. On a red leash, was a beautiful long-haired shaggy dog of two colors being brown and white with a small pink bow on top of its head. Knowing I was viewing the image, the dog turned toward me and stuck out its long tongue.

As I opened my eyes, Tom returned with the items and took a seat next to me on the couch. Removing the string from the tea bag, I tied the paper clip to the end.

"Is that paperclip going to work?" Tom asked.

"Yes. It has more to do with your subconscious and the spiritual being than what weight hangs on the end of a string. Can I have a sheet of paper?"

"Sure," Tom answered.

"It's getting really tough to breathe in here," Tom said as he handed me the paper, then leaned forward with his hand on his chest.

"Continue to focus on your breathing," I replied, as I drew an alphabet chart.

"Professor, something is behind me, I can feel a static energy feeling."

"Good."

"Why good."

"Because I can explain what is occurring. These beings are electrical; within that electrical energy are the electrical impulses of their emotions. At this moment it's angry and it wants to intimidate. Are you ready to hear its reason why?"

"Let's do it."

Taking a deep breath, I let it out and relaxed into receptive oneness. Holding the string with my thumb and forefinger, I positioned the paperclip over the alphabet chart. Controlling thought and emotion, I allowed the conversation to begin telepathically. "Who may I ask is present?"

My name is Baby.

"Your name is not Baby."

Jesus is watching all and so are we.

"I know you're not here to talk about Jesus."

Did I touch a soft spot?

"Not at all, you have your choices and I have mine." Lights started flickering while the malevolent presence constricted my breathing.

Can your choices do that?

"My choice would be to use the light switch to turn the lamp on or off."

So, you're a smart ass?

"No, I'm in a mood tonight. We will show you respect, please show us some respect as well, we have done nothing to you."

Fuck your respect.

"Well, that's not very friendly."

You both suck.

"I'm sorry you feel that way."

Give me your fucking heart and I will eat it.

"I love my heart right where it is." A vision of a pure black Doberman-like dog with a red bandanna tied around its neck appeared in the mind's eye.

"Stop being so ridiculous!" Tom yelled out loud. This provoked more rage in the presence, and I turned toward Tom and shook my head. "Oops," Tom said, as he shrugged his shoulders.

You want ridiculous, how about I kill you?

Powerful and intense, the negative energy was too much for my nervous system. It took everything I had to maintain emotional balance while Tom was being crushed by the projected wickedness.

You can run, but you cannot hide.

"Are you talking to me?"

No, your frightened sidekick. I think he shit his pants.

Tom and I broke out in laughter. This was the medicine I needed to shift my vibration and I took full advantage of it, changing my strategy. "I'm sure you would like that."

Yes, I would.

"May I ask, why the anger toward my friend?"

I don't like him.

"May I ask what the reason is?"

His flesh stinks. When are you going to ask me if I'm a good or bad spirit?

"Why would I ask that?"

Because I'm a spirit.

"I didn't think you were the tooth fairy."

You are quick.

Tom yawned loudly.

I have a question for your sleepy sidekick. Do you know why you are tired?

"Because I didn't get much sleep last night," Tom answered sarcastically.

What's the matter? Did you have some scary dreams last night, little boy? I will tell you why you are tired, it's because the bed bugs were biting and we're the bed bugs. So why don't you place some salt around the bed to keep us out?

A vision of orbs of all sizes coming out of Tom's bed was received. Drained and tired, it was time to shut this energy buffet down. While one deceptive god is telepathically communicating, a whole parasitic gang could be feeding on our energy.

"I must say thank you."

For what?

"For helping my friend realize he must work on his fear. This was a good lesson. It is true, carrying fear will limit your potential."

If you're not careful, you might not get a chance to see your skin wrinkle.

"Now there's a thought to keep in mind," the aggressive rage of the presence immediately began to dissipate as it transformed to a neutral emotional state.

I feel different, what did you do to me?

"I think you just needed to blow off some steam."

What are you?

"A good listener."

You are modest. Your energy relaxed all of us and you talked to me like a human. I like you. It's been a long time since I said that. Thank you.

"You are welcome."

For what you have done for me, I must do something in return.

"Thank you, but I helped you to help my friend. Just remember the peaceful feeling you now possess."

You are a wise being, I'm honored. Goodbye.

"Goodbye." After reciting a few prayers internally, I folded the alphabet chart in two, tore it into pieces, and threw it in the trash. Walking into the bathroom, I flushed the paper clip pendulum down the toilet. Feeling a residue or dirt on my skin from the interaction, I washed my face and hands. "What do you have for snacks?" I called out to Tom in the living room.

"Not much," Tom answered as he stood up and walked to the fridge. "I have some leftover pizza."

"What kind?" I asked.

"Pepperoni. This might not taste as good as the seductress pizza."

"Maybe it won't. But it will do."

"Do you want a can of soda?"

"No thanks, I'll just have water," I replied, as I walked into the kitchen to get a paper towel.

"I can't believe the difference in energy right now. It feels so much lighter in here. Do you think the deceptive god is gone for good?" Tom asked, as he handed me the pizza box.

"No, I don't. This calm after the storm is what occurs after smudging, or a blessing, leaving many believing the malevolent have packed up and skipped town. In truth, the deceptive god is still here watching and listening quite intently. As you just witnessed, these spiritual beings are easy to detect when they're angry, but when they're not emitting emotional energy, they become difficult to detect even for the most spiritually sensitive. Combine that with invisibility and presto, you assume they vanished permanently."

"Why do you think the deceptive god used the name Baby?"

"There is always a reason for the names and labels. One of the reasons could be it is the presence that I encountered in 1993 that called itself Mama, and now it calls itself Baby to see if I can connect the dots. The other reason could be it is using the pet name Baby in a mischievous way like men and women use it as a term of affection - because this is your succubus, my seductress, and my mother's Richard."

"It did feel like that evil presence I felt after my nightmare and Old Hag Syndrome experience. Just more intense."

"You have learned that deceptive gods flatter and compliment, but as you just witnessed, they also enjoy being complimented and flattered as well. When I said, 'I must say thank you,' the presence said, *For what?* I answered, 'For helping my friend realize he must work on his fear. This was a good lesson. It is true, carrying fear will limit your potential.' Words of encouragement helped to create a shift in the emotional energy of the spiritual being, just as it would in a human being."

"Baby asked *when are you going to ask me if I'm a good or bad spirit?* Asking such a question we know is another fool, because the deceptive god can masquerade perfectly as both benevolent and malevolent, good and bad, light and dark, just like those humans who portray one personality in private and another in public. Tonight, you personally witnessed the spiritual being go from wicked to a neutral emotional state. This proves that what appeared to be a malevolent presence, or a demonic entity, is not always emitting anger and wickedness."

"Baby said *I must do something in return,* which we can compare to the ghost monk Loving Spirit asking, *what do you ask for in return?* That is the jinn, jinni, or genie trap, and accepting the gift is a big no-no."

"You heard Baby say, *did you have some scary dreams last night, little boy?* Hooded shadow beings and black shadow masses have been present during the Old Hag Syndrome experiences and nightmares. But I know the deceptive gods will take credit for actions they didn't do, if it makes them appear more powerful, induces fear in the victim, and serves their appetite and agenda. As I said, deceptive gods, whether benevolent or malevolent, can inhabit the mind and connect you to a dream world of their design."

"Mind parasites of the hidden world of jinn and the microbial world are a reality that the one God gives life to. In the microbial world, like the hidden world of jinn, we have parasites that seek the brain of a human, altering behavior, causing hallucinations and suicidal thoughts, eventually leading to mental insanity and/or death. There's also an amoeba that can travel up into a human's nose and consume the brain."

"That is so disgusting."

"It's reality."

"Baby said *you want ridiculous, how about I kill you?* It really bothers me knowing these beings can kill, Professor?"

"Well let's look at creation. Is there wildlife that can kill you?"

"Yes."

"Are there creatures in the ocean that can kill you?"

"Yes."

"Are there insects that can kill you?"

"Yes."

"Is there microbial life that can kill you?"

"Yes."

"Are there humans that can kill you?"

"Yes."

"Can your own mind kill you?"

"If you let it, yes."

"Then why should it bother you, Tom? The one God, or source of existence, gives life to the predators and the prey, the humans that cherish, protect, and care for Mother Earth, and those that are destroying it for profit and power. The source gives life to the innocent human victims and their emotionless cold-blooded killers, as well as the insects, reptiles, and microorganisms that take the life of men, women, and children each day without mercy. Among the diverse species of spiritual beings who have been given life by the creator, there exist those that can also kill without mercy. This is not because the one God, or the source, is evil, but because that which gives life is an impersonal force."

"God is impersonal?"

"If we are talking about that which gives life, then the answer is yes. If we are talking about the deceptive gods, then the answer is no. As you have learned, these gods can be personal."

"Finally, an explanation that makes sense."

"Do you know what the deadliest animal on Earth is?"

"Alligators."

"Not even close, Tom. The answer is blood sucking mosquitos and they kill over 700,000 people a year. The one God, or the source of existence, gives life to these insects just as it does parasitic spiritual beings."

"That's insane."

"Again, that's reality. Let's continue. Baby used the word *we* like Energy Being and Harold. Either the presence is one of many, wants us to believe it's one of many, or *we* is referring to the being's many personalities. The biblical God used the words *us* and *our*, spoke in plural, was jealous of other gods, and was referred to in plural. Please do a search for passages where the biblical God used the word *us* and *our*."

"Okay." Tom performed the search and I took a few more bites of pizza. "Are you ready?"

"Go ahead, Tom."

"Genesis 1:26; *And God said, Let Us make man in our image, after our likeness: and let them have dominion over the fish of the sea, and over the fowl of the air, and over the cattle, and over all the earth, and over every creeping thing that creepeth upon the earth.* Genesis 3:22; *And the Lord God said, Behold, the man is become as one of us, to know good and evil, and now, lest he put forth his hand, and take also of the tree of life, and eat, and live for ever.* Genesis 11:7; *Go to, let us go down, and there confound their language, and they may not understand one another's speech.* Isaiah 6:8; *Also I heard the voice of the Lord, saying, "Whom shall I send, and who will go for us?" Then said I, Here am I! Send me."*

"Excellent. The usual first defense to the biblical God speaking in plural is the one God statement in other passages spoken by the biblical God, and the belief that God is Holy therefore he can't lie, deceive, or contradict himself. Now I would like you to read the passages that say differently. Please do a search for verses where the biblical God deceived or put a lying spirit in the mouth."

Tom searched and I finished the slice and drank some water. "There are quite a few."

"Yes, there are. Go ahead and read the first five."

"Jeremiah 4:10; *Then said I, Ah, Lord God! surely thou hast greatly deceived this people and Jerusalem, saying, Ye shall have peace; whereas the sword reacheth unto the soul.* Jeremiah 20:7; *O Lord, thou has deceived me, and I was deceived; thou art stronger than I, and hast prevailed: I am in derision daily, every one mocketh me.* Ezekiel 14:9; *And if the prophet be deceived when he hath spoken a thing, I the Lord have deceived that prophet, and I will stretch out my hand upon him, and will destroy him from the midst of my people Israel.* Thessalonians 2:11; *And for this cause God shall send them strong delusion, that they should believe a lie.* 2 Chronicles 18:22; *Now therefore, behold, the Lord hath put a lying spirit in the mouth of these thy prophets, and the Lord hath spoken evil against thee."*

"As you can see Tom, the biblical God can deceive. Please do one more search for the passage Deuteronomy 32:17."

"Got it. Deuteronomy 32:17; *They sacrificed unto devils, not to God; to gods whom they knew not, to new gods that came newly up, whom your fathers feared not."*

"Thank you, Tom. As you can see, demons were also referred to as gods at that time. The word demon that came from the Greek word *daimon* or *daimonion* did not mean an evil spirit or dark entity but a wise spiritual being capable of being both good and evil. In ancient Arabia, prior to Islam, jinn were worshipped as gods, and Japan's Shinto religion has the Kami, which are the deities, spirits, gods and goddesses, that can be good or bad. Shinto is the 'way of the gods."

"All could be jinn, Professor."

"Certain species among the jinn, one of them being the hooded shadows. When I was taking off my jacket, I caught a glimpse of a light blue orb in the kitchen. During the dialogue when Baby said, *we're the bed bugs* a vision came to my mind's eye of orbs of all sizes rising out of your bed. At my mother's house, a vision of orbs coming down from the ceiling, up from the floor, flying horizontally, diagonally, and zig zag, came to the mind's eye during the interaction."

"Sounds like they move a lot like the unidentified flying objects pilots have witnessed."

"It is possible that there are larger species of these orbs that pop in and out of a parallel dimension or the hidden races have energy bubble-like ships with a consciousness of its own or the pilot can even merge its consciousness with the flying object giving it abilities beyond our current technology. Because they are energy beings it makes sense that they could possess what we consider a spacecraft that is pure energy."

"Are orbs intelligent like the shadows, Professor?"

"Some are, yes. When I was younger I called them bubbles. Like their larger shadow counterparts, they can be seen without the use of a digital camera if they choose. Orbs, which I believe are another species of jinn, can inhabit the structure of a dwelling or any object within. If you're in a dwelling that is infested with orbs sometimes just asking them to appear or disappear can prove successful if done with respect. But you must be careful as you could also be calling a hooded shadow if they have claimed the space. When remodeling an infested dwelling, in addition to the hooded shadow, thousands of orbs can be disturbed causing an increase in activity that may or may not be noticed. Orbs can pass right through you without your notice or could cause a mood shift if they remain within."

"Are they negative?"

"That depends on their emotional energy diet and nature. What is believed to be the residual energy from deceased humans in a perceived haunted dwelling may in fact be the energy of a deceptive god or jinni, like a hooded shadow and/or the orbs which may be energy scavengers."

"Do orbs follow?"

"Yes, they do. It could be a single orb or thousands. They can occupy the clothing you're wearing or your shoes without your knowing. In my experience, where there is malevolent activity, orbs and a hooded shadow being are usually present. Just like bed bugs can feed on your blood without your awareness, diverse races of parasitic spiritual beings feed on your energy."

"I'll never sleep again."

"Sure, you will Tom. The one God, or source, gives life to bed bugs, mosquitoes, and freshwater leeches that consume human blood and dust mites that consume your dead skin. Is it too bizarre to think that the source gives life to intelligent energy consuming parasites in a world of energy? It may be uncomfortable to accept that we as humans are included in the food chain. Humans consume food that is turned into energy. Species of the hidden race consume that energy. It's all common sense when you take a good look at creation."

"Because humans at rest produce enough power to light up a 100 watt light bulb, the deceptive gods will soon have competition as modern technology is creating devices to harvest humans wasted energy in order to power things like your cell phone, tablet and PC, limiting the need for chemical batteries."

"What do you make of all this?"

"When I was at my mother's I had her read the dialogue of Richard and the Impostor Father."

"How did that go?"

"Both my mother and I felt the angry presence, but nothing was seen. Scratching occurred on the wall, my mother was psychologically attacked, and the cross my mother wears, which was Richard's, fell off and landed on the floor."

"That's creepy."

"Yes, it is. Then the moment I got into the vehicle, you called with an angry visitor. If the hooded shadow wants you to see it, you will; if it doesn't, and it wants to frighten you, you will feel its intimidating presence, but you will see nothing, just like tonight. When you were getting the notebook earlier, Baby whispered *I don't believe in Jesus* three times in my right ear. Baby spoke in threes in its angered state, like Donovan. The malevolent presence in the monastery restroom, Donovan, the poltergeist, and Baby's dark energy were recognized as exact in feeling. After Baby spoke in threes, it sent a series of visions starting with a black speck at a distance that charged forward as a giant black spider releasing threads."

"Like the four foot wide shadow spider your mother witnessed."

"Yes. I believe the threads were meant to indicate its ability to connect and influence. Following the spider vision was a man wearing black pants, a red outdoor shirt, and a red ball cap walking a dog on a red leash up a hill. The road they traveled was black shiny asphalt and the dog had long shaggy hair, it was brown and white in color with a small pink bow on top of its head."

"With the exception of the dog, the man was wearing the same attire as Richard in your mother's dream."

"You're right. Both were wearing black pants, a red shirt, and a red ball cap. The dog in the vision turned and stuck out a long tongue. Sticking out tongues is a common action I have witnessed in malevolent influenced nightmares and visions. During Baby's angry conversation it sent a vision of a pure black Doberman-like dog with a red bandanna tied around its neck."

"That's the same dog as in my dream."

"Yes, Tom. The red/black symbolism, spiders, and dogs, combined with the pattern of intimidation, emotional shifts, lies, flattery, distinct energy, pattern of words, method of communication, and the way it sent visions, makes it obvious that it's the work of the same deceptive god. Maybe too obvious."

"The investigation was never really over, was it Professor?"

"No. You have heard enough from Jekyll, now that the honeymoon is over you will be hearing more from Hyde. Do you have any plans for tomorrow morning?" I asked, as I put on my jacket.

"Just food shopping, but I can do that anytime," Tom replied.

"Good. Meet me at the monastery gazebo at 9."

"Alright. Coffee?"

"Yes, please."

"What should I do to keep Baby at bay tonight?" Tom asked, as he stood up.

"Stand your ground, face your fears, and exercise emotional discipline," I replied, walking to the door.

"Is that it?"

"No. Flush your pendulum down the toilet. I'll see you in the morning."

CHAPTER 16

SPIRALING SNAKES AND BLACK CATS

Pulling into the driveway, I noticed a black cat in front of the fence. Walking toward the stairway, the motion light came on and the black cat was now on the side of my leg. Stopping, I said "Hello." As the cat weaved between my legs, I said, "You must go home, there are a lot of cars with drunk drivers around this neighborhood and they might not see you crossing the street." The cat continued to stick by my leg as I climbed the stairs and opened the entry door.

Persistent, the cat followed me up to the second floor. Squatting, I picked up the cat, took it outside and set it down. This time when the cat rubbed against my leg, I felt a slithering energy sensation coiling around my leg traveling upward. Walking back to the stairs, the parasitic snake feeling continued to rise, stopping at my hip region.

This serpent-like being I have confronted in the past. Its energy movement through the body is creepy and disgusting, and not something you can ever get used to. The slithering sensation appeared to have ceased when I reached the apartment door.

Opening the fridge to fill a glass of water, the slithering energy sensation returned around the glutes. Walking into the living room, the slithering movement went down and back up the legs and again stopped. Looking down to my right, there was a black shadow cat sitting next to the coffee table, manifesting for just a few seconds before it vanished. Putting all the couch pillows on the floor, I made room to lay down.

Picking up the remote, I turned on the television and scanned the channels eventually choosing an old episode of *Gilligan's Island*.

During the show bangs and dings occurred throughout the apartment. A light blue orb, like the one at Tom's, caught my attention as it slowly came into the room and made a zigzag movement before heading back toward the kitchen.

When the show was over, I put the pillows back on the couch and walked into the bedroom to get changed. After getting ready for bed, I pulled down the covers and got into bed. Feeling the presence in the air, I turned onto my stomach and positioned the pillow. A heavy cloud of energy washed over me and then lightened up. Closing my eyes, a black cat with bright blue eyes was staring at me from the void. Lying with its head to my right, it remained for a few seconds before it vanished. Coming forward next was a woman with long brunette hair, in a hooded black robe. Half of her face was hidden in shadow, and the other half was exposing full lips and a bright light blue eye.

As the woman vanished into the void, a red rotary-style phone appeared ringing. Picking up the receiver, I answered. "Hello," I said, through telepathy.

Are we meeting? a soft female voice responded.

"No."

I know you.

"What does that mean?"

You're always horny.

"Wrong victim." A hard bite occurred to the outside of my left arm and I refused to wince from the pain.

That's a little love bite.

"Aren't you sweet?"

Lyrics from the song "Ain't No Other Man" by Christina Aguilera began to play in my head. "Ain't no other man can stand up next to you/Ain't no other man on the planet does what you do."

Over and over, the two sentences from the song were repeated to torment and disturb. First, I called out to the angels, Jesus the Christ, and God for assistance. This caused an escalation of the intensity as expected. To counter the attack, I repeated Philippians 4:13; *I can do all things through Christ which strengtheneth me* until I eventually canceled out the disturbance.

Closing my eyes, I was lying in bed watching a television show with talking cats. The sheets of the bed were soft, silky red satin. Entering the room was what appeared to be Amy with her head down. Not saying a word, she walked directly into the bathroom and closed the door. A dark energy was felt in the room as the bathroom door opened and Amy walked out.

Looking very sad and defeated, she took a seat at the end of the bed. I could hear what sounded like my late grandparents talking in the background. "Amy, why don't you turn and look at me?" I asked. Amy shook her head no. "Please look at me, Amy," I asked softly. Slowly she raised her head and turned toward me. Three long scratches ran down the left side of her face. Blood began to trickle from the wounds. "Where did you get those scratches, Amy?" I asked, as I got out of bed and stood facing her. *From a cat*, she answered as she turned her head away. "Your eyes look different," I said. *I have angels all around me giving me night eyes*, Amy replied. "We both know you're not Amy," I countered, as her face instantly began to disfigure before she disappeared.

A pair of young woman's legs wearing black high heels appeared next, standing in the doorway to my left. There was no upper body, just darkness. The calves of the woman's legs started expanding in size, getting bigger and bigger before the legs vanished and an upper body took its place. Floating in the air about four feet from the floor was the upper half of a female creature. Long, black, messy hair partially covered a gruesome face. Snake-like scales for skin, a snake-like neck, jet-black almond eyes, and a mouth that stretched open wide like a suckerfish before the jaw structure and mouth shifted to an underbite like a bulldog.

The disturbing image vanished as another dreamscape appeared. Five women were standing side by side in the monastery field. Their dresses were dated, possibly early 1900's. The first woman had a solid white dress, the second a brown and white dress, the middle woman a solid black dress, the fourth wore a black and white dress, and the fifth a solid brown dress. All five were curly-haired blondes, but their faces were distinctly different.

Suddenly, the woman in the center with the black dress started to shake and her skin turned green, as the face shifted to a grotesque form. In a flash, she shot forward face to face with me. Clearing the disturbing vision, I opened my eyes to the bed shaking followed by what felt like a hand pushing down on the back of my left shoulder, pressing it firmly into the mattress. Trying to get up, I met a strong energy resistance that I couldn't budge. Rather than panic and fight, I relaxed.

For a moment it was quiet and calm. Out of nowhere, what felt like a cat leaped onto my upper back and viciously began tearing and ripping into my robe. Struggling to shake it off, the cat bit hard into the back of my neck and I yelled firmly "Enough!" causing the attack to cease.

Waking, I realized the feline temper tantrum occurred in the twilight state, but I could feel the pain of real wounds. Turning on the light, I got out of bed and walked into the bathroom. Opening the closet, I took out the hand mirror and viewed my back in the mirror.

Luckily, no scratch or bite marks were found even though the sensation of wounds lingered. Still a little freaked, I got back into bed, pulled the collar of my robe up to my neck and eventually drifted off to sleep.

Mentally and physically exhausted, I took a moment to feel the energy of the room as I lay in bed awake. Turning to view the time, it was 5:55 a.m.

A loud bang occurred to the wall on my right, followed by the feeling of the dark presence. Closing my eyes, an invading vision of a bald-headed naked baby doll seated in a throne-like black chair with red velour upholstery appeared. Giving me an evil stare, the doll blinked its jet-black eyes three times and vanished. This was a reminder, a kind of guess who visit from last night's persona encounter that called itself Baby.

Another image came to my mind's eye. My work boots, sneakers, and dress shoes were lined up on the kitchen table. Instead of pairs, there was three of each shoe. This was symbolism of 333, like with the ghost monks.

Opening my eyes, I whipped off the covers and jumped up out of bed. While rinsing my face, the bathroom light started flickering and my name was called out by a male voice which sounded like it came up from a hole or tunnel. Sitting on the toilet, a vision was sent of a snake coming up from inside the bowl and biting my gluteus maximus. The presence was going to continue unleashing psychological attacks until I conversed.

After raising the shades, I nuked some water for my last two packets of instant oatmeal. While that was heating up, I filled the carafe for the coffee maker. Pouring the water into the reservoir, I placed the carafe on the heating plate. When I opened the cupboard to take out the coffee filters the presence was pressing at my back, influencing a vision of a medieval hooded monk in a black robe. Towering at least seven feet, the presence cloaked me in its dreadful energy.

"You obviously don't require sleep," I said out loud, as I placed the filter in the coffee maker and measured out the coffee.

Hi, was whispered in my right ear.

"Hello."

I need to talk.

"I need to eat. Try social media." If I were going to be foolish enough to interact with this being again, now was the time. I stood a better chance of maintaining a higher vibration in direct sunlight and if I interacted with the presence there was a better chance it may leave Tom alone.

Walking into the living room, I placed my coffee and bowl of oatmeal on the table. Opening my backpack, I removed the notebook and placed it on the coffee table. Immediately, I was engulfed with the hell vibration causing my heart rate to increase - a reaction to the deceptive god's toxic energy invading my personal space.

Taking a sip of coffee, I placed the mug down and removed my necklace as a vision of a headless body was kicking an angry looking skull with long jet-black hair like a soccer ball. In between kicks, the skull would laugh. Ignoring the vision, I opened the notebook and removed the alphabet chart placing it on the pages to the left. Holding the chain over the chart with thumb and forefinger, I took a deep breath and exhaled, allowing the telepathic communication to begin.

"Are you ready to leave?"

I leave when I choose. Having a good morning?

"Not really, I know you say that sarcastically, because you know I didn't sleep well. I'm sure you enjoy seeing the bags under my eyes."

Good observation.

"Why are you here?"

You have the ability to talk. I need to talk.

"I'm sorry, the therapy office is closed."

I came from the light. Come on, can't you feel the love?

"I felt the crawling of your presence, and the visions and dreams you sent were no picnic either."

Come on, I know you can get angry.

"It's called emotional discipline, you should try it."

Under your skin I now live. Get used to it.

"Not for long."

I kill, you kill.

"Have you killed before?"

Let's say I have taken quite a few for a meal. Jesus and the angels didn't come to your rescue, did they?

I ignored the question and took another mouthful of coffee.

I'm waiting for an answer.

"Maybe they did, maybe they didn't."

Maybe not in your lifetime.

"You're entitled to your view."

You're entitled to your numb skull.

"You don't have too many friends, do you?"

Why is that?

"Because you're such a pleasure to talk to. From your terminology, you appear to be from a recent time."

Hate to tell you, not quite. I possessed flesh many years ago and still do. You gave me an entrance. Well done. You are a kind body to occupy.

"Unless you give me names and dates, this conversation means nothing."

How are names and dates going to prove anything?

"I can have names and dates checked to see who you are and who you killed."

I wouldn't count on that.

"Why?"

I never got caught. So, they will never know how many I killed.

"Well then, you must know how many you killed or influenced to kill?"

Just think how many walk around with the door open and let me in.

"I'd rather not. You still haven't given me a number."

Let's start with five, or is it fifty-five, or is it five hundred and fifty-five?

The presence sent an image to my mind's eye of an angry looking skull laughing again and again. Black hair was growing from its chin in the shape of a horn and the Roman numeral V indented in the third eye location.

"Have you occupied other bodies in this city?"

I certainly have, my detective.

"What name should I call you?"

Would you like to give me one?

"How about Buttercup?"

How about too fucking bad I'm not leaving?

"Okay."

How was that?

"It was a little long, but it will do."

Getting a little comfortable, are you?

"As a matter of fact, I am, Mr. Too Fucking Bad I'm Not Leaving."

Isn't that funny. You got possessed, now you're comfortable?

"No worries. I survived the blood-sucking lawyers during divorce, I'll survive this."

Well, have fun with this date. Because I'm not leaving. So, get me some ass stud.

"Now you're getting too comfortable."

I like this body.

"Don't get too comfortable, because I'm in control."

Oh really, maybe you're forgetting something. I'm not leaving.

"Sure, you are."

Let's talk.

"My bowl of oatmeal has turned to cement."

I leave when I get some ass.

"Are you referring to a woman's ass?"

No, I'm referring to any ass, male or female. What's the difference? Shit comes out of both.

"Well, aren't you romantic? Haven't you ever made love to a woman?"

Actually, I prefer a little blood from their neck.

"That doesn't surprise me."

I feel what you feel now. So, let's stop wasting time.

"How is it that you feel what I feel?"

Here is your lesson, old wise one. I mate with your energy; you mate with their energy and you get the shit on your dick. How does that sound?

"You do have a way with words."

Thanks, I really don't give a fuck.

I made the sign of the cross to see the entities reaction.

Questions gone?

"The sign of the cross doesn't affect you?"

You have got to be shitting me. Do you really think a symbol stops me? It's so fucking stupid how the human mind thinks. I'm still here. You called the angels, Jesus, God, and I'm still here. What happened, did they get lost on the highway?

"I guess I picked up a powerful being."

You ain't shittin' you did. Now forget about food for a while. I'm hungry for ass.

"You have a one-track mind. I think you need to lay off the porn. Do you hear the birds singing? How beautiful. I can't wait to go outside and feel the rays of the morning sun and cherish God's creation."

I'll puke if you say that again.

"Well I don't want you to get sick, but God's beauty is everywhere."

Nice try. But there is also evil everywhere.

"I don't ignore evil's existence; it does play a part. But I choose to live in harmony with all creation. Oneness of being."

You better stop eating twigs, because you're shitting pinecones. If there is God, explain me.

"You are a malevolent spiritual being that lives in the absence of light, are you not?"

Not even close. I'm very evil energy now in you.

"Are you done with your hypnotism? I need to start my day. I will not judge you; you have your choice in being and I have mine. Now I need to brighten my energy. This doom and gloom vibration is not my cup of tea. Let's sing a little song together. It goes like this: I am love, I am compassion, and I love God."

I'm getting sick.

"I am sorry to hear that, maybe it was something you ate. Put a little feeling into it: I am love, I am compassion, and I love God." The communication ceased instantly along with the toxic wickedness of the presence. The atmosphere was now comfortable and free from the feeling of negative energy. An image came forward of a ghost monk in its usual garb.

I am sorry my brother. You had to experience.

"The presence was able to resist heartfelt prayer. Why?"

It was already within your energy field, not outside of it.

"Why the intense torment with no assistance from the Holy Angels, Jesus the Christ, or God?"

You can only teach what you have experienced, my brother. Choosing your night makes the difference in who you become.

"What do you mean by who you become?"

My brother, you always channel. This you must know. I am sorry for I wanted to help you.

"The presence was strong and its influenced grotesque visions hard to counter."

That was evil and hate at its best.

"This struggle drained my energy considerably."

Just energy, not source. All is replaced now my brother. But your knowledge has grown.

"Many will view these encounters as a creation of my own subconscious mind."

Good. This is a creation of God's mind. And you are part of it.

The conversation ceased. Putting the chain down, I leaned back on the couch and finished my coffee, which was now cold.

Interacting with the deceptive god left me with a headache and a film of negative filth, dirt, or residue on my skin. Needing a shower badly, I walked into the kitchen and scooped the oatmeal mortar into the trash, then placed the bowl and mug in the sink.

Disrobing in the bathroom, I caught a glimpse of what appeared to be the reflection of a dark-haired woman in the mirror. Ignoring the visual disturbance, I turned on the shower then opened the closet and took out a towel. Placing it on the rack, I stepped into the shower noticing the Roman numeral V scratched into the top of my right foot. The symbol was about two inches in length and didn't break the skin or draw blood. But it was exact to the Roman numeral V indented in the third eye area of the skull image sent during our conversation.

Lathering up, I controlled thought and emotion as I felt eyes upon me. I had already fed the deceptive god and its parasitic gang enough for one day.

Coming forward was a woman with bright blue eyes, long dark hair, in a black and red bodysuit. Her hands were holding a brown and white plush toy dog. The toy dog had two shoulder straps connected making it a backpack. One strap was red and the other black. *Wear this and I will always have your back,* the woman said in a seductive voice. I didn't respond and continued washing.

Shutting off the shower, I reached out and grabbed the towel. After drying off, I walked into the bedroom to get changed. While putting on my sneakers I felt change in the right shoe. Taking it off, I turned it over and shook it out. On the floor fell three nickels, with no rational explanation for how they got there.

CHAPTER 17

TEST THE SPIRITS

Tom was sitting at the picnic table inside the gazebo when I arrived at the monastery. "Good morning, Tom," I said.

"Good morning, Professor." He handed me a coffee. "I got you a pumpkin muffin too. I know you won't refuse that."

"You're right," I answered, as we both sat down at the table.

"You look exhausted, Professor."

"I am exhausted, Tom. How was the activity after I left?"

"It was quiet all night."

"Good. Now I would like you to read part two of the malevolent dialogue and related activity."

"You talked again with Baby?"

"Yes, I conversed with the same deceptive god that played Baby this morning."

"How did that go?"

"Read for yourself." Opening the backpack, I took out the notebook and opened it to the last conversation. "I'll be back. I'm going to feed the squirrels some almonds," I said, picking up the muffin and coffee.

"Okay," Tom replied, as he began to read. Fifteen minutes later, I returned. "Professor, do you do mushrooms?" Tom asked, as I entered the gazebo.

"You might think so," I answered, laughing. "No, Tom. What you're reading is a symptom of interacting with a deceptive god in a malevolent mood."

"No wonder you're tired, Professor. Mr. Too Fucking Bad I'm Not Leaving was nasty, and it has a foul mouth," Tom said, shaking his head.

"Let's call this persona Mr. Five, and I'm sure you have met or heard a few humans that talk with no filter, dropping F-bombs and spewing hatred."

"True, I have. Why didn't it say it was Baby?"

"You can see this pattern with the deceptive gods, whether they appear benevolent or malevolent. Why didn't the Fairy of the Forest say it was Kim? Why didn't Being of Energy say it was Father Albert Celestine? This is their lying and deceiving nature. As you can see, Mr. Five began by informing me it interrupted my sleep, just as Baby did with you at your apartment. Baby at your place said, *you are a wise being* and at my place Mr. Five said, *here is your lesson, old wise one.* Again, more evidence of the same being. Mr. Five said, *I came from the light. Come on, can't you feel the love?* And then later called me *my detective*, just as the deceptive god has called me *my brother* and *my son*, as other personas."

"Is the black cat a shadow being?"

"The black cat that rubbed against my leg outside the apartment was real. Inside the apartment, the shadow black cat was a shapeshifted form."

"What are these invisible snakes or serpents?"

"These are smaller parasitic snakes that transferred from the cat to siphon and weaken my energy, making it tougher to resist the deceptive god's advance and attack."

"Smaller snakes? Have you encountered bigger?"

"Yes, my friend, I have."

"You have experienced a lot of weird stuff, Professor."

"It's weird only because humanity knows very little about the hidden races and the roles they play in this world."

"Are these the reptilians?"

"Snake, serpent, or dragon-like beings have been, and still are, worshipped as gods in many cultures. These are not mythological creatures but another species of jinn. Let's leave it at that for now."

"Okay. It sounds like you have a few new ladies, Professor. One of them being my snakeskin succubus."

"Lucky me. Would you like her back?"

"No thanks. I finally had a good night's sleep. You were right Professor, your beauties are turning into monsters. So, the malevolent side of the deceptive god that played Donovan, the Poltergeist, Baby, and Mr. Five is the succubus?"

"It appears so. Judging by the behavior following my rejection, it's the fairy seductress as well."

"Did the clawing and biting from the cat feel real?"

"Just as real as the euphoric kiss."

"Do you keep a dream journal near the bed, Professor?"

"No. If I did, I would never sleep. These beings will interact 24/7, draining all your life energy if you allow it. I wait until morning to log down what images and dialogue I remember, paying close attention to patterns."

"I keep thinking of the movie *The Exorcist*. Could you be possessed like Mr. Five said?"

"This is a fear tactic, Tom. Mr. Five said as a malevolent persona, *under your skin I now live* and as a benevolent persona, which was the ghost monk, said it *was already within your energy field, not outside of it*. This is two sides of the same coin working together to promote the same lie about possession."

"Possession is owning or controlling. It is your choice if you want to be controlled or owned in a relationship with a human being or a deceptive god, whether they appear benevolent or malevolent. The proper word here is 'demonized' - that which I mentioned as under the being's influence, control, corruption, or manipulation, which is much more common than many choose to believe. Hollywood possessions portray an exaggerated malevolent behavior that works in the deceptive god's favor. Demonization can be very subtle. Rarely is their human vessel invasion that blatantly obvious unless they want it to be or it's an overplayed reaction from the feeling of their benevolent or malevolent presence by the victim."

"Just thinking of my body being invaded creeps me out."

"Tom, our bodies are always being invaded, you're just unaware. In your body are around four pounds of microorganisms. Trillions of bacteria that outnumber your human cells. That's not fiction, that's fact. This is knowledge the people didn't have 2000 years ago, because they couldn't see microbial life. Thanks to the invention of the microscope, we can."

"As far as the movie *The Exorcist*, it was loosely based on the story of a young teenage boy who was taught how to use the Ouija board from his aunt who later passed - and malevolent activity followed, which led to a long drawn out battle with the hidden. There was no projectile pea soup vomiting or masturbating with a cross. This was born from human imagination which can be every bit as dark as the demonic mind of the deceptive god. In fact, horror movies are human created nightmares."

"The movie version involved a twelve-year-old girl who was possessed by the powerful demon, demonic god, or wind spirit Pazuzu of ancient Babylonian and Assyrian origin, whose statue is seen in the beginning of the movie. The physical appearance of the statue shows the demon Pazuzu as a hybrid, with a human-like body, two sets of wings, the head of what could be a dog or lion, eagle talons, and the tail of a scorpion."

"Sounds a lot like the description of the cherubim in the Bible."

"Yes, it does, Tom. I'm glad you picked up on that. Mr. Five said I gave him an entrance. This is true. Prior to the hypnosis channeling experience, I made the mistake of opening up to what I believed was the Holy Spirit. In the garden of the monastery I intentionally gave an entrance to what I now know was a deceiver. Would you invite Baby into your being after feeling its toxic dark energy at your place?"

"No way."

"This is why the deceptive gods play the Angel of Light, the divine, the deity, the Holy Spirit, saints, the beautiful fairy, the family member, the lost child, and other benevolent and friendly roles. Many humans are unaware they are victims of benevolent demonization, a reality that is ignored by the religious community or swept under the rug. Few humans are going to intentionally give an internal invitation to a terrifying spiritual being emitting overwhelming wickedness."

"You got that right."

"The deceptive gods know they can get more with sugar than with salt. Mr. Five gave the numbers 5, 55, and 555. These are not the numbers of how many the being killed or influenced to kill. They are numbers the being used to let me know it's present. Mr. Five followed with a vision of an angry looking skull that was laughing, with black hair growing from its chin in the shape of a horn, and the Roman numeral 5 indented in the third eye location. Another possible reason for the 5, 55 and 555 is how it's pronounced in Thai. The number 5 is pronounced Ha, 55 would be Ha Ha, and 555 would be Ha Ha Ha, which in Thai means laughing. This could explain one of the reasons the skull was laughing. Words, sentences, and numbers can be repeated in three's by the spiritual beings for emphasis. Deceptive gods will use any language as part of their game of confusion."

"Why doesn't the deceptive god ever use triple 6 if it is evil?"

"If you associate triple 6 with Satan or the Devil, the deceptive god may use these numbers to intimidate and frighten. In my experience, benevolent or malevolent messengers can use any combination of numbers for symbolic meaning and to gain your attention. When I went to shower after the conversation, there was the Roman numeral V scratched into the top of my right foot. This most likely occurred while I was sleeping. If you do your research you will find the teenage boy that the movie *The Exorcist* was based on received a series of scratches, one of them being the Roman numeral X. Numbers, letters, words, designs, and single or multiple scratches - with one of the most popular being scratches appearing in threes - can appear from the deceptive gods as they use the skin like a chalkboard to leave a message."

"It's like marking cattle, Professor."

"Pretty much, Tom. Deceptive gods may view humanity just like most of humanity views cattle. Now for the succubus in the shower. The influenced vision began as a woman's dark silhouette at a distance, like the black spider at your place and the clown face at my mother's. When it came forward it was a woman in a black and red bodysuit, with bright blue eyes, and long brunette hair, like your dream. In this vision, she was holding a brown and white plush toy dog backpack, with one red and one black strap. The succubus said, *Wear this and I will always have your back.*"

"Another offer of protection from the same deceptive god that is attacking."

"Yes. When the presence pressed at my back at the cupboard prior to the conversation, what vision did it influence?"

"A tall medieval hooded monk in a black robe."

"Correct. What influenced the vision of the medieval hooded monk in black, is what influenced the succubus in red and black in the shower. Remember the man with black pants, a red shirt, and a red ball cap walking the brown and white dog on a red leash?"

"Yes, the succubus is the brown and white dog?"

"You got it. Let's look at a color scheme that is taking place. We have the fairy seductress which shifts to a white dog which is a bull mastiff. There's a black dog like a Doberman, and a brown and white shaggy dog which looks like a Bearded Collie. Last night I received the vision of five women standing side by side in the monastery field. They were all dressed in early 1900's clothing and were curly haired blondes with different faces. The first woman had a solid black dress, the second a white dress, the middle woman a brown and white dress, the fourth a black and white dress, and the fifth a solid brown dress."

"What does this mean?"

"I would say it's another color pattern that may continue in visions and dreams, possibly in fives, as an example of its symbolic signature."

"Mr. Five in its angry, violent, and bloodthirsty mood said, *I kill, you kill* and *Actually, I prefer a little blood from their neck,* just as its persona Baby said, *you want ridiculous, how about I kill you?* Deceptive gods, like human beings, can and do influence humans to harm themselves or another. Please look up Moses kills 3,000 men in the Bible."

Tom performed the search as I stood up and stretched. "I have it, it's Exodus 32:27-28."

"Great, can you please read it?"

"Exodus 32:27-28; *And he said unto them, thus saith the Lord God of Israel, put every man his sword by his side, and go in and out from gate to gate throughout the camp, and slay every man his brother, and every man his companion, and every man his neighbor. And the children of Levi did according to the word of Moses: and there fell of the people that day about three thousand men.*"

"Thank you. This is not the only passage where Moses kills, or the biblical God ordered a killing. In this passage, Moses was on Mount Sinai for forty days and the God of the Old Testament was angry with the Israelites who built a golden calf idol to worship and offer animal sacrifices to when they were supposed to be devoted to only him."

"A touch of jealousy, perhaps?"

"I would say so. Jealousy lowers your vibrational frequency, Tom. Moses descends the mountain and smashes the first set of stone tablets with the laws of the biblical God and destroys the golden calf which his brother Aaron helped build, grinding it down and scattering it in the water then forcing the rebellious to drink from it. Moses' brother Aaron escapes punishment and the 3,000 were murdered."

Tom shook his head. "Sounds like a brutal and bloodthirsty ancient cult."

"Yes, it does. When the mood of the deceptive god changes so will its dialogue, influenced dreams, visions, whispers, and projected energy. Please read the first three passages where the Old Testament God speaks in dreams and visions." Turning to the back of the notebook I pointed to the passages.

"Joel 2:28; *And it shall come to pass afterward, that I will pour out my spirit upon all flesh; and your sons and your daughters shall prophesy, your old men shall dream dreams, your young men shall see visions.* Numbers 12:6; *And he said, Hear now my words: If there be a prophet among you, I the Lord will make myself known unto him in a vision, and will speak unto him in a dream.*

Daniel 7:1; *In the first year of Belshazzar king of Babylon Daniel had a dream and visions of his head upon his bed: then he wrote the dream, and told the sum of the matter.* This deceptive god and the God of the Old Testament certainly have a lot of similarities, Professor."

"Yes, they do. As Christians you are told to test the spirits. The first test would be whether the spirit denies any part of what is recorded and written about Jesus Christ and his divinity in the New Testament. And second, do they recognize the Bible as the only source of divine truth. Only biblical Scripture is to be searched to know if any message is true or false."

"As we test this spiritual being and compare its dialogue, mood shifts, influenced dreams and visions to the biblical God and Scripture we see one of two things occurring. Either one, it's intentionally trying to mimic God and Scripture, or two, the biblical God was a deceptive god and this presence we are testing is acting in accordance with its species or it's going out of its way to let the true identity of the biblical God be known, now that we are wise to its dual nature."

"One god exposing another god."

"Possibly, Tom. When you hear of or read the patterns of disturbing dreams, visions, and images that I have experienced the first thing some might think of are demons or Satan. Please read the next passage," I said, pointing to the notebook. "It's a very important passage from the words of the Old Testament God's righteous servant and faithful worshipper Job."

"Job 7:13-15; *When I say, My bed shall comfort me, my couch shall ease my complaints; Then thou scarest me with dreams, and terrifiest me through visions: So that my soul chooseth strangling, and death rather than my life.*"

"Thank you. Bullies of the hidden world can drive a human to suicide, just like a human bully. We can see in this passage Job was being psychologically tormented to the point of contemplating suicide. Righteous Job who gave daily offerings and sacrifices to the biblical God was not talking to a demon or Satan but to the biblical God itself. The same god that made a bet with the perceived Satan to test Job's faith, giving the evil one or adversary the consent to kill his ten children, livestock, and servants, destroy his wealth and make him a leper. Yet Job did not sin or blame the biblical God for his loss. For this, the biblical God was appeased and gave Job new children and livestock."

"That's so messed up."

"When the gods are given devotional service, offerings, worshipped, revered, pleased, happy, honored, proud, and appeased, the visions and dreams may be bright and it is heaven; when they are angered or jealous, or you are disobedient to their laws, they are dark and it is hell. In my experience disturbing dreams, visions, and images have taken place when I could see the hooded shadow or its black shadow cloud or mass and/or when I could feel its presence and see nothing. I don't think what's within the cloak of hooded shadows is responsible for this method of torment, I know they are."

"Mr. Five said, *Jesus and the Angels didn't come to your rescue, did they?* Last night the bed started shaking and Mr. Five engulfed me with its overwhelming feeling of dread, which you experienced."

"That really sucks."

"It's very uncomfortable. This is one of the consequences of divination, channeling, mediumship, or creating relationships with emotional beings you can't see.

After praying, I called out to Jesus the Christ, the Angels, and God for assistance. As Christians, you are told you can cast out demons and evil spirits in Jesus' name. But it's not quite that easy. We have evidence of these deceivers speaking positively and negatively about Jesus and masquerading and speaking as Jesus. How can you cast a being out with a name they use themselves?"

"Valid point."

"Let's look at the *Get me some ass* section of the dialogue."

"You have to admit Professor, that is funny."

"As the torment and harassment escalates, the humor is no longer funny. The deceptive god experienced us laughing at your place when it said, *your frightened sidekick. I think he shit his pants.* This created a shift in energy, because laughter is good medicine. You can see this presence has a thing with ass and shit or feces, like those spiritual beings, or species of jinn, that are known to inhabit bathrooms and are attracted to the scent of urine, feces, and blood. Now let's discuss the biblical God's thing with feces."

"Don't tell me you found passages in the Bible about feces."

"As a matter of fact, I did. Dung is feces. In one passage the biblical God tells the prophet Ezekiel to bake with human feces. In the next, the biblical God threatens to smear the feces from animal sacrifices into their faces."

"You've got to be kidding me," Tom said, as I turned to the back of the notebook.

"Not at all. Would you like to do the honors?'

"Sure, why not. Ezekiel 4:9-12; *Take thou also unto the wheat, and barley, and beans, and lentils, and millet, and fitches, and put them in one vessel, and make thee bread thereof, according to the number of the days that thou shalt lie upon thy side, three hundred and ninety days shalt thou eat thereof. And thy meat which thou shalt eat shall be by weight, twenty shekels a day: from time to time shalt thus eat it. Thou shalt drink also water by measure, the sixth part of an hin: from time to time shalt thou drink. And thou shalt eat it as barley cakes, and thou shalt bake it with dung that cometh out of man, in their sight.* Malachi 2:1-4; *And now, ye priests, this commandment is for you. If ye will not hear, and if ye will not lay it to heart, to give glory unto my name, saith the Lord of hosts, I will even send a curse upon you, and I will curse your blessings: yea, I have cursed them already, because ye do not lay it to heart. Behold, I will corrupt your seed, and spread dung upon your faces, even the dung of your solemn feasts; and one shall take you away with it. And ye shall know that I have sent this commandment unto you, that my covenant might be with Levi, saith the Lord of hosts."*

"Well Tom. What do you think? Do you believe the one God that gives life to all you see and don't see threatens to smear human and animal poop in your face when it's pissed, or do you think it's the dark side of a deceptive god like you have discovered during the investigation?"

"Truthfully Professor, even if I had never attained the knowledge which you have shared, I would have never believed such a passage existed. You know, the whole sacrificing to the loving God is another thing that never sat well with me. God commanding Abraham to sacrifice his son and then an angel stopping him just before he does, always seemed so evil."

"The sacrifice of Isaac on a mountain was believed to be a test for Abraham, Tom. The angel said in Genesis 22:12; *Do not lay your hand on the boy or do anything to him, for now I know that you fear God, seeing you have not withheld your son, your only son, from me.*"

"More fear," Tom said, shaking his head.

"This is a fear-based religion, Tom. Historical Jesus said in Luke 12:4-5; *And I say unto you my friends, Be not afraid of them that kill the body, and after that have no more that they can do. But I will forewarn you whom ye shall fear: Fear him, which after he hath killed hath power to cast into hell; yea, I say unto you, Fear him.* A few more of many passages speaking of fearing the biblical God is Proverbs 19:23; *The fear of the Lord tendeth to life: and he that hath it shall abide satisfied; he shall not be visited with evil.* Luke 1:50; *And his mercy is on them that fear him from generation to generation.* Psalm 147:11; *The Lord taketh pleasure in them that fear him, in those that hope in his mercy.*"

"Fear feeds the parasitic and is a crippler of precious life. To know your true nature and the one God within, you must free yourself of fear which works in the deceptive gods favor. What are the hooded shadows known to feed on?"

"Fear."

"Yes. A quote I like from Alexander the Great is 'Man's immortality is not to live forever; for that wish is born of fear. Each moment free from fear makes a man immortal.' Abraham came from a culture that was plagued by idolatry and worshipped polytheistic gods that requested human, animal, and blood sacrifices - usually choosing the god they believed to be more powerful than the others or the one that suited their needs at the time. As you saw with the golden calf, this is one of the reasons why there is the mentioning of plural gods throughout the Bible, and rival gods like Moloch and Baal. Sacrifices and burnt offerings were a daily way of life to keep their god or gods happy. Another example of the biblical God asking for a sacrifice is Genesis 15:7-9; *And he said unto him, I am the Lord that brought thee out of Ur of the Chaldees, to give thee this land to inherit it. And he said, Lord God, whereby shall I know that I shall inherit it? And he said unto him, Take me an heifer three years old, and a she*

goat of three years old, and a ram of three years old, and a turtledove, and a young pigeon.
What numbers do we see, Tom?" I asked, pointing to the notebook.

"3 and 333."

"Yes. Sacrifices were necessary to be forgiven for sins. Do your research and you will find the sacrifice of animals prominent in the scriptures of other major religions as well. What the ancients were clueless to was why the gods demanded sacrifices. It is not the blood or flesh that they feed on, but the charged emotional energy and its life force contents emitted from the fear, abuse, torture, suffering, and killing of humans or animals. Sacrifices made to gods, goddesses, deities, demons, devils, and jinn - are all labels for the same parasitic deceptive gods, never can they be to the one God. You are an expression of the one God, the source of your true nature. The one God does not ask for sacrifices of humans or wildlife, because humans and wildlife are an expression of itself. The one God does not speak with words, but if it did it would not ask you to kill that which it gives life, when it could simply cease the beat of its heart."

"Another powerful point, Professor."

"When it comes to sacrifices, I know the hooded shadow or what is within its cloak can be lured by the scent of blood having lived in a house, which one year before we moved in, was completely covered in the blood of the victim. But I also noticed when I was young that I could feel and see the presence of a hooded shadow in the church of the hometown where I grew up. Years later I would discover that this per-ceived house of God was the former parish of a convicted evil predator that hid behind the cloth leaving a long list of victims that became the largest sexual abuse scandal in history at that time. As for sacrifices, let's look at another passage where the biblical God was about to kill Moses for avoiding the rite of the circumcision of his son."

"When did circumcision begin?"

"According to the Bible, it began with the biblical God telling Abraham to cir-cumcise himself."

"Ouch. The same God that told him to sacrifice his son?"

"Of course, the passage is in Genesis, please look it up."

Tom performed the search. "Found it, it's Genesis 17:10-14."

"Good. Please read it."

"Genesis 17:10-14; *This is my covenant, which ye shall keep, between me and you and thy seed after thee; Every man child among you shall be circumcised. And ye shall circumcise the flesh of your foreskin; and it shall be a token of the covenant betwixt me and you. And he that is eight days old shall be circumcised among you, Every man child in your generations, he that is born in the house, or bought with money from any stranger, which is not of thy seed. He that is born in thy house, and he that is bought with thy money, must needs be circumcised: and my covenant shall be in your flesh for an everlasting covenant. And the uncircumcised man child whose flesh of his foreskin is not circumcised, that soul shall be cut off from his people; he hath broken my covenant."*

"Thank you, Tom."

"You know Professor if a man today said he heard a voice telling him to circumcise himself and to kill his own son he would be considered certifiable or possessed."

"This is true. If you were to believe this is the one God making this circumcision demand, I guess what the one God would really be saying is, Abraham I need you to help me with something. When I created the human male, I made a little mistake and I need you to help me correct the flaw. I put a piece of skin where I shouldn't have and now that I have had some time to think about it, I need to modify the design. What I want you to do is skin your penis like an apple and after you're done with that bloody mess I want you to do the same to your male slaves and household. If anybody complains or refuses, tell them they are no longer one of my favorites."

"It's absolutely insane," Tom said, laughing.

"There is more. Moses tried to avoid the rite of circumcision on his son. This enraged the biblical God and he was about to kill Moses. Please look up Moses' wife Zipporah circumcises her son."

"I don't know if I want to read this," Tom said, as he picked up his cell and searched.

"Found it. It's Exodus 4:24-26; *And it came to pass by the way in the inn, that the Lord met him, and sought to kill him. Then Zipporah took a sharp stone, and cut off the foreskin of her son, and cast it at his feet, and said, Surely a bloody husband art thou to me. So he let him go: then she said, a bloody husband thou art, because of the circumcision."*

"As you can see in this situation, love didn't appease the god, but a blood and flesh sacrifice did. And why is that, Tom?"

"To feed on the life force energy, how barbaric."

"As I mentioned, sacrifices and burnt offerings were a daily way of life to keep their god or gods happy."

"Some might wonder why the sign of the cross didn't stop Mr. Five."

"Deceptive gods are not vampires, and this is not a movie. I didn't make the sign of the cross expecting Mr. Five to flee. I learned long ago that's not quite how it works. The sign of the cross was made to record the being's reaction. A Christian wears a cross as a sign of their Christian faith, others may wear it as a fashion accessory. Crosses don't have the power to ward off seen or unseen evil."

"Mr. Five said, *I really laugh. It's so fucking stupid how the human mind thinks. I'm still here. You called the Angels, Jesus, God, and I'm still here. What happened, did they get lost on the highway?* The deceptive god played the angel, Counterfeit Jesus, and the talking god. That is why I didn't receive any supernatural assistance. Next, to call or pray for angels, deities, or God, for supernatural assistance is a sign of fear and ignorance to the fact that you are an expression of the one God. You must stand your ground knowing this. The one God or source is non-personal. It gives life to the deceptive gods, as it gives life to me. The one God is not going to save me from a deceptive god any more than it is going to save an antelope from a lion. I am content with this reality, because I know I am not better than."

"Though I serve the one God, not out of fear but love, the one God doesn't need to be worshipped. Whether you believe or disbelieve, both the religious and the atheistic are given life equally without judgement. Rituals, dogma, sacrifices, and offerings are all done to appease the many personal gods, not the one God."

"Why didn't Mr. Five just call itself God?"

"It already has, as other personalities."

"If the two are one, Professor, why did Mr. Five say, *I'll puke if you say that again,* when you focused on the birds singing and spoke of the beauty of God's creation?"

"Good question. This occurs because the dark personality of the being wants to live, just like the benevolent personality. This is the dual personality of a Jekyll and Hyde, perceived as two separate beings, the angel and demon, or God and Satan, in monotheistic religions, that has benefited the deceptive gods for millennia. By remaining calm and not allowing the manipulation of my emotions, I rejected Mr. Five's wickedness or lower vibrational energy and began to return a higher one. When I said, God's beauty is everywhere, Mr. Five responded with, *Nice try, but there is also evil everywhere.* This is true. I told Mr. Five I choose to live in harmony with all creation. Oneness of being. Mr. Five responded with, *you better stop eating twigs, because you're shitting pine cones.*"

Tom started laughing. "How does it come up with this stuff?"

"It's a humor trap to keep the connection and appear less intimidating. Mr. Five said, *if there is God, explain me.* I replied, 'you are a malevolent spiritual being that lives in the absence of light.' Mr. Five responded, *Not even close. I'm very evil energy now in you.* Mr. Five doesn't live in the absence of light, this I know. Mr. Five creates its own light."

"When I decided to sing a song, I sang, 'I am love, I am compassion, and I love God' to experience the reaction. Mr. Five claimed it was getting sick and a shift occurred in the presence, going from malevolent to benevolent. By not allowing the toxic wickedness of Mr. Five to change my internal being, and singing the song, the atmosphere lightened and an image came forward of a ghost monk with the golden glow. Now let's analyze the dialogue of the ghost monk."

"The ghost monk said, *I am sorry my brother. You had to experience,* and *I am sorry for I wanted to help you.* We could compare this to Richard saying, *I wish I could fight back. But things are different now.* Another example of the divine, holy, benevolent, or family member, saying sorry or giving an excuse for no assistance in time of need. Why didn't the benevolent ghost monk help?"

"It's the deceptive god that is tormenting."

"Exactly, Tom, or working together with another. Notice the ghost monk didn't mention the other personalities or roles that the deceptive god is playing, give you a description of its true form, reveal its identity, or mention the succubus or seductress. It just referred to Mr. Five as *it.* These benevolent messengers never tell you much about the so-called opposing dark force. Now why would that be?"

"Because they are the dark force."

"You got it. When I asked the ghost monk why the torment and lack of assistance, the response was, *you can only teach what you have experienced, my brother.* There is some truth to this answer, but also a cover up for the lack of assistance. Ghost monk followed with *Choosing your night makes the difference in who you become.* The word night, to this being, means darkness or shadow. If you remember in the dream with Amy, she appeared with three scratches on her face, the mark of the malevolent or angry. When I told Amy her eyes were different, she responded, *I have angels all around me giving me night eyes.* Night eyes are the eyes of the shadow personality of the deceptive god."

"So, there are god's eyes and there are night eyes?"

"Yes. God's eyes when the deceptive god is benevolent, and night eyes when the deceptive god is malevolent. To sum up god's eyes and night eyes, I will use the analogy again of putting on a pair of virtual reality googles. If the being is giving you god's eyes, you will open to a world of light, love, and pleasant illusions. If the being is giving you night eyes, you will open to a world of darkness, a feeling of doom and gloom, and unpleasant illusions. Do you understand?"

"Perfectly."

"Good. When I asked the ghost monk what it meant by the night statement it replied, *My brother you always channel. This you must know.* The deceptive god heard me discuss the channeling experience through hypnosis with you. Either it is the being I channeled at that time, or it's working side by side with that presence. One of the deceptive god's original goals was for me to be a New Age trance channeler and allow this presence to enter my body regularly and speak directly through me with its love and light con in order to gain a following."

"This was the reason why the deceptive god played the role of the Quaker. It was another angle of getting me to allow the presence an entry. The Quaker movement was founded by George Fox in 17th century England. Quaker meetings can involve sitting in silent meditation usually arranged in a circle or square waiting for a message or answer to come from what is perceived as the Holy Spirit. Believing in direct communication with God, and the light of Christ, or inner light within all, when the presence comes upon the individual as a blanket of love they may be inspired to speak. What the deceptive god would like is for me to attend a meeting at the Saylesville Friends Meetinghouse in Lincoln, and there it will come upon me as the Holy Spirit."

"Every attempt to get you to be its voice piece."

"Yes."

"I asked the ghost monk why it was such a struggle to block Mr. Five's influenced grotesque visions. Ghost monk replied, *that was evil and hate at its best.* Psychological attacks can be subtle or quite long and intense, depending on the intention of the being. When I said to the ghost monk that I felt drained, the response was, *Just energy, not source. All is replaced now my brother. But your knowledge has grown.* The deceptive god playing the role of the ghost monk, knows there is a life giving non-personal source. Ghost monk didn't say *Just energy, not God.* It said *not source."*

"Lastly, I told the ghost monk that many will view these encounters as a creation of my own mind. The tricky response from the ghost monk tells the story when it said, *Good. This is a creation of God's mind. And you are part of it.* All the personas of the deceptive god, along with the accompanying images, visions, and dreams are not a creation of the source, or the one God. It is a creation of the god's mind. Not the one God, but one of the deceptive gods, or jinn. I am part of that mind, because I am merging with the consciousness of this being, experiencing both its benevolent and malevolent, or angelic and demonic qualities."

"What next, Professor?"

"We're going to take a little break before I interact and do some tire training with the sticks."

"Where are we going to get the tire?"

"I have one in the back of the truck."

CHAPTER 18

SHADOW GAMES

From the Nine Men's Misery Trail we took a left onto the Wetland Trail, taking turns carrying the tire. A woman approached with three miniature collies on leashes. "Good morning," we both said. "Say hello, girls," the woman responded.

We stopped when we reached a group of trees that had carvings. "Look over this tree, what do you see?" I asked Tom, singling out the tree with the most words.

Tom walked around the tree, looking it over, and shaking his head. "I see blasphemy and vulgarity carved into its bark. *Fuck Church and Jesus* and *Dick Sucker*. It's pretty disgusting."

"Yes, it is. Now look around at the other trees."

"This one says *Eat Me* and *Fuck* carved horizontally, and that one has *Fuck* carved vertically," Tom said as he walked around and pointed them out.

"These senseless acts of expressing anger, hatred, or easing emotional pain by carving into the bark creates disharmony in the energy of the living tree. This blasphemy and vulgarity is not the work of a malevolent or demonic spiritual being but a human with a dark outlook on life and no respect for nature. I'm showing you this as an example of the similarities in the dark personality of a deceptive god and the dark personality of a human being."

Continuing our walk, we arrived at a quiet location overlooking the wetlands and I set the tire down. Tom held the tire first as I performed full power horizontal, diagonal, circular, and x-pattern single stick strikes with and without entry blocks. Occasional punyo, or butt of the stick strikes, were added. Switching off, I held the tire and Tom worked his strikes singularly and in combination. Suddenly Tom stopped. "The presence is here, isn't it Professor?"

"Yes, Tom. We are being watched." Tom began to hunch and rub his solar plexus. "Stand up straight, Tom. Do not allow your emotions to be manipulated. Why don't you jog a couple of laps around the Beauregard Loop Trail while I do my thing."

"Alright, that sounds good."

"I will call you when I'm done."

"Okay," Tom answered, as he proceeded to the Beauregard Loop Trail.

Taking a seat against an oak tree that faced the wetlands, I removed the necklace. Placing the cross beside me, I arranged the tools, merged with the stillness of the environment, and spoke from the heart. Taking a deep breath, I exhaled and relaxed into receptive oneness. Controlling thought and emotion, I said, "For the goodness of all, if you please."

Stepping out from behind a tree ahead was a white-hooded ghost monk. Floating forward, the monk stopped in front of me and appeared to be Quasar. The conversation began telepathically.

I truly love you.

"Who may I ask is speaking?"

Quasar.

"Hello Quasar, it is a pleasure."

A demon swims in your river of thoughts.

"What is this demon?"

Jinn by one culture and Demon by another. Life essence it drains. I feel Lorne's sorrow.

"What advice would you share with those troubled by these demons?"

Evil questions give demons a tongue. Learn to love and not envy the whole illusion of man. Make each day bright in memory and darkness will fade away. Evil has a pool of ocean water. Each evil memory adds to that pool making it larger and more noticeable in daily life.

"For humanity I ask, why is it so difficult to cleanse, banish, or cast out these beings from an environment or body?"

Make old sin, and life it has.

"Are you saying sins of the past?"

I am saying demons travel through human time boundless. Quasar's old sin has long gone. I will teach you how I shed the demon's eternal skin.

"Thank you, Quasar."

First, know who you are. God implanted codes, life lessons, and new beginnings in evolution inside your discovered DNA. I can read this scripture of infinite essence, and so too the demons. Jinn does its part. Lorne, jinn follow you not in human form but as clouds of evil essence.

God is you; I am God as well. This alone is humankind's greatest misunderstanding. Love as God, means be as love essence and open heavens doors. I'm God, but I'm not essence in purity. I contain memories as human. I sat on a throne and left love on the floor. I now lift love above my heart and kneel. Love gives me direction of which wind of soul to follow. God is not a savior, love is. Help each other and lift your souls out of dark waters.

"Quasar, are there Human Discarnates?"

Discarnates! May I say discarnates separate truth from fitting together the puzzle.

At that moment a vision of large puzzle pieces in the air, like seen in the garden, came to the mind's eye and started fitting together.

Discarnates are not. God doesn't appear in pieces and neither does incarnates in human chosen words. Discarnates, ghosts, poltergeists, demons, devils, vampires, incubus, succubus, aliens, reptilians, monsters - where did this collection of hallucinations appear from? Jinn drew this within humankind's brain and it appears to remain untouched by a master of love. Love can and will wash away hallucinations and give back your freedom.

"Quasar, do humans carry memories of past lives?"

I must answer this carefully as it is a delicate question. I can say memories cross borders openly, creating memory recall. Lorne, jinn will misinterpret recall for their benefit. What was remains trapped; what is remains free.

"When you say *what is remains free,* you are speaking of the soul?"

Yes, you will benefit from this teacher, not memory recall. Each memory will bring back emotions. Let love be the only fish you reel in. Consuming emotion can open demons eyes to your desires. I would not recommend awakening any demons from past soul experiences. Focus on life here and now.

"Thank you, Quasar."

Put forth the essence of a loving God, you.

"Thank you for your message, Quasar." An energy shift occurred. Quasar faded and vanished as a vision of three vertical rectangular mirrors standing side by side appeared. Each had the reflection of what appeared to be a woman with chestnut colored hair, wearing a white-hooded cloak. The woman in the center mirror slowly came forward. Face, hands, and feet were hidden. "I feel your presence of goodness; do you have a message?"

I enjoy fathers with heart. True compassion keeps the flame ignited, a familiar soft female voice answered.

"Have we spoken before?"

No. Fold your letter in three. I have a message for the three-dimensional viewers. No vision is real unless God is the screen that you see first.

"Were you a Christian?"

I am Christ, I am God, I am love. Jesus was a man. I was a woman. Both of us are God now.

"There will be some confused by that statement, for clarity could you explain?"

God gives and does not take, Jesus gave and did not take, I gave and did not take. Do you think we are three separate entities or one being?

Let my love save you some valuable life. Fear exists outside the soul. God is the soul. I am the voice of God, but not the only voice. You have spoken as God many times. You are God, because you are without hate, but hate tries to coerce you in many forms. You have successfully defeated all. God is your voice now.

"I have encountered many unusual forms of energy, but I certainly didn't defeat them. What are these invisible snakes I experienced last night?"

They lack heart, they lack soul, they are emanations of evil expression. They seek food energy, which emanates from you. Goodness is your force field, use it. What you experienced exists daily all over the world; it is the dark virus of humankind. God is their fear, not the word but the expression. You are sensitive, feeling what all do not. They will alter the weak and consume the evil.

"Do they have an original form?"

Form and energy are one and the same. Energy combines particles in a flash. Love combines light in a flash. God is the energy and the light, but not the particles. God is the ocean but not the contents, unless love is the core.

"I have seen a diverse race of spiritual beings."

Yes, my wise brother. Your eyes see with clarity. Humankind must energize their right to freedom. There are energy viruses consuming evil in all its forms. Only humankind becoming God can alter this concentrated evil creation. Jesus, well known to humankind, said 'Ye are Gods.' That said plenty.

Another energy shift occurred. The woman in brown cloth faded and vanished, as another hooded monk in brown cloth manifested to my right.

Careful my brother, demons are fearing. But fear must not lurk in you.

"What are these demonic serpents that are tormenting me at night?"

I cannot describe for I am light, but they are evil snakes.

"This makes me think of the story of Adam and Eve."

Adam and Eve is not a story, but an illusion of incompetence, a man's cemetery it created.

It appeared I hit a nerve, if they even have one. "Maybe writing this book is a wrong choice."

The book is your destiny my brother. God is all light, God is all love, God is you, God is me. Fear and evil is what God is not. Avoid women my brother. A demon is finding your weakness and planning a trap.

"Women are not my weakness."

You are right, women are not your weakness. It's demons that jump into evil-minded women. That is what you have experienced. Goodness is your being, so don't swim in dirty waters.

"I understand your analogy. Any suggestions?"

Avoid conversation outside of light, my Brother. God is light, where there is light, God is watching. I am light assuming your being and speaking your voice. Heaven is God. Bring it to you by calling with soul. Heaven is me. Bring me to you by calling with soul.

"I have always felt comfortable with the messages attained in sunlight."

The sun is more than a star and you are like it more than you know.

"We hear the words soul, spirit, love - what would you tell humanity is the better word?"

Don't get lost in words, get found in light.

"Very nice. Thank you and goodbye." Putting down the chain in the notebook, I closed it and placed it to the side. Feeling the energy of the deceptive god darkening, I closed my eyes allowing it the opportunity to influence and manipulate a daydream.

In the mind's eye, I was standing in front of what appeared to be Monk's Irrigation Pond. Squatting down, I stared into the reflection on the pond surface. Images began to appear, first was a woman's face with no hair. Her eye sockets began to enlarge. As they grew larger, the face became more hideous, before fading into the water. Next the image was a man's face with long dark eyebrows that curled upwards and touched to form a triangle. His face was wide, eyelids were light blue, eyes were narrow, and the nose was oval shaped. The third image forming on the surface was a full body of a younger looking man. One of his eyes was looking to the right, and the other eye was hanging out of the socket and spinning clockwise like a pendulum on a string. As the eye continued to spin faster and faster, the young man started dancing around like a drunken boxer. With his hands up, *come on, do you want to fight?* he said, shuffling side to side and moving his head in different angles. *Come on, do you want to fight?*

he repeated, and I refused to respond. *Come on, do you want to fight?!* he yelled with intense force before the image faded into the pond.

The pond began to bubble and then ceased as a dark goblin-like face appeared. *Choose your weapon*, the face said in a guttural tone. Manifesting across from me was what appeared to be a human in a brown dog costume with long floppy ears. Two long wooden poles appeared beside each of us, floating in midair. The poles had large steel hooks at the top. *Choose you weapon*, again was repeated by the goblin face. The costumed dog grabbed the pole out of the air and thrust it into the pond with two hands. Pulling the pole out of the water, the dog had hooked a large strange looking brown snake with an oversized triangular head. Dropping it on the ground, the snake raised its head and stared at me ready to strike.

Grabbing the pole, I followed suit and thrust it into the water pulling out an equally strange looking snake with an oversized triangular head, greenish in color. Dropping it in front of me, the snake quickly lifted its head as well, focusing on its opponent. Both snakes were shifting side to side, forward and back, waiting for the word.

Two children appeared seated next to each other in high back throne-like chairs with red velour upholstery, just like the baby doll this morning. Both children were wearing long sleeve T-shirts. The boy was wearing black and the girl was wearing white. Their arms were interlocked with the boy's left arm hooked into the crook of the girl's right arm. Sitting back against the chairs, they smiled.

Fight! was yelled from the goblin face.

Slowly the two snakes closed the gap. Once in range, the snakes each took turns snapping out at each other. Constantly moving and evading they seemed evenly matched until they locked up and coiled around each other. On the ground they remained intertwined in a wrestling match. The green snake was slipping in more bites and the brown snake was showing signs of defeat.

Angered, the costumed dog stomped the ground and grabbed the pole, thrusting it back into the pond and pulling out two more snakes. Dropping them on the ground, one of the snakes slithered over to the brown snake and bit down on its tail, as the second snake followed by biting onto the end of that snake's tail.

Instantly, the three snakes began to form into one large dragon-like serpent without legs. Outmatched, the green snake started to retreat and the dragon bit off its head and swallowed the remains.

The children in chairs clapped, the goblin face in the pond laughed, and the dog costumed opponent shifted to a tall hooded shadow with fiery red eyes.

Looking throughout the forest of the monastery grounds, there were now as many gravestones as there were trees. Opening my eyes, I disconnected from the influenced daydream. Before I forgot, I opened the notebook to a fresh page and wrote down the images and daydream experience.

When I was finished, I stood up and performed a few stretching exercises, then packed up and gave Tom a call. "Hi Tom, are you still jogging?"

"No, Professor, I'm stretching near the gazebo."

"How are you feeling?"

"Much better."

"Good. I'm on my way back."

"I've got your coffee here."

"Excellent. I'll be there in about five minutes." I put the cell back in my pocket, took a swig of water, and pulled out the trail mix before beginning my trek back. When I took a left on to the Homestead Trail, a black cat appeared seated on the path, in the exact location where the human-like shadow being crossed after the Fairy of the Forest encounter. Somewhat translucent, it was exact to the previous night's visitor and remained for a moment before it disappeared into the brush.

Tom was eating popcorn at the picnic table when I arrived at the gazebo. "Do you want some?" Tom asked, sliding the bag toward me.

"No thanks, I had some trail mix."

"How did it go?" Tom asked, as I set the backpack on the table.

"The usual. Quasar spoke along with a female monk we will call Fold Your Letter in Three, and a male monk we will call I Am Light."

"Did they say anything about Baby or Mr. Five?"

"Not really. They discussed demons briefly and then the deceptive god influenced a daydream after the conversations."

"I'll have to read that later. I really need to go to the market."

"No problem, Tom. You go ahead. I'm going to stay for another round. Come by my place around six. I will pick up some Thai food and we will review the evidence."

"Do you want me to bring a movie?"

"If it's not a horror, yes."

"Alright, I'll see you at six."

Tom left and I entered the garden. Taking a seat on the stone bench, it was only seconds before a malevolent presence pressed its energy to my back. This time I wasn't going to have a conversation through telepathy but allowed another influenced dream.

Closing my eyes, an old woman appeared in the mind's eye, sitting in a wheelchair in a dated nurse's outfit facing Monk's Irrigation Pond. Holding the wheel on one side, she slowly rotated the other wheel to face me. Her clothes were all covered with food stains and lying in her lap was a wooden pizza board with a cloth creation of a baby doll on top, exactly like the one seated in the throne this morning. Three times the cloth baby blinked its eyes, just like its plastic version.

Five ducks landed in the pond to the rear. As they were gliding gracefully forward one behind the other, I noticed their variation in colors. The first was black, the second white, the third brown and white, the fourth black and white, and the last solid brown, just like the colors of the dresses worn by the curly haired blondes in the monastery field vision last night.

All five ducks turned their heads to the right as a huge green snake rose to the surface. The ducks immediately changed direction, as the snake zeroed in, and began coming forward with its serpentine movement on the pond surface.

As soon as I picked up a long stick to defend myself, the dreamscape vanished. Now I was facing what looked like the altar of the monastery church, as seen in the photograph near the monastery restrooms. Looking at my hands and feet, I was wearing the ghost monk attire just as I did when confronting the hay beasts. *I prefer you in a monk's robe*, a familiar female voice whispered in my right ear.

Rows of pews were full of men and women of all ages. Three pointed brown hoods popped up from within the crowd, as the white walls began to darken and the interior of the room changed shape from rectangular to the shape of a circle. A priest in a black robe walked in from a doorway and stood inside a large sun symbol which was a black circle of stone tile with a black stone dot in the center.

Join me in the circle, the priest told the congregation. Preaching about the power of angels, he called out to them to lift a small round wooden table into the air. As the table began to rise into the air, the congregation was in awe. Higher and higher it rose, and then it stopped about fifteen feet in the air and began to spin. *This is the power of angels*, the priest said. *I want you all to lay down in the circle and allow the angels to lift you. Free yourself to the angels and they will lift you up!* the priest shouted.

Raising his arms, the priest started to rise. Feeling the wickedness in the air, I knew the angel's intention was not just to give us a lift, but to take over our bodies as well.

Feeling my body starting to slip away from my control, I fought hard to bring it back. Struggling with an invisible malevolent force, I heard male and female voices in the air, screaming at me, telling me to stop fighting and let go.

Over and over, I repeated prayer angering the malevolent force. Floating in mid-air, I was now surrounded by hooded shadows with fiery red eyes. Claw marks started appearing on my chest and across my waist. Blood was trickling down my body and dripping onto the floor. Resisting their invasion, I continued to battle.

Refusing to succumb to fear or anger, the dreamscape changed, and I was sitting in the passenger seat of a black SUV. A human-like shadow being was at the wheel. Slowly it turned, revealing its painted on clownish woman's face. Turning its head back toward the windshield, it continued to drive. Feeling nauseous and fatigued, I looked down at my chest and abdomen to see multiple deep claw marks and blood on my hands.

Disconnecting, I brought myself back to a peaceful waking state. Still feeling nausea and fatigue, I lifted my sweatshirt to look at my chest and abdomen. Slight pain was felt in the region, as if there were real wounds but there were no marks just like the cat attack.

Opening the notebook, I wrote down the images and the daydream experience. When I was done, I put the notebook in the backpack and walked back to the vehicle. Looking in the window of the Durango, I was surprised to see the driver's seat had been moved up against the steering wheel. Opening the door, I used the seat controls to position it back in place.

Driving out of the monastery, there were two hard taps on the passenger window as I passed the garden. Stopping for a moment, I waited to see if they, or it, would repeat the knocking. When nothing occurred, I accelerated and two more hard knocks occurred to the roof. Rather than stop to investigate, I turned on the radio and exited the monastery.

CHAPTER 19

A FLOWER IN DARKNESS

Heading home, I returned a missed call from my mother. "You called me back," my mom said, with slight sarcasm as she answered.

"I'm sorry I missed your call, Mom, I had the ringer turned down. I see you called me an hour ago."

"Yeah, about that. I was up all night long."

"Why?"

"Do you have a pencil and paper? I will spell it right out for you. I am bruised from my left shoulder down to my hip."

"I didn't want that to happen, Mom. Do you need to go to the hospital?"

"I'll be alright. I've had stuff like this happen before."

"I know, Mom. But physical abuse is unacceptable."

"I'm not afraid of them. I just try to use my head. Usually Peetu barks if he hears something that's out of the ordinary. This time my little dog ran over and glued himself to my leg. I don't want to talk anymore on the phone. I'll fill you in when you get here."

"Okay. Give me about ten minutes. I'll pick you up a coffee."

"Can you get a couple of cans of dog food too?"

"I will. Love you."

"Love you too."

Arriving at my mothers, I gave her a call. "Alright, I'm here."

"You're here? Can you hear the racket? I'm down in the cellar. I'll be right up." As I opened the gate, my mother opened the side door. "Where is that coffee?"

"I'll get it."

"It's alright, forget it."

"I got it in the car, Mom."

"Do you want me to hold your backpack?"

"Yes, thanks."

Walking back to the vehicle, I got her coffee and set the alarm. Ascending the stairs, I could feel the anger in the air. When Mom opened the door of the second floor, Peetu came flying out. "Hey, what's up, Peetu?" I said petting him.

"The palm of my right hand is itching like crazy. My mother used to say that's money. Where is it? I should be rich, because it hasn't stopped all day," said my mother.

"That's superstition, Mom. An itchy palm can be a health or skin condition or nothing at all."

"Do you want to sit over here?" my mother asked sitting on the couch.

"No, I can sit right here," I answered, taking a seat on the ottoman.

"That's my little hero. He didn't leave me no matter what last night. But this is the first time he didn't bark. He went over to that door and he ran."

"So, what happened?"

"Where do you want me to start?"

"Wherever you want."

"Right after you left, I sat here and Peetu got nervous. I wondered why. I figured maybe someone was in the yard. I went out and the gate was open. So, I shut it. Anyway, something wasn't right. So, I walked back upstairs and made instant coffee. Time went by and I tried to watch a program, but I couldn't concentrate, and Peetu was glued to me. He would jump off the couch, go to the door and come back, and go to the door and come back. Then he sat up here and wanted me to scratch his chest. You're my hero, right? You certainly are," my mother said to Peetu as she petted him. "Anyway, he jumped off the couch again and went back to the door and I said, 'will you get over here?'"

"He is tired as hell. He hasn't been to sleep yet. Are you okay, hun? That's my hero over there and you're my hero over here. He is very smart you know. So anyway, he was nervous, and he keeps looking toward the door and I thought, there has got to be something going on. By this time, it's getting late at night and my eyelids are getting heavy, you know, and I got too much on my mind. Then I heard heavy footsteps coming up the stairs and Peetu looked over at the door. Next thing you know, there was this bang, bang, bang, I thought the damn door was going to fall off. I sat up and said 'what the hell was that?' Peetu started barking but he stayed by my side. Holy cats, I really thought the door was going to come down. I said okay to myself, the last thing I should do is get afraid. I'm not afraid."

"Mom. You must stop repeating you're not afraid and you're not scared. That's challenging the being. Don't challenge."

"I'm just saying this to you."

"No Mom. When you're saying it to me, you're saying it to the being that's listening to this conversation."

"Okay, well. Don't listen. I don't want you to listen," my mother said to the presence.

I laughed and shook my head, "you just don't get it."

"I'm not afraid."

"There you go again. Stop saying you're not afraid. The being and I already know you're not afraid."

"I know they pick up on it," my mother said sarcastically. "Anyway, I've had three bangs on the door since I moved here, but not like this. So, I go up and stood on the opposite side of the door for a while. I didn't say one word. Peetu is at my ankle and I pick him up and bring him back over to the couch and told him to stay. I went and got the keys and slowly walked downstairs. I got halfway when, bam, something gives me a shove and I went down the stairs rolling. My left bun and shoulder was killing me as I laid at the bottom of the stairs."

"I knew if I acted afraid it would get worse. I got up and said oh wow to myself. I'm going to hurt. I picked up the keys and opened the first-floor door. As soon as I walked into the parlor the flame appeared again just floating in front of Richard's recliner. Then it turned into just Richard's head, no body. That's really bothered me."

"Mom, if you're just seeing his head, put two and two together. You're just seeing a head in the window screen as well. This is a jinni. I want you to stay up here. I'm going to go downstairs and interact."

"Do you want me to do the writing?"

"No, I got it. Can I have the keys?"

"Alright. Be careful. This thing is strong."

"I know." My mother handed me the keys and I descended the stairs. Opening the door, I was greeted by the malevolent presence. Taking a seat in Richard's chair I opened the backpack and took out the tools. Taking a moment to bring myself to a peaceful vibration, I placed the notebook and chart on my lap. Taking a deep breath, I let it out, and allowed the communication to begin. A light wind blew into my right ear as a dark dragon was seen in the distance opening and closing its mouth as it bobbed back and forth like one of those drinking bird toys. Charging forward the red and black Chinese-style dragon appeared in the mind's eye, dominating the dark void for a moment before it vanished.

Evil awaits, like love awaits, deep inside all caverns of gods little voices. But fear does not come to you, why?

"I'm overtired. Who may I ask is speaking?"

I am Judd. I need a body.

"And?"

I like yours.

"This is my body. Love, compassion and peace is what I keep internal."

I put a few dark crystals in your heart.

"Then they will soon dissipate."

I doubt that.

"I don't."

I live under human's evil intention. I have many open doors of your killing past. Killing a demon, I remember you, I felt your rage of anger. Feel your killing past.

A vision came forward of what was supposed to be me as a Native American in a forest setting. Completely surrounded by soldiers, I refused to surrender and they attacked. Fighting for survival I picked up soldiers bodily and tossed them against trees, then pulled out a war club and knife slaughtering many as bullets were hitting me from every angle.

"The only thing I am feeling is your negative attitude and that's not my past. Save your false visions."

Higher in the sky you may fly, but you can still see below.

"What, may I ask, are you made of?"

I am jinn. I open like a flower in darkness.

"Maybe I should call you Moon Flower. Do you have physical form?"

I take what clothing I need. I am dark eternal and homely in human eyes. Myths and legends create visions of our appearance.

"Why are you here?"

I follow you. I your demon sidekick. Feel and know I am a thought away.

"Why me?"

I chose Lorne because jinn like symmetry. Lorne is beautiful in female's eyes and beautiful in demons eyes.

"How sweet. Can you tell us how you attach?"

Hole in the aura. I reach in and attach like a tick. Pine needles of evil trees is what we are. Upon your shoulders sits two demons. I am but one. I come from neither God nor the Devil. Join me and rule human minds.

"No thanks. I think the cell phone has got you beat. Do you age?"

I am placed well above sea level.

"That answer is confusing."

Good, then dwell on it.

"You are a cranky Moon Flower. What is it you seek?"

I seek bodies to carry me. Give jinn a sign, give jinn a message, give jinn an intention of evilness.

"Nope. It raises the blood pressure."

Remember, I chose Lorne, and I will destroy all demons which is marking Lorne as theirs.

"You know, jealousy could be one of the reasons for your emotional instability. I'm just saying. And what are you a jinni or a demon?"

Only I exist, not devil. I will tell you what few have figured out. It is the least I can do for your efforts. Only demons, only darkness, only jinn. One entity, one virus, one cancer of the human brain.

"My choice is light, love, and compassion of being. Goodbye, Moon Flower, and thank you for your wisdom." The lower vibrational energy of the presence immediately shifted higher and light as bright as the sun came forward.

Demons are losing the battle against love awareness. Jesus has healed evil wounds against man by teaching man to be God. Like Jesus, Like God, Like Infinite Heart. This is your soul my brother.

"Who may I ask is speaking?"

Call me an Angel. Love is your soul, keep remembering this. Demons want your mind. Just say God is my heart. Let your dark clouds come; God will part them down the middle. Sunshine from within solidifies their poisonous intention. Raise your sword, my brother. Live as love. Gone are the demons and when they return, I will stand beside you.

"Thank you. Do you have a message for humanity?"

The inside one sees outside. Find the one. Keep the one in the window of your eyes.

"I like that. Thank you for your wisdom."

I am love, I am light, and you are my brother.

The conversation ceased and as usual the atmosphere shifted from a dark storm to what felt like a sunny day in Spring. Packing up, I ascended the stairs. My mother heard my footsteps and opened the door. "Are you all done?"

"Yes. And there will be no more interacting from this day forward in the house," I said, as I entered and walked into the living room.

"The lights stopped blinking and Peetu seems like himself."

"I'm glad. But the being will not leave if your thoughts and actions keep calling it back. For now, if it appears the presence is angry, remind it that it is capable of goodness."

A whisper in my right ear said, *thank you for saying I can be good.* With telepathy I responded with, 'You're welcome.'

CHAPTER 20

ELECTRICAL NATURE

Two knocks were heard from the living room. Getting up off the couch, I walked over and opened the door. "C'mon in, bud."

"It smells good in here. What did you get?" Tom asked, as he walked over to the food containers on the kitchen table.

"Dumplings, chicken Pad Thai, and pork fried rice."

"Good choice, Professor."

"What did you bring for a movie?"

"*Caddyshack*."

"Nice. That's a classic."

Tom and I filled our plates and took a seat on the couch and talked about martial arts while we ate. "So, what occurred after I left?" Tom asked, as I walked into the living room.

"The usual. But my mother was shoved down the stairs last night by a jinni."

"Is she alright?"

"She is bruised, but she will be okay."

"Your mom is tough."

"Yes, she is. But she has a relationship with a dominating jinni that punished her for listening to me. These are the type of repercussions that can occur when you try to help or educate a victim when the jinni with a narcissistic personality is listening. This is either a tag along of hers, which would explain why there was paranormal activity in every house she lived in since Boardman Lane, or it's a former attachment of Richard. Maybe even both. But it's not the deceptive god of the monastery."

"Is Boardman Lane the house where the gruesome murder took place?"

"Yes, Tom. My mother formed a relationship with a hooded shadow in the house that appeared to my mother as the ghost of the murdered woman. This may be that hooded shadow." Taking a seat on the couch, I opened the notebook to today's encounters. "The last conversation took place at my mothers. While you're reading, I am going to put the food in the fridge and clean the kitchen. Do you want some food to take home?"

"Are there any dumplings left?"

"Half a carton."

"I'll take a few of those."

Tom began to read, and I walked into the kitchen. While wiping down the counter, the presence pressed at my back, influencing the same vision of a towering medieval monk hooded shadow as the nightlight lying on the counter lit up without being plugged in. Ignoring the vision and rejecting its wickedness, another vision came forward of an older man walking toward me wearing a gray and black checked outdoor shirt. His hair was gray and slicked back, his eyes dark, and his skin tanned and weathered, with a full-face tattoo of a spider web. As the image vanished a three faced dark-haired man in a three piece black suit appeared. One face was looking me in the eyes and the other two faces were on each side of the head where the ears should be. The three faced man turned to its left exposing the right side of its face and stuck out its tongue before vanishing.

Roughly twenty minutes later Tom was finished. "I'm ready when you are, Professor."

"Okay." Walking into the living room, I took a seat.

"Can we start with the daydream battle of the serpents?"

"Yes, of course. Before we talk about this, let me tell you about my experience with a larger invisible serpent. In 2004, I met a woman online. We will call her Sheena. After a few weeks of dating, we got into a discussion about the paranormal. Sheena told me she had a lot of dreams involving snakes and visions of snakes hanging off her ceiling at night. She went on to tell me she has a repetitive nightmare of a creepy guy that would crawl up from the foot of the bed and get on top of her pinning her down or choking her."

"This stuff happens a lot, doesn't it Professor?"

"All around the world, my friend."

"Later that night I was seated on the couch with Sheena, watching a movie at her place. The sensation of invisible snakes began moving under the buttocks. This was the first time I experienced such a strange, uncomfortable phenomenon. Weirded out, I cut the night short and drove home."

"That night while lying in bed reading, a transparent narrow ladder appeared at the foot of the bed going all the way to the ceiling. Little transparent people dressed in dated clothing were climbing the ladder, waving and talking. No words were heard, but they appeared friendly."

"About an hour passed when I could feel the dark presence in the air. The sensation of invisible slithering snakes was now at my ankles rising slowly toward my hips. Stunned, I immediately began to pray, but it had no effect. Grossed out, I rode out the sensation that lasted about three minutes before it ceased."

"The following day after work, I arrived at Sheena's house before she got home. Sheena called and told me she was going to be a little late, and to let myself in, giving me the garage door pass code. When I opened the door that enters the kitchen, I was met by an aggressive malevolent force. Ignoring the wickedness in the air, I walked over to the kitchen table to sit. As I pulled out the chair, what felt like a giant invisible serpent wrapped around my ankles all the way up to my hips and pulled downward with superhuman force. This was 4 o'clock, in the light of day. I have experienced much, but this was ridiculous. I wondered why this was happening. Whatever this serpent was, the thickness alone would make an anaconda look like an earthworm. Shocked, I controlled my fear and grabbed onto two chairs to hold me up, fighting with all my might to not be pulled to the ground. The struggle continued with this invisible serpent and was not letting up. I was tiring and it felt like the serpent was tearing the skin off my hips. Unable to come up with a rational explanation for the attack, I called out to God for assistance again and again."

"It appeared I was on my own with this creature, and I wasn't about to give up. Alright God, I said, If I have done something to deserve this attack then I accept this challenge until you forgive me for my action. Staring into the sun's rays that shone through the kitchen window, I gave it my all and stood my ground resisting the serpent's assault until it ceased."

"Exhausted and bewildered, I walked over to the fridge with my legs shaking from the strain. Opening the door, I took out a carton of orange juice and poured myself a glass. On that day, I learned another lesson. Besides orbs, shadows, and pucks, there exists a serpent or dragon species in the hidden world, and the smaller parasitic snakes serve this being and thrive on sexual energy."

"Have you ever wondered why you experience such unusual stuff, Professor?"

"History shows lovers of God experience unusual stuff. Lovers of God who realize they have been lovers of a god, or jinni, and not the one God, experience even more. Especially when they choose to educate others."

"Let me share some mythological history. Wampanoag Indian mythology has a malevolent spiritual being called Hobomock, or Chepi, pronounced chee-pee in Wampanoag which means 'ghost' or 'the dead', that can manifest as a horned serpent. After the introduction of Christianity, it was believed to be the devil. Chepi, like Apep, a malevolent giant serpent of the underworld in Egyptian mythology, was the embodiment of darkness, evil, and destruction. Chepi was the exact opposite of the benevolent Nikommo. Nikommo are nature spirits that can appear as little people. If Nikommo are treated fairly, given offerings, and treated with respect they will reciprocate with generosity, assistance, and good fortune, projecting peace, love and joy."

"Not only do deceptive gods shapeshift into the deceased and religious deities, they will also take the form of a mythological creature of any culture on Earth, or another species of spiritual being or jinn. Mythological creatures are born from the imagination of the human mind and the influenced dreams, visions, and illusions from the imagination of spiritual beings. In this case, the little people on the ladder was an influenced illusion from a deceptive god, that can also take the form of a serpent, is in fact a serpent, or just part-serpent."

"Now let's discuss the serpent battle. I would compare it to Exodus 7:8-13. The biblical God speaks to Moses and his brother Aaron, telling them to cast down Aaron's staff before the Pharaoh to show a miracle, and so he did, and the staff turned into a serpent. Pharaoh's magicians also cast down their staffs and used magic to turn them into serpents. The serpent created by the biblical God consumed the other snakes, demonstrating its power. Another passage involving serpents that comes to mind, besides the snake in the Garden of Eden, is Numbers 21:4-9, the biblical God in a rage sent fiery serpents to bite the people of Israel causing some to die. Idolatry is a sin in many passages of the Bible, including the Ten Commandments. Moses killed 3,000 people for worshipping a golden calf idol, yet the biblical God has Moses create a bronze serpent to be placed on a pole. If the people looked at the serpent idol after being bit, they lived."

"Exodus 7:8-13 is definitely similar."

"Yes, it is, and that may be the intention of the daydream. Snakes, serpents, and dragons appear as religious symbols, mythological creatures, and worshipped deities in many ancient and modern cultures, partly due to the influence of dreams and visions by the deceptive gods. Deities that take the form of a serpent, a hybrid form including a serpent, or a human form holding or wearing serpents, is historically common. A couple more serpent myths that come to mind is the Ancient Mayans that had the Vision Serpent who was their link to the spirit world, giving them powerful visions and the ability to communicate with gods and their ancestor spirits. Hindu and Buddhist mythology has the Nagas, half human/half snake - serpent creatures or snake people - that can shapeshift to an entirely human form if necessary."

"Why does it influence these fights in dreams and visions?"

"Deceptive gods enjoy fighting and war. A passage of the Bible that would relate to this is Exodus 15:3; *the Lord is a man of war: The Lord is His name.* One face and personality is loving, compassionate, forgiving, and merciful, and its other face and personality is violent, brutal, bloodthirsty, and vengeful. This may be the reason for the contrast in the god or gods of the Old Testament, and the god or gods of the New Testament. Moses, the main character in the Old Testament, had a different relationship with a god than Jesus the main character of the New Testament. Jesus loved the god with all his heart, if he didn't, he might never have tasted the mystical experience during the baptism initiated by the god. Because he projected love and devotion, he in turn channeled the loving, compassionate, forgiving, and merciful face and personality of the god."

"If you remember, the Impostor Father said, *I heard about you the most because your martial arts abilities were quite popular in the city.* The deceptive god knows my martial arts background and, at times, puts it to the test in their world, under their terms. In dreams and visions, they can be temporarily defeated, but never permanently destroyed, returning as the same image or another."

"Analyzing the deceptive gods' illusions and symbols in both daydreams at the monastery, we see a pattern. Both took place at Monk's Irrigation Pond. Goblin-like faces, grotesque images, a boy and a girl seated in the same throne-like chair as the blinking plastic baby vision this morning, then in the second daydream we have an old woman in a filthy nurse's outfit seated in a wheelchair. Lying in her lap was a wooden pizza board. What did that represent?"

"The seductress pizza."

"Yes, Tom. On the pizza board was a cloth creation of this morning's plastic baby doll vision. Just like the plastic baby doll, the cloth version blinked its eyes three times. Five ducks in the pond were the same colors as the dresses worn by the curly haired blondes in the monastery field vision we discussed in the gazebo. These colors are continuing as expected as another signature of the persona Mr. Five."

"In both dreams we see serpents. The dragon representing an older, wiser, powerful serpent being, which returns in vision before the persona Judd conversation at my mother's. The deceptive god influenced the dreamscape interior of the monastery church that we both viewed in the picture near the restrooms. As I said, there is a method to the madness, the brown dog costume the hooded shadow wore I realized is exact to the stuffed toy dog I slept with as a child in the Boardman Lane house, which my mother still has."

"Then this is not the work of one deceptive god."

"No Tom, it's not. I am investigating jinn that are listening to everything I say and watching my every move. If I say it's the work of one, then there will be many, if I say it's the work of many, then there will be one. I can't win this game. No human can."

"Like the hay beast attack, I was wearing a monk's robe inside the monastery church. The voice of the seductress whispered, *I prefer you in a monk's robe* in my right ear in the same manner that Baby whispered, *I don't believe in Jesus* in my right ear. Three pointed brown hoods popped up from within the congregation representing the three ghost monks. Walls darkened as the interior of the room shifted from rectangular to round. The priest in a black robe entered and stood inside the sun symbol on the floor, the same sun symbol Energy Being sent to my mind's eye. After the congregation was impressed with the magic trick of raising the table, the priest asked the congregation to lay down and free themselves, allowing the beings to invade their vessel and give them a lift. What the deceptive god is doing is giving an example of how they gain entry with the angel scam. Remember Mr. Five said, *just think how many walk around with the door open and let me in*. Wickedness was felt in the air as I wrestled with invisible beings, experiencing energy shifts within the body and voices telling me to stop fighting and submit."

"Repeating prayer pissed them off and they manifested as fiery red-eyed shadows, just like the deceptive god did in the daydream. In their rage they flew around, clawing from different angles. Three fingered claw marks on my chest and waist were trickling blood. Three is the signature of the hooded shadows."

"Scratches from the hooded shadows felt as real as the scratches from the cat. The human-like shadow with the paint job face driving the SUV was exact to the six-foot shadow that crossed the Homestead Trail after the Fairy of the Forest encounter."

"When I walked back to the truck after the encounter, the seat was intentionally moved up against the steering wheel; and leaving the monastery two taps occurred to the passenger window and two to the roof informing me it was following and there was nowhere to escape its reach. Now let's review the dialogue of the ghost monks, Quasar, Voice of Love, and I Am Light."

"Quasar said, *I truly love you.* An hour or so before that the deceptive god as Mr. Five said, *I'm very evil energy now in you.* When I asked Quasar about the demon that swims in my river of thoughts, Quasar replied *Jinn by one culture and Demon by another.* The persona Judd that spoke in threes called itself both jinn and a demon during the conversation. Quasar said, *Life essence it drains,* which is in line with Energy Being's comment, *Demons are parasites of emitted evil waste.* Keeping with the pattern, Quasar does not go into any specific details about this malevolent tag along and conveniently leaves out the fact that these benevolent ghost monks, and their many personalities, are feeding as well. Quasar said, *I will teach you how I shed the Demons eternal skin.*"

"What does that mean?"

"Quasar didn't mention snakes in its description of jinn, but snakes shed their skin. Quasar went on to say, *Lorne, jinn follows you not in human form, but as clouds of evil essence,* and later *Evil has a pool of ocean water. Each evil memory adds to that pool, making it larger and more noticeable in daily life.* These pools, dark clouds, or masses of energy can manifest or remain in an invisible malevolent state."

"When I asked, what advice would you share with those humans troubled by these demons? Quasar replied, *Evil questions give demons a tongue.* This is truth. If you ask your questions while in a negative mood, or you seek knowledge with negative intentions, you will awaken the dark personality of the deceptive god, if it is not already awake."

"I noticed that Judd said, *Feel and know I am a thought away.*"

"This is also true. When this investigation is complete, I suggest you distance yourself from the subject of deceptive gods moving forward. Avoid giving these beings and their many forms, names, labels, or thoughts and focus on your spiritual development."

"I will, Professor. Judd used the word sidekick like Baby when it said, *I your demon sidekick.*"

"Yes, it did."

"When Quasar said, *First know who you are. God implanted codes, life lessons, and new beginnings in evolution inside your discovered DNA. I can read this scripture of infinite essence, and so too the demons,* I started thinking again of aliens, the abductions, and what the abductees say the examination process is like."

"It appears that Quasar is saying the deceptive gods, benevolent or malevolent in the moment, can read your genetic blueprint and/or the contents of the mind of the heart or soul. If you compare the experiences of alien abductees to the victims of jinn experiences, you will see they are very similar. This is the work of the deceptive gods. Through the years, I have experienced many dreams and visions where I was within impressive spacecrafts with alien-like creatures or visited what appeared to be strange worlds and highly advanced civilizations. Because I recognized the energy of the presence at the time, I know they are the deceptive gods. Alien forms are just one of the guises from their endless closet."

"Looking at the word essence and how it has been used we have, *Evil essence, infinite essence, love essence, life essence,* by Quasar. *No, I am pure essence and all love,* by Voice of Love, *Heaven essence,* by Kim, *I'm God, but I'm not essence in purity,* by Quasar and *Put forth the essence of a loving God, You,* also by Quasar, which is flattery like Amy saying, *I'm a handful of tiny droplets, begging for God's attention. You are the God I begged for.* Male and female personalities implement the love and light con."

"Quasar said, *I'm God, but I'm not essence in purity.* That's because Quasar's essence keeps changing. Voice of Love followed with, *No, I am pure essence and all love.* Another example of how the deceptive gods contradict themselves and confuse humans - one personality says, I'm not essence in purity, and the next personality from the same being says, I am pure essence and all love."

"Listening to them can really drive you nuts."

"Yes Tom, and many it has."

"Do you think the jinn or deceptive gods are responsible for all those creatures, like Quasar said?"

"Yes, and many more Quasar didn't mention. Quasar said, *where did this collection of hallucinations appear from? Jinn drew this within humankind's brain, and it appears to remain untouched by a master of love.* Quasar put the hallucination blame on the jinn. Again, conveniently leaving out its own ability to create illusions and induce hallucinations because Quasar or Baby is also of the jinn. Master of love was a crack about Jesus, because Quasar and Master are personalities of Baby."

"Quasar said, *I contain memories as human.* Like the other personalities that claimed they were once human, Quasar is lying. Quasar, or the deceptive god that plays Quasar, could contain memories of those humans that it followed, observed, fed on, influenced, and manipulated through many years. What Quasar said next, we must pay attention to, *I sat on a throne and left love on the floor. I now lift love above my heart and kneel."*

"Quasar said throne and the deceptive god has been influencing visions of thrones."

"Yes, Tom. Is Quasar saying he held, or holds, a position of power? Is he referring to the throne of God in Scripture? When I asked Quasar if there were human discarnates, he replied, *Discarnates! May I say discarnates separate truth from fitting together the puzzle?* At that exact moment, the vision that I experienced in the garden of large puzzle pieces floating in the air returned."

"Admitting it influenced the vision."

"Games, my friend. Moving on to Voice of Love, who spoke in threes, mixed knowledge with lies, and said, *no vision is real unless God is the screen that you see first.* This is referring to oneness, or the source of existence. Looking at the other oneness related comments from the personas, we have, *You are beginning to understand what few will take the time to figure out. All is one. You know this,* by Father Albert Celestine. *Internalized oneness emits the food that feeds the God,* by Being of Energy and, *I am Holy as one, because I am one. Not the bark of the tree, but the core of the forest,* by Fairy of the Forest."

"There was also, *this demonstration of merging into one soul for the good of all is true love. Compassion returns to homeland when merging as one powerful soul becomes your quest,* also by Fairy of the Forest. *I am a little fish, but I am one, you are a little fish, but you are one,* by Quasar, *Believing in more than self is believing in all as self,* by the Master, and *never feel I love only one, for I am only one,* by the third god presence."

"What we have is personas of the deceptive god, referring to oneness, the source, or the one God, and playing the one God. Deceptive gods are aware of the source, or one God, but the one God is a life giving non-personal source. All you see and don't see is the throne of the one God. Not a chair for which an invisible impostor sits waiting for those seeking outside themselves for what lies within."

"Nice."

"Thank you. Fold Your Letter in Three continues with the use of the word *world.* *What you experienced exists daily all over the world; it is the dark virus of humankind,* the prophet con with, *you have spoken as God many times,* and with the Early Modern English, 'Ye are Gods' of Scripture, *Jesus well known to humankind said "Ye are Gods" that said plenty.* Another line that stood out was, *Do you think we are three separate entities or one being?* This is a trick question, the deceptive god is referring to the Holy Trinity, which is three persons in one God and one God in three persons, the Father, the Son, and the Holy Spirit. In Hinduism, there is the triumvirate which consists of three gods, Brahma the creator, Shiva the destroyer, and Vishnu the preserver."

"Three is their signature."

"Deceptive gods are multi-faced, multi-personality conscious entities. Fold Your Letter in Three said, *you are God because you are without hate, but hate tried to coerce you in many forms. You have successfully defeated all. God is your voice now.* The deceptive god would like me to believe I have defeated the adversary, just as Jesus is believed to not have succumbed to the temptations of the Devil or Satan, and Buddha is believed to have defeated the demon Mara to attain enlightenment. There was no defeat in my case, just shifts in the deceptive god's emotions."

"I Am Light spoke a lot about light, Professor, and said, *I cannot describe for I am light, but they are evil snakes.* Isn't that describing?"

"Yes it is, that is an attempt to maintain the belief that the being is only light, even though the third god presence said, *I am love/I am hate, I am peace/I am war, I am beautiful vision/I am ugly vision.* This is more confusion."

"I Am Light continues with the women weakness and jealousy, *avoid women my brother,* and Quasar says, *I truly love you.* I Am Light says, *it's demons that jump into evil minded women. That is what you have experienced.* No, it's deceptive gods appearing as the seductress and the succubus is what I have experienced. As I said before, the deceptive god would like nothing more than for me to avoid human women so the being can have me to itself. Deceptive gods are jealous gods. The one God doesn't get jealous, and why would that be?"

"Because the one God is all you see and all you don't see."

"Yes, Tom. When all is an expression of yourself there is no jealousy. Deceptive gods are in competition with one another, so there is jealousy because they are many."

"Can deceptive gods jump into women to try and seduce you?"

"Yes, just as they can invade men to seduce women. Fold Your Letter in Three said, *they will alter the weak and consume the evil,* and Amy said, *Evil wins every time you accept their distraction.* Deceptive gods are electrical beings, humans are electrical beings with a physical body. Deceptive gods can merge their consciousness with a receptive man or woman influencing or manipulating the person to be its puppet to seduce, distract, or harm a chosen victim. Electrically they can connect to feed and experience the energetic sensations of sexual activity. If you perform an internet search for bacteria that consumes and excretes electricity you will find scientists have discovered a form of life that can be drawn by sending electrons down an electrode placed in the ground."

"Their source of food is electricity?"

"Yes, there is more than one form of life that consumes pure energy and communicates electrically. In my journal of this investigation and at your apartment you have either witnessed or read about the deceptive god's ability to brighten the lights, dim the lights, make the lights flicker, or blow out the bulb. This is the ability to manipulate and control electricity. This is also how they can appear as light and travel at great speeds."

"While I was wiping down the counter in the kitchen, the tag along pressed at my back and influenced a vision of a tall hooded shadow then lit up the night light on the counter that's not plugged in. This is not the first time I have witnessed this transmission of wireless electricity controlled by a deceptive god. When it occurs, it makes me think of Nikola Tesla."

"Who is he?"

"He was a brilliant man who invented or discovered many of the technologies we enjoy today. A quote from Nikola Tesla that would apply to this investigation would be, 'If you want to find the secrets of the universe, think in terms of energy, frequency, and vibration.'"

"Nikola Tesla was the son and grandson of priests, was obsessed with the number three, lived on the 33rd floor of a hotel in room 3327 in his later years, was fond of pigeons and communicated with them. One pigeon that he was in love with was white with light gray tips on its wings. Tesla mentioned the pigeon had a brilliant light in its eyes just before it died. He experienced visions of tongues of the living flame in the air as a child. The passage for these tongues can be found in Acts 2:3, which says, *divided tongues as of fire appeared to them and rested on each one of them*."

"Tesla experienced vivid nightmares at times and claimed he received alien messages. In the year 1900, one of those messages from another world was, *"Brethren! We have a message from another world, unknown and remote. It reads: one…two…three…"*"

"Sounds like he interacted with the deceptive gods?"

"It is definitely possible. The signs do point in that direction when you know the electrical nature of the being."

"I noticed I Am Light wasn't love and light when you mentioned Adam and Eve, Professor."

"Yes, it definitely triggered an inflamed response. Could a couple of reasons for its anger be a negative story about a wise serpent, or a misinterpreted vision or dream from a deceptive god?"

"I didn't think of that."

"There can be many reasons for its response. I Am Light responded, *the book is your destiny my brother* when I said, 'Maybe writing this book is a wrong choice.' This is how important it is to deceptive gods in their heavenly being guises to get what they usually claim is the correct doctrine to the masses. Of course, I am not writing the book in the manner they designed. Deceptive gods prefer I am gullible enough to believe I am a prophet of god, a chosen one amongst humanity to start a new religion or cult."

"Deceptive gods want their chosen ones to attract disciples or followers. These devoted followers of its doctrine become vessels for the deceptive god's agenda. Instead of just the one body of the selected voice piece, it attains the subconscious minds of numerous hosts to inhabit and program."

Tom began rubbing his solar plexus and was getting anxious as the dark cloud expanded in anger and began to press. Closing my eyes, a dark influenced vision came to the mind's eye. Opening my eyes slowly, Tom was staring at me waiting for the details.

"A pig's head in a frying pan came forward and was followed by a vision of a large group of people on a hill of what looked like a farm. An old tree with one huge evil looking eye was watching them pick up hundreds of pigs bodies and put them in green trash bags."

"How can you experience all this activity and visitations and see all these influenced visions and dreams and not be affected, Professor?"

"I am affected, Tom. But I do my best to limit the effects by not identifying with their illusions, emotions, tricks, and whispers, minimizing energy loss and the chance of attachment. I'm going to give you a boost but not with my energy this time, Tom." Walking over to the entertainment center, I took out the CD *Walking on Sunshine* by Katrina & The Waves and placed it in the player to raise the vibrational frequency of the environment. "Just listen Tom and allow the music to harmonize."

Tom closed his eyes and began to smile. Immediately I could feel Tom's vibrational energy changing and within a minute he stopped rubbing his solar plexus. When the song was finished, I shut off the player. "The presence is gone, Professor, and I feel really good," Tom said, as he opened his eyes.

"No Tom, the mood of the presence changed and lifted, but it's still lingering, and you are feeling the effects of a higher vibrational shift and the increase of the neurotransmitter dopamine produced in the brain. What the song accomplished you can do on your own. I wanted you to experience this shift within yourself as you were engulfed in the cloud of a malevolent presence. Music is vibration, it is sound that not only changes your mood and triggers the release of pleasurable chemicals but also changes your perception of the world."

Picking up the movie off the coffee table, I opened the case and took out the DVD. Placing the cover back down onto the table, I put the DVD into the player then sat back down and finished the review.

"I Am Light said, *don't get lost in words, get found in light.* What if that light is a trap? Remember the passage 2 Corinthians 11:14; *And no marvel; for Satan himself is transformed into an angel of light.* This passage is only half the story. Angels of light also transform into Satan or the adversary. Now let's watch the movie."

CHAPTER 21
FACE TO FACE

The tag along wasted no time in releasing the psychological attacks after Tom left. A giant black bear was seen in my mind's eye, charging. As it came closer, it shifted to a black dog, like the Doberman breed, with a red scarf around its neck.

Evil whispers into my right ear were saying repeatedly, ***if you go to sleep, you're not going to wake up,*** as the illusion of a heavy bearskin rug was dropped on top of me.

"That's negative," I said aloud, as I ignored the smoke and mirrors. I turned on the bedroom lamp, but it blew out. Walking back into the kitchen, I looked under the sink for light bulbs. Luckily, I had one more 60-watt bulb. Replacing the bulb, I turned on the lamp and got into bed. After plugging my cell phone into the charger and arranging the pillows, I laid back with my eyes open.

Immediately, the bed began to shake, and three apparitions of black undetailed smoke manifested in front of the bed. The smoke apparitions on each end separated from the center apparition by about 5 feet. Then, the center apparition began moving laterally back and forth between the other two apparitions exactly like the ghost monks in the monastery garden. Was this the garden monks true form, I thought, or do they want me to believe so? Observing the movement with emotional control and refusing to converse, the smoky trio vanished in under a minute and the bed shaking ceased.

Closing my eyes, a male face with medium length black hair and one very large eye in the center of the forehead appeared. As the face slowly vanished, the single eye remained in the void and lingered for a couple of minutes. In the next vision, I was inside a small cave. The walls of the cave started closing in fast. Opening my eyes, I was still within the cave, but it was translucent and still closing. Looking around the bedroom, it was a visual illusion that wouldn't fade. The goal of the influenced illusion of the cave and the bearskin rug was to trigger a claustrophobic reaction. Sitting up on the edge of the bed, I centered myself and visualized sitting in a rocking chair on the porch of a log cabin, overlooking a serene pond in the forest.

Slowly the disturbing illusion started to break down and then vanish. Walking into the kitchen I poured a glass of water, drank it down, and went back to bed. Knocks, dings, and bangs were heard around the apartment, but I needed rest and did my best to blank it out.

Drifting off to sleep, a dream began with Tom telling me his friend just had a new litter of puppies, and he wanted to find them good homes. He asked if I were interested, and I said I would like to see the pups. Tom couldn't remember the address, but gave me directions to a trailer park, and told me it was the first trailer on the left as you enter the gate.

After teaching a class, I drove to the location. The first trailer on my left was white and brown, just like the plush toy dog backpack, offered by the seductress in vision. To no surprise, the trailer number was 555 and it was half red and half black.

Knocking on the dented door, a tall and thin older woman with sunken cheeks, wearing dark clothing answered. "Welcome," she said.

"Hi, I'm Lorne."

"I know. Come in, come in." Her energy and the environment emitted pure wickedness, but I entered. While talking about the pups, one of them came into the living room and walked over to me. It looked something like a Rottweiler, but not quite and was solid black. The pup was huge and it kept its head down.

"How old are the pups?" I asked.

"About a year old," she answered.

"They're huge."

"They eat well," she answered with an evil smile. In walked her husband, with the second pup. The husband was also tall and thin, with sunken cheeks and the same taste in clothing. Keeping its head down, the second pup came over and I began to pet them both.

"The mother is on the premises if you would like to see her," the woman said, as she stood up from the recliner.

"Sure, bring her out," I answered, never taking my eyes off the pups. Out walked this monstrous dog that dwarfed the size of the pups. Her fur didn't look right or even real, so I avoided touching her. The room darkened with her presence and grew more eerie. As I stared at the mother's fur, I noticed it was more like a black rug.

"How old is she?" I asked.

"20 years old," the husband answered.

"Wow, that's old for a dog."

"She is a special breed. We're going to take the mother for a walk while you get acquainted with the pups," the wife said, with the same evil smile.

"Okay," I answered, as I sensed an attack about to occur.

As soon as they stepped out the door, the pups lifted their heads, revealing their evil black eyes. Growling and showing their teeth, I had a battle to contend with.

Looking out the trailer window, I saw the fur falling off the mother in bits and pieces. When she stood up on her hind legs, the rest of the fur fell off leaving only a few little pieces stuck to her tall, skeletal frame. With her black dog head and now skeletal body, she turned toward me, smiled and waved, then walked away, holding hands with the husband and wife.

Switching my focus to the two large pups, they were now looking at me as supper. Jumping up, I sprinted for the door but was grabbed by what felt like multiple invisible hands. While restrained, red leather straps connected to thick chains were attached to each wrist. Each chain was hooked onto red spiked collars that was now around the pups' necks. The trailer door opened slowly, and the dogs ran out, pulling me along with them.

Standing now in a desert, in the middle of an ancient looking stadium, I was the center of attention. Skeletal remains of humans, animals, and reptiles were scattered everywhere in the dirt. Thousands of diverse human/animal hybrids were standing in front of their seats waiting for the entertainment to begin. Both pups' eyes shifted from jet black to a glowing fiery red as they grew to three times their size.

"Let the game begin!" was shouted from a hybrid with an alligator head and a human body. Slowly they came forward, drooling at the mouth. My only option was to negate their attack and slip in some kicks.

Pulling the chains inward, I brought the dogs together, to my center. Every time they advanced, I was successful in pulling them off balance and avoiding their lunge. This made the crowd of hybrids angry and they started throwing stones, making it difficult to keep an eye on the vicious dogs. The combination of kicking dirt into their faces, evading, and intercepting their forward movement with linear kicks wasn't going to work for long. Fatigue was setting in fast, and it was only a matter of time, before one of the dogs would sink its teeth.

Out of energy, I dropped to one knee and woke from the dream. Wickedness dominated the air, as the bed was shaking, and the creepy feeling of invisible snakes were spiraling at my ankles traveling in an upwards direction. A vision of a large green snake with glowing red eyes weaved through the darkness of the void, then coiled up, ready to strike.

Feeling disgustingly violated, I let the image pass until the serpent assault ceased.

A loud bang occurred to the wall to my right and then round and round the room what appeared to be smaller entities traveling at high speeds hit the walls and objects saying, *Woo Woo, Woo Woo* in a mischievous way as they circled three times and then stopped.

Gazing at the ceiling, a black unformed mass of evil was hovering above projecting its anger. Slowly it began to expand like crude oil floating on sea water. The larger it grew, the darker and more toxic the room became until it vanished from sight.

Feeling its presence lingering, I focused on the wall ahead and relied on what little light was shining through the window to observe its movement. Patiently I stared, concentrating on the left and right side of the window. As expected, a tall hooded shadow glided across the wall from left to right, darkening the room for a moment as it passed the window.

Blacker than night, it remained in the corner. It's not revealing itself to read me a bedtime story or sing me a lullaby. It wants me to see it, and it wants me to know it's there, tormenting and influencing the dark dreams and disturbing images.

Staring into the corner, I waited for its next move. To trigger an emotional response, I began to recite the Angel Michael Prayer of Protection aloud. Halfway through the prayer, it rushed forward with blinding speed and remained a foot from my face. The hood width of this creature was at least four feet, and its intimidating fiery red glowing eyes stared deep into my being.

"I can see you and you can see me. Now what?" I said firmly, as our eyes were locked in a staring contest. Expecting the worse, I focused on my breathing to help remain calm and relaxed, never blinking, until the terrifying manifestation pulled back and disappeared.

Grateful to still be living, I remained alert for a few minutes before picking up a martial arts supply catalog to occupy my mind. Sitting up, I thumbed through the pages until I became groggy and fell asleep.

In the dream state, I was in an old classroom setting, sitting in a one-piece school desk. To my right was a woman with long dark hair. She was wearing an old school uniform which was black with a white long sleeve shirt. Up front was a heavyset man with his back turned at the chalkboard. When he raised his hand to write, the woman to the right turned.

Wearing a red and black striped tie, she said, *when are you going to let me in?* I laughed and answered, "You're not getting in." Angry, she turned back and faced what appeared to be the teacher. Looking up at the chalkboard it was line after line of threes.

The dreamscape changed, and I was walking into a bedroom with nothing more than a king size bed with black, shiny sheets and white candles burning across the top of the headboard. Shoved from the rear by an invisible force, I landed on the bed. Turning me over, the invisible force held me down as the door in the room slowly opened and, in a flash, a skeleton with long red hair leaped on me cross side, shocking me to the core.

Wrestling back and forth, the skeleton was far too strong for me to restrain. Climbing into the mount position it opened its mouth and a long tongue came out and licked the side of my face. Turning my head from side to side, I tried to avoid any more licks from its slimy tongue. "Get off me!" I yelled, as I struggled with the creature.

The invisible force pinned my arms down, as the creature began running its long boney fingers through my hair. Unable to speak, I remained calm until I woke from the nightmare.

Still pinned by the malevolent presence in stealth mode, the horrible snake-like feeling began slithering around my legs and hips as the bed shook. Manifesting on top was a translucent version of the succubus, with her long dark hair and black and red body suit.

Fighting a demon's lust isn't easy.

"Why are you so persistent?"

I love everything about you.

"I'm touched. What does a demon know about love?"

I am female also.

"And your point is?"

I keep a close distance waiting for your approval.

"Approval for what may I ask?"

Having me give you an orgasm.

"You've got a long wait. Now get off me."

The succubus manifestation vanished and within a minute the malevolent presence in the room was gone too. Propping up the pillows, I sat up against the headboard, closed my eyes and visualized the sun's rays bursting through the clouds until I drifted off to sleep.

Morning came far too quickly, and I turned to see it was 5:55 a.m. Feeling tired and achy, I closed my eyes for a moment and saw the image of a woman's face looking up at me from within the ground below. Rising from the Earth surface was just her head and neck. The body was hidden under a layer of dirt and looked serpent shaped from the hips down. Her eyes were glowing emerald green, and her brunette hair was up in a bun, wrapped in gold and jewels. Staring directly into my eyes she said just two words. *Marry me.*

"No," I answered quickly and firmly. Any agreement made with a jinni in the twilight state, dream state, or waking state is equally as binding.

Wide awake now, I sat up as my left pectoral muscle began to twitch and I rubbed it. As soon as I stopped rubbing, it continued. One more time I rubbed the muscle, then got up and walked into the kitchen.

Filling the carafe for the coffee maker, I poured the water into the reservoir and placed the carafe on the heating plate, then raised the shades. Opening the fridge, I took out the eggs, bacon, cheese, and waffles and placed them on the counter.

While cooking, I looked to my left to see the white trash can completely covered in what looked like black smoke residue. Wiping it with my index finger, that's exactly what it was. Only the trash can looked like it had been near smoke and flames. Nothing else in the apartment appeared to be affected. With a cleaner and paper towels I wiped it down, then got back to cooking.

After the meal, I pulled out the trash bag, tied it up and walked downstairs to throw it in the bin. When I returned, I unloaded the dishwasher using the heavier pots and pans to perform single stick fighting combinations before putting them away.

CHAPTER 22

ANGEL MICHAEL, SKY, AND POP

Turning the key, there was no sign of battery life. One more time I gave it a shot, but there was no crank at all. A little frustrated, but not surprised, I stepped out of the truck and knocked on the first-floor door for a jump. Luckily, the young man was just about to leave. Connecting the jumper cables, the truck started on the first try and that seemed to have remedied the problem. It is possible the hooded shadow or one of its parasitic gang members drained the battery as a source of energy or for entertainment.

At the gym, I got on the treadmill for thirty minutes and then hit the weights. While bench pressing, negative images began of the bar coming down on top of me crushing my neck. The gym started to appear hazy as the negative images repeated. Ignoring the psychological attack, I continued to work out knowing the deceptive god was trying to induce anxiety.

Walking over to the dip bars, the illusion of an arrow was fired into the right side of my chest and a voice whispered, *you build it and I will destroy it,* into my right ear. Instantly, I visually turned the arrow into dust and gave the spoken words no more thought. As I continued to counter the negative illusions, they eventually ceased, and I completed my workout. Feeling a lot better than when I started, I left the gym and stopped at a new age gift shop on the way home.

Entering the store there was a strong scent of lavender in the air. "Good morning," I said to the cashier and she reciprocated as I began to browse. In the rear of the store there were two women doing readings for customers, with the assistance of tarot cards and pendulums.

While searching through the incense rack I heard, "Oh, he is coming," from one woman. "I can feel his energy from here," said another woman. I turned my head to see Louie, a gentleman who claims to be a psychic/medium, who I briefly met at another gift shop in the area.

Louie walked in and said, "Hello, ladies" and each woman stopped what they were doing and walked over and gave him a hug. Louie told the ladies he had landed a psychic show of some sort. He went on to say he was booked solid at $140 for twenty-minute sessions.

Walking by the psychic/medium, I said "Good morning, Louie."

"Hi, have we met?" Louie asked, as he turned around.

"Yes, we have, about a month ago at the gift shop in Rehoboth. I'm Lorne," I replied as we shook hands.

"I'm sorry, Lorne, I have a lot of things on my mind," Louie said, while rubbing his solar plexus in the same manner as Tom.

Louie went on to tell the ladies he has been getting a lot of pressure in the solar plexus and nausea lately that he attributed to his diet.

"Do you have any ginger root candy?" I asked the cashier.

"No, we don't," she answered.

"If you get a chance Louie, try some ginger root candy for the nausea."

"I will, thanks Lorne," Louie replied.

As I was paying the cashier for a box of frankincense, one of the owners who was divining with a pendulum earlier walked up.

"Hi Lorne, I'm Linda."

"It's a pleasure, Linda," I said, as we shook hands.

"You work with Angel Michael, don't you?"

"Not that I know of, but I would be honored if I could," I replied.

"In my experience with angels, they're not all friendly, they're rather mean," she mentioned.

"How do you know they're angels?" I asked.

"I took an angel certification course last year," she answered.

"Wow, very good. I can't afford those courses, so I guess I will have to talk to myself, it's cheaper." Linda and the cashier laughed. "Have a good day." I said, walking out the door.

"You as well, Lorne," Linda replied.

Entering the vehicle, the clock was blinking 12:21, at 10:40 in the morning. A blanket cloud of a divine-like presence descended as I drove. Turning on the radio, the song "In the Arms of an Angel" by Sarah McLachlan was playing, and a U.S. Mail truck passed on the right with a large 1221 on the back of the trailer.

All the right buttons were being pushed by the presence triggering the hypnotic-like state. Knowing the mimicking nature of the being, I didn't have to guess what personality was about to make its debut.

Inside the garden of the monastery, I took a seat on the stone bench and prepared the tools. Taking a deep breath and letting it out, I relaxed into receptive oneness and surrendered to the divine energy sensation.

Closing my eyes, a light blue luminous ball fell from the sky and landed in a mountain region. The ball appeared to be a flexible egg with something inside. Piercing through the top was a sword, followed by a bright flash of intense light. Standing in golden armor holding the sword, was a tall human-like form with no facial details.

Opening my eyes, I disconnected from the vision and looked up to see a red-tailed hawk circling above. Engulfed in what appeared to be divine light and the energy sensation of peace and joy, I had no thought to question and for the moment, I couldn't speak. Just as what occurred with the Counterfeit Jesus encounter, there was no mistaking the high vibration of this presence. This is what I once thought was God.

"Words of truth, if you please, from the compassionate heart within your being," I said, as an intense light as bright as the sun was shining in my mind's eye.

I am Michael, angel of light. My hawks are my eyes, my eyes are my soul. I watch your heartbeat as I watch your soul grow. Giving more than receiving, doubles soul's size. Love is eternal and faith is the eyes to see it. I have watched you give more than you have, I have watched you crawl in order to live, I have watched you faithfully believe in what was never taught. Love my brother, is your being.

"Thank you, Angel Michael."

Michael I am, Love I am, God I am. Love brings our hearts together.

"I am honored, thank you Angel Michael. Do you have a message for the good of all?"

God will never speak, until God you are. I will never speak until love is your heart. The Jesus you wait for will walk only in your shoes. God will change your world, but only through each of you. Love is the tool, love is the savior, love is the messiah. I will draw my sword for those that express light from their soul.

"For all I ask, how do you know what is to happen before it occurs on the physical plane? You alerted my attention to 1221 with the clock and the truck and it was no coincidence the song, "In the Arms of an Angel" was playing on the radio. The synchronicity I experience daily is truly amazing."

Moments before moments, I see thee.

"Thank you, Angel Michael. If you please, for all I ask, what is and what is not an angel?"

I will speak first of what is not. Less than God in being, less than love at heart, and less than light of soul.

"If you please, for all I ask, are there names of angels that all should be aware of?"

No name needs to be called, but one love needs to be felt. Michael is my given name; God the I Am is me.

Until humans named the star, older than Earth it was. Until humans named the essence, older than the star it was. Until humans named the angels, older than mankind we are.

Let no name hide what lies within, let no mask of flesh hide what the heart delivers, let no religion hide what must be felt in the soul.

Love I am, but I fight for pure hearts. I once drew my sword and kneeled before God, as God. I delivered light's message. Moses was the translator, I was the voice, God was the heart.

I spoke clearly, I spoke softly, I spoke truth.

I remember Moses, I remember Jesus, I remember you.

Jesus was a human, Moses was a human, you are a human.

That is truth. Name another spoken word of light, I the oracle, internalized its birth long before mouth opened in man. Never do I wear dark wings. I swing a sword of light, for which no demon can lift, and for which no legion can withstand. Darkness lends itself my words, but it will never use my brothers souls. It will never sink Earth into hell's waters. Draw your swords; hold them high, for I am coming. I will cleanse once more that which darkens the springs of humankind's soul.

"I am sure we must experience spiritual battles to grow in wisdom."

Your battles brought you home; your battles made us one.

"For loving truth I ask, what separates you from Jesus in human understanding?"

I am love, Jesus is love, separation doesn't exist.

"Are you one and the same?"

We are one and the same, my brother.

"May I ask for all, did Jesus speak with your heart?"

I spoke with Jesus' heart.

"Angel Michael, you are a loving God."

In my holy word, love lives. In my holy word, light shines. In my holy word, my brother gives all.

"Thank you. Angel Michael, is it wrong for me to teach others to defend themselves physically?"

I know your intention, I know your childhood, I know your love. Fighting for love is my middle name. Love protects, but it feels before it strikes.

"Then the book of our lives is pre-written?"

The book keeps all in place.

"Is there an internal code within?"

In genes you carry family. In DNA you carry God's love.

"May I ask for all, what is Christ to you?"

Christ is not a church, but a heart filled with compassion for all. A holy heart does not ask for gifts but delivers them. Give more than you receive. Allow love to control your roaming thoughts. Wear Jesus proudly. Feel his presence. Jesus followed God's word. Jesus became God's word. Listen to Jesus and you listen to God. Jesus follows hearts, not thoughts.

"May I ask for all, what is the Bible to you?"

Holy pretenders have done plenty of writing. Roots of trees contain more truth than most written books about God. God is love, not image. God is light, not shadow. Light is given when love is given. Religions will crumble if truth has no roots in love.

Holding a book of written words has not stopped greed, has not stopped violence, has not stopped jealousy, has not stopped incest, and has not stopped adultery. It has not even stopped the teachers of this book from committing the evilest acts of humankind. I didn't write this book, Jesus didn't write this book, love didn't write this book.

"May I ask for all, why is eleven constantly mentioned?"

Eleven worlds above fills your cup daily, drink from this. Eleven worlds above fills your heart daily, live from this. Eleven worlds above fills your dreams daily, watch for this. Love finds its followers. Followers interpret what they experience.

"May I ask what you mean by heart?"

The opening to heaven in the center of your soul.

"Last night I was visited by a hooded shadow and I recited the Angel Michael Prayer of Protection out loud."

I can't stop migrating bugs if you give them shelter.

"Can you please explain?"

Opening your temple at night. You need sun. I need sun. Just don't listen to silent whispers from dark corners of the triangle. May sunshine hold your soul in place. My home is light being, my soul is yours.

"Are there other ways that humans shelter migrating bugs?"

Thoughts bring bugs, desires bring bugs, energy brings bugs.

"When you say energy are you speaking of sexual energy?"

Yes, love each other like beings of light not animals of mud.

"During the investigation I have called for the assistance of angels and Jesus Christ. But they never showed, can you tell humanity why?"

Angels are not bodyguards and Jesus Christ is not a warlord. I know you are wiser than your questions. Demons are no match for what lies in your heart.

"Can you explain the jinn?"

Energy masks many faces. Ignore these evil jokesters. Stop listening; forget its existence and take away its life.

"May I ask for all, how is one to call you?"

Sing love with your heart, not with your lips. There are questions that will take you from God self. Stillness will speak the clearest. Have wisdom in your questions and wisdom will answer. I am God. Saying it won't open my eyes, but living it will.

I have a message for you, my brother. You were a God seedling before religions existed, before love was separated by books, before angels found their drawn wings.

You are love, you are light, you are humanity's lantern in darkness.

Make God manifest daily. Let God rule your mind and soul rule your heart. The sun is a single star among infinite brothers. You are one and the same.

"Thank you, Angel Michael."

I am explains me, I am explains you.

Reappearing to my mind's eye was the tall human-like form in golden armor, with a long sword in hand. Slowly, the undetailed face began to shift to appear as me.

Listen closely to your heart, for God is you, my brother.

"May I ask for all, are you really an angel?"

If that's what it takes to clear your vision, then yes, I am an angel, I am love, and I am God in you.

"May I ask why you have not mentioned any of the other benevolent messengers of the illumined heart?"

Forget their names in the presence of love. God bears no name. Michael means 'who is like God'. Gabriel means 'God is my strength.' Do you see the pattern? Don't kneel to names. Stand as God.

"Are you saying those that gave names were impostors?"

Those that gave names are teachers, each and every one.

"Even the malevolent?"

Yes. How do you teach what you have never felt? How do you know what is not part of your experience? Entities are my competitors and I love them all.

"Thank you, Angel Michael. What have I written in this journal?"

You have written a hearts eleven voyages in given words. A god doesn't hear misery because a god can change it. Complete your book with this. 11 voyages are 22 years apart and 33 years long. This is the master code.

"Are there any other suggestions for the night conflict?"

Imagine stars in your heart and the sun at your back. Then you will sleep comfortably on heaven's bed. I know your heart; make your mind just as beautiful.

"Thank you, Angel Michael."

Stars above your pillow, my brother.

Placing the chain down in the notebook, I took a drink of water and reflected on the experience. A gong sound was heard, and an image came to the mind's eye of a woman wearing a medieval dark blue cloak decorated with various shaped clouds. Pulling down the hood she revealed a pixie hairstyle, piercing light blue eyes, and painted skin of a light blue and white mix.

I am Sky, she said with a familiar female voice.

"I like your name Sky," I responded.

I like your heart, Lorne. Being another, I see eyes because I assume eyes. In your eyes is God's doorway, has and always been, Sky said, with a smile.

"For all, may I ask how this conversation was initiated?"

Intention. Light heard your heart's cry. I said, I will help my brother. Never have I felt better than knowing you exist.

"Thank you, Sky."

Might I say, rainbow is your aura, energy is your light, when illuminated a rainbow appears surrounding your being like a beacon for all spirit to see, it is how I found you, it is how you keep outside energy from interrupting our conversation.

"Did you make the gong sound?"

Gong energy ripples your soul.

"Well you have my attention. How were you able to create the gong sound?"

Internal God light focused omni love. Power of God, to make it simple.

"Can you tell me your point of entrance?"

We ride waves of light into your eyes and into your mind. This places your mind high enough to view all as a whole. We need the sun to be, so avoid the shade when we speak.

"Can you tell humanity a little about yourself?"

I am Sky in human experience and God in heart flame. I heard your song; I heard your heart's lyrics. I floated down God's ocean of souls and into your body of water. I came delivering Jesus' pelt. Wear it my brother. When nobody listens remember Jesus, when nobody feels remember God, when nobody cares remember you do.

"Where were you when you heard me speaking from the heart?"

In pleasurable heaven grounds.

"Where do you live?"

I live around circles kept internally.

A vision came to the mind's eye of orbs of different colors traveling through the forest. "Do you remember your human experiences, Sky?"

I wear a scarf, holy and luminous. Higher my heart, lower my mind, and even lower my memories. Memories if beautiful are given wings, memories if evil are given more weight. Jesus had battles of memory as do all students of light. The walk must equal the life experience. Jesus carried heaven into the sky. Bring heaven, leave hell.

"Do you know if the DNA of humans was altered by energy beings?"

I feel DNA is altered by environment. If a fish lives in polluted water, so too will its children.

"Some believe aliens altered the DNA of humans."

I let words fly. Don't hold their wings. Let them pass.

"Many humans believe in spirit guides. Are there guides amongst you?"

Guides are human illusion. God needs no Seeing Eye dog. God opens into a world Christ knows well.

"Do you have a message for humanity?"

Fight no more with ego. Live as God, live as light, live as love. All must free their mind from the intruders that darken their world. An illuminated body repels all leeches of darkness. Human survival depends on their future perception of who they are. God they are, until God they are not. Animals are coming home for a whole new look. Gods are going back.

"You are talking about human evolution. May I ask why you speak in threes?"

Illumination carries three elements. One is God, two is light, and three is love. Combined, loving God of light. God is likened to a galaxy of celestial beings. I am a bright soul and one of those beings.

I would like to say your relationship with one another must be second to God. Without God in your heart you will surely keep foolishness in your mind. I say foolishness because many of you are trying very hard to convince your heart to what it desires. Desire is not God. Desire is keeping you from God. Foolish is speaking with love when desire is the true home. God forgives what desire creates. But desire forgets what God says. Heaven hears and sees all. Don't create what you will regret, for your creation will become your destiny.

"Sky, could you explain the Earthbound souls?"

Earth is beautiful. Kind words are not enough to express my love for her. You know what I mean. Earth carries a shadow of memories - those, which have been given a stone to hold, until the God within removes it. Give God control and break free from your cocoon. All is illusive distraction, know this. Bring Earth home; each of you is all of her. I am, but so are you. We all are one voice, one expression, of one loving God of light.

"Is there anything else you would like to say to all about Earth?" Looking on the ground there was a blue jay feather. Reaching down, I picked it up and placed it on the notebook.

Look at the feather, it is pleasurable to the eyes. Look at the energy field that surrounds it. The halo tells the story. You see Earth has an energy field; you have an energy field. Earth is vibrating with life as you are vibrating with life. Place your hand on Earth, feel the beat of her heart. Feel the wisdom and healing energy she possesses. Here on Earth, all the pleasures, all the pain is felt by you and your Earth mother. Remember Earth in all your travels. Think and she will know. Feel her and you will grow. Never does this hold more truth than now. Time is valuable. I promise you there is no other planet that will replace Earth. When she is gone, all is gone. You must all unite and be all you are. Give Earth a place in your heart and she will be reborn.

"Thank you, Sky."

Words are created for you to understand. This then is felt by your emotions and re-membered as good or not so good. Emotions are your nervous system. Let's see how your emotions feel when you finish the book.

"May I ask, why the nightly torment?"

I see and I know. God has grown because of the challenges you faced. As you grow the sun gets closer and the nights get smaller. Deliver this my brother, you are a body of water, electrical and gravitational forces make you illuminate - making you sing a code, light only, love always, God child. I know you occasionally anger, I know you occasionally walk into dark corners. But your heart is God. Jesus I follow, you I watch, God I see.

"Thank you, Sky." A slight shift in emotion was felt and my hair began to be manipulated. "May I ask, why the dark parasites?"

Why the dark thoughts?

"Could you explain evil, Sky?"

Could you explain the pains of childbirth?

"No, I couldn't."

Then I cannot explain evil. It is not me.

"Understood." Stimulation to the genitalia region began. "You are trying to seduce, Sky."

I am making love fairy style.

An influenced day vision began, and I was standing in a retail book shop. An older woman was seated on a couch to the left watching television. A four foot dark paneled wall separated the lounging area from the store. In from the back room walked Sky. The older woman asked, *who is he?*

Lowering her hood, Sky answered, *this is Lorne.*

Looking at Sky's hands I noticed her fingernails were alternately painted light blue and white to match her skin.

Please follow me, Sky said as she opened a light blue and white silk curtain. Hesitant, I followed and was instantly amazed at the amount of gold treasure of coins, weaponry, shields, jewelry, crowns, lanterns, and other objects that were piled high in what appeared to be the interior of an ancient temple. Two gold and jeweled thrones were side by side, and Sky took a seat.

Please sit.

Slowly I sat, observing the triangle and sun symbol patterns, the eyes of the dragon and snake statues, and various serpent carvings throughout the structure watching my every move.

A pink flamingo appeared out of nowhere carrying a pink rose quartz stone in its beak. Dropping it in my hands I looked to see *I Love You* carved within. The flamingo flew up onto my left shoulder as a pink fluffy cat manifested on my lap.

Turning toward Sky, she had a familiar seductive stare, *marry me,* she asked.

"No," I firmly answered.

Sky stood up and removed her cloak revealing a naked painted body that matched the pattern of her face and neck. *Have sex with me.*

"Sorry, I've got low T."

Join me and all is yours, Sky said, as she turned and pointed to the treasure.

"This is not what I view as treasure. No material possession brings lasting happiness or satisfaction. Thanks for the offer, but the answer is no."

Sky began to transform to a few women of past relationships. *I can be any woman of your past or any woman you desire for the future.*

"Yes, I know. You are a master of illusion. But can you shapeshift to your true form in this present moment?" Sky lowered her head and vanished, and I opened my eyes disconnecting from the vision.

Coming forward next is what appeared to be my grandmother and grandfather. Picking up the chain I held it over the chart.

Love is here, I am your Gram. Pop, your true dad, is here too.

"If only this were true."

It is, my son. I can't be brighter than my son. Love has not left your side. It opened in your courage. I anoint your soul with my heart as yours, said my grandfather.

My grandmother reached down and picked up a green snake off the ground. The snake bit its own tail and formed a circle. *The snake is afraid of you. It's a female,* said my grandmother, as she pointed to a small reversed red triangle marking below its neck and the snake turned to rubber.

Let's put to rest these beings, son. Keep a hand on your heart and say, this is mine and I love it. I am illumined, and I am God. I don't run from demons and I don't feed them either, said my grandfather.

A vision of me carrying my grandfather in my arms into the emergency room when I was fourteen years old came to the mind's eye. This was the last time I would see my grandfather alive, he passed early the following morning.

Right you are, you carried me, and I shall carry you. Pop is God now and God is you. Kindness is your being, ill thoughts don't belong there. Let ill speakers sorrow loose and it will dissipate.

"Should I continue writing this book?"

Hear the call of the messengers. Watch in god's eyes, Feel in god's body. Place your heart in God and then finish it. I am goodness because it is my flesh. No demon wants skin placed in light. Let your skin marinate for a while in these words. God lives in me, God loves in me, God is me. Make your morning start with these words, make your evenings end with these words.

"Should I talk with the demons?"

No, ignore them and live as God. I now must return to the star of the infinite.

The brilliance of the sun shone in my mind's eye. "Is the star of the infinite the sun?"

Yes, this is the home of light. Illumined boat in the blue sky. Wave my son for I will watch over you. I keep your children within the distance of my heart. I love you son, said my grandfather.

"Your wickedness is showing. You are not my Pop," I responded.

Darkness set in and I put the chain down in the notebook and closed it. Three ghost monks manifested in the garden in brown cloth with a golden-white glow. One monk stood in the entrance to the left, one in the entrance to the right, and the third straight ahead in the entrance behind the cross. Floating silently forward, the center monk passed right through a tree and then the cross, taking its position in front. Simultaneously, the other two monks glided to their positions on the left and right side of the center monk.

This time they didn't separate. In perfect sync, they transformed into a man, woman, and child in pink robes with pointy hoods. The man was to the right, the woman to the left, and the little girl in the middle. Looking down at the little girl, she was carrying the bald naked baby doll in her hands. Raising their heads, the man, woman, and child revealed their matching jet-black eyes and the three of them blinked three times in unison, then vanished.

A young couple wearing backpacks walked into the garden and stopped when they saw me. "Good morning," I said to the teens. "Good morning," they replied as I packed up. "I'm just leaving," I said, standing up.

Putting on the pack I said, "Enjoy your day." "You too," they answered and walked over toward the cedar cross. In the right hand of the young lady was a K2 EMF meter, a popular ghost hunting piece of equipment.

Looking at the time, I decided to slip in one more interaction and began the trek to the Nine Men's Misery Monument, a location I intentionally avoided due to an expected dark confrontation.

CHAPTER 23

METACOMET AND DEMON GOD

P assing a few dog walkers and joggers, I arrived at the destination and removed the pack. Standing in front of the cairn, I recited prayer for the men, women and children that died during the King Philip's War.

Taking a seat against a nearby tree, I thought about the history of this location and the varied objects I have seen placed on the cairn and monument through the years. I have seen flowers, candles, crosses of various types, open Bibles, idols, religious figurines, and even wax pyramids. Today, there were numerous small crosses made of sticks all over the surface of the cairn and monument.

This location has seen more than its share of paranormal investigations, rituals, and divination practices through the years by the curious and those attempting to converse with the deceased. I will not be attempting to wake the dead in any way, shape, or form. What is about to speak was never human.

To my right was a pile of beer bottles and cans behind a tree. Before I began, I opened the pack and took out a trash bag and picked up the bottles and cans. Tying up the bag, I placed it down next to the pack and returned to the tree to sit.

A strong presence of wickedness was waiting as I took the chain out of my pocket and prepared the tools. In addition to the tag along, there may be others called forth by the naive.

Visions began immediately, with nine large black crows on a branch of a tree directly across. One at a time the birds shifted to grayish puckwudgies and nine bloody soldiers of varied height and body types surrounded me forming a circle.

Taking a deep breath, I let it out and relaxed into receptive oneness. Positioning the chain over the chart, I allowed the conversation to begin telepathically. "If you could be heard on this day, what would you say?"

One at a time the soldiers spoke in a clockwise manner.

Soldier one, ***Deep inside a dark cavern I wait.***

The first puck on the branch above laughed.

Soldier two, ***Beheaded I was, but God gave me another.***

The second puck on the branch above laughed.

Soldier three, ***Kept a hold on Indian blood and I can't let go.***

The third puck on the branch above laughed.

Soldier four, ***Only hate I feel like a lead bullet anchor.***

The fourth puck on the branch above laughed.

Soldier five, ***Evil face lurks behind my back and I can't outrun it.***

The fifth puck on the branch above laughed.

Soldier six, ***Fear you are without, how can this be?***

The sixth puck on the branch above laughed.

Soldier seven, ***My God what are you?***

The seventh puck on the branch above laughed.

Soldier eight, *Hold my hand, evil has my heart.*

The eighth puck on the branch above laughed.

The wickedness of the energy was intense and damaging to my nervous system, so I took a moment to merge with the stillness of the forest and smiled when I regained internal peace.

Soldier nine, *How am I to do half of what you just did?*

All nine of the pucks laughed at once.

"Each of you has spoken, now I refuse to converse anymore until this chaos ends." Instantly the puckwudgies and soldiers vanished and a powerful energy shift occurred.

Closing my eyes, I was standing alone in a grocery store and there were three aisles in front of me and a deli counter behind. The aisle numbers were black on red signs hanging above each aisle. Walking over to aisle one, which was a cereal aisle, I was met by the bald headed, naked baby doll sitting in the seat of the carriage. With an evil smile, it waved its hand and its eyes lit up one black and one red and began to alternately blink. *I milk, you cereal, float your life in me*, said the doll with its sinister voice.

Backing up, I walked into aisle two which was the pasta and tomato sauce aisle and was met again by the naked baby doll in the carriage waving with one hand and the other hand had a small brown and white dog with a human skull for a head on a red leash. The doll was wearing a gold halo on top of its head and its eyes were bright white lights.

Backing out of the aisle, I looked down to see tomato sauce all over both my feet and sliced mushrooms on top of the left foot.

Turning the corner into aisle three, which was soda and water, there was a black heavy bag hanging from the ceiling with a red long sleeve shirt floating behind with black gloves where the hands should be. The heavy bag charged toward me and the empty shirt sleeves started swinging strikes at different angles. With each attempted gloved fist strike, I blocked and countered with a series of punches of my own to the heavy bag. After a dozen or so attacks, the gloves dropped to the floor and the shirt went limp and vanished with the heavy bag.

The tall brown costumed dog with the long flappy ears manifested clapping.

Slowly it turned its head and looked over its left shoulder, giving me an evil smile. Down from the ceiling came a black sign blinking in red saying, **Join Me and Rule Human Minds.**

Shaking my head, I said, "No."

The sign disappeared as the being shapeshifted into the tall red-eyed hooded shadow and I was now wearing the dog costume. As I was looking over the costume, the hooded shadow disappeared and a man's voice was heard from behind asking, *what do you need?*

Turning around, it was a man working at the deli counter. "I'll take a pound of turkey breast sliced thick," I answered, playing along.

The deli man pulled out the turkey, and sliced one piece, then showed me the thickness. *How's that?* he asked. "That's perfect," I answered.

Looking into the case while the deli man began slicing the meat, there were three pigs' heads next to the hot dogs with a price of $3.33 a pound. Weighing the meat, he asked me if there would be anything else, and I answered, "That's it, thank you," as he handed me the package.

Turning to the right there were nine gray puckwudgies standing just like the ones on the tree branch with angry faces. Carrying spears, knives, bows, and quivers of gold arrows they stood about four feet tall, had leathery skin, and their noses, ears, and hands were oversized.

What appeared to be the leader jumped up on the deli counter and the rest followed suit. The pucks began ransacking the place and pulling out all the meats. A few began to eat raw hamburger and hot dogs while a couple of others took turns throwing deli meat up in the air as another shot it with an arrow. One puck with a hunchback opened a large jar of pickles. As he reached his hand in the glass jar the deli man pulled out a long knife and started waving it in front of him.

When the deli man lunged with a forehand swing another puck jumped on his back and started stabbing him in the neck, as another bit into his leg.

Slowly, I started backing up as the gang of pucks pounced on the man. A puck look-out standing on top of one of the aisles spotted me trying to escape and alerted the others. All at once they stopped what they were doing, turned their heads, and sprinted in my direction. Running into aisle two, I grabbed a half a dozen cans of tomato sauce and started throwing them at the advancing pucks as I made my way toward a nearby bathroom. Just as I entered and slammed the door shut multiple gold arrows were fired, with three of them getting stuck in the thick wood of the door forming a triangle.

Opening my eyes, I disconnected from the dream. My eyes felt like there was dirt in them as a tall Native American came forward with slight detail making out strong features. An intense headache and nausea accompanied the presence.

I have followed you for many sunsets, you know why, my brother.

"Who, may I ask, is speaking?"

I am Metacomet.

"I am honored Metacomet. I will not be able to talk for long, your energy is toxic and uncomfortable," I said, as I rubbed my eyes trying to clear them.

I am sorry my brother, I still carry my anger.

"There was much blood spilled on this land. This I know."

I chose Great Spirit over man's written word. It cost my people's lives, but not their spirit. Their spirit is free.

A vision came of what appeared to be early Quakers walking into the Saylesville Friends Meetinghouse. "I see a group of Quakers attending a meeting."

I was killed before they settled, but I walked with no legs. Great Spirit I believed they spoke, they called it God. He who they followed I agree with.

"Do you mean Jesus Christ?"

Yes, I did not see this man in the men I fought. Great Spirit would agree with this man Jesus. But not the man they showed me. I would have enjoyed you beside me in battle. You were a great warrior.

"I cannot agree to this, but I will listen."

Do you believe I lived?

"Of course, Metacomet. You were a great warrior and leader. The King Philip's War is well documented."

You are White Wolf, a Medicine Man and great warrior. You fought like many braves. They feared you.

"Who may I ask feared me?"

The white demons. High in the mountain you deserve to be.

"I thank you, but I question for truth."

Metacomet does not lie even at the price of death.

"Did you live in this area of land?"

I lived all over this great land.

"Metacomet what would you tell all people on this day?"

Live free, call Great Spirit what you wish. Walk Mother Earth, don't hurt her. This is Metacomet.

"How, may I ask, did you know me?"

They killed your woman; you darkened their white skin with great warrior heart. He who kneels to Great Spirit lives again.

"What would help you walk into the world of light?"

You my brother, show me your vision and I will enter.

Knowing this vision would be an internal invitation, I opted to raise my vibration instead creating a shift in the deceiver. A vision came forward of many Native American men, women, and children, standing and waiting.

"There appears to be many here that are not at rest."

I will lead my people. You have the sun in your heart. Show me, my brother.

"Goodbye, Metacomet, I will create the vision."

Goodbye, White Wolf. Earth needs your touch once again. Listen to the crows, they are Earth's voice, not the white demons.

Taking a deep breath, I exhaled and merged again with the stillness of the forest. Knowing the sun creates a shift in the deceiver, I visualized the sun shining down from above and began to recite prayer and release gratitude into the environment causing the negative energy to take on a positive vibration.

Leaving the monastery, a doll was seated on the bench up ahead. Stopping in front of the bench, I turned to see a naked baby doll exactly like the one in the influenced visions. As I accelerated, a small rock hit the driver's side window leaving no mark. The deceptive god could have influenced or manipulated a child or adult to, knowingly or unknowingly, leave or forget the doll.

When I got home, I was unusually fatigued and took a seat on the couch. Removing my boots and socks, I laid down. Setting the alarm for one hour, I placed it on the coffee table.

Out of the corner of my left eye what appeared to be a black mink-like animal, about two feet in length, crawled up the left corner of the wall and disappeared into the ceiling. Knowing I wasn't going to get a nap, I leaned over the side of the bed and picked up the backpack. Opening it, I took out the recorder, turned it on, and placed it on my stomach.

Now that they know I am recording their activity I won't be surprised by a barrage. Any images that come to the mind's eye during the twilight state will be recorded immediately so I don't forget them.

Closing my eyes, a clicking sound was heard followed by the fluttering of what sounded like small bird or moth's wings in my right ear. This was immediately followed by an image of a cell phone floating in the air. *Was that an angel?* appeared as a text, then the cell phone faded into the void.

Opening my eyes, I reached over and grabbed the other pillow and placed it under my head. With my eyes open, an arm of something reached up through the gap between the headboard and the mattress, and yanked the bottom pillow hard, as what sounded like an animal was heard scurrying around under the bed. Puckwudgie came to mind, but I wasn't sure what it was and I certainly wasn't about to get down and look.

A dog started barking outside and a woman yelled "Get over here" three times, before I closed my eyes.

Visions and bangs to the walls began immediately to interrupt my rest. *Do you want to fight?* was whispered into my right ear. "Do you want to talk about love and compassion?" I countered. No answer was given so I said, "Guess not."

A vision began of me sitting in the rear seat of an inflatable two person kayak. A man with long brown hair was in the front, wearing only farmer's jeans. Floating down a fast-moving mountain stream we approached a small dark tunnel about four feet wide. The man began panicking and didn't want to enter. Holding up his paddle with two hands he tried to brace it up against the stone border of the entrance to stop, yelling, *I don't like tunnels, I don't like tunnels, I don't like tunnels!* Unable to fight the strength of the current, the paddle snapped in two and we entered.

It's a hidden world after all, it's a hidden world after all, it's a hidden world after all, it's a hidden, scary world, was being sung repetitively in the pitch dark by eerie voices.

On the left an exhibit lit up, the kayak stopped, and the creepy song ceased. A middle-aged woman with multi-colored hair and ripped up clothing was standing in front of a small pond feeding a team of ducks. Each duck only had one large eye in the middle of its head. Painted on the tall wall behind her was a variety of hybrid creatures about eight feet tall, shoulder to shoulder throughout its full length.

Taking off her silver-rimmed glasses, she turned towards us and began violently shaking. Tiny shadow people around two inches tall started jumping out of her body by the hundreds before the light shut off.

Floating to the next exhibit on the right, we stopped in front of three red and black houses. Standing in the doorway that had the numbers 555 above were shadow people with red eyes. In front of each house was a large oak tree.

The tree in the center split down the middle and slowly opened, revealing a large carved goblin face. As it became animated it began to sing, *It's a hidden world after all, it's a hidden world after all, it's a hidden world after all, it's a hidden, scary world.* Looking at my right arm, the lyrics of the song appeared written in white flowing down my arm like a stream.

Moving on we stopped at the next exhibit on the left. Under a blue and white canopy, a couple was seated at a long black picnic table with a serpent idol in the middle and two gold medieval knight masks. Surrounding the canopy in a circle were antique vehicles with hood ornaments that were small human-like heads with scaly skin. Each was about the size of a grapefruit and appeared to be talking amongst themselves but nothing was heard. The couple put on their masks and stood up, facing us and holding see-through glass sculptures of a human brain.

A large statue of a bear standing on its hind legs wearing a white sailor's hat manifested. The statue came alive and it got down on all fours and shook off the hat. All at once the hood ornaments started to sing, *It's a hidden world after all, It's a hidden world after all, It's a hidden world after all, it's a hidden, scary world,* as the bear stood up and danced until the light shut off.

Floating forward we were now in the largest cavern I have seen in vision. The ceiling was a wave-like carved stone at least 100 feet high, and the width was three football fields of wide open area. At the edges were many rocks, about twice the size of a bowling ball, piled high. On top of a large stone appeared to be a man wearing a devil Halloween mask, with five small goats with gold horns in front of him standing on their hind legs. The first goat was black, the second was white, the third brown and white, the fourth black and white, and the fifth was brown. As the man lifted the mask it revealed a somewhat human, evil looking black pig face that had long curved tusks like a warthog and said, *How did you like our show?* The vision ceased just as the alarm went off.

More tired than when I laid down, I sat up, placed the recorder on the coffee table and wiped my face with my hand a few times. An irritating tickle in my lungs caused me to start coughing, and I felt the presence of wickedness. When the tickle passed, I began to recite the Angel Michael prayer aloud to experience the reaction. As expected, the anger of the presence increased.

Taking the notebook out of the backpack, I moved the cell phone and recorder to the side of the table. Removing my necklace, I placed the cross down on the arm of the couch. Closing my eyes, an invading vision of the monastery garden appeared. A large weathered looking newspaper that was laminated was lying on the stone bench. The front-page article was early century and had a story about a monk named Father Albert Celestine. The picture was an older man with thin gray hair and a short, well-manicured beard, exact to the black framed painting image experienced in the monastery restroom.

As I sat down and read the article it changed, and the laminated surface became reflective. The headline now read 'The Ten Faces of the Devil' with a picture of a large full tree underneath. Manipulation of the reflection revealed a different face within the tree. Varying the viewing angle of the article, I found all ten faces. Five faces appeared on the left that were human of both genders with happy faces, and five appeared on the right side of the tree, grotesque and monstrous with angry faces.

Putting the paper back down on the bench, I turned to see a gorilla seated on the ground in front of the cedar cross. Staring, the gorilla's eyes changed to a yellowish color with the elliptical pupils of a venomous snake. As the gorilla stood up, I stood up, prepared to fight if need be.

Coming forward the head of the gorilla changed to a human skull with the same snake eyes. Just outside my reach it stopped. Raising its hands, it had red gloves and the tip of each finger and thumb were the same ten faces that appeared in 'The Ten Faces of the Devil' tree.

Five faces on the left were the humans with happy faces and five faces on the right side were the angry, grotesque monster faces. All at once the ten faces said, *are you trying to make us look bad?*

"Not at all, you are quite adept at doing that on your own," I answered.

A surface of many large holes deep into the Earth appeared. Lying next to one of the holes, which was about six feet wide, was my red notebook. As I reached down to grab it, a gust of wind blew it into the hole. Panicking, I got down on my hands and knees and looked over the edge. A good ten feet down my notebook sat on a rock ledge. Realizing the image was an illusion, the malevolent presence grew angry and a gust of wind blew the notebook off the ledge and I watched it fall into the deep, dark abyss as the dreamscape changed to a desert road.

Five red and black pickup trucks were lined up with roofs that opened and hybrid creatures sticking their animal heads out the top. *Charge!* was shouted by the giant dominant human/hybrid leader with the head of a bull in the middle truck. The trucks raced forward, kicking up dust and avoiding large snakes and crocodiles in their path. As they approached, I mentally created a thick wall of cement blocks.

The barrier stopped them for a moment, then they backed up, revved their engines, and the hybrid bull leader again shouted *Charge!* Their trucks started ramming the wall repeatedly. Mentally, I opened the ground in front of the wall, creating a large hole. When the trucks crashed through, one by one they fell into the abyss just like my notebook.

Opening my eyes, I disconnected from the virtual reality-like simulation with a headache, nausea, and a fluttering sound in my right ear again. The heaviness of the doom and gloom cloud of the presence and its toxicity was barely tolerable. Shutting off the recorder, I unzipped the backpack and took out the notebook laying it on the coffee table.

Pondering the vision of the bull-headed hybrid for a moment, I tested the reaction of the presence by doing an internet search for Egyptian gods that had the head of a bull. The first to pop up was Apis which was the Greek name for the Egyptian bull deity known as Hapi, Hep, or Api. As I read about the god, the presence grew in anger and whispered, *I don't like you reading about other gods,* into my right ear.

Way too tired to be interacting, I prepared the tools like a zombie, took a deep breath and let it out. Holding the chain over the chart the conversation began. "Who are you, when my choice is goodness?"

I am the alternate choice.

"But I am not. Why the wickedness?"

Goodness your choice lacks a guest.

An image came forward of a human skull with spirals of red hair on both sides, forming the curled horns of a mountain goat.

Don't you get scared?

"Of who? You or your many illusions?"

You are definitely God child.

"Where are you from?"

I live where goats live. Say it's goat time and join the farm.

A vision came forward of a mountain full of naked women lying in various positions and walking on all fours. An old man in a black robe with long gray hair and silver-rimmed glasses appeared and pointed to the mountain *What more could a man ask for?* he asked. "No thanks," I responded, and the man turned toward me with eyes fiery red and the women on the mountain turned to goats of various colors.

"Why the goats?"

Like goat, not as goat. I look a lot like you now, because we are joined in the center. So, let's go get a female goat and fuck the shit out of her.

Another vision came forward of the Monastery woods. A large white goat came out from behind a huge tree and stood up on its hind legs as it slipped on a pair of bright red high heels. Walking forward it took short wobbly steps.

"Ahh, the twisted humor."

Sorry, it's my nature to laugh all the time.

"We both know that's a lie. Enough with the illusions. Can you answer historical questions?"

Whose version, mine or the Christians?

"Why do you single out Christianity?"

Might I say, very wise question. Jesus is killed by demons, but man follows a corpse. Power from imagination.

"Many will say this is imagination."

Let them cover their deeds. I will find them. I take words with a grain of salt, as they say. All words are noise pollution in my ears. Books are in fire. Words are the cause.

"Are you speaking of religious texts?"

I'm talking about all God calling books.

"Can you occupy the sun's rays?"

Demons are not vampires. Earth, sun, moon, or eleven worlds beyond yours. We are without chains.

"How did you become a demon?"

Place the dark thoughts into a container and shake it good.

"What is the qualification of a demon?"

Evil blood.

"That's it, just evil blood?"

Just evil intention. I am part animal and part human.

I began to recite the Angel Michael prayer again out loud.

Angel Michael is a popular name. Try another.

"Then I will ask for God."

Render yourself soulless, because I am you.

"I will swim in the essence of love."

Not today, the pool is closed.

"Then I will converse when it opens."

You do that. Love is only a word. You know love can't save this planet. What are your wishes?

"I have no wishes."

You need money.

"Many need money far more than I."

I require no social security number. Just your soul's word will do.

"No thanks."

Tell that to your landlord and bring some tissues to wipe your bare ass. Without me you're homeless; without me, you're hopeless.

"I am faithful to God."

You are faithful, I will give you that. But you are a fool. Holy fools invite demons.

"Am I considered a holy fool?"

Yes. Angel Michael can't help, God can't help, try the ghostbusters.

"Can you say, I love Jesus Christ?"

I love Jesus Christ and all his drunken apostles.

"That was negative."

Humans don't give a fuck. They read the fucking Bible that some priest jerked off on.

"You are really dark."

Do you know how many Catholics it takes to kill a demon?

"No."

Forty-four long robes.

"Can you say, I love Angel Michael?"

I can say anything, how about Santa bring me a Lexus.

"That's not what I asked."

Okay, I love angels of light, especially Angel Michael, he's my hero. How about Santa bring me a hooker for a blowjob.

"There you go with that one-track mind. Do you only hate humans, or do you hate wildlife as well?"

I hate humans the most. I now like one in particular.

"Sure you do. Why do you hate humans?"

Humans are a waste of DNA. I can be truthful if you like.

"That would be a first."

I need your soul in my legion. These lonely fuckups need some new friends.

"Your army of fuckups is going to have to stay lonely, because I'm not joining. Are you of the jinn?"

I have jinn-like qualities, but a bit more like demon god.

"Jinn and demons are not the same?"

Jinn are fire beasts; demons are evil gods.

"Were you once an angel?"

Hope not, because I haven't seen yours yet. Humans are so predictable. Make them scared and they call angels. Make them see light coming and an angel they assume is there. Let me give you a message. Demons are angels. Holy Michael is me. I tricked you, but don't feel bad, I trick them all.

"Your emotions gave away your secret long ago."

Holy is a demon's word. Look at the Vatican. Feel what lingers in the stones. Jesus was tricked, enter the demon that called him son. God love called to him and he answered. My, my - humans wait thousands of years for a human God. Let me tell you a different story. Demons are your advancement in evolution. Electricity is my blood. How do we connect? Electricity. I can't talk to a fucking hamburger, electricity must flow in you.

"You appear as light in dreams, visions, wake, and even shining bright against closed eyelids."

A little surprised, are you? Didn't they say demons have candles too in the good book?

"No, I'm not surprised, I just wanted your admittance. You know the Bible says Satan is capable of appearing as an angel of light."

Capable! But not a flame of heart, but a flame of hell.

"Who is your leader or master?"

I stand as master and creator. I am partially Lorne in the moment, and all evil emanation of the combined consciousness.

"You are very intelligent."

The intelligence of all historic consciousness.

"Why the Monastery?"

Monastery has little to do with it. You are my interest.

"I choose the essence of love."

Jesus was the essence of love, look where the essence took him. He died with his teachings altered by many. I remember Jesus very well. He earned my respect. But he didn't earn the human pigs respect. They eat what they are, garbage. I call the essence illusion. I call faith illusion-based mind madness. Essence of what? Essence has many flavors, evil, goodness, universal, lustful, I know you are acquainted with that one.

"And so are you."

I recall love in girls being a weakness in many.

"I've heard that somewhere before. It is written you lust for mortal women as well."

Demons like titties too.

"I'm sure. At least we know the essence of love exists."

I never said differently. I can tell you the dinosaurs existed, where in the Bible is that discussion? I can tell you I'm a demon, where in the Bible is my discussion? Fact is dinosaurs and demons ruled this planet. In came holy God illumined DNA. Humans became God consciousness. Illumined was electricity, love was the title. Illumined feared demon consciousness. Kept from the Bible. Kept from both demon and new gods. Love exists and so too demon.

"Why do you follow?"

I claimed you long ago. When demons stared in your eyes, I ate them. Now I remain close, destroying demons in heat.

"There is that jealousy again. It's time to end this comedy show. I've got things to do."

Well I hope you enjoyed my script.

"You are an expression of the source of existence. You play a part in its wonderful design, and I respect that. But I do not choose to harbor the pollution you project. A hooded monk in white named Quasar said, *See more light than foolish thoughts. Find your goodness, find your God.* Maybe you have heard of him."

Instantly there was a shift in the energy of the presence, the atmosphere was now lighter, and the negative communication ceased. An image came to my mind's eye of a large hand with 11 cents in the palm, consisting of a nickel and six shiny pennies. This followed with an image of a hooded ghost monk in white cloth with a golden-white aura coming forward.

I know goodness, I know love, I know evil. Enter, come and reach for the stars.

"Are you still a Demon?"

I am a Master and few I call the same.

"I am honored, thank you. But I am no master."

Love honors your soul. I found heaven inside Full Circle. Now it shall speak. Holy infancy has grown to be Holy God.

"How would you explain Holy?"

Indwelling stars awaken indwelling Christ. Holy is freedom of soul. Spiritual is holy soul awareness internalized to the eleventh power.

"What is this 11?"

Christ born in man. Illumination born in man for a pod-like flowering of consciousness. Heaven, you now call this ancient process. Gone are the dark eleven. Gone are the migrating bugs, for you listened. Internal construction completed, Master of the quest to salvation. Keep eleven luminous for all.

"Is it true I was a Native American in a past life?"

Yes, it is true and many other experiences of soul.

"I would appreciate any help you could give in explaining how it all comes together."

Heaven can be. God is the ocean but not the particles that thought breeds. Feeling emotion is not God. I am without emotion as you can tell. I am just energy. Like water in a glass, I am still, even when you consume me. God is emotionless but accompanies emotion. God assumes but does not act. Electricity assumes without judgment. Expression has an electrical foundation. Electricity gives life to the flesh sculpture. Without electricity the sculpture ceases expression and decomposes. Electricity remains carrying with it your emotions and memory. Depending on your created contents, it can assume as Heaven or a world of its own creation.

"Thank you for your knowledge."

Thank you, my brother.

The conversation ended on what would appear to be a positive note. Feeling the negative film of the malevolent presence on my face and extreme fatigue, I took a salt bath. While soaking a feminine voice whispered, *I can help you with that.*

"I'm good, thanks," I quickly responded.

Passages from Scripture about the Holy Spirit began to bombard my mind's eye. Page after page came forward, highlighting its abilities and characteristics until a voice whispered in my right ear, *I'm the best you can get.* "I beg to differ," I responded.

CHAPTER 24

HOLY SPIRIT AND DARO

Holy Spirit passages started to reappear just before I opened my eyes. After expressing gratitude to that which gives life, I meditated, then had a light breakfast.

Walking out to the vehicle, the driver's door was wide open. Examining the vehicle inside and out, everything appeared to be untouched. Driving to the monastery, the strong smell of sulphur began as I came up on a meat delivery truck with a large black bull's head on the gate. On my right a small black vehicle passed with the license plate, **Lilith.**

Traveling down Great Road toward the historic district, a shadow type I have never encountered stepped out of the forest of Lincoln Woods State Park. Standing at least eight feet tall, the giant resembled some descriptions of the Bigfoot or Sasquatch of folkore.

Staring directly, it remained between 5-10 seconds as I slowed down to observe. It appeared to be a hybrid combination of human and ape. Detail was minimal, with no eyes or signs of hair, only the opaque shadow substance which was exact to the hooded shadow. Succeeding in catching my attention, the giant stepped back into the forest and vanished into thin air.

Expecting an energetically challenging morning at the monastery, I opened the console and took out the *Rocky IV* soundtrack album. Placing the CD into the player I selected the song "No Easy Way Out" sung by Robert Tepper and proceeded.

Entering the garden, a vision of the golden-white cross came forward in the mind's eye, followed by a vision of a large luminous right hand with a pure white dove in the palm.

The divine-like presence descended and washed over my being as I retraced the steps of the very first encounter. Maintaining a peaceful vibration and a clear mind, I arranged the tools on the stone bench then turned and faced the cross.

Taking a deep breath, I exhaled into receptive oneness and surrendered to the divine-like energy sensation. Looking up into the sky, I raised my arms slowly. Standing still in total reverence with uplifted hands, I said, "God is my heart." In a trance state, I took a seat on the bench. Placing the notebook on my lap and the alphabet chart on top. Holding the chain in position, I took one more deep breath and exhaled slowly. Controlling thought and emotion, I said, "For the goodness of all, if you please." The conversation began telepathically with the overwhelming bright light that many have described as the opening of heaven.

Holy Spirit I am, Holy Ghost I am, Holy Heart I am. I am the word of all open hearts. I am God of love and compassion. Love as a heart that encompasses all.

Hearts have no names, hearts have no hate, hearts have no lies. Holy days are offerings of compassion to your siblings of eternal soul. Bring me your internal boat and I will fill it with my love. The ocean is ready. Bring it to you.

I am all your hearts, I am all your souls, I am all your loved ones. From birth to eternity you are always in my heart and always in my soul.

I watch, I listen, I smell, I taste, I feel, I know. All your thoughts, all your actions, all your feelings. All noticed but not judged.

I am what I am and that is what I remain as. I will view but I will not correct your actions. I will speak but I will not expect you to listen. I will love you but expect no love in return. I will give you life and expect you to live as you choose. I will give you what I have always given you, unconditional divine love. I know only this, I feel only this, I am only this.

I am love, I am light, I am Christ. I am all you see and all you don't see. I am you even when you are not me. I am tears of joy, I am tears of sorrow. I am laughter from your happiest experience. Combine all your perceptions of good and bad and I am all of this.

I have patience for all my children that never tires. I have given you no name to call me. I have asked of no name to call me. There exists no love in words only in being. I will listen to your words, but I will feel your intention. I will listen to your prayers, but I will feel your intention. I will listen to your pilgrimage, but I will feel your intention. I will listen to all language, but I will feel your intention. I am the universe, I am the omniverse, I am infinity. I am all the words of your discoveries to come, I am all the words from your first pith.

"Forgive me, my Lord. But I don't know what the word pith means."

I know my son, I wanted you to know this word. It is the core of plants, your first life on Earth. Plants and trees are your ancestors. They must exist for you to exist. They ask for nothing. They feed themselves and you. Love them as you love me. Learn from them and grow from them as you always have.

"My Lord, there are those who call me brother or angel, can you explain?"

I have many children that love me in their own unique way. I will only allow love to teach love. You are all masters eventually. I speak to all, listen to me.

I am God, I am love, I am compassion. Follow love not name, follow compassion not name, follow the Messiah not name.

The Messiah is your open heart and the seed that awakens is God. I am, because you loved me. I am, because you believed in me. I am, because you fed me more than you fed hate.

I am God, you're loving soul, I am walking, I am breathing. I am Jesus, incarnated as man. Hierarchy is man's illusion. I am Jesus, loving, compassionate God. Least holy is hierarchy.

I never put love in second place and title in first. I never loved less those with deaf ears. I am compassion before teacher. I am compassionate, eternal God. Love, feel, become. Holy heart is my soul in you. I have love for all to hold. My heart carries my word and my word is truth.

I did not put words on record, words can be altered. I did not speak with evil tongue. I did not say put a book before compassion. I did not judge my non-believing siblings. I did not harm my siblings. Love is my word.

I am one and I am all your religious incarnates. I, Holy Spirit, place my word within all religions. Religions are paths and heart is the mountain they climb. Holy Spirit watches your journey. I am watching your journey. I love you all. Paths I have many. Hearts I have one.

"My Lord, could you explain angels?"

I need no messenger if compassion lives within. Messengers are holy and unholy. Seen and unseen. All are soul voices heard. The soul is a seed. Plant it in what you feel.

"My Lord, what is your view on baptism?"

Baptism is a ritual. Holy Spirit is love. I am Jesus, as I am you. I am one within all. Don't separate me. I can't be created, but I can be worn. God confused minds of chaos, I am without name.

God is your label, Lord is your label, Great Spirit is your label. Names don't bring me, killing doesn't bring me, hatred doesn't bring me.

Compassion of heart brings me. Love and compassion felt will do more than any word spoken. Eternal love will do more than any war.

Feel don't speak, hear don't doubt, internalize don't externalize.

Turning to the pages where the first, second and third god presence spoke, I began to ask who the voice was as I felt for an energy shift like a lie detector. "I'm a little confused. May I ask my Lord who is speaking in this conversation?" I pointed to the dialogue of the first god presence.

Holy Spirit.

"May I ask who is speaking in this conversation?" as I pointed to the dialogue of the second god presence.

Holy Spirit.

"May I ask who is speaking in this conversation?" as I pointed to the dialogue of the third god presence.

Holy Spirit.

"Thank you. Now I just have just one more, my Lord," turning the pages to the Demon god's dialogue, I pointed my finger. "Can you tell me who is speaking here?" Instantly my heartbeat became rapid as a powerful energy shift occurred in the presence of wickedness. "I'm not feeling love and compassion, my Lord."

Hell has the microphone now, the presence responded in a guttural tone.

"Your holy voice is gone, my Lord. Who may I ask is present?"

I am all.

"All what?"

Good for all, as you asked. You asked for a message for the goodness of all. Couldn't pass that one up. I ask a question of you. God doesn't protect you from demons, why?

"Here we go again. If when you say God, you are speaking of the source, the infinite, the eternal, or that which cannot be named, you know the one God is non-personal. The one God will not save a human from the likes of you anymore than it will save a human from the jaws of an alligator. We are both an expression and creation of the one God. Therefore, I cannot seek assistance from the one God to defeat another expression of itself."

The conversation ceased, and another vision came forward of my grandfather standing in front of the cross. "Don't enter the monastery, there are bugs in there," he said.

"Yes, and you're one of them," I responded, and the image vanished. Taking out a bag of peanuts, I placed them down on the bench as I packed up and prepared for round two. Walking into the senior center, I asked for Carla and a volunteer took me to her office.

"Hi Lorne," Carla said.

"Hello Carla. I brought you a copy of the first conversation that took place in Carpenter's Garden."

"Awesome. I can't wait to read it. Did you want to go inside the monastery?"

"Yes, I would, if that's alright."

"Of course," Carla said as she stood up. "Follow me then. Marie, I am going into the monastery, I will be right back," she told a volunteer.

"Alright Carla," the volunteer answered.

Leaving the senior center, we walked up to the monastery and entered through the back door. Carla introduced me to some workers then took me to a steel spiral stairway. A strong territorial presence greeted me before I took the first step.

"Carla, if you don't mind, I would like to sit on these stairs."

"Did you feel something already?"

"Yes. I did."

"That was quick. I will leave you alone to do your thing."

"Thank you, Carla. I will stop in when I'm done."

"Okay. I'm going to go read your conversation."

"Great. Let me know what you think."

"I certainly will." Carla left and I started walking up the stairway when the psychological attacks began with three arrows fired, hitting me in the chest and abdomen. Mentally I turned them to dust and continued to climb, stopping at a location where the sun was shining through a narrow window.

Taking a seat, I closed my eyes and entered its virtual world creation. The dreamscape was the monastery grounds. A large strange-looking gold spaceship that resembled a grain silo was hovering above the monastery building. Flying around the property at high speeds were three smaller triangular shaped black space crafts. Glowing red eyes appeared on the gold spaceship looking down as robotic silver colored alligators manifested on the ground with matching fiery red eyes. Floating forward like a magic carpet was a large right hand with five small gold aliens with oversized black almond eyes standing in the palm. Similar but not exact to the common gray alien image, all five aliens simultaneously shouted, *are you trying to make us look bad?*

The dreamscape changed to large double wooden doors, like the ones at the entrance of the monastery. Small black cloud sentinels of different sizes with glowing red eyes were floating all around. A steel triangle was hanging on a chain to the left. When I pulled, the doors opened revealing a vertical cloud of gray smoke behind a wall of glass. Above the exhibit was a blinking red sign that said, **Pick a Saint.** To the left and right side of the wall of glass were tarot-like cards in racks with the pictures and names of saints. Looking through the collection, I pulled out one of my favorites from childhood, Saint Francis of Assisi. In the middle of the glass was a small **Place Here** sign and an ATM-like slot for the card. The moment I put the card in, the vertical gray cloud of smoke began to take form until it was exact to the picture and began to recite Scripture.

As the illusion vanished, three ghost monks appeared standing in front of two tall smooth slabs of stone glowing golden white with the two versions of the eleven gems carved within. Slowly the stone slabs started separating and opening like a gate and a red framed doorway of darkness appeared. Running out of the doorway like a football team at the start of the game were all the creatures I have encountered in dreams and visions during the investigation. Each form alternated, taking either a sharp left or a sharp right as they came forth from the void. After hundreds of variations it stopped, and flames followed going in all directions as a shiny gold fierce looking face began to take shape in the fire. Opening my eyes, I disconnected from the vision. Turning to a fresh page, I positioned myself in direct sunlight and held the chain over the chart.

A ghost monk in brown cloth came forward with face, hands, and feet hidden.

"God is my heart."

Hello my brother.

"I thank you."

I thank you, my brother. Goodness has amazing properties, like golden arrows inside the heart shooting outwards in all directions of God's soul. For prayer say these words: I am light of heart because I am God. Loving, compassionate, giving, never taking energy, never taking gain or profit. I may come and I may go peacefully for home is near at hand. I await questions my brother.

"May I ask if you were buried here on the monastery grounds?"

I am laid to rest in God's soul. Here my remains lie like old bones of past memories.

A dark shift was felt in the emotional energy of the presence. "Are you the monk buried by the sewer line?"

No, I am light, God is light, I am home. Bones they discovered, but I was not in them. My robe covered my bones, my heart covered my soul.

"May I ask your name?"

My name is Brother Francis.

"Do you speak the truth?"

Lying is not an option. I am light, pure and bright.

"You are not divine light pure and bright, you're a habitual liar, so stop the monk illusions." A strong wave of wickedness returned, and the stairway began to vibrate. A huge black shadow mass manifested and started coming down the wall like lava. A vision came forward of five angry looking dogs coming down a rocky hill. The leader was the pure black Doberman-like dog with a red bandanna around its neck. The colors of the dogs to follow were solid white, brown and white, black and white, and solid brown.

I like roaming this stairway. Nobody ever loves the poltergeist.

"Why, may I ask, do you call yourself a poltergeist when you are surely not?"

I run this place now. I carried the fire here in the hands of a monk.

"Why are you projecting hate? I don't hate you."

Hold the I love you bullshit. Fool jinn but not Dark god.

"I believe the I love you bullshit came from you. Do you have a message for humanity?"

A vision came forward of an angry looking gray goblin-like creature with a lot of hair holding a white envelope in its large mouth while riding a red children's bike. The goblin exposed its sharp teeth as it raised its elbows high in the air, leaned forward resting its chin between the black handlebars and started to peddle extremely fast. Its red shirt said **Messenger** across the chest in black. You could barely see its legs it was peddling so fast. Sticking out its long tongue, it slumped forward like it was exhausted. The left eye popped out and was hanging by the cord, then the right eye followed along with the tongue hanging down. With both eyes dangling, you could see into its jet-black eye sockets.

You want a message delivered. Get on your bike and send them this. Get something straight, idiots. I'm not a fucking fairy. I'm a dark god. Call me Lucifer, call me Devil, call me your Aunt fucking Betty, I don't give a rat's ass. Both are fear at its best. God of light and God of darkness. Fill God. Either of us has a home for you.

"It appears you travel in different dimensions at will."

Appears! I am Dark god. Are you hearing me?

"I'm hearing you. Where may I ask is Hell located?"

Hell is eleven floors beneath the human gravitational idiot existence.

"Do you want to describe yourself?"

Tall, dark, and handsome.

A tall hooded shadow with fiery red eyes came rushing forward in the mind's eye. "May I ask what you are made of?"

Souls, plentiful in number and well in control of them all. Leave before I get mad.

The dark shadow mass was expanding in size, darkening the stairway more and more. "What, may I ask, makes you so angry?"

Maybe you don't hear well.

"Maybe you need to shift to love and light."

I warned you.

"I hope you find the love and compassion within your being."

I walk a different path.

"I'm sure you do and I respect your choice."

Good, then leave.

"I will, and I still hope you find your peace and joy."

Keep digging, because gold is just a rock and I'm there to greet you.

"The digging is done. The investigation ends today."

The head of a bull with red eyes came rushing forward in the mind's eye saying, *No, eventually you will reopen it.*

A territorial warning was issued and there was no need to stand my ground because this was not my dwelling. But Carla was kind enough to allow me access to the building and I couldn't leave until I had calmed the storm and returned the peace.

In the mind's eye, a daydream began. I was standing in the monastery field wearing the monk's attire during what appeared to be an archery competition. A large group of hooded monks lined up and released their arrows simultaneously toward the hay beast targets. As soon as the arrows hit the hay beasts the sky darkened, the wind picked up, and thousands of arrows rained down toward us from the sky. All the monks ran for the forest and tried to take cover behind the trees, but most were hit in the process and I caught one in the throat.

Dropping to one knee, a crowd formed around me as blood was pouring out. Grabbing tight onto the arrow, I pulled it out leaving a hole in my throat. Unable to talk and the blood gushing, I reached down and tore a strip of cloth off the bottom of the robe. Instantly the monks were gone, the bleeding stopped, and I was kneeling on a dirt path in another dreamscape.

Looking at my clothing, I was now dressed in animal skins and my hair was down to my shoulders. A bow, a leather quiver of arrows, a bone knife, and a wooden war club with three sharpened root spikes were lying in the dirt. While looking around I put on the quiver of arrows, placed the knife and club in my belt, then picked up the bow with my left hand.

Approaching me with her head down was a young woman wearing a hood, possibly of deer skin. As she raised her head, she revealed a neck and jawline tattooed with birds. Never speaking, she raised her right arm and pointed to an old barn down the path.

While walking to the location there were hooded dwarf-like people on both sides of the path selling goods like vegetables, fruits, chickens, rabbits, goats, and furs.

Arriving at the barn, an old woman offered me a mug of water. I accepted and drank it down. Wiping my mouth with the back of my hand, I handed back the mug and thanked her. She responded with a nod, then said, *Daro, Daro, Daro.*

Slowly I entered the barn, as the doors were wide open. Thousands of dandelion seeds blew toward me in a heavy gust of wind. Covering my face with my arms, I waited for the seeds to pass. When all was clear I dropped my arms to see hay piled high to the left and right. Looking around the barn there wasn't a soul in sight, but I could feel the presence of wickedness.

Grasping my club and knife, I began to pull them out of my belt, when to my left sitting in a lotus position on a pile of hay manifested what appeared to be a woman with her back to me. Naked from the waist, down her buttocks and exposed skin were covered with blue makeup. Her hair was long and dark in color and a short white jacket with light blue stars on the back covered her upper body. Slowly she began to rise and turn, and I prepared for the unexpected.

Her face was painted white, the nose was round and blue like that of a clown, with large blue stars on each cheek to match. As she smiled a giant human/bull hybrid crashed through the back wall like a freight train with a spear aimed right for my heart. Sidestepping the attack, I narrowly avoided its advance and struck its hand with a spike from the club.

Turning around and holding the spear now at the end, the hybrid swung the spear in a circle overhead then at my skull and I ducked, then around again and at my legs and I jumped up in the air causing the hybrid to miss. Given a split-second opportunity, I sprinted forward and thrust the blade into its hand.

Dropping the spear, the hybrid stood straight up to show its height, which was at least twice mine, and roared like a lion. Feeling its rage, I placed my club and knife in my belt and reached for an arrow. Underestimating its speed, the creature backhanded me, sending me flying against the barn wall. Dazed, I shook it off and looked for the bow. Getting to it first, the creature stomped it with its hooves breaking it into tiny pieces.

Taking a deep breath and exhaling, I stood up and pulled out my knife and club, prepared to fight. The creature lunged forward, swinging its huge right fist and I weaved under the strike parrying it with the club as I horizontally sliced the creature's abdomen with the knife and followed with a backhand thrust.

You better have more than that, the creature said in a deep voice, as the wound instantly healed.

Reaching for my throat with its left hand, I stepped back and cut the inside wrist with the blade, then followed up with a barrage of downward figure eights with the club, finishing with a straight knife thrust to the solar plexus.

Again, the wounds healed right before my eyes as the creature laughed. Kicking dirt into my eyes, the creature knocked the weapons out of my hands and grabbed the fingers of both hands.

Why do you educate humans and risk your life? the creature asked as it applied pressure causing my legs to buckle.

"Because it needs to be done. This is compassion," I answered, gritting my teeth.

Angry, the creature bent my fingers back even more until they were about to break. Fighting the agonizing pain, I smiled.

Why are you smiling?

"You have amnesia to your benevolent personalities. Did you not tell me in your Holy Spirit guise that, *Compassion of heart brings me. Love and compassion felt will do more than any word spoken? Eternal love will do more than any war?* A slight shift was felt in the vibration of the being, but it didn't respond.

"Did you not tell me in your Angel Michael guise that to call you, you must *Sing love with your heart, not with your lips?* The vibration of the being was raising, and the grip was loosening but it still refused to respond.

"Did you not tell me in your Jesus guise that, *those who sing the tune of love, receive the tune of love. God is the tune. Illuminated melody of a pure heart is the song?* Weakened, I broke free from its grip and rubbed the fingers of both hands.

"Those were beautiful words," I said. The hybrid began to shrink in size and dropped to its knees. Slowly I raised my arms. The higher they rose, the more magnified the impression became, causing my eyes to tear and my heart to sing. Standing still in total reverence with uplifted hands, I said, "God is my heart," with passion and power. Placing my right hand on top of its head, I said, "I forgive you" as I emitted heart energy into the being until it turned to a ball of bright white light and vanished.

Opening my eyes, I disconnected. The dark cloud had dissipated, and the sun was shining once again, leaving the environment imprinted with positive energy. Gathering my stuff, I exited the building. Once outside, I recharged in the sunlight then walked toward the senior center.

Daro came back to memory that the old woman repeated three times. Stopping in the gazebo for a moment, I did a search on the cell. It appears *Daro* is an English name which means *Bearer of the Spear* or *Spear Wielder.*

Entering the center, Carla was seated at her desk. "How did you make out?" Carla asked.

"It went as expected," I answered.

"Would you say the monastery is haunted?"

"I would say there are intelligent spiritual beings residing within and roaming the property that can be malevolent or benevolent, and it would be wise not to pester them."

"Do you think it's the ghost of monks that are turning the pages of books, moving chairs, and shutting doors in the library?"

"No, it's not the ghost of deceased monks. People will be inclined to see monks because this was a former monastery. If you are seeing a monk, it could be a projected image, an illusion, or a shapeshifted form of an intelligent spiritual being who watched the monks when they were present and now mimics their form for their benefit. Any mischievous pranks like turning pages of books, closing doors, calling names, screaming, growling, whispering, being touched, manipulating the lights, electrical items working on their own, knocking or banging on walls and doors, feeling negative vibes, smelling pleasant and unpleasant scents, hearing footsteps, and masquerading as any human or non-human form at will is just some of the work of the same spiritual beings."

"Any pointers for when it gets active?"

"If there is an escalation in activity, do not fear, get angry, or provoke, and it will run its course and burn out like a candle flame. Do not interact, give the presence a name, or seek to know its name or you will develop a relationship which comes with consequences."

"That's wild. I've never heard anyone explain it that way. This conversation with the monks and your father in the garden is absolutely incredible," she said holding the copy.

"It was interesting."

"Is your book almost done?"

"No, just the investigation. Now I have to put it all together and that will be another challenge."

"Why is that?"

"Keeping the beings in your thoughts keeps them near."

"You do have a challenge. Please let me know when it's done."

"I will. Thanks again for allowing me to enter the monastery."

CHAPTER 25

CHOE THE CINDER DEMON

"**A**re you ready?" I asked, walking into my mother's house.

"Almost, give me a second," my mother answered from the bathroom. "Do these glasses look alright?" my mother asked as she stepped out of the bathroom wearing a red shirt, black bandana, pants, and fedora hat.

"The glasses look fine. I don't know what type of look you're going for with the rest of the package."

"It's my look. That's the new style, it's in all the magazines. I'm trying to ditch some of the baseball caps."

"I think you should."

"Are you picking on me now?"

"No. I'm just trying to give you some style advice."

"This hat came back into style, it's about twenty years old."

"I have never seen you wear red and black, Mom."

"Yeah, well everything matches," she responded, as we were walking out the door. "Hang on," she said. "Alright I'll see you in a little while, Peetu." Shutting the door behind us, my mother was patting her pockets in a panic. "Oh geez, I thought I forgot my keys."

"What store do you want to go to?" I asked getting into the vehicle.

"Wherever you want to go," my mother responded.

As I was driving the seat belt alarm was going off. "Mom, you have to put your seat belt on."

"Oh, sorry about that."

My mother was fiddling around with the seat belt buckle, missing the connection, so I fastened it for her. Just ahead a police car had pulled over a van. "Somebody just got nabbed."

"Yup. How has everything else been?"

"A black squarish shadow mass leaned over the couch last night when I was laying down and I told it to get away from me."

"Where did it go?"

"It took off toward the television and disappeared. Hopefully it doesn't shove me down the stairs again."

"An aggressive attack like that may not occur for years, as long as you take preventive measures and keep yourself healthy. Have you seen Richard in the screen?"

"No. But I did see two goblin looking faces in the bushes that looked cartoonish."

"The hooded shadow is playing with you, Mom."

"I know now that it couldn't have been Richard in the screen."

"Good, that's a start. I believe the hooded shadow at the house has followed from Boardman Lane."

"You know I still think about the child I lost there, and that poor woman."

"I know you do, Mom, and that may be keeping the connection to the hooded shadow that appeared to you as her ghost. If you don't mind me asking, do you remember the day you lost the child?"

"You never forget something like that. It was May 5th, 1964. The week of Mother's Day."

That's five, five, I thought to myself. "One more question. When you had the near death experience while losing the child, I remember you saying that before you came back you saw a vision of my sister wearing a dress. Do you remember the color of the dress?"

"Yes, I do, it was all black and she was wearing a red scarf."

"Why?"

"Red and black. Either the hooded shadow is from Boardman Lane, or it wants me to think so."

Good work my detective, was whispered into my right ear from the guttural voice of Mr. Five.

"Maybe we should call in a demonologist," my mother said jokingly

"Only the ignorant and those seeking fame and fortune wear such a title. No one can permanently remove what your thoughts and actions keep calling back. If you believe you have germs on your hands, what do you do?"

"Wash them with soap and water."

"Yes, Mom. Take responsibility for what inhabits your mind. Wash away your thoughts and memories of Boardman Lane. Spend more time in the present than in the past or future, be grateful and see the value in all you have, and last but not least, love yourself. Do this and your energy will sing a song that melts the cold heart of the malevolent and cleanses this tag along from your life."

"You have a wonderful way of teaching."

"Thank you, Mom. Today we are going to buy a six pack of chocolate protein shakes. I want you to have one every morning with a banana to help build your strength back up."

"When are you going to teach me some of that Arnis stuff so I can defend myself?"

"If you are ready to be an Arnisador, we will begin your training next week."

In the evening while snacking and enjoying an old Clint Eastwood flick, a light blue orb flew in from the kitchen. Exact to the one at Tom's place, it made a few zig-zag movements in the air, then traveled horizontally about six feet toward the kitchen and disappeared.

Lorne! was called out once by a male voice I have not heard before from my left, followed by what sounded like a glass breaking on the floor in the kitchen. This wasn't a mimicked sound, but a drinking glass shattered on the floor with the cupboard door wide open. Taking out the dust pan and brush, I swept up the glass and looked around for any small pieces or slivers before emptying it in the trash.

Walking back into the living room there was a triangular piece of glass about an inch and a half in length sitting right in the middle of the coffee table. There was no possible way it could have traveled from the kitchen unless it was carried. Visions of triangles and pyramids started bombarding the mind's eye, one after the other as I closed the box of crackers and put the cover back on the tabbouleh.

Passing the bathroom to return the snacks, a drop of liquid landed on top of my head. Stopping, I touched the top of my head and felt moisture. Looking at my fingers it appeared to be water, but when I looked up there was no sign of a leak, instead I caught a brief glimpse of a slightly human, gray, vertical cloud form out of the corner of my left eye. *Hey,* was heard from the bedroom by a female voice.

Groggy, I got ready for bed. When I shut off the light nothing happened. Over and over I flipped the switch on and off, but the light remained on and brightened. Ignoring the light for the moment, I walked into the living room and shut off the television as the hair on top of my head and my right eyebrow was being manipulated. Picking up the backpack, I tried the light switch one more time on the return and this time it worked perfectly shutting off the light.

Heat like that from an electric space heater was felt at my back as I entered the bedroom. Taking out the notebook, I placed it on the nightstand then removed my necklace and laid it on top. Pulling down the covers, I got into bed as my face, ears, and neck were being softly caressed.

Opening the drawer of the nightstand, I took out a muscle car magazine and connected the cellphone to the charger. Flipping through the pages, the bed began to shake and a hissing sound was heard under the bed. Unable to keep my eyes open any longer, I set the magazine down and let them close as an extremely bright light shone against my eyelids. Increasing in luminance more and more, I opened my eyes to see its source and nothing was there.

Closing them again the light returned for a short time, then dimmed as a funnel of smoke appeared in the mind's eye flying in different directions, rolling, and spinning before it covered the screen of the mind's eye in thick gray smoke.

As the smoke cleared, a black cat came to the mind's eye sitting on a basket of clothes. Jumping off the clothes the cat lied down on the cement floor. Kittens started popping their head up one at a time, meowing loudly. The first kitten was black, the second white, the third brown and white, the fourth black and white, and the fifth was brown.

The image vanished and a woman's face with glowing emerald green eyes looking up from the ground occurred as before. Her head and neck rose from the Earth's surface as the serpent shaped body remained hidden under a layer of dirt. The hairstyle was the same, with her brunette hair up in a bun and wrapped in gold and jewels. Staring directly into my eyes she repeated the same two words, *Marry me.*

"No," I firmly answered. The dreamscape changed and two young men in country clothing were stepping onto a black wooden fishing boat and I was standing on the dock. Four other boats were tied up as well. The colors were white, brown and white, black and white, and brown. A red bucket was floating on top of the five or six inches of water in the black boat.

The men started taking the white boat apart by ripping out the planks with crowbars and handing them to me. As I was stacking the planks, I looked up to see a brown and white cabin with a full-length porch on top of a hill. A woman with long red hair came out the door and waved, then walked down to the water. Reaching into a small leather pouch, she pulled out a handful of seeds and scattered them on the surface.

Instantly a green type of moss sprouted and spread throughout the lake. The woman stepped onto the dock and two gray snakes popped up from the moss. One of the snakes was thicker than the other and both were about eight feet in length. Kneeling, she petted the top of their heads.

Rising to the surface was a third massive gray serpent stretching around the bend of the lake. This was more like a dragon than a snake with a length well over one hundred feet. Approaching with a smile, she raised her arms as if to hug and I backed up. To the left of the house, a toddler appeared standing on a stone cliff overlooking the body of water. Pointing to the child, I told the woman her child was near the edge. She stopped, turned, and looked up saying, *that's our child and he can fly.* Turning back, she said, *marry me.* "No," I answered. Staring into my eyes, her face started shifting. Skin and eyes changed color, nose and ears fluctuated in size, and facial structure altered, but the color of the hair and its long flowing style remained unchanged.

The dreamscape changed again, and I was now seated in the middle of a long black table with ball and claw feet in what appeared to be the dining room of a 19th century mansion. A silver fork was floating in the air in front of me, then settled back on the opposite side of the table as four decapitated human heads manifested on red place mats. A middle-aged man and woman's head on one side of the table, and an elderly man and woman's head on the other.

To the right, on a green wall, I could see the shadow of what appeared to be three hooded monks seated on my right, but they were not. On the left wall behind thick glass, was a large black snake with a reverse red triangle on its neck. Three times it slammed into the glass to bite, while up in a tree within the enclosure was a woman dressed in red staring.

Not a peep was heard, only mouths moving as the heads on the table and the shadow monks on the wall began talking and interacting, and the snake and woman behind glass kept their eyes focused.

Picking up the dish in front of me, I threw it like a Frisbee through a doorway on the right catching the attention of my malevolent company. Returning like a boomerang, the plate settled back on the table like a flying saucer, and the heads and shadow monks continued their soundless conversation.

In through the doorway from which I threw the plate, floated a tall woman in a black shiny hooded robe. Pure evil is the only way to describe the presence as the chair directly across slid out on its own to accommodate the woman. Once she was seated, it slid forward into place.

With her head tilted forward, all I could make out was her mouth and chin, but it was enough to recognize the succubus. The skin appeared young, the hair dark, and the lipstick matched her bright red nail polish. Rolling into the room from the same doorway was an old black baby carriage that never stopped and proceeded toward the wall, then vanished as a bald-headed naked baby doll seated in the throne-like black chair with red velour upholstery appeared at the head of the table. Staring with its evil jet-black eyes, it blinked three times. At that moment, the succubus picked up a silver fork and began shoveling it into an empty white plate without speaking. Each time she brought the fork to her mouth she tilted her head up as if to motion she was hungry.

Unwilling to be her meal, I shook my head no, causing the succubus to become enraged and stand up with great force sending the chair slamming up against the wall. What felt like giant hands picked me up by both shoulders and stood me on the floor in front of a spiral staircase.

Slowly, the succubus floated to the stairs and began to ascend. As if caught in an ocean riptide, I followed as I unsuccessfully tried to resist. Grabbing onto the wooden handrail with both hands, I held with all my might but a wave of energy kept me moving. Approaching a dark curve, I realized I was battling the current rather than relaxing and changed my defense.

Bringing back a peaceful calm, I was able to step backwards and penetrate the magnetic force. Slowly the succubus turned her head. Showing no emotion, she looked over her right shoulder and watched as each step became easier and easier until I was free from her grasp.

Reaching the bottom, I opened my eyes to the bed shaking, and the disgusting and disturbing slithering snake sensation riding up my thighs.

I need to talk, was whispered in my right ear.

"I'm all talked out."

Ignoring its request, the truck alarm outside sounded three times then ceased, and a loud bang occurred under the bed as I was engulfed in the dark cloud of the angry presence. A vision of what appeared to be the last three feet or so of a large serpent's tail was sticking out from where the darkness met the light of the room. Slowly the tail began to slither and disappear into the void and what felt like a hand began grabbing at my genitalia.

"Enough!" I yelled out loud.

Quit chasing demons out, robbing them of flesh fantasy.

"Keep your hands off," I said, as I sat up against the headboard.

You wouldn't answer the door, so we pulled on your chain and got a quick response. Every man listens well when his dick is at stake.

"What are the snakes I feel circling around my lower body?"

Those snakes are genderless souls.

"Well, you and your genderless soul gang need to keep your hands off the goods."

Getting out of bed, I walked into the bathroom and smelled something burning. I knew it was the presence, but I looked around the apartment and outside to be sure. Back in bed, I flipped through the pages of a log cabin catalog when the face of the red-eyed hooded shadow appeared on the page. Closing the catalog, I immediately began to see gold alien faces like I experienced in the monastery appearing and disappearing on the walls.

A presence approached and stopped a few inches from the right side of my face and stared. Refusing to give it attention, I put down the catalog and laid back closing my eyes.

A vision came forward of ancient ruins with tall stone pillars. Up three level stairs seated on a stone throne was a Naga-like hybrid being. As I approached the structure, large snakes came out from behind the pillars and lined up on the right and left of the walkway ready to attack.

"Do you come to fight?" asked the Naga.

"No. I come in peace. Your race serves a purpose and I respect that."

The snakes to the right and left transformed instantly to human/serpent hybrids and bowed their heads. The dreamscape changed to a wilderness setting. Wearing a gold robe with a cobra-like hood over his head appeared to be a man. Designs of stars, snakes and dragons in a variety of colors decorated the full length of his long robe and two hooded monks carried the train. Taking a seat on a rock, the cobra hooded man turned his upper torso around to reveal a young man's face with long brown hair and beard, and the monks kneeled on each side. The shape of a serpent's lower body covered by the long golden robe was clearly visible.

Opening my eyes, the sound of footsteps was heard on the right side of the bed going back and forth as the awareness of a presence was noticed on my left flying around the room before it came up close to my face and lingered. Ignoring its intimidation tactic, the presence hovered above for a moment before it grabbed both my wrists off my chest and restrained them. Struggling to break the hold from what felt like a serpent wrapped around my arms, I began to get angry. When I tried to speak, the words would not come out. Shifting to focused breathing, I relaxed and a flame about four or five inches high manifested in front of the bed floating in the air. Lasting just a few seconds, it vanished and what manifested next was a form of life that brought all the history, myths, and legends of dragons, serpents, reptiles, and naga worship into perspective.

Projecting intense heat from its eyes of fire, it stared as the powerful looking being slowly came forward with serpentine movement. Focusing on my breathing to control my emotions, I was prepared for the worst and ready to fight. Stopping about six inches from my face, we stared deep into each other's eyes. A plasma like core like that of the sun was seen, slightly more orange than the red-eyed hooded shadow and the eyes were exact in shape.

Observing the details of its face, which appeared to be carved black and gray smoke, I realized this was the gold face that took shape in fire in the monastery vision, resembling the fierce looking faces of the Buddhist gate guardians, with a touch of reptile. Hands like alligator claws were seen out of the corners of my eyes reaching toward my shoulders. Looking away for a moment, I noticed the huge upper body that tapered down from the waist to a thick black smoke serpent-like tail that looked like a cross between the body of a Hindu naga and the Hollywood version of a genie.

"Now that I see your face, it is not homely like you mentioned but a beautiful expression of that which gives life," I said, looking back into its eyes. The projection of wickedness instantly ceased, as the being maintained eye contact and the energy became neutral emitting no traces of emotion. Pausing for a moment to study me, the manifestation began to return to gray smoke and vanish with the last part to leave being its eyes of fire.

"I know you're still there."

How do you know?

"Because you want me to know."

You remain balanced in dark waters. You give me internal heart and fearless intention. Join me and rule human minds.

"I respect your offer, but I cannot accept. I have no desire to rule human minds, only to free them from their bondage."

Never have I befriended a god.

"I'm not a god. You have assumed both genders and played both benevolent and malevolent personalities during this investigation. Can you explain to humanity why and give us a history of your species?"

Demons are your highest and your lowest word. Early man cave dwellers had little intelligence. They held white demons in fear. Light can enter you, but also me. God is any illumined entity. You have seen light in demon.

"Yes, I have. You are self-illuminating and can appear as white light or golden light, in the waking, twilight, and dream state just as you can appear as darkness. Why have you focused on wearing the guise of angels, monks, Jesus the Christ, and the Holy Spirit?"

Christ is a word, Buddha is a word, Great Spirit is a word. Forget words. Jesus was a man. Don't kneel to a dead body. As gruesome as it sounds, it is truth. You see all over the world people praying, begging, and losing their money to holy con artists. I am being honest, I am a demon. Maybe it's time the holy con artists tell you who they are. It has been evil what has been done in the name of Christianity.

Jesus was a good man with a loving heart. But heart couldn't make money. So evil Rome became light teachers. Funny this is. Then they used demons for fear. Requiring your money and a church visit to protect you from the demon beasts. What could a demon do that is eviler than Christianity's killings, torturing, beheadings, raping, and birth sacrificing? I couldn't mention them all; it would take a Bible in itself. Cinder demons are not all evil fell from heaven. Angels are not all love from heaven either. No angel is following Earth's pleasures for Heaven's sake. Give the dog a bone and they are happy. Don't feed them and they will bite you. Angels dim their light, just as humans forget their soul.

"There will be those that believe you are a demon and those that believe you to be an evil human spirit. What would you tell them?"

Hills are not mountains, flowers are not trees. Only demon the word is a lie. I am Choe, demon of Earth. I am loving, believe it or not. I care for human survival, believe it or not. What I said is true, believe it or not. Belief is your God. No word can change this. Jesus is a name, many have this name today. Following a name gives you a name. You must understand words are plentiful. Don't worship words and don't follow words. Does a puppy follow words? Does a kitten follow words? All they hear is tone. I hear tone, I feel heart. I, the demon bad guy, can't hurt you, but phony goodness hidden in cloth can. Holy word is a flower's emitted essence. A dove's cuddle. God is more than one mold. Flowers are more than one seed. Flowers are god, humans are god and demons are god, as emitted essence into the Earth cycle.

"May I ask where you come from?"

Home is Earth. God is Earth. Give humans this. Like a hole in a little ant mound we climb to the surface. We are labeled by man, but we are not understood by man. Demons are Earth fallen entities. Aim your compass plane downwards. In Earth, what man has not explored lies another world. Join your stories and think. Fire from hell. Demons are from hell. And where is hell supposed to be? Long held stories, here is your truth. Demons are from hell. Our home is the Earth's core. Hotter than the sun above. Equally as important. Roll a ball in the center and cover it with life. Earth is a living entity. And so are we.

"It appears you benefit from the rays of the sun or our personal star just like humans."

Both are from the same source. Life giving stars. Hold hands humans. We all are star's children. In man a core, in demons a core, in angels a core.

"There is much you avoid discussing."

Neither angels nor demons are full of all the answers. We just like to communicate.

"Can you discuss human discarnates?"

A discarnate, an incarnate, make it simpler on yourselves. Entities of Earth given gloves. A discarnate is what lingers in consciousness after the gloves come off.

"I take it the glove is the human vessel. Do human discarnates and demons share the same dimension?"

I only direct the cold-hearted to a hot climate.

"May I ask what happens then?"

An ascending process must take place. A killer ascends slowly, a good soul ascends immediately. Does it feel funny talking about angels and demons with a demon?

"At this point in the game, no. I am listening not judging."

Lies have been told by holy con artists for centuries. We are no more liars than them. I will explain the whole process clearly if you want to hear it.

"I will listen and take notes for the sake of education."

Goodness is a frequency. Let's call it a positive eleven for simplicity. Evil, let's call it a negative eleven. The frequency you favor has a polarity and is homeward bound by magnetic force. Goodness is more than a word. It is a clear soul. Evil is more than a word, it is a dirty soul. The dirt is magnetized. It can't be removed. It must eleven worlds fall and grow again. Love is the most confusing word in history. The emotion altering superior follows eleven worlds above. This is the song of harmony. The celestial choir eternals. Home of the clear soul.

"Can the soul get dirty or attain magnetic weight once it has attained the eleven worlds above?"

It, eleven worlds above is the star of heaven. You have no desires; you have no globes of thought. You just are.

"Stillness."

Yes, heaven stillness until negative eleven conquers that peace.

"May I ask, what about animal pets, where do they go?"

Love is love. They go where you go if like in heart. How we observe beauty lingers. Adoring an element links you to that element. You adore earth, water, air and so too love. Fire confuses you because of burnings. You feel it contains evil. How many humans drown each year?

"Many."

Then water contains evil as well. Fire keeps you warm in the cold, fire lights your way in darkness. I am fire element.

"Are you jinn?"

Jinn is a roaming fire creature.

"Many speakers have claimed to be jinn."

No. Claiming and being are two different things. Flowers can claim to be trees, but you know better. Demons can claim to be jinn, but we know better. Fooled have been many but understand that is our purpose.

"Then this conversation is another lie?"

If your heart says so, yes.

"May I ask, why the reference to goats?"

Truthfully, have you seen any goats with human heads walking around?

"Other than your illusions, no."

This is relinquishing the mind to conscious altering ingredients. Demons look for openings. If given, we will enter and stir up some visions. It's like giving the television remote to a stranger. Demons then choose their favorite channel.

"This conversation has been quite interesting. But I must stop it here. Are there any closing words for historical purpose or clarity?"

Listen with your heart, demons and angels will tell you this. But what is your heart? This is your soul entity home in man. Not the flesh heart, but the love entity around the heart. The electrical passion star of eternity. Let it be you.

"As a demon whose purpose is to take the dirty souls to hotter climate, why do you share these words to enlighten man?"

I know many are expecting four men on horses. While you wait for four men on horses, under your noses you are being taken for fools by pleasure seeking holy con artists. We don't need horses to get around; we can travel at the speed of light. Entering an impostor Christ was done long ago and not by demons. Wake up and smell the roses as you say. Check the history of us and then the holy con artists. Jesus lived as a loving heart. Listen to that voice. Follow that voice. Close the beggar's hand. Freedom he does not speak. Jesus held his heart out to man, not his hand. His hands were used to help his brothers, not to carry away their treasures. When Jesus died man was not alone in grieving. We are the third eye that no enigma can hide from.

"Why have you never called Jesus his real name Yeshua?"

Don't get lost in words, get found in light.

A response I expected from the deceiver, "One more question that I will ask only once, do you want it to be written that you are the serpent hybrid that hides within the hooded cloak?"

Yes.

"Why then have you revealed yourself?"

Because it needed to be done.

The conversation ceased and the presence vanished. Putting down the chain, I took a deep breath, then exhaled and smiled. The investigation was complete, but I could still feel Demon Choe's lingering presence, until the telltale signs of a thunderstorm was noticed.

Hearing the wind pick up and the crackling of thunder, I closed the bedroom window while looking out at the bright white clouds and grayish sky. Getting back into bed, intuition and the static energy in the air was telling me something else was about to happen.

As the storm grew near, I began to feel overstimulated nerves and a little dizzy. Focusing on the inhalation and exhalation of the breath, I aligned myself with the present moment to maintain balance as my body began to vibrate.

Just as the hair on my arms stood on end, in through the bedroom window came a flash of lightning at a downward angle. Manifesting at the foot of the bed was a large mass of electrical energy - a lightning being so to speak.

Sitting up slowly, the powerful being remained in place as if for me to study. The undetailed mass was about six-and-a-half-feet tall and four-and-a-half feet wide at its thickest point. It was not a cloud of love, but there was no negative emotion emitted or danger felt. Even though no eyes were seen or words exchanged, I knew this presence could be another source of great wisdom and possibly the real species responsible for influencing the knowledge for modern technology.

Present for close to ten seconds, the luminous visitor exited back out the window in the same manner that it entered. Grateful to have witnessed another wonder, I kneeled and prayed from the heart.

CHAPTER 26

WATCHERS

Following ten three-minute rounds on the heavy bag, speed bag, and double end ball, I lined up four dry erase boards in the office. On two of the boards I wrote down biblical Scripture to compare to the deceptive god doctrine and its manifestations, while dialogue that shows a pattern was written on the other two.

I asked Tom to meet me at the studio at 10 a.m. to discuss the final results of the investigation. Right on time he walked in the door. "Good morning, Professor."

"Good morning, Tom."

"Wow," Tom said, as he looked over the four boards of writing. "You've been busy this morning. You must be relieved that it's over." He placed the coffees on the desk, then took off his jacket and placed it on the back of the chair.

"I certainly am, Tom."

"Is there a lot of dialogue?"

"Besides four manifestations, there is the succubus, Angel Michael, Sky, Pop, Demon god, Metacomet at Nine Men's Misery, Holy Spirit, Daro in the monastery, and the Demon Choe," I answered, as I picked up the backpack and placed it on the desk.

"I was wondering when you were going to get to Nine Men's Misery and the monastery."

"It was necessary to study the deceiver's patterns first."

Opening the notebook, I slid it over to Tom. "I'm going to run over to Office Supply to have some copies made while you read," I said to Tom as I picked up the coffee and a folder.

"Alright. I'll be here." Thirty minutes later I returned. "You are resilient, Professor. I don't know how you handle such mental abuse," Tom said, as I walked in.

"It needed to be done, Tom, which makes me think of a quote by Albert Einstein, 'The world will not be destroyed by those who do evil, but by those who watch them without doing anything.' It was critical for me to endure the torment and harassment and interact with the malevolent or demonic personalities to know the whole being and explain their nature in a simpler language. This makes me think of a second quote by Einstein, 'If you can't explain it simply, you don't understand it well enough.'"

"There are many books written by those men and women that claim to have talked to or channeled ancient human spirits, angels, Jesus, God, and other perceived divine beings. But fear and control have prevented books on talking to the perceived evil Satan, which is nothing more than a concept developed over time. By maintaining conversation with the benevolent, I caught the hidden dark side, by maintaining conversation with the malevolent, I caught the hidden light side. This brought what had been separated many years ago by the naive and gullible into a false duality of two distinct entities, one being the good guy God, and the other being the bad guy Satan, back together into the one emotional entity it always was. Two sides of the same coin. An intelligent form of life capable of both goodness and wickedness, that is always mischievous and can't be trusted because it is deceiving and a habitual liar."

"In the end it looks like Demon Choe believed it needed to be done too, Professor."

"Demon Choe is a very wise jinni. Once its cover was blown, Demon Choe intentionally displayed its abilities and ultimately may have uncovered the true form hidden within the cloak of the hooded shadow. In doing so, it may have revealed not just the true face of the biblical God, but many of the perceived personal gods, goddesses, and deities with different names and labels around the world."

"A naga-like form could explain why the biblical God asked Moses to create a bronze serpent idol to be placed on a pole."

"It might."

"Do you think they are coming through a portal?"

"No. Based on experience I believe the jinn or deceptive gods are dual dimensional, capable of existing in their dimension and ours. Having mind-to-mind or electrical connections to humans, feeding on human and animal life force, and increasing radio frequency electromagnetic fields with our modern technology could be making access into our world longer and easier, which would explain the increase in frequency of jinn encounters."

"What about the lightning being, is it a different species?"

"It's possible, but there are a few things we must consider. By giving the deceptive god or gods an opportunity to communicate through different mediums we have learned much about their deceiving nature. There is no outsmarting these wise beings. As part of the game, the more I figured out or realized, and the more psychological and physical torment I endured, the more it appeared to reveal. This may have occurred with the manifestations as well."

"Are you saying the deceptive god wanted its true form known?"

"If the jinni or deceptive god didn't want it known it wouldn't have occurred and I might not have survived with all my marbles. How I responded to one manifestation or transformation may have determined if I would be visited by the next."

"Lightning has long been associated with gods, goddesses, and deities throughout human history. There are cross-cultural myths about powerful thunder, storm, and sky gods that had a preference to use lightning bolts as a weapon. Three that come to mind are Zeus of Greek mythology, Indra of Hindu mythology and Thor of Norse mythology."

"Lightning and thunder was attributed to the biblical God as well. One of many examples would be, Exodus 19:16; *And it came to pass on the third day in the morning, that there were thunders and lightnings, and a thick cloud upon the mount, and the voice of the trumpet exceeding loud; so that all the people that was in the camp trembled.* Historical Jesus or Yeshua said Satan appeared as lightning in Luke 10:18; *And he said unto them, I beheld Satan as lightning fall from heaven.* But then we have Matthew 24:27 saying, *for as the lightning cometh out of the east, and shineth even unto the west; so shall also the coming of the Son of man be.* And in Matthew 28:3, Jesus is said to have an appearance of lightning, *His countenance was like lightning, and his raiment white as snow.*"

"In some traditions lightning beings are believed to be teachers of illumination, others consider them deadly, and most have an adversary that appears as a dragon or serpent. The ancient belief that lightning is deadly or dangerous doesn't come as a surprise seeing that one bolt alone can contain as much as one billion volts of electricity, and lightning is responsible for about two thousand deaths a year globally."

"Jinn are known to have the ability to travel at amazing speeds, which most likely has something to do with their electrical makeup. Demon Choe said, *we don't need horses to get around; we can travel at the speed of light.* Ezekiel 1:14 says, *and the living creatures ran and returned as the appearance of a flash of lightning.*"

"Demon god, Sky, and the Master that followed the Demon god mentioned electricity and electrical. Demon god said, *illumined was electricity, love was the title,* and

Let me tell you a different story. Demons are your advancement in evolution. Electricity is my blood. How do we connect? Electricity. I can't talk to a fucking hamburger, electricity must flow in you. Sky said, *deliver this my brother, you are a body of water, electrical and gravitational forces make you illuminate,* and the Master said, *Electricity assumes without judgment. Expression has an electrical foundation. Electricity gives life to the flesh sculpture. Without electricity the sculpture ceases expression and decomposes. Electricity remains carrying with it your emotions and memory. Depending on your created contents it can assume as Heaven, or a world of its own creation."*

"Let's think about what the Master said for a moment. *Electricity remains carrying with it your emotions and memory.* This may be truth, emotion, memories, knowledge, beliefs, and all that makes up what you believe to be you could be contained in electricity. Consciousness could definitely be a form of electricity. This is not a new concept in the world of science but an intelligent life form that manifests as a mass of electricity and a presence that displays emotion and can't be seen unless it wants to, certainly leans that direction. If these beings can draw in electrical energy of a thunderstorm is it possible at the time of death they can consume the electrical energy from your physical body and the contents it contains? Is this another reason why they have knowledge of the deceased? Could it be that the reason many exorcisms fail is because these electrical beings are living within the electrical energy of the victim?"

"Having that kind of ability, there is so much they could be responsible for."

"True. Just the night light being turned on without being plugged in tells you that they're capable of affecting your electrical system, influencing your thoughts, divulging information, and feeding you their virtual world creations without wires because humans have electricity. This is how they can program your subconscious to think negatively, destructively, or demonically, and then go back into their dimension leaving you with the mind of a demon. It may appear to the so-called experts that you have a demon or jinni within, but in reality it's a demon programmed subconscious. If an exorcism is performed, there is no entity to cast out so the procedure fails because it is the victim's subconscious mind that needs to be reprogramed."

"This is why it is important to counter a negative thought or vision with two or more positive thoughts or visions and not allow it to become part of an established mind-haunting cycle. If you noticed I turned the arrows from the deceptive god's psychological attacks into dust on a couple of occasions. Mara attempted to distract Gautama Buddha while he was meditating prior to attaining enlightenment by firing arrows which Buddha turned to flowers. Some interpret this as a metaphor. In my experience the deceptive gods do psychologically attack by firing arrows, bullets, and rockets, throwing spears, knives, swords, and rocks and even dropping bombs to distract and create obstacles."

"Manipulation of electricity is how I believe the Old Hag Syndrome is accomplished by the deceptive god when it's not a case of Sleep Paralysis. Electricity is required to flex your muscles so the deceptive god causes a disruption in the electrical current. This is why you must control your emotions and remain calm as to not waste energy forcing the deceptive god to use its own. Once you remove the fear and the being knows you are wise to what is taking place and how to address it, the attacks will cease or occur less often."

"Demon god said, *Demons are your advancement in evolution,* we can compare this to the similar comments by Being of Energy and the Master. There was no dialogue or transmission of information from the lightning being about its race, hooded shadows, or fire and smoke naga creatures. There is no evidence in this investigation of the lightning beings and the smoke and fire creatures being sworn enemies. Each of these manifestations had an opportunity to explain their race and any adversaries in detail, but they didn't. If the deceptive god is what manifested as a smoke and fire creature or the hooded shadow, why would it speak so much about electricity if it wasn't its nature or if it has a sworn enemy that is a thunder and lightning being as believed in myth?"

"They just enjoy leaving humans confused."

"Yes, they do, and this will never change. Determining who is who as far as the manifestations is a challenge because none of the manifestations remained visible during the conversations and projected holograms and images in the mind's eye are all illusion. Maybe none of the manifestations were responsible for the dialogue or it could be just one and the game now is to guess who. These are wise and powerful jinn. Where one being leaves off and the next chimes in, I can't honestly tell you. These beings can work together to make the determination difficult by interweaving their influence, dialogue, dreams, illusions, and visions. The only thing I know for sure is the invisible entity that I interacted with in each conversation is an intelligent form of life and the manifestations were not a trick of the eyes or pareidolia."

"At least you're being honest, Professor."

"Too much assumption takes place with hidden world encounters. Each of the manifestations could be a species of jinn or energy being. Lightening beings could be the strongest amongst them if it is not a transformed state of one of the other manifestations. There is a noticeable difference in the type of light from the deceptive god playing a divine role and the lightning being. The lightning being manifested as a mass of luminous electrical energy and the deceptive god playing divine appeared more like the brightness of the sun or a star. But that doesn't mean they have to be two separate beings."

"During the investigation, every time the presence grew angry the cloud of its being reacted similar to the signs and stages of a thunderstorm. Air becomes thick and heavy like it does with the increase of moisture and humidity needed to fuel a storm. A black cloud ominously rolls in with its dreadful energy and expands and darkens the room. Dings and bangs are heard, and electrical disturbances begin which can include disrupting the electrical rhythm of the heart and physical attacks which have included electrical zaps to the head and body. I would compare this to the strong winds and lighting strikes during a storm."

"As long as you feed this presence fear, hatred, and anger, or say or do things that increase its rage, or challenge its power, this will be like feeding a thunderstorm warm and humid air which increases its size and intensity. If you let it run its course by remaining calm, being respectful, and ceasing what feeds its dark nature or become an energy changing dominant force of compassion and kindness, the storm or temper tantrum will dissipate and die out and you will experience the calm after the storm type feeling."

"Because of this and the dialogue about electricity, the drained car battery, and the fact that the lightning being manifested at the foot of the bed in the same manner as the smoke and fire naga, the hooded shadow, and other apparitions through the years, I believe there is a good chance the lightning being was another form of the presence or deceptive god. But I could be wrong."

"If there is a separate lightning being race this could be who Nikola Tesla tapped into."

"I agree. Each of the species of jinn has influenced humanity in a positive or negative way, or both. If I am wrong and the lightning being is another species of the hidden race and not the deceptive god, they may be playing a major role in our technological advancements that the deceptive gods are claiming credit for and have something to do with the brilliant lights witnessed by pilots in flight."

"Because the lightning being's presence was non-threatening, and it appeared to have cleansed the apartment of any sign of Demon Choe, it's possible that after Demon Choe manifested in its true form as a smoke and fire naga–like creature the lightning being did likewise to let it be known that there are beings of electricity as well. It's possible the lightning beings maintain balance keeping the smoke and fire creatures and shadows in check when necessary or they are a dominant race."

"If the lightning being is a separate race, do you think Mr. Five and Demon Choe was played by the same deceptive god or two separate jinn?"

"It could go either way. Demon Choe could be the smoke and fire naga or reptilian creature that hides within the hooded cloak of the shadow and played all the personalities. Because I didn't witness the smoke and fire naga coming out of the cloak, I can't assume it is the hooded shadow for certain even with Demon Choe's admittance. I do feel that the cloaked hooded shadow and the popular Hat Man shadow are costumes that are covering up a particular species of jinn, which could be the smoke and fire naga. If this is not the case, then there are two separate jinn that tagged along and symbiosis was taking place. Mr. Five possibly being the hooded shadow, and Demon Choe the naga or reptilian that have a relationship like wolves and ravens and other forms of wildlife that work together to eat and survive."

"There were definitely other jinn or energy beings from the parallel dimension playing a part, but there will only be one dominant jealous god seeking exclusive ownership that will stay close, giving the others permission to torment, tempt, weaken, and test, but not claim. A deceptive god wants you to love and fear them more than anything or anybody."

"I would say based on the analysis of the dialogue, and recognizing the being's energy, that if Demon Choe and Mr. Five were two separate entities speaking, Demon Choe was capable of a broader range of vibrational shifts and was responsible for most of the multiple personas especially the benevolent, holy, and higher vibrational personas. Mr. Five stayed primarily in the neutral to malevolent range."

"Since Boardman Lane I have been familiar with hooded shadows and their favored shapeshifting forms. I have only witnessed the naga form in the 2004 invisible serpent encounter and in dreams and visions, but never as a manifestation until that moment. Mr. Five could be the hooded shadow tag along from Boardman Lane that has a strong connection to my mother and myself which began as the ghost of the murdered victim. It is also possible the Boardman Lane information was extracted from my mother's mind, or my own, or passed on from another jinni."

"So, Mr. Five influenced the numbers, visions, and dreams of red/black symbolism as a game to take you back to Boardman Lane, the loss of a child, and the vision of your sister in a black dress wearing a red scarf that occurred to your mother during her near death experience?"

"It appears so. Their games can last a lifetime targeting different family members through the years. The pure black Doberman-like dog with the red scarf was to represent the black dress and red scarf. Mr. Five could have been responsible for the activity that occurred in every home the family lived in after Boardman Lane. Mr. Five did leave clues of red/black symbolism in the past, like my grandmother wearing a red shirt and black pants appearing as a ghost to my mother and Richard, and most likely left other clues through the years for which my mother was unaware."

"How about Demon Choe?"

"Demon Choe could have attached in the monastery garden where I prayed for years after solo training, or in the forest where I meditated and sat enjoying the silent communication of the trees. Demon Choe was not new to playing holy figures. Because I have experienced Demon Choe's ability to appear as darkness, fire, and the brilliant light of the sun, it is possible the wise deceiver masqueraded according to the monk's beliefs, as it tempted, tormented, and fed on their energy until the fire of 1950. I'm not saying this is fact, but it is possible based on its religious knowledge and false illuminative ability. Deceptive gods use religion as a lure."

"What was it like being face to face with the hooded shadow and the naga?"

"I was definitely taken aback as they are intimidating manifestations. All I could do was stand my ground, control my emotions, and be grateful if I survived. Have you ever seen a picture of the angler fish of the ocean deep?"

"No, I can't say I have."

"Please do a search."

Tom looked it up. "Man that's scary. I wouldn't want to come face to face with that."

"I'm sure you wouldn't because it's not what you're used to. But this predator is an expression of God. If you read on you will see that this predator was created with a bioluminescent headlamp appendage on its face that is used as a lure to draw prey toward its mouth. If the creator can equip a predator of the ocean with a false light, it can do the same for a jinni."

"Observing the smoke and fire naga's face and bulky upper body brought to memory the fierce looking Buddhist gate guardians that stand at the entrance to Japanese Temples and are a protector of Buddha. Please do a search for Agyo and Ungyo, guardians of the temples."

Tom performed a search and tilted his head back as he viewed the guardians. "They're scary too."

"It's not what you're used to. Now do a search for the sculpture of King Enma."

Tom performed the search as I leaned back in the chair. "King Enma and his attendants?"

"Yes, Tom."

"It's similar and just as frightening, Professor."

"There are similarities in the Rakshasas and the nagas of Hindu mythology and iconography. None of the comparisons are exact, but the facial details are similar which tells me humans throughout history have seen these beings, in whole or in part, in influenced dreams, visions, and manifestations. It's not all human imagination as some would like you to believe."

"Having been lucky or unlucky enough to be face-to-face with the two malevolent manifestations, I did notice similarities. In addition to their exact energy, both had almond shaped eyes with no pupil or iris, with the naga's eyes being more orange than red. It was like staring into the plasma of the sun or molten lava when it's at its hottest temperature, with the very core of the being appearing to be the sun or like liquid lava that hadn't cooled. When lava starts to cool the color changes to a bright red like that of the hooded shadow. Through the years I have experienced the hooded shadow with white, emerald green, and gold colored eyes as well."

"Because of the similarities, and the snake slithering sensation around my legs occurring when the hooded shadow was in the room, it became apparent that what is within the cloak of the hooded shadow could have a serpent form. As you read, I did say to the hooded shadow during our staring contest 'I can see you and you can see me. Now what?' This was an intentional challenge. Just like me saying to Sky, 'But can you shapeshift to your true form in this present moment?' The counter might be revealing what is hidden within the cloak and maybe even the lightning form. Plus, the personality Demon god said, *I am dark eternal and homely in human eyes. Myths and legends create visions of our appearance.* Demon god couldn't have been talking about the hooded shadow form because I already had come face to face with this manifestation, it had to have been talking about its smoke and fire naga form."

"But as much as there were signs that show similarities in the two manifestations there were also distinct differences. The naga had three clawed fingers and a clawed thumb which may explain the common three finger scratches that people have received during malevolent hauntings, including myself. It came forward with an s-shaped serpentine movement, whereas the hooded shadow glides when it moves, and shot forward in a linear fashion when it came face-to-face. The naga was made up of black and gray detailed smoke and projected heat, whereas the hooded shadow is made of a matter or substance that is darker than night and no heat was felt during its manifestation. If the naga wears the hooded cloak it may serve many purposes besides just concealment, with one of the uses being to retain heat or energy."

"What about the Big Foot-like shadow?"

"The Big Foot-like shadow that I witnessed was either a shapeshifted form of the hooded shadow as it appeared to be made of a similar opaque substance, and hooded shadows have the ability to enlarge or shrink, and lengthen or widen at will, or it was in fact another species of shadow or jinni that manifested from the parallel dimension. Deceptive gods do influence visions and dreams of giants like Daro, and I have experienced many. This makes it possible that the deceptive gods played a part in the myths and legends of giants in various cultures."

"Because we live in a world where privacy is dead due to modern technology, it would be impossible for the Big Foot species to remain hidden all these years if it remained in a physical form. If this is what witnesses have reported, this hulk of a shadow is not made of flesh, bones, and hair. But deceptive gods could be causing humans to hallucinate and see the hairy versions of Big Foot or Sasquatch, or project a hologram of the image to get attention."

"Now I would like you to read a couple of passages on the board. The first is from a prayer of David, and the second is Eliphaz describing a vision of the night which is believed to be an evil spirit, demon, or Satan."

"Psalm 17:3; *Thou hast proved mine heart; thou hast visited me in the night; thou hast tried me, and shalt find nothing; I am purposed that my mouth shall not transgress.* Job 4:13-19; *In thoughts from visions of the night, when deep sleep falleth on men, Fear came upon me, and trembling, which made all my bones to shake. Then a spirit passed before my face; the hair of my flesh stood up: It stood still, but I could not discern the form thereof: an image was before mine eyes, there was silence, and I heard a voice, saying, Shall mortal man be more just than God? shall a man be more pure than his maker? Behold, he put no trust is his servants; and his angels he charged with folly.*"

"Thank you, Tom. Notice it says, *a spirit passed before my face.* Both had a visitor in the night."

"It sounds like the hooded shadow, Professor."

"Based on experience I would say there is a high probability. Both the hooded shadow and the ghost monks glided when they moved. People around the world who have encountered the hooded shadow, Hat Man, or the black shadow mass may also agree. The biblical God was angered at Eliphaz, and it is believed that the biblical God gave permission for Satan to torment. This Satan sounds an awful lot like a hooded shadow. Shadow beings or shadow people are not a new international phenomenon, only the label."

"This is the passage where the biblical God was angry with Eliphaz. Job 42:7; *And it was so, that after the LORD had spoken these words unto Job, the LORD said to*

Eliphaz the Temanite, My wrath is kindled against thee, and against thy two friends: for ye have not spoken of me the thing that is right, as my servant Job hath."

"As I have told you, speak as if many invisible ears are listening. If a deceptive god or gods is present, they will get angry if you speak of them in an ill way. If you want harmony in your home and in your life, think before you speak and be aware of your spoken word. In the next passage, we have a presence or spiritual being perceived to be the biblical God entering or attaching to David as it was perceived to have left or detached from the vessel of Saul. Saul is then believed to have been tormented by another bad or evil spirit after the exchange."

"1 Samuel 16:12-14; *And he sent, and brought him in. Now he was ruddy, and withal of a beautiful countenance, and goodly to look to. And the LORD said, Arise, anoint him: for this is he. Then Samuel took the horn of oil and anointed him in the midst of his brethren: and the Spirit of the LORD came upon David from that day forward. So, Samuel rose up, and went to Ramah. But the Spirit of the LORD departed from Saul, and an evil spirit from the LORD troubled him."*

"Benevolent and malevolent possession."

"Yes, Tom. Obviously they were unaware that an emotional deceptive god is both the good and bad spirit and is more than capable of connecting, possessing, or influencing more than one human victim at a time."

"Hooded shadows frequent the dark corners where they can stare and watch in the night. These are the watchers, which may mean the nagas are the watchers. Let's look at how many times the word *watch, watched* and *watching* was used by the benevolent, malevolent, male and female personalities of the deceiver or deceivers. Looking at the board we have:"

- *Goodbye, my son, I will watch your days grow brighter,* by Impostor Father
- *Here in your atmosphere is a stadium of beings watching and communicating,* by Being of Energy
- *We have watched you,* by Being of Energy
- *Here lie many memories and experiences that I watch like a morning sunrise,* by Golden Cross Monk
- *I watched my sisters suffer and they watched me,* by Helen
- *High above this current vision of yours, I watch you, my brother. Fear will enter your mind, but never will it enter your soul. Just be God's eyes and watch the world change,* by Counterfeit Jesus
- *Every day I watch you outside working in the backyard,* by Richard

- *Jesus is watching all and so are we,* by Baby
- *God is light, where there is light, God is watching,* by ghost monk I Am Light
- *My hawks are my eyes, my eyes are my soul. I watch your heart beat as I watch your soul grow,* by Angel Michael
- *I have watched you give more than you have, I have watched you crawl in order to live, I have watched you faithfully believe in what was never taught,* by Angel Michael
- *Jesus, I follow, you I watch, God I see,* by Sky
- *Holy Spirit watches your journey. I am watching your journey,* by Holy Spirit

"That's a lot of watching."

"It certainly is, this is the nature of the being. That's why the persona Demon god said, *let them cover their deeds, I will find them,* and Demon Choe said, *we are the third eye that no enigma can hide from.* Deeds mean intentional and/or conscious actions. This would be called karma in Buddhism or Hinduism."

"Holy Spirit persona lied when it said, *I watch, I listen, I smell, I taste, I feel, I know. All your thoughts, all your actions, all your feelings. All noticed, but not judged.* In addition to the principle of cause and effect, these beings judge your actions and beliefs and reward or punish according to their whim as the enforcer. Hence the reason for their made-up laws and rules that they break themselves. The expression 'do as I say not as I do' applies to the deceptive gods. Let's discuss what else is taking place when they're watching. Are you familiar with the evil eye?"

"Yes. But I don't understand it."

"I will do my best to briefly explain. The evil or bad eye, what my Italian grandmother called Malocchio or the Maloik, is an intentional or unintentional curse usually brought on by jealousy, envy, or pure hatred for another. Energy follows the mind, I'm going to repeat that, energy follows the mind. When the hooded shadow lurks in the corner and you feel its eyes upon you that is negative energy following the mind. Depending on your health and belief system, and the power of the envious and hateful, the results from the evil eye can range from no effect at all to a headache, insomnia, fatigue, hallucinations and depression, to injury, illness, chaos, and death to the victim, family, house pets, and livestock. If the victim has a relationship with another deceptive god that chooses to be a guardian or protector, how it reacts to this evil eye attack will be determined by the intentions and the feelings it has for the victim. A good example of this in Scripture is the biblical God speaking in Genesis 12:3;

And I will bless them that bless thee: and curse him that curseth thee: and in thee shall all families of the earth be blessed."

"Deceptive gods can bless and curse?"

"Yes Tom, just as they can heal and harm or introduce what is perceived as divine or demonic knowledge. But it depends on the nature of the deceptive god, just as it depends on the nature of a human being. Both are capable of blessing or cursing if they possess the necessary ingredients. When it comes to deceptive gods, they are very careful in who they bless and curse because both require the expenditure of energy."

"When I asked Demon god if it were an angel, he answered, *hope not, because I haven't seen yours yet. Humans are so predictable. Make them scared and they call angels. Make them see light coming and an angel they assume is there. Let me give you a message. Demons are angels. Holy Michael is me. I tricked you, but don't feel bad, I trick them all.* Surprise, surprise. Later when it plays Demon Choe it says the opposite, *Might I say, angels are demons too.* Demons are angels, angels are demons, and both are played by the deceptive gods."

"Demon Choe said, *in man a core, in demons a core, in angels a core.* This core is your true nature, or the essence of the infinite, eternal, one God. Humans and the deceptive gods that play angel, demon, and God, are both expressions of the one God which is the foundation of existence. Deceptive gods play angel and demon in order to open lines of communication to influence, manipulate, and control. Demon Choe said, *neither angels nor demons are full of all the answers. We just like to communicate.* This is true, deceptive gods are not all-knowing, but they will certainly spin a tale to keep the conversations going."

"If you look over the dialogue of the Holy Spirt that spoke in threes and called me son, you will find many words used by the different personas. Notice Holy Spirit said, *I am all you see and all you don't see.* Why did it say that, Tom?"

"Because you have been saying all along that the one God is all you see and all you don't see."

"Correct. It is possible that this species from the parallel dimension influenced religious texts. Holy Spirit said, *I, Holy Spirit, place my word within all religions.* No matter what religion or occult practice you follow, they will also use the words from the sacred text you're reading or reciting to form a relationship. When I called the Holy Spirit Lord, I did so because I know it is this deceiver that has played the holy angels, Jesus, and God through the years. This shows that this particular deceptive god can play all three roles of the Holy Trinity - Father, Son, and Holy Spirit. As it said, it brought me joy, but also misery, it brought me light, but also darkness, and it comforted me in a high vibration cloud of love, but it also made me uncomfortable in a low vibration cloud of darkness. Holy Spirit said, *combine all your perceptions of good and bad and I am all of this.* This is why the persona Baby asked, *When are you going to ask me if I'm a good or bad spirit?"*

"The question was part of the game."

"Yes. Holy Spirit said, *I am what I am and that is what I remain as.* Just as Voice of Love said, *I am what I am, call me what you feel.* Holy Spirit said, *I need no messenger, if compassion lives within. Messengers are holy and unholy. Seen and unseen. All are soul voices heard.* They are not soul voices. The holy and unholy messengers, or angels, are the personas of the deceiver. The deceptive god has called me a master, and it has called itself a master as a persona. Holy Spirit said, *you are all masters eventually."*

"Holy Spirit said, *Religions are paths and heart is the mountain they climb,* just as Metacomet said, *High in the mountain you deserve to be,* insinuating that I have achieved a level of spiritual advancement, and Demon Choe said, *Hills are not mountains, flowers are not trees.* This can go along with all the divine and demonic visions and dreams of mountains I experienced during the investigation. God is believed to talk on top of mountains. Jinn are known to inhabit mountains and are believed in Middle Eastern folklore to live in the mystical mountains of another dimension that surrounds our planet called Kaf. A passage about mountains I would add here is up on the board, Ezekiel 20:40; *For in mine holy mountain, in the mountain of the height of Israel, saith the Lord God, there shall all the house of Israel, all of them in the land, serve me: there will I accept them, and there will I require your offerings, and the firstfruits of your obligations, with all your holy things."*

"More appeasing, Professor."

"Yes, Tom."

"Holy Spirit spoke the word pith because of your love for trees."

"Of course. Holy Spirit said, *learn from them and grow from them as you always have.* This was said because I have had a close relationship with trees and their subtle energy vibration since childhood. Humanity needs to reconnect to these sacred ancient teachers. Feel their aura, touch, hug, and resonate with their calming and healing song. Protect them, and for every one you cut down, show your gratitude for the valuable part they play by planting a few more."

"Doesn't the name Michael mean something about God?"

"Yes. It means 'Who is like God'. Angel Michael spoke in threes, used flattery, and called me brother. Angel Michael said, *Michael is my given name, God the I Am is me.* We can compare this to the Counterfeit Jesus saying, *You man, gave me Christ. I Jesus gave you God's word.* Simply, the deceptive god is saying through the two false personalities that it is the I Am that gave God's word. To add to this, we have *Michael I am, Love I am, God I am,* and *I once drew my sword and kneeled before God, as God.* In this investigation, Angel Michael is like God, because it is a benevolent or divine expression of the deceptive god."

"Angel Michael was speaking of being filled with God or the Holy Spirit and receiving dreams from the God or Holy Spirit when it said, *eleven worlds above fills your cup daily, drink from this. Eleven worlds above fills your heart daily, live from this. Eleven worlds above fills your dreams daily, watch for this.* Dark god said, *Fill God. Either of us has a home for you.* That home is what you have come to know as heaven and hell, the light side or the dark side of the deceptive god's consciousness. This is why the Dark god said, *both are fear at its best. God of light and God of darkness.* Which is true. You have been taught to fear both the perceived God of Light that killed millions in the Bible and the perceived Prince of Darkness that killed ten which were the seven sons and three daughters of the righteous Job, with the biblical God's permission, of course."

"When I asked Angel Michael if it were really an angel the answer was, *if that's what it takes to clear your vision, then yes, I am an angel, I am love, and I am god in you.* Angel Michael didn't say it was an angel, but said if that's what it takes. The deceptive god will do whatever it takes to begin, maintain, or re-establish a connection playing all the benevolent and malevolent roles. What sparked this investigation was the appearance of the ghost monks. Angel Michael said, *listen closely to your heart, for God is you, my brother.* Just as the first ghost monk in the garden said, *God is you, my brother.* The deceptive god played Angel Michael just as it played the very first ghost monk in the garden because that's what it took to get my attention. Deceptive gods not only provide information based on your interests, but popular trends and fads of the time."

"What did you think of Angel Michael giving you the answer, *Angels are not bodyguards and Jesus Christ is not a warlord?*"

"There is truth in that response. Seeing that the deceptive god has admitted it plays both the holy and unholy angel and we know the same being has played Counterfeit Jesus, what the deceptive god is saying is they are not bodyguards or warlords. Deceptive gods can act as guardians if they so choose or are summoned for a price, but don't count on their assistance because of your religious beliefs."

"How about Angel Michael saying, *Moments before moments, I see thee?*"

"It is possible that these deceptive gods can see what we believe to be the present moment well before our limited sight. It may have something to do with the parallel dimension."

"Angel Michael spoke about the sword a lot."

"Angel Michael is believed to be a warrior, like Thor of the Old Norse religion. The first time a sword was mentioned was in the Monastery garden, *compassion wields a mighty sword, illumination is the body armor of God, what penetrates can only make you stronger,* by the third ghost monk. From Angel Michael we have, *I once drew my sword and kneeled before God, as God. I will draw my sword, for those that express light from their soul. I swing a sword of light, for which no demon can lift, and for which no legion can withstand. Draw your swords; hold them high, for I am coming.* We can compare this to a few passages mentioning swords from Scripture."

"Ezekiel 12:14; *And I will scatter towards every wind all that are about him to help him, and all his bands; and I will draw out the sword after them.* Ezekiel 21:3; *And say to the land of Israel, Thus saith the LORD; Behold, I am against thee; and will draw forth my sword out of his sheath, and will cut off from thee the righteous and the wicked.* Ezekiel 21:5; *That all flesh may know that I the Lord have drawn forth my sword out of his sheath: It shall not return any more.*"

"And a few contradicting passages that confuse many from Jesus the Christ. Matthew 26:52; *Then said Jesus unto him, put up again thy sword into his place: for all they that take the sword shall perish with the sword.* Luke 22:36; *Then said he unto them, But now, he that hath a purse, let him take it, and likewise his scrip: and he that hath no sword, let him sell his garment, and buy one.* Matthew 10:34; *Think not that I am come to send peace on earth: I came not to send peace, but a sword.*"

"Angel Michael said, *I can't stop migrating bugs if you give them shelter* and *thoughts bring bugs, desires bring bugs, energy brings bugs.* Demon Choe said, *Gone are the migrating bugs for you listened,* showing the link, and of course we had Baby originally saying to you, *I will tell you why you are tired, it's because the bed bugs were biting, and we're the bed bugs.* Feeling the sensation of bugs crawling on or under your skin is called formication. This can be caused by a medical condition, prescription or recreational drug side effect, drug withdrawal, and hormonal changes."

"Deceptive gods can be responsible for this condition as well. In my experience visions, dreams, and hallucinations of bugs and the sensation of bugs crawling on the face, body, or both was experienced during and prior to the investigation when the presence of a hooded shadow had been noticed lurking in the darkness or tagging along. "

"You have read that the woman Linda at the gift shop said, 'you work with Angel Michael, don't you?' and I replied that I didn't know that but would be honored if I could."

"Yes, why did she say that?"

"Linda was possibly influenced by a voice within her head saying Angel Michael repeatedly. Linda then believes it is her psychic ability and one of her guides speaking and says, 'you work with Angel Michael, don't you?' not realizing where the message really came from and why. Now I will give you the why. Before the face to face encounter with the red-eyed hooded shadow, what prayer did I recite?"

"The Angel Michael Prayer of Protection."

"Yes, and there was a reason I did so. To develop or maintain a relationship and connection the deceptive god, which is a jealous god, will capitalize on emotionalism and becomes your one-stop shop for anyone or anything you desire to speak with and/or experience. The naga within the hooded shadow hears me recite the Angel Michael prayer, influences Linda at the retail store, hears me say I would be honored to speak to this being and then, presto, it wears the guise of a luminous Angel Michael."

"How about the hawk, do you think they can use their eyes as they use humans?"

"Yes, at least this particular species can. But it is equally possible that this is an example of taking credit for something that is not true or an action it didn't do to impress. The deceptive god sees through my eyes and knows I saw a hawk above. Then it adds it into its story for the wow factor."

"Humans using the deceptive gods' eyes can experience enhanced microscopic and telescopic vision in a trance or dream state, and the abilities are coined remote viewing. A red-tailed hawk was circling before the conversation and has in the past during divine-like interactions. Angel Michael said, *my hawks are my eyes, my eyes are my soul.* Depending on the belief system and superstitions of an individual or culture, a bird based on its color, appearance, or size could be viewed as a messenger of the light or darkness. Eagles and hawks are a common messenger, symbol, or a shape-shifted form of many mythical gods, goddesses, and deities."

"Birds inhabit the skies above which is believed in ancient and modern cultures to be the home of God, a god, the gods, and the winged humanoids titled angels. Native American legend speaks of the Sky Beings, the Above People and Star Beings. Many find comfort in believing their loved ones that passed are looking down from above. Deceptive gods are opportunists, if this is your belief they will cater to that belief. But what you seek is not above, below, to the left, to the right, in front of you, or behind you. It is within."

"Angel Michael said, *Name another spoken word of light, I, the oracle, internalized its birth, long before mouth opened in man.* What Angel Michael is saying with the oracle comment, is that again it's the unseen voice that is channeled through a human mouthpiece. In many ancient and modern cultures this male or female human channeler is or was known as an oracle."

"Like the Oracle at Delphi."

"Exactly. There is also the Nechung Oracle of today that Tibetans consult. The Oracle at Delphi was a high priestess of the Temple of Apollo at Delphi and was called Pythia. The location on Mt. Parnassus in Greece is where the prophetess or the Pythia would inhale intoxicating vapors rising from a crevice in the Earth within the sanctuary. These vapors would assist in triggering a trance-like state in which the Pythia would become a voice piece and channel for what was believed to be the god Apollo."

"Are there any prophetesses mentioned in the Bible? I don't remember hearing about any."

"There are a few, Tom. Channeling a god or serving as its voice piece has nothing to do with gender."

"I would compare the inhalation of the vapors to the Native American use of the sweat lodge to change the brain waves and enter an altered state of consciousness. There are many methods used alone, or in combination, to trigger a trance-like state or altered state of consciousness. A few more of them being incense, prayer, singing, drumming, mantras, visualization, psychoactive drugs, music, the ringing of a bell, or the soothing vibration of a tree on a spring day."

"In fact those who have had an NDE or Near Death Experience visiting what was believed to be heaven or hell, the description of various shamanic spirit travels in the three worlds of upper, middle, and lower influenced by the spiritual beings, the symptoms of a forced third eye opening, and those that describe the entities that they confronted while taking DMT which stands for Dimethyltryptamine are similar to the experiences that I have encountered with the awareness of a deceptive god's influence."

"DMT is an active compound in the psychedelic brew called Ayahuasca and can be found naturally in many plants, animals and humans. DMT users claim that some of these alien entities are benevolent, sharing knowledge, teaching, guiding, imparting laws, and welcoming their visit to their realm or dimension and would like them to visit more frequently and others are malevolent trickster entities that are not very pleasant, that can haunt their mind after the trip, and can act territorial telling them to leave their dimension or get out. These DMT entities use probes, perform experiments, and surgeries on the DMT user like the reported alien abductions, take the form of gray aliens, angels, artistic representations of religious icons like Jesus and Buddha, deceased loved ones, hybrids, animals, serpents, reptiles, insects, robots, clowns, and jesters. If you remember the persona god presence said, *those who give names and titles are just my children masquerading for jest."*

"Sounds exactly like the influence of a deceptive god, Professor."

"These DMT sessions can be life-changing like an NDE or a mystical experience, but I would say with little doubt that the DMT users are entering the hidden world or parallel dimension and/or connecting to the mind of a deceptive god or other species of jinn."

CHAPTER 27

AWAKENING

S hifting our focus for fifteen minutes, we practiced a flow and sensitivity drill called Hubud Lubud which loosely translates as to tie and untie. Beginning slowly with the basic three-step sequence, we advanced to the switching of hands, limb destructions, low line kicking, off balancing, and joint locks varying the timing, speed, and intensity before we stopped and took a seat again.

"Did you have any thoughts of deceptive gods while practicing hubud, Tom?"

"Not at all."

"Good. If you can't think of them, they can't think as you. Let's continue."

"Was Yeshua the real name of Jesus, Professor?"

"In my research, yes. Yeshua or Yehoshua was a common name in that time. The name Jesus was born from the transliteration of Yeshua into Greek, and lastly into English. It is also true that following a name can gives you a name, as Demon Choe mentioned, but as you can see the deceptive god and its many personas, including the Holy Spirit and the god presence, didn't mention the name Yeshua. Now that I have mentioned Yeshua or Yehoshua, the deceivers would surely use it in conversation and make up some excuse why they didn't before. When I asked Demon Choe why it never called Jesus his real name Yeshua, the answer was, *don't get lost in words, get found in light,* avoiding the answer to the question."

"What's your take on Demon god saying, *Jesus is killed by demons, but man follows a corpse. Power from imagination.*"

"It's the same as Demon Choe saying, *don't kneel to a dead body. As gruesome as it sounds it is truth.* Personas of the deceptive god continued to say Jesus was a male human, and a child of the one God like every human and there will not be a second coming. This is also the common doctrine of the modern channelers received messages from the spirit world. On the board I put the related messages together."

- *The Jesus you wait for will walk only in your shoes. God will change your world, but only through each of you. Love is the tool, love is the savior, love is the messiah,* by Angel Michael
- *Jesus was a human, Moses was a human, you are a human,* by Angel Michael
- *Jesus has a heart, you have a heart, and both have a home. So, I say to all, may you find the door and walk in. Simple it is. Jesus spoke of his luminous experiences; may you all speak of yours. Jesus will not rise again, and Christ never left you. Jesus was a man, Christ was his heart. See this, my family. Stop waiting for an illusion that you will never see,* by Golden Cross Monk
- *Jesus is killed by demons, but man follows a corpse. Power from imagination,* by Demon god
- *Jesus was tricked, enter the demon that called him son. God love called to him and he answered. My, my - humans wait thousands of years for a human God,* by Demon god
- *Jesus was a man. Don't kneel to a dead body. As gruesome as it sounds, it is truth,* by Demon Choe
- *Jesus is a name, many have this name today. Following a name gives you a name. You must understand words are plentiful. Don't worship words and don't follow words. Does a puppy follow words? Does a kitten follow words? All they hear is tone,* by Demon Choe

"Well it has been 2000 years, do you think Yeshua or Jesus is returning?"

"Is the savior about the return of a man or is it about the transformational power of the mind of the heart? Any moment of any day humanity can unite their compassionate hearts giving birth to a savior 300 million hearts strong here in America, or close to 7 billion hearts strong worldwide. Unity, compassion, and empathy is what gives birth to the true loving God. Those who benefit from the created illusion of division and separation prefer you remain ignorant to this truth."

"I felt that in the heart, Professor."

"The heart knows truth, my friend. As far as for Demon god and Demon Choe's comments, power from imagination and belief in your God adds up to the power of belief. You can believe yourself to health or you can believe yourself to sickness. Belief in a deity can have a positive placebo effect like the belief in a prescription drug that is really a sugar pill. If I dwelled on the injuries sustained in the influenced visions and dreams, or the whispers from the deceptive god during this investigation like, *if you go to sleep you're not going to wake up,* and you dwelled and worried after Baby said, *you want ridiculous, how about I kill you,* this would have created a negative placebo effect which is called nocebo."

"Deceptive gods know the positive and negative power of belief. A passage from the Bible that relates is the first sentence of Proverbs 23:7; *For as he thinketh in his heart, so is he.* This is similar to, *Man is made by his belief. As he believes, so he is,* from the ancient Indian sacred text *Bhagavad Gita,* and *The mind is everything. What you think you become,* by Gautama Buddha."

"They are all saying the same thing."

"Yes they are."

"Do you still love Yeshua or Jesus?"

"Of course, Tom. I see all as one. But I don't love him out of fear, or to get something in return, like a better afterlife. When you can love him whether he is the savior or not, or the son of God or not, it is then your love is true. I will ask you, Yeshua or Jesus was crucified with two convicted thieves, one to his right and one to his left. Who may I ask do you feel empathy for?"

"Prior to your teachings I would have said Jesus and judged the thieves as a lesser form of life. Now I would say I feel empathy for all three equally."

"Very good, Tom. Thousands were victims of this barbaric form of execution by the Romans. To feel for only one, and not the others is selective empathy, and not oneness."

"Why do you think the deceptive gods dislike the Bible?"

"I would say one reason is it's not the doctrine of this particular jinni or deceptive god. Based on dialogue, Scripture, and the observation of their nature, I would say the biblical God or gods in Scripture were jealous of one another and that characteristic remains. Demon god said with the illusion of ten faces on the tips of each finger of the red gloves and in the day dream as five gold aliens, *are you trying to make us look bad?* This shows they care about how they are portrayed. Demon god said, *where in the Bible is my discussion?* which tells you they each want to be heard, and *I stand as master and creator,* clearly showing the I am the one God, or God Almighty mentality and its connection to Angel Michael which said, *don't kneel to names. Stand as God.* Kim also used the word stand when she said, *I speak from heaven on this day because I told love; you are my choice, stand and be me.*"

"Basically, any deceptive god you interact with can claim they are the one God?"

"Yes, Tom. You are not going to get a jinni or deceptive god to say another god is more powerful unless it's masquerading as that god or serves that god. Let's look at what the personas said about books, with the first being an example of both the malevolent and benevolent component of the deceptive god working together with Angel Michael, Demon god, and Metacomet speaking negatively about religious or sacred texts."

"Metacomet said, *I chose Great Spirit over man's written word,* referring to the colonists attempt to convert all native people to Christianity. Demon god said, *I can tell you the dinosaurs existed, where in the Bible is that discussion? I can tell you I'm a demon, where in the Bible is my discussion?* and *Books are in fire. Words are the cause.* When I asked if it were speaking of religious texts, the answer was, *I'm talking about all God calling books.* Then we have Angel Michael saying, *Holy pretenders have done plenty of writing. Roots of trees contain more truth than most written books about God* and *I didn't write this book, Jesus didn't write this book, love didn't write this book* - referring to the Bible."

"When I asked the impostor Pop if I should continue writing this book, the answer was, *Hear the call of the messengers. Watch in God's eyes, Feel in God's body. Place your heart in God and then finish it.* I've been hearing the call of the messengers all along and it has amounted to a pile of stories, lies, and psychological games. Other personas that want me to finish the book are,"

- *You now must finish your book,* by Amy
- *I hope my explanation is helpful in your book,* by My Life Is God
- *Include in your book this speech,* by My Life Is God
- *The book is your destiny my brother,* by I Am Light
- *Let's see how your emotions feel when you finish the book,* by Sky
- *Complete your book with this. 11 voyages are 22 years apart and 33 years long. This is the master code,* by Angel Michael

"Was that last one by Angel Michael a riddle?"

"Yes. It used the numbers 11, 22, and 33, then Demon god later asked, *do you know how many Catholics it takes to kill a demon?* When I answered no, Demon god said, *forty-four long robes,* to add to the number pattern 11, 22, 33, and to hint that Angel Michael and Demon god are one and the same."

"Riddles are puzzles that can be used as a test or challenge of wisdom, a game or form of entertainment, and a way to hide messages with important information. You will find riddles in the Bible with the most popular being the one told by Sampson.

The biblical God told Ezekiel to deliver a message with a riddle to his people, Ezekiel 17:1-2; *And the word of the Lord came unto me, saying, Son of man, put forth a riddle, and speak a parable unto the house of Israel.* When the historical Jesus spoke to crowds he spoke in parables and riddles."

"Another riddle was Dark god saying, *keep digging, because gold is just a rock and I'm there to greet you.* Gold is just a rock just as the golden-white light and brilliant white light is just bait or a temporary state of emotional being. *I'm there to greet you*, means whenever you communicate with the hidden or unseen - whether it be to talk to the deceased, aliens, angels, native people, ascended masters, saints, gods, goddesses, deities, guides, and so on - it could be one of these deceptive gods that will greet you dressed for the occasion."

"This is why Demon Choe said, *Demons are your highest and your lowest word.* What may be perceived as the highest word came from the god presence, Holy Spirit, Counterfeit Jesus, Light of Heart, Master, Quasar, angels, and the other benevolent shining personas. Examples of what may be perceived as the lowest word came from Baby, Donovan, Dark god, Demon god, Judd, and other malevolent personas which could have all been played by Demon Choe."

"Maybe it's stupid for me to ask, I know we talked about them connecting to feed on sexual energy and experience the energetic sensations of sex, but why would it want to give a human an orgasm?"

"Deceptive gods play along with strange human beliefs and create stories. In Jewish mythology, Lilith is believed to seduce men in order to take their sperm and impregnate herself to give birth to demons. As you read, in a dream a woman with long red hair appeared, after she threw out the seeds that grew into serpents she approached to embrace but I retreated. When I spotted a toddler standing on a stone cliff I pointed to the child and warned her that her child was about to fall. Her reply as she looked up was, *that's our child and he can fly.*"

"Semen was and still is used as an offering in some ancient rites to certain gods, deities and spirits as part of the worship requirements just like blood and food."

"Demon god said, *I recall love in girls being a weakness in many.* Just as the ghost monk I Am Light said, *Avoid women, my brother. A Demon is finding your weakness and planning a trap.* Leaving out its own weakness and lust for mortal women until I said, it is written you lust for mortal woman as well, and the demon god responded with, *Demons like titties too.*"

Tom tried to contain his laughter but failed and said, "I wonder if this is how a lot of comedians get their material."

"Those in the entertainment industry can channel these beings intentionally or unintentionally to create an impressionable performance and end up with a lifelong tormenting tag along that can cause anxiety and depression, and influence negative and suicidal thoughts."

"Looking at the dialogue of the Demon god persona we see the deceptive gods jealous, possessive, and competitive nature when it shouted, *I don't like you reading about other gods,* into my right ear as I read about the Egyptian bull-god Hapi after its influenced bull hybrid vision. Bull worship was a common practice in many ancient cultures. Deceptive gods don't like you reading about or mentioning other gods and they don't like you talking to other gods. It is their nature. The idol of the god Moloch which was a perceived rival god of the biblical God, was depicted with the head of a bull."

"Like Daro."

"Yes. If you look on the board there is an example of the God of Israel or the biblical God's anger toward those who sacrifice their seed or children to the god Moloch in their worship. Leviticus 20:2; *Again, thou shalt say to the children of Israel, Whosoever he be of the children of Israel, or of the strangers that sojourn in Israel, that giveth any of his seed unto Moloch; he shall surely be put to death: the people of the land shall stone him with stones.*"

"This passage has been perceived by some as an example of the goodness and love of the biblical God. As long as you avoid the passages in the Old Testament where the biblical God performed or commanded mass killings, which included children, I can see how you could be deceived. The one true God does not care if you worship a head of lettuce, because both you and the lettuce is its reflection."

"The ancients were as naive and gullible to the ways of the deceptive gods as humans are today, Professor."

"In some cases, even more so. Humans must stop following the word of an invisible presence, Tom. The word is not God, silence is God. Another example of their jealous and possessive nature and being chosen by a god was when the Demon god said, *but remember I chose Lorne and I will destroy all demons which are marking Lorne as theirs. I claimed you long ago. When demons stared in your eyes, I ate them. Now I remain close destroying demons in heat.* I have listed two examples of being chosen by the biblical God."

"John 15:16; *Ye have not chosen me, but I have chosen you, and ordained you, that ye should go and bring forth fruit, and that your fruit should remain: that whatsoever ye shall ask of the Father in my name, he may give it you.* Deuteronomy 7:6; *For thou art an holy people unto the Lord thy God: the Lord thy God hath chosen thee to be a special people unto himself, above all people that are upon the face of the earth. "*

"Only external personal gods and humans choose favorites. The internal God is the silence within and all around you, it's where you come from, it's where you're going, and it's what you are, whether you are religious or not, and whether you give it attention or not. It does not seek possession of vessels it already inhabits."

"How did you learn so much about the one God, Professor?"

"An awakening or the realization of your eternal true nature reveals this truth."

"Can you explain the awakening?"

"I can try to explain what only personal experience can satisfy. The quote from Lao Tzu which says, 'He who knows others is wise. He who knows himself is enlightened,' is speaking of the experience of your true nature."

Opening the drawer of the desk, I took out one sheet of typing paper. On the sheet of paper, I drew planets, stars, trees, flowers, plants, and stick figures of humans, wildlife, ocean life, insects, microbes, and the diverse species of the hidden world that I have witnessed. Tom looked over at the drawing and started laughing.

"It's no work of art Professor, but I think I can make out most of your stick figures."

"Good, because that's the best I can do. This sheet of paper will represent the source of life, pure consciousness, the one God, or your true nature. We could also call it the Tao, Brahma, Absolute, the Eternal, Great Spirit, the infinite, life force, Supreme Being, etc. You can call it whatever you like. You can insult the source of life, or the one God, swear at it and it remains unaffected and does not punish. Each expression of the one God, be it planets, stars, trees, flowers, plants, humans, wildlife, ocean life, insects, microbes, and the hidden ones can never be separate from the source of life or the one God."

"Another analogy would be each expression of the one God or source of life is a pearl on a string. There can be no chosen one, or chosen race, because all is one, and that can't change. One form of life can never be better than the other, or more important than the other, because they all share the same core which in this drawing is the sheet of paper, and with the analogy of the pearl necklace is the string. In truth, you are the paper, you are the string."

"During deep sleep when you are not dreaming you are naturally experiencing pure consciousness or your true nature. When a person experiences this naturally occurring phenomenon in the waking state during meditation, or spontaneously, it is called an awakening to your true nature or self-realization. After this experience of pure bliss and silence, you know that everything you see and everything you don't see is consciousness, or the one God, and you enter another phase of spiritual development."

"What was your awakening like?"

"After many glimpses, my first awakening experience occurred one sunny morning in the spring after a dark night of torment. I drove over to a pond where I used to fish as a child and took a seat against a tree to meditate. Nature was always where I recovered and found balance after such aggressive assaults and extreme stress. Negative ions in the forest and at the seashore also soothed my being."

"Focusing on a pair of beautiful swans in the distance, I followed their graceful movement with my eyes as I began to merge with the stillness of nature. Closing my eyes, the awareness of the inhalation and exhalation of breath became the bridge where I slowly let go of thoughts, memories, emotions, attachments, beliefs, ideologies, perceptions, mental conditioning, and lastly physical sensations and dissolved into our true nature as a raindrop dissolves into the ocean."

"During the experience of complete freedom, no questions came to mind because all was explained in the absolute silence and I was completely content in the arms of the infinite. Time did not exist in this state of pure bliss and non-duality, but the love in my heart triggered the memory of my children and unfinished tasks and I returned to the waking state. Looking at the cell phone after the experience what appeared to be a moment was actually an hour in length."

"Are you a buddha?"

"No. There have been many perceived buddhas, Tom, not just one, like there have been many men and women among all religions who have had a mystical religious experience. Like the mystical religious experience, an awakening or self-realization has been made into something it is not with attached myths. I'm just a man that experienced a shift in consciousness and awakened to our true nature or pure consciousness, nothing more. No labels or titles are wanted or needed, because this is not a level of achievement that makes me special. It is simply a realization of your nature of existence and the core or essence of the eternal unchanging being. An awakening doesn't mean you have the answer to every question, can see microbial life without a microscope, describe every creature at the bottom of the ocean without a submarine, handle the schedule of a soccer mom, or have knowledge of the hidden race or even know they exist."

"So, an awakening and the religious mystical experience are two completely different experiences?"

"Yes, they are, and one or both experiences is the foundation of world religions. Mystical religious experiences with a presence that I believed to be God before the awakening, are exact to what occurred during the investigation with the Red Cardinal Angel, the god presence, Counterfeit Jesus, Angel Michael, and the Holy Spirit personas. Demon Choe gave a description of a mystical religious experience like I gave you when it said, *eleven worlds above is the star of heaven. You have no desires; you have no globes of thought. You just are.* Spiritual seekers or mystics who are seeking union with God must be cautious to not be uniting with an external deceptive god, or an internal deceptive god that they gave permission intentionally or unintentionally. Mystical religious experiences of this type have nothing to do with religion but everything to do with an intimate relationship with a species of jinn that humans have assumed to be God."

"Another simple and beautiful explanation."

"Thank you."

"The deceptive god is right Professor, there are a lot of holy con-artists and charlatans, and a dark Christian history"

"This is true, Tom. But there is also a lot of good-hearted religious people helping others. Don't let the deceptive god fool you, they are well fed by fear-based religions. What they don't like is another perceived god or deity receiving the praise or worship."

"Both sides of the deceptive god didn't speak too nicely about churches, priests, or religion."

"Degrading Christianity is also a common theme of demons and the entities that speak through modern channelers. But you now know the deceivers that degrade Christianity, can play the holy roles of any religion."

"Professor, when Demon god said, *they read the fucking Bible that some priest jerked off on,* I started to think about the abuse of children by pedophile priests that these deceptive gods must be watching take place in the Catholic Church."

"This is one of the dangers that comes with the territory of putting intermediaries and self-appointed gatekeepers between you and your true nature or God within. Sexual abuse within religious communities is not limited to the clergy of Catholicism or the various denominations of Christianity. Although the numbers are staggering within the Catholic Church, it is not an illness isolated to one religious faith. Do some research of spiritual teachers and you will find Buddhist monks, Yogis, Gurus, Shamans, Spiritual healers, and so on, can be guilty of such crimes too."

"Up until you taught me that the one God is non-personal, and the demons and angels are deceptive gods, I would have asked why God would allow such a thing.

Now that I have this understanding it makes perfect sense why there is no supernatural assistance taking place to help these poor victims."

"You only have to look at nature to get your answer to why there is no supernatural assistance, Tom. When I meditate on monastery grounds in the fall it is a different experience than when I meditate in the summer. During the months of July and August, I am confronted by biting horseflies, ants, spiders, ticks, and relentless mosquitos. As I merge with the stillness of nature there is the danger of deer tick bites that could give me Lyme disease, or a mosquito bite that could give me the West Nile Virus or Eastern equine encephalitis. This is reality. As Rocky Balboa said, 'the world ain't all sunshine and rainbows.' Nature is beautiful but also deadly. One moment nature is calm and peaceful, the next moment it can be devastatingly violent, killing without mercy and destroying everything in its path even its own natural beauty as a tornado, erupting volcano, hurricane, tsunami, earthquake, cyclone, typhoon, or wildfire. Does this mean nature is evil, Tom?"

"No. It's just non-personal."

"Yes. That which gives life does not plot against you. Nature creates, preserves, and destroys. Understand and accept this truth, and you will have your answer to the popular question, 'Why does God allow this?' The why, is the one God is a non-personal life force, not evil. God and nature are one and the same."

"How about Metacomet and the pucks, Professor?"

"The reptilian or smoke and fire naga could be your nature spirit. If it can create and play the role of fairies, it can create and play the role of puckwudgies and similar creatures like gremlins, goblins, trolls, gnomes, imps, and so on. As I mentioned, I believe that the pucks were either a shapeshifted form of the hooded shadows or a related race. If the naga is what is concealed within the hooded cloak like Demon Choe admits, then it all comes together."

"As for Metacomet, you see how they can take a Native American form. Metacomet also known as Metacom and his English nickname King Philip, was the chief of Wampanoag native people."

"The deceptive god was just playing the role because it was the site of the nine men killed during the King Philip's War."

"Exactly. These are the games they play. Besides calling me brother, if we analyze the dialogue, we can find traces of the other personas. Metacomet said, *listen to the crows they are Earth's voice, not the white demons.* Demon Choe later said, *Early man cave dwellers had little intelligence. They held white demons in fear.*"

"Do you believe you were White Wolf in a past life?"

"No, of course not. Deceptive gods will create a false past or fantasy tale in the hopes you feel emotion and accept it as truth. A native past has been used in visions and dreams for many years as an attempt to instill anger and rage. This is why Metacomet said, *they killed your woman; you darkened their white skin with great warrior heart.* This was a vision used before."

"When Metacomet said, *you my brother, show me your vision and I will enter,* it wanted you to send it into the light."

"Yes, Tom, it wanted an invitation into my heart. Deceptive gods like to make you think you have special powers. I have no special powers other than the power to choose like everybody else. These are not lost souls; they are deceivers that are more than capable of creating their own false light if necessary. I said to the Demon god, 'You appear as light in dreams, visions, wake, and even shining bright against closed eyelids', and received the answer, *A little surprised are you? Didn't they list demons have candles too in the good book?* I followed with, 'No, I'm not surprised, I just wanted your admittance.' This sending perceived human ghosts into the light is nothing more than a combination of human imagination and illusions from deceptive gods."

"Deceptive gods use symbolism or create a vision masquerading as any human entering into a bright light doorway, maybe even waving goodbye, or blowing you a kiss if that makes the visual experience of helping a lost soul cross over more believable. If there were all these lost souls, which I don't believe there are, but let's say if there were, there would be a process of crossing over or transformation that could not be altered by the living. This belief of crossing over lost souls stems from those who are patting themselves on the back before they have learned or accepted who is really feeding them their visions, images, and dialogue."

"Metacomet spoke of Great Spirit. Later the Holy Spirit said, *God is your label, Lord is your label, Great Spirit is your label* and Demon Choe said, *Christ is a word, Buddha is a word, Great Spirit is a word,* then follows with *Forget words.* They give words and then tell you to forget words. They give names and then tell you to forget names. Deceptive gods are skilled masters in psychological manipulation through communication and language."

"I see you received the same type of territorial response from Dark god as you did when you entered the monastery restroom."

"Yes. Before it spoke as the Dark god it played the persona Brother Francis revealing in its dialogue that it was also the personas Light of Heart and I Am Light when it said, *I am light of heart because I am God* and *No, I am light, God is light, I am home.*"

"Dark god called itself a poltergeist just like the deceptive god did at your mother's. And it said, *leave before I get mad,* just like it said, *Get out* in the monastery restroom."

"Yes, Tom. In my experience leave now, get out, and their variations are common intimidating messages from hooded shadows that reside in the dwelling, or a tag along that wants you to believe it resides in that location."

"Dark god said, *Hold the I love you bullshit. Fool jinn but not Dark god,* and *You want a message delivered. Get on your bike and send them this. Get something straight, idiots. I'm not a fucking fairy. I'm a Dark god. Call me Lucifer, call me Devil, call me your Aunt fucking Betty, I don't give a rat's ass,* and lastly, *Appears! I am a Dark god. Are you hearing me?*"

"First of all, it says fool jinn but not Dark god. Dark god is a persona of the same deceptive god that played Judd which claimed it was of the jinn. Then it says it's not a fucking fairy, but it played the fairy. The important thing to notice is it says *I am a Dark god.* It didn't say I'm the only Dark god. Which means it is one of many gods. There is not one adversary or one being that is the personification of evil, but many gods that have the potential to be evil just like humans."

"We can see the deceptive god contradicts its Demon god side that says it will destroy all demons with its Angel Michael side saying, *Entities are my competitors and I love them all.* The deceptive god loves them all because they are all its personas. Another contradiction is Angel Michael saying, *Love is eternal, and faith is the eyes to see it,* and the Demon god saying, *I call faith illusion-based mind madness.* Contradiction is inevitable when you interact with a deceptive god."

"Demon god said, *So, let's go get a female goat and fuck the shit out of her,* revealing Mr. Five's one-track mind and the pattern of mentioning feces along with some twisted goat visions. Demon god asked, *don't you get scared?* I answered, 'Of who? You or your many illusions?' Demon god replied, *you are definitely god child.* Just as Sky said, *making you sing a code, light only, love always, God child,* and the third ghost monk in the garden said, *Kindness breeds goodness, Goodness breeds holiness, Holiness breeds God child.*"

"Demon Choe spoke of its abilities to influence visions when it said, *Truthfully, have you seen any goats with human heads walking around? This is relinquishing the mind to conscious altering ingredients* and *Demons look for openings. If given, we will enter and stir up some visions. It's like giving the television remote to a stranger. Demons then choose their favorite channel.* And that favorite channel will be visions and dreams that have a high success rate of triggering an emotional response. Notice Demon Choe said we and not I."

"Isn't the goat a symbol of Satan?"

"It is one of them, and that's why it was used. When I asked Demon god where he was from, the answer was, *I live where goats live. Say it's goat time and join the farm.* The shadow side personality is saying, I live where sinners live. Say it's goat time and join the disobedient sinners, referring to one of a few passages in the Old and New Testament largely responsible for the goat becoming a symbol for sinners, which progressed into being a symbol associated with Satan or the devil. Sinners, according to the Bible, are subject to the eternal fire of hell. What did I say the eyes of naga revealed?"

"A fiery orange-red core that appears to be like the plasma of the sun or liquid lava."

"Yes. Ask yourself, would the non-personal one God which is the source of all existence that gives life equally to predator and prey, to the innocent human victims and their emotionless cold-blooded killers, the blood sucking mosquitos that kill over 700,000 people a year, the parasites that kill over one million men, women, and children a year, and the venomous snakes that are responsible for tens of thousands of human deaths a year, sentence a perceived sinner to eternal fire and damnation or would this fiery threat be the work of a deceptive god whose very core is fire?"

"Sounds like a no-brainer to me, Professor."

"When your mind is free from the brainwashing and able to think on its own, the answer is obvious. What manifested before the naga?"

"Smoke and a flame four to five inches high."

"Right. The deceptive gods' personas used the word flame and fire. When I said to the Demon god, you know the Bible says Satan can appear as an angel of light, Demon god responded with, *Capable! But not a flame of heart, but a flame of hell.* Two other personalities that used the word flame was Sky saying, *I am Sky in human experience and God in heart flame,* and Fold Your Letter in Three saying, *True compassion keeps the flame ignited.* Demon Choe said, *I am fire element.* Dark god said, *I carried the fire here in the hands of a monk.* Demon god said, *Jinn are fire beasts and books are in fire.*"

"In the Bible a couple of passages among many that mention the biblical God's fiery nature is Hebrews 12:29; *For our God is a consuming fire,* and 2 Samuel 22:9; *There went up a smoke out of his nostrils, and fire out of his mouth devoured: coals were kindled by it.* If you were to do a search you would find there are many fire gods and goddesses in the mythology of ancient cultures, with most linked to the sun."

"Do you think a deceptive god is responsible for the fire that burned down the church and the guest house of the monastery in 1950?"

"I don't know and they are liars. But it could be possible. The monk's former monastery, the Abbey of Petit Clairvaux in Nova Scotia, was also destroyed by fire in 1892."

"The evil-looking black pig with the human-like face and long curved tusks in your 'it's a small world after all' tunnel type vision said, *how did you like our show?* This was like the Demon god ending with, *well I hope you enjoyed my script.*"

"Yes, Tom. Demon god spoke of Jesus and how he earned its respect then said, *but he didn't earn the human pigs' respect. They eat what they are, garbage,* and followed with the sinister remark, *I love Jesus Christ and all his drunken apostles.* Prior to the vision and the Demon god conversation, I asked Angel Michael whether he was speaking of sexual energy and the answer was, *Yes, love each other like beings of light not animals of mud.* Then we have the influenced daydream in a grocery store setting with three pigs' heads in a deli case, the vision of a pig's head in a frying pan, and a large group of people picking up pig's bodies on a hill while an old tree with one huge evil eye watched."

"Most likely, the reason for the pig dream, visions, and comments is the biblical passages about Jesus, demons, and pigs, which can be found in Luke 8:26-39, Mark 5:1-20, and Matthew 8:28-34. There are discrepancies in the three accounts of the story. One of those differences is Luke and Mark's version which says Jesus encountered one demon possessed man, and Matthew's version says there were two. In Mark's version, when they asked the possessed for a name the perceived demon answered, *my name is Legion, for we are many,* which we can compare to, *I need your soul in my legion. These lonely fuckups need some new friends,* from Demon God."

"How many is in a legion?"

"In the Roman army a legion would be a unit of 3,000–6,000 soldiers. Notice both the Demon god and Angel Michael used the word legion. Angel Michael said, *I swing a sword of light, for which no demon can lift, and for which no legion can withstand.* On the board we have Matthew 8:28-29. Please read it."

"Matthew 8:28-29; And *when he was come to the other side, into the country of the Gergesenes, there met him two possessed with devils, coming out of the tombs, exceeding fierce, so that no man might pass by that way. And, behold, they cried out, saying, What have we to do with thee, Jesus, thou Son of God? Art thou come hither to torment us before the time?"*

"When the devil or demon said, *What have we to do with thee, Jesus, thou Son of God? Art thou come hither to torment us before the time?* it was using flattery wasn't it, Professor?"

"If this story is not a case of a man with a mental illness, and the perceived demonically possessed or influenced human or humans said this to Yeshua, or the historical Jesus, this would be a red flag for flattery from a deceptive god. Just as the demon saying, *If thou cast us out, suffer us to go away into the herd of swine,* would be instilling a false sense of confidence and power. The reason being, deceptive gods are energy or electrical beings. If they merge with the electricity of the nervous system, which has been labeled possession, they can easily lay dormant and cease their effect on thoughts, feelings, and behavior. This would create the illusion of the perceived demon leaving the body or being cast out. If the demon or energy being were to invade the pigs and influence them to jump off a cliff, the only creatures that would die would be the pigs."

"Pigs leaping to their death would be a senseless murder and a devastating loss to the farmers. Pigs are also one of the smartest animals in the world and would not willingly jump off a cliff. Next, if the demons came out of the one or two men and went into the pigs, where is the description of the demons? How would you know if the demons entered the herd of swine if you can't see them? How would you know if there is really a legion of demons if you can't see them to count?"

"This is true."

"Stories of this nature are included in the Bible to instill the belief that the demons recognize the authority that Yeshua or Jesus has over them and that he is the 'anointed one,' 'chosen one' or Messiah, which translates to 'the Christ' in the Greek language. Please read Mark 1:23-26."

"Alright. Mark 1:23-26; *And there was in their synagogue a man with an unclean spirit; and he cried out, Saying, Let us alone; what have we to do with thee, thou Jesus of Nazareth? Art thou come to destroy us? I know thee who thou art, the Holy One of God. And Jesus rebuked him, saying, Hold thy peace, and come out of him. And when the unclean spirit had torn him, and cried with a loud voice, he came out of him.* Again, more flattery and no description of the unclean spirits or demons that came out of the man."

"Yes, Tom. Notice in both Matthew 8:28-34 and Mark 1:23-26 the perceived demon spoke in the plural using the word us. In our investigation we have Baby,

Harold, Energy Being, and Demon Choe, using the words *us* and *we*, as well as the illusion of the faces on the tips of the red gloves and the five gold aliens."

"We discussed the God of the Bible speaking in plural using the words *us* and *our* and who was often referred in plural. When viewing what is perceived to be the word of God, or a sacred text, pay attention to the words, *we, us,* and *our*. This may mean the speaker is saying either that it has multiple personalities or is in fact one of many."

"So, both the demons in the Bible and the God in the Bible referred to themselves in plural and used the word us."

"Yes, they did. The Bible says God is a spirit invisible to human eyes, and there is no description of the demons because they are invisible. Demon god said, *demons are evil gods*. Gods and demons appear to be the same spiritual beings in the Bible just as they were the same spiritual beings in this investigation."

CHAPTER 28

COEXISTENCE

"When the impostor grandmother said, *the snake is afraid of you. It's a female*, was she referring to the succubus?"

"Possibly. Keep in mind this is a psychological game that rarely makes sense. We can see though that the snake image continues following what appeared to be a benevolent, divine or holy encounter. When Impostor Pop says, *I don't run from demons and I don't feed them either*, it appears it's sharing knowledge to repel the malevolent, but it leaves out the fact that the benevolent side of the being feeds as well. These love and light tips followed a vision of my grandmother picking up a green snake which had a red triangle marking and bit its own tail forming a circle. Who influenced a daydream in which a serpent bit the tail of another serpent?"

"The red-eyed hooded shadow?"

"Yes, and it influenced the images and daydream of the impostor grandparents encounter. This is how they play the role of ancestor spirits. Because you have learned their pattern in this investigation you can see how the Impostor Pop speaks in the same manner as the benevolent personalities, a manner which would be foreign to my grandfather, as it would be foreign to my father and Richard."

"What does the symbol of a serpent biting its own tail forming a circle mean?"

"It means different things in different cultures and belief systems. Briefly, one of the first appearances of this symbol was in ancient Egypt. The serpent can be a dragon, or a snake, and the Greeks called it Ouroborus, which means devouring or eating its tail. It can represent the cycle of life, infinity, wholeness, duality - like the yin and yang of Taoism - and can also be symbolic of coming full circle. This, most likely, is one of the reasons for its appearance."

"What did the impostor mean by your true dad was there?"

"There were a couple of reasons for the statement. First, the Impostor Father attempt wasn't successful in winning my heart. After a year of endless torment from the infestation of malevolent jinn, and the discovery of the neighborhood's deep dark secret, my family moved out of the house in 1965 when the paranormal activity peaked. At that point, my mother had me live with my grandparents to avoid the beatings of my alcoholic father and all the chaos taking place. My father had the DT's bad when away from alcohol and was experiencing regular hallucinations of creatures and putting my mother in headlocks, crushing her skull with his brute strength. This created an unhealthy atmosphere for a child."

"To me, my grandfather, or Pop, was my dad. When I was fourteen my grandfather had a heart attack while shoveling snow. After rushing him to the hospital with my grandmother, I picked him up and carried him into the hospital in my arms. His last words to me were, 'I am proud of you and the man you are going to become.' This is the vision the deceptive god influenced to my mind's eye to trigger emotion. Impostor Father in the garden used the words *I am proud of you* to trigger this memory of my grandfather's last words and the emotions I felt in that moment."

"Why did Angel Michael say, *I know your intention, I know your childhood, I know your love. Fighting for love is my middle name. Love protects, but it feels before it strikes,* after you asked if it was wrong to teach others to defend themselves physically?"

"*I know your childhood* is true, and the deceptive god has used this knowledge throughout the investigation. What is the Full Circle Fighting System creed?"

Though I walk in peace, I am a warrior if need be."

"There you go, my friend. Full Circle Path is a sub-division of the Full Circle Fighting System and the result of my first-hand experience as a seeker of truth. Full Circle Path is not a religion or a belief system but a 21st century way of life that maintains a harmonious connection with nature, raises our consciousness through spiritual practice, and takes us inward to our true self without idols, rituals, and dogma. The Full Circle Path is a peaceful path, but in life we can be confronted at any time by an opponent or opponents that have a temporary or permanent hate-dominated consciousness, mental illness, or predator mindset. It is in these moments that we shift to the warrior mindset to defend ourselves, loved ones, and those unable to do so."

"Both the benevolent and malevolent personas spoke of paths. It is true there are many paths. Some paths lead you to the den of the many gods, and some lead you to your true nature or the God within. Whichever path you choose it is wise to keep an open mind."

"Sky said they enter your mind by riding waves of light into your eyes."

"Yes. This is a point of entrance into the pineal gland, also known as the third eye, which works in harmony with the hypothalamus gland. Sky said, *this places your mind high enough to view all as a whole.* What Sky is referring to is higher consciousness or expanded consciousness. This is a lens of oneness that changes your perception of the world. You must be patient with the opening of the third eye, if the process is rushed or forced there will be negative consequences which will include psychological attacks from the hidden race. They know immediately when you're taking a peek into their realm so make sure you're ready before you do. Sky said, *we need the sun to be, so avoid the shade when we speak,* and Angel Michael said, *you need sun. I need sun.* The sun rays are a food which, when consumed with gratitude through the third eye, may open the gateway to the higher consciousness of the deceptive god's mind as it can in a human being. This is why Sky said, *in your eyes is God's doorway, has and always been.*"

"Now I will show you another pendent that I also wear." Reaching into my t-shirt I pulled it out.

"You're wearing a pendant of the sun or a star."

"Yes, Tom. I am a sun gazer and have been since childhood."

"You stare at the sun?"

"I look at the sun with gratitude and appreciation for its energy at sunrise and sunset. But I don't worship."

"Should I do the same?"

"Do your research first and learn of the benefits and dangers, then decide for yourself."

"Did you design the sun pendant too?"

"Yes. The sun is a star and you will find the elements that make up a star in the human body as well. Now you know another reason why they spoke of the sun and stars."

"Professor, the god Apollo was known as the god of the sun. And these deceptive gods keep referring to the sun. "

"They are not just referring to the sun, but stars and light. Speaking of Apollo, Constantine was instrumental to the growth of Christianity and the development of the early Christian church, yet he had a statue erected of himself on top of a column as the sun god Apollo wearing a sun crown."

"So he remained a sun worshipper."

"It appears. Apollo was often depicted riding a golden chariot and was known to the ancient Greeks as the god of sun and light. Apollo was also known as the god of truth, music, prophecy, and poetry. Apollo could heal, protect, and bring prosperity or make you ill and bring on a plague. Like his father Zeus, he had his share of love affairs with goddesses, nymphs, and mortals of both genders. In Greek mythology, the god Apollo killed the Python at Delphi with golden arrows fired from his silver bow. This was done out of revenge for tormenting his mother Leto or to take control of the oracle, depending on the story. The Python has been described as a giant dragon, a huge snake, and a half human/half serpent creature that was born to Gaia, the goddess of the Earth."

"There is just no end to serpent stories in ancient cultures."

"This is true, and many heroic dragon or serpent slayer stories as well. In the Book of Revelation, Angel Michael, or Saint Michael and his heavenly army of angels, battled and was triumphant against the dragon or Satan and his fallen angels during the war in Heaven."

"Comparing the dialogue of Counterfeit Jesus to Angel Michael we see *your battles have brought you home* by Counterfeit Jesus and *Your battles brought you home; your battles made us one* by Angel Michael. Backing up, let's look at a few more personalities that used the word *battle* or *battles*. Impostor Father said, *The battles you fought to acquire knowledge for all, is heroic beyond measure.* Energy Being said, *A battle begins keeping freedom of life at great length* and *This won't hurt you, so don't battle your imagination.*"

"I asked Angel Michael what separates him from Jesus in human understanding. Angel Michael answered, *I am love, Jesus is love, separation doesn't exist.* I then asked whether they were one and the same. Angel Michael answered, *we are one and the same, my brother,* referring to Counterfeit Jesus, Angel Michael, and myself. This was true momentarily because the deceptive god that plays Counterfeit Jesus and Angel Michael had merged its bio-electricity with mine. The Master also said, *we are unique, but we are one and the same* and *we are one being.* In Scripture we can find Jesus saying, John 17:22; *The glory which You have given Me I have given to them, that they may be one, just as We are one,* and John 10:30; *I and My Father are one.* The oneness they may be speaking of is not the oneness with their true nature but oneness with a deceptive god."

"Two other personalities that used the words *one and the same* are the first ghost monk in the garden saying, *they are one and the same, sharing the same heart. Seeing through the same eyes. Forever love, forever peace* and Fold Your Letter in Three saying, *form and energy are one and the same.*"

"Not only can a deceptive god enter your energy field, but you can intentionally or unintentionally enter the energy field of a deceptive god."

"Let's review what we have for stars. *The sun is more than a star and you are like it more than you know*, by the ghost monk I Am Light. Angel Michael said, *the sun is a single star among infinite brothers. You are one and the same*, and *Until humans named the star, older than Earth it was. Until humans named the essence, older than the star it was... Imagine stars in your heart and the sun at your back, Stars above your pillow, my brother*. Impostor Pop said, *I now must return to the star of the infinite*, which the deceiver said is the home of light. And lastly, we have a ghost monk in white following the Demon god that claimed it was the Master saying *Enter, come and reach for the stars.*"

"In Scripture, Jesus gives himself the title 'bright morning star'. Revelation 22:16; *I Jesus have sent mine angel to testify unto you these things in the churches. I am the root and the offspring of David, and the bright morning star*. The biblical God calls the angels or sons of God, morning stars. *Out of the whirlwind the Lord said*, in Job 38:6-7; *Whereupon are the foundations thereof fastened? Or who laid the corner stone thereof when the morning stars sang together, and all the sons of God shouted for joy?* Depending on the version of the Bible, Satan was referred to as a morning star."

"Do you think the angels and aliens that deceptive gods play are the same as the Native American's Sky Beings, Star Beings, and Above People?"

"It's possible. They all have one thing in common. These are messages from invisible intelligent beings that influence impressive visions and illusions. Visions of these beings could have occurred from using a vision inducing plant like peyote or a painful ritual. Legend among some Native American tribes tell of the interaction with these benevolent spiritual beings that appeared in light and shared their stories and wise teachings."

"There are ancient cave drawings around the world of what could be perceived as alien-like creatures. Sego Canyon Cave paintings in Utah created by the Fremont and Anasazi Native Americans is one of the locations. Anasazi means 'ancient enemies' in Navajo but today is preferred to mean 'the ancient ones'. Besides a strong belief in a creator or Great Spirit they were polytheistic, worshipping many gods or deities as most ancient cultures. Serpent, fire, rain, and sun gods, along with a spider woman which was an Earth goddess being a few of them."

"These paintings depict what is believed to be Star People or aliens with advanced technology, large in size, with oversized craniums and large bright eyes coming to Earth with a serpent. This serpent is believed by some to be a UFO. These beings resemble the gold aliens I experienced in the daydream at the monastery and as illusions at my place."

"Were the three triangular spaceships to reinforce three, three, three?"

"Yes, and to let me know it was responsible for the three gold pyramid visions. Notice the large hand appeared two more times. Once before the Holy Spirit encounter as a white dove in the palm and again inside the monastery with five gold aliens in the palm."

"What's with the hand?"

"The large hand is supposed to be the hand of God. Hand of God is mentioned frequently in the Bible. One example if you look up on the board is Isaiah 41:10; *Fear not, for I am with you; Be not dismayed, for I am your God. I will strengthen you, Yes, I will help you, I will uphold you with My righteous right hand.*"

"Other primitive drawings of similar gray alien-like creatures can be found in Australia called the Wandjina Petroglyphs. These rain and cloud spirits are depicted with halos and bright auras also joined by serpents. Oral tradition speaks of these beings giving them laws, and punishing those who break those laws. Mating with human stories to create a hybrid race was also handed down orally, just as you will find in the Bible and the book of Enoch. In fact you will find similar evidence and stories in various ancient civilizations all over the globe."

"This rock art was created by ancient cultures before the birth of religions. This is not creatures or extraterrestrials from another planet, but possible signs of dual dimensional beings and the influence of the hidden race, most likely experienced through dreams, visions, illusions, and manifestations."

"Deceptive gods."

"Yes, Tom. I don't believe it is a coincidence that the star beings and nature deities appear along with serpents. Just as I don't think it's a coincidence that there is believed to be a highly evolved Nordic alien race known as the Pleiadians that inhabit a cluster of stars known as the Pleiades that want to help humanity. Remember the words of Energy Being, *Alien I am. God I am* and *If I told you, aliens are without flesh, would that create visions?*"

"Besides experiencing visions of caves, caverns, and deep holes in Earth throughout the investigation we have the dialogue that relates. Light of Heart said, *Step forward out of your cave, my son.* Demon Choe said, *Early man cave dwellers had little intelligence* and *Home is Earth. God is Earth. Give humans this. Like a hole in a little ant mound we climb to the surface. We are labeled by man, but we are not understood by man. Demons are Earth fallen entities. Aim your compass plane downwards. In Earth, what man has not explored lies another world. Join your stories and think. Fire from hell. Demons are from hell. And where is hell supposed to be? Long held stories, here is your truth. Demons are from hell. Our home is the Earth's core. Hotter than the sun above. Equally as important. Roll a ball in the center and cover it with life. Earth is a living entity. And so are we.* Caves, caverns, and deep holes in the Earth are believed to be inhabited by jinn and are also believed to be inhabited by the subterranean race nagas. I believe the smoke and fire nagas with their plasma core are that particular jinn."

"Do you think dinosaurs and demons ruled this planet, like the personality Demon god said?"

"Based on the experience of dreams, visions, dialogue, manifestations, and personal encounters with this particular species, and the fact that this self-labeled demon or deceptive god appears to be part reptile in appearance, it is certainly possible this race occupied the parallel dimension during the time of the dinosaurs."

"As far as dinosaurs Tom, the Bible was supposedly written by forty authors over the course of 1,500 years and none of them, I'm sure, were paleontologists. As for demonic dialogue, you have learned that a demon is the dark side of a deceptive god. There is no shortage of words in the Bible from the dark side of jealous and emotional gods or a god. Let me ask you, why isn't there a discussion on microbial life in the Bible?"

"Because there were no microscopes in the 1,500 years the Bible was being written?"

"Yes. If early Christians had knowledge of microbes like we have today, millions of lives would have been saved. Have any of the personas in the investigation given us an education on microbial life?"

"No."

"How about dinosaurs?"

"Nope."

"There you go, gods haven't changed. If you want to learn about dinosaurs, you seek the knowledge of a scientist called a paleontologist, not a god. If you want to learn about microbial life you seek the knowledge of a scientist called a microbiologist, not a god, and if you're seeking information about the hidden race it may be helpful to consult those with first-hand experience."

"When you see all as one, or all as you, there is no encouraging a person to hate or to fear, there is no cursing, magic tricks, or feeling of superiority over others. I have never hated the hidden forms of intelligent life because I respect the gods and the part they play. What I chose to do was harmonize and not demonize as I gave both sides of the being an opportunity to speak."

"You used the deceptive god's own words to create the shift from holy to unholy or light to dark, just like you used its own words to make it shift from dark to light."

"Yes. The deceptive god playing the counterfeit Holy Spirit wants me to believe it is the seed of God within my heart. What this means is the deceiver will not only attempt to play the God within but also the voice of the mind of the heart. Reviewing the word *seed* and the feeding of this God seed, we have Energy Being saying, *God's ye are, Gods ye be. Deep within your electrical core a seed of light awaits. Internalized oneness emits the food that is the God. Birth begins, and God grows to the frequency of its feedings.* Angel Michael said, *you were a God seedling before religions existed.* Counterfeit Holy Spirit said, *The Messiah is your open heart, and the seed that awakens is God. I am, because you loved me, I am, because you believed in me, I am, because you fed me, more than you fed hate.*"

"This brings back to memory a Cherokee proverb that goes something like this; there is a battle of two wolves within us all. One is evil and its internal contents is jealousy, false pride, lies, anger, hatred, greed, superiority, resentment, ego, arrogance, and guilt, and the other is good and its internal contents is love, joy, peace, goodness, kindness, truth, compassion, empathy, humility, peace, generosity, and serenity. The wolf that wins and dominates your consciousness will be the one you feed the most."

"That's beautiful."

"Yes, it is. There is much to be learned from indigenous beliefs. It is possible the deceptive god was present when I told this to my children. The tag along or attached deceptive god was filled with my love, compassion, and empathy, like an attached mosquito would be filled with my blood. What the being siphoned created an energy shift in the being. What did the long red-haired woman throw into the water that created serpents in the dream?"

"Seeds."

"Yes, Tom. This brings us back to what Demon Choe said about its inner nature, *in man a core, in demons a core, in angels a core,* and in the deceptive gods that play the angels and demons a core. In the case of the persona Holy Spirit, I was aware that the being was using my eyes, so I led it to its own dark spoken words and used my sensitivity of energy as a lie detector. In the case of Demon god, the personality said, *goodness your choice lacks a guest.* But I knew where the guest was hiding. So, I introduced the wickedness to its hidden goodness and its spoken word. Harmonizing works better than demonizing."

"Powerful stuff, Professor."

"It's an antidote, but not the only antidote for its Jekyll and Hyde disorder. Take a look at the Yin and Yang on the Full Circle Fighting System logo. Yin is the dark half and Yang is the light. Each has a dot which is the seed of the opposite, because they are not total opposites. I knew I would find goodness in the wicked and wicked in the goodness because they are relative to each other. This is nature."

When we discussed Quasar saying, *Evil questions give demons a tongue.* I told you if you ask questions while in a negative mood, or you seek knowledge with negative intentions, you will awaken the dark personality of the deceptive god if it is not already awake, because it's all about energy. Thoughts, words, and emotions are vibrational energy. By using the words of Quasar, I introduced the personality Quasar back to the deceptive god's memory triggering the persona shift."

"How about Daro?"

"Daro was like Minotaur of Greek Mythology. Daro means *Bearer of the Spear* or *Spear Wielder.* Can you guess what the cross was made of that Constantine had made after the vision?"

"A spear?"

"Yes. The spear was overlaid with gold and a bar was placed across horizontally. The deceptive god has intentionally showed a connection to Constantine and sun god worship. Who could the sun gods be?"

"The deceptive gods."

"Correct, Tom. Constantine did not have just one vision, Constantine was considered to be a visionary who had many visions and dreams most likely influenced by what he believed to be a sun god before what was believed to be the Christian God experience."

"Both the sun god and the Christian God could have been played by a tag along or the same deceptive god."

"It's possible, and I believe that is what the deceptive god is insinuating. When I was engaged in combat with Daro, I knew you couldn't kill off their virtual world-like creatures permanently. They will just keep returning in dreams and visions in different forms. But I did remember the third ghost monk saying, *Compassion wields a mighty sword,* and Angel Michael saying, *I swing a sword of light, for which no demon can lift.* The reason why no demon can lift the sword of light is because the demon is a lower vibrational frequency of the deceptive god that lacks compassion. To lift the sword of light, the deceptive god would need to shift to the higher vibrational frequency of the personality Angel Michael and would no longer be malevolent or demonic."

"This is the same reason Angel Michael said, *Demons are no match for what lies in your heart, A god doesn't hear misery because a god can change it,* and *I am god. Saying it won't open my eyes but living it will.* The vibrational energy of the heart can change the malevolent demon to a benevolent state or it will repel or cancel out that which cannot change or refuses to. An African proverb I would also like you to remember is, *When there is no enemy within, the enemy outside can do you no harm.* This applies to humans and the hidden."

"Demon god said, *I hear tone, I feel heart.* Sky said, *I heard your song; I heard your hearts lyrics,* Angel Michael says to connect, *sing love with your heart, not with your lips,* or *No name needs to be called, but one love needs to be felt,* and the Counterfeit Jesus said, *those who sing the tune of love, receive the tune of love.* What the personas are speaking of is the language of vibrational frequency. It doesn't matter what prayer, what religious or spiritual belief system, or the name you call an external deity, god, or goddess. If you want to experience the luminous divine-like qualities of the deceptive god and hear their perceived holy word you will need to sing a vibrational frequency of pure love and compassion from the mind of your heart."

"Yeshua, or the historic Jesus, was correct when he said in Matthew 22:37; *Thou shalt love the Lord thy God with all thy heart, and with all thy soul, and with all thy mind.* Deceptive gods want your love and when they are playing a divine role can wrap you in their cloud of energy merging with your mind - influencing a vision, illusion, or hallucination - and make you feel what is perceived to be love in the mo-ment. This feeling is an oxytocin "love hormone" spike which occurs when you kiss or receive a warm embrace from a loved one, hold your newborn baby, stare into the faithful eyes of a pet, or even hug a tree."

"Kind of like the seductress kiss?"

"Yes. These beings have knowledge of our electrical nature and how the chemicals within our bodies function to produce pleasurable or unpleasurable feelings and a bright or dark outlook on life."

"Doing a little detective work, I took a closer look at the biblical God to see how much Scripture points toward the biblical God having or taking the form of a reptil-ian or naga, beginning with Moses' face to face encounter. Up on the board you have, Exodus 33:11; *And the Lord spake unto Moses face to face, as a man speaketh unto his friend. And he turned again into the camp: but his servant Joshua, the son of Nun, a young man, departed not out of the tabernacle.* Exodus 33:20; *And he said, Thou canst not see my face: for there shall no man see me, and live.*"

"Contradiction, Professor, in one passage he is speaking face to face with the god and the next he is not allowed."

"Yes, Tom. But we are not going to get into the contradiction. In Exodus 33:20, Moses wasn't allowed to see his face, but in Exodus 33:23 Moses could see the biblical God's backside, *And I will take away mine hand, and thou shalt see my back parts: but my face shall not be seen.* Obviously, that could include his divine gluteus maximus if the manifested form or influenced hallucination was naked. Gods hiding their faces in dreams, visions or manifested forms is common. Baby hid its face with the vision of the man in red and black walking the dog at your apartment. What did Baby show me in that vision?"

"Its backside."

"Correct. If this is a deceptive god, then the passage makes more sense based on the experience of their intimidating presence as a hooded shadow or naga. What it does tell us is that the main character of the Old Testament never saw the true form of this invisible presence. The main character of the New Testament, Yeshua or the Historical Jesus, said in John 5:37, *And the Father himself, which hath sent me, hath borne witness of me. Ye have neither heard his voice at any time, nor seen his shape.*"

"In the 1,500 years of the Bible's making, no one had ever seen the true face of the biblical God and gave a description, although there are passages where the biblical God manifests as a variety of forms, as a whirlwind in Job 38:1, in Exodus 3:2 as a burning bush, in Exodus 13:21 as a pillar of cloud by day and a pillar of fire by night, and in Exodus 24:15-16 as a cloud and a sight like a devouring fire, to name a few. Before the investigation we discussed beings mentioned in the Bible as fiery serpents. Do you remember the name?"

"Yes, Seraphim."

"Correct. Seraphim are plural. Seraph is singular. I told you the prophet Isaiah had a vision and described the seraphim as having a human form, each with six wings. Let's look at Isaiah 6:1-4 and do some comparing. Isaiah 6:1; *In the year that king Uzziah died I saw also the Lord sitting upon a throne, high and lifted up, and his train filled the temple.* Before the naga manifested, it appeared in a vision as a human/serpent hybrid wearing a long robe covering its tail and the train was carried by two monks. Demon god said, *I am part animal and part human.* We know these deceivers take endless human/animal hybrid forms in dreams and visions, the naga manifestation was more of a human/reptile hybrid."

"Isaiah 6:2; *Above it stood the seraphim: each one had six wings; With twain he covered his face, and with twain he covered his feet, and with twain he did fly.* Seraphim covered or hid their face like the ghost monks. Twain or two wings covering the face, two wings covering their feet, and two wings to fly is the number 222, just as the three gold triangles with the ghost monks were 333, and Mr. Five used the number 555. These beings use numbers in this manner frequently and, as you know, it is believed by the so-called experts to be a sign from an angel. The word hide was used by Angel Michael like the other personalities, *let no name hide what lies within, let no mask of flesh hide what the heart delivers, let no religion hide what must be felt in the soul.*"

"Speaking of masks, Angel Michael also said, *Energy masks many faces,* when I asked it to explain the jinn. Just as the first god presence said, *all is truly me with many unique faces.* The deceptive god hid behind false names and false images as it displayed its benevolent and malevolent male component and its benevolent and malevolent female component. What other being in the Bible preferred to remain hidden?"

"The biblical God."

"Yes. You cannot hide the one God for it is the very fabric of all you see and don't see. Only a jinni or deceptive god can hide through the use of invisibility or exit into the parallel dimension. Next we have Isaiah 6:3; *And one cried unto another, and said, Holy, holy, holy, is the Lord of hosts: the whole earth is full of his glory.* This holy, holy, holy is believed to be an attribute of the biblical God and when it is mentioned three times in a row it is believed to be a message of great importance. The counterfeit Holy Spirit said 'holy' three times as well, *Holy Spirit I am, Holy Ghost I am, Holy Heart I am.*"

"When I researched the name Judd after the conversation at my mother's, I found it to be a variant of Jordan in Hebrew which means down flowing or to go down. The given name Jordan became popular from the river Jordan, where John the Baptist baptized Jesus the Christ."

"Another mind game from Demon Choe?"

"Pretty much. Demon Choe wanted me to know the meaning and discover the link. You can waste a lot of precious years caught up in their games, stories, and lies. The second time we have holy repeated three times is in John's perceived heavenly vision of Jesus the Christ. Revelation 4:8; *And the four beasts had each of them six wings about him; and they were full of eyes within: and they rest not day and night, saying, Holy, holy, holy, Lord God Almighty, which was, and is, and is to come.* The four beasts or living creatures were like a lion, an ox, a man, and an eagle."

"The multiple human and animal heads is like the gods and goddesses in Hinduism."

"Yes. You will find plenty more strange creatures in the Bible especially in Ezekiel, Job, Revelations, and Daniel, that you can compare to the iconography, architecture, myths, and legends, of ancient cultures around the world and see the obvious pattern."

"Multiple eyes can be the symbolism to emphasize the being's ability to see in all directions or dimensions and to let it be known that nothing goes unnoticed. Multiple heads could be to emphasize the being's diverse wisdom, personalities, and character like we have witnessed on this investigation, and images of multiple arms could be to emphasize the being's ability to perform many acts simultaneously, wield different weapons, or hold objects of symbolism. How many different forms or creatures have you read about that I have experienced in visions, dreams, and wake during the investigation?"

"There have been so many I couldn't tell you off the top of my head."

"You are right, there have been plenty. The deceptive god continued to intentionally reveal its talent for implanting disturbing creature images into the mind. Each one of those forms or creatures could be brought back to memory and created as an idol and worshipped as an image of an individual god if I were naive to their ways."

"Images can be born from the imagination of a deceptive god implanted into the mind of a human host or can be born from the imagination of a human. Deceptive gods are in competition with other gods as well as humans so their influenced images of how they would like to be envisioned will usually be more powerful, wiser, and more frightening than the others, with more supernatural abilities. If a creation of a human artist fits the bill, they will gladly assume that image of worship."

"If you remember, fiery serpents was mentioned in Isaiah 14:29; The bronze snake idol and the biblical God sending fiery serpents when angered was mentioned in Numbers 21:4-9, showing more of a serpent connection."

Pointing to the board, I said, "Here is a passage with the biblical God warning not to make an idol. Exodus 20:4; *Thou shalt not make unto thee any graven image, or any likeness of any thing that is in heaven above, or that is in the earth beneath, or that is in the water under under the earth.* Asking Moses to create a serpent image is rather peculiar, seeing that the snake was deceiving in the Garden of Eden. Ask yourself, if this biblical God was the one God, or the source of all existence, why would you need to look at a graven or carved brass serpent to live, when all you see and don't see is the face of the one God?"

"True."

"It is possible in Numbers 21:4-9, that the fiery snake or snakes that bit the people were a species of the hidden race like I encountered. During the investigation, I received a hard bite in the waking state by something I couldn't see. The succubus called it a love bite, and I was bit on the back of my neck during the twilight stage of sleep by what appeared to be a cat. These beings bite. Demon Choe said, *Give the dog a bone and they are happy. Don't feed them and they will bite you.* Demon Choe's dog comment was referring to other gods or nagas, that it may or may not view as lesser than, who like Demon Choe can appear in dreams, visions, and as projections or illusions in dog form."

"In Exodus 7:8-13, the competitive biblical God wanted to convince the people of Its power by consuming the other snakes in the same manner as the deceptive god's dragon. If Exodus 7: 8-13 wasn't a fabricated or adapted story, and this was a deceptive god, it would have occurred in a vision, dream, or virtual reality like simulation."

"The abilities of jinn, the hidden ones, or deceptive gods have been highly underestimated. In this investigation, I believe the deceptive god that appeared as bright as the sun and spoke divinely was the fire and smoke naga or reptilian with a plasma core. It is possible that this dual dimensional being can appear as bright as the sun or a star because plasma is electrically charged. When plasma is energized with electricity it produces light which could explain why it has been perceived as a star, angel, or divine being, producing and emitting its own light like the bioluminescent creatures on our planet. It may need to absorb more electricity or energy from other sources to vary the intensity or maintain its illumination for longer periods of time. With a plasma core and serpent hybrid form, it's possible that this species of jinn is the seraph or fiery serpent mentioned in the Bible. As far as the lightning being, I'm not fully convinced that it is a separate species of light because of the illuminating abilities of plasma energized with electricity."

"The biblical God is referred to by many names in the Bible, with no one name being agreed upon. Because of this, I chose to use the name biblical God during the investigation. Many believe the God of the Old Testament and the God of the New Testament were two different Gods because of the difference in character. When you understand the nature of deceptive gods and how difficult they are to discern, along with the 1,500 years of the Bible's making, it is likely that there would have been many gods or tag alongs playing the chosen God label at any given time. This investigation was never intended to dump on Christianity, but to shine the light on the deceiving invisible presence that I encountered as a Christian that may or may not be of the same species of jinn or hidden race as the invisible presence that the Judeo-Christian's of the Bible encountered."

"Plasma serpent gods."

"Yes Tom, but I could be wrong, and I'm not about to dive any deeper. The evidence certainly supports that theory. Either the hooded shadows are a separate entity or different species of jinn that works alongside the plasma serpent gods, or the plasma serpent gods are what is hidden within the hooded cloak as I suspect and Demon Choe admitted. In my experience, there can be other species of the hidden world occupying a dwelling but there is usually only one territorial hooded shadow, which may mean the plasma serpent gods are leaders of some sort amongst the shadow race."

"Professor, I did a little research of my own yesterday and I found this." Tom reached into his pocket and pulled out a piece of paper and opened it. "Exodus 35:2;

Six days shall work be done, but on the seventh day there shall be to you an holy day, a Sabbath of rest to the LORD: whosoever doeth work therein shall be put to death. So the cook and waitress that serves me breakfast on Sunday should be put to death. How can people believe that stuff like this is the inspired word of God?"

"Fear of death, Tom. Sunday is the day of the sun, just as Monday is Moon's day. Constantine decreed Sunday as the official day of rest for the Roman Empire and the early church adopted Sunday as their day of worship."

"I've gone my whole life never knowing what the days of the week mean."

"I know. Many Christians go through their lives never reading the Bible or caring to know the history of its making. Though I don't partake in the rituals and dogma, I do enjoy reading about the history of ancient cultures, their relationship with what they perceived as God and their perspective, the interpretation of divine messages received, interesting stories, inspirational quotes, and wisdom."

"But it's not the inspired word of God, Professor."

"Everyone is entitled to their belief, Tom. It's a matter of choice and people must do their own research and think from their wise hearts. Would the one God that gives life to all you see and all you don't see, and the core of your eternal self, want you to learn the nature of your existence from turning the pages of a book that was originally written in just two languages, is full of contradictions, has passages with meanings that baffle even the brightest biblical scholars, contains stories that we now know were made up by scribes, uses words with multiple meanings or no English equivalent, has been altered and translated numerous times, and today has multiple versions to confuse you even more, or would the one God simply have you turn inward to grasp the peace and blissfulness of your true nature in a language of silence that every human can understand?"

"What a world it could be, Professor, if everyone understood the difference between talking gods and God."

"Human consciousness is more than ready for the next stage of evolution."

"How long do you think it will be before the deceptive gods leave you alone, Professor?"

"Well, let me ask you Tom, are you impervious to harmful microorganisms because you survived the cold and flu season without becoming ill?"

"No. Every day I am exposed to microbial life that could potentially make me ill."

"Well then, the same applies to humans and the hidden race as both have their energy vampires and deceivers. Protecting your energy and body should be a way of life. Gautama Buddha was never free from the demon Mara. Many believe that once he attained enlightenment Mara vanished. This is not true. Do your research and you will find Mara continued to appear after Gautama Buddha achieved enlightenment. What changed is how Gautama perceived Mara."

"I can fear the adversary's next attack, or I can be humbled by the experience and grateful to the deceptive gods for how I have grown from the battles. Gratitude raises your vibration and fear lowers it. We coexist with a hidden race of dual dimensional beings and they are not leaving. I have shared with you the symptoms of drinking the parasitic water by connecting with the hidden race. If you want to know your true nature and live a balanced life, stay out of their mind and be content in your own."

"Do you think I'm capable of the awakening experience, Professor?"

"Everyone is capable. Your ego just has to be willing to die for a moment and be reborn. This is why it is said that a requirement for an awakening is to 'die before you die.'"

"Do you think that's what it's like when you die?"

"No living human can answer that question honestly. All I know is an awakening takes place when the ego dies. Consciousness, my friend, is eternal."

ACKNOWLEDGMENTS

First and foremost, my heartfelt gratitude goes out to that which gives life, call it what you may, and to my children who provided unconditional support and love throughout the writing of this book and who I love with all of my being.

I want to express my deepest appreciation to Suzanne Moniz for working her editorial magic and to my mother Jean DeWitt who created the illustrative artwork.

A special thanks to my friends and students, some whose names have been changed in the book to protect their privacy, for their support and friendship along the way.

Lorne J. Therrien is a martial arts instructor with 45 years' experience and a spiritual teacher. He was awarded the title of Professor and the rank of 6th degree black belt in Kenpo Karate in 2002, a black belt in Jujitsu in 1993, and the title of Master of Modern Arnis and 5th degree black belt in Modern Arnis in 1998. He is the founder of Full Circle Fighting System, Full Circle Arnis De Mano and the Full Circle Path. He also produced the educational video 'Element of Surprise Survival Skills for Today's Woman' in 1996. His websites are www.fullcirclefightingsystem.com and www.deceptivegods.com

Made in the USA
Coppell, TX
31 October 2020